R Statistics Cookbook

Over 100 recipes for performing complex statistical operations with R 3.5

Francisco Juretig

BIRMINGHAM - MUMBAI

R Statistics Cookbook

Commissioning Editor: Pravin Dhandre
Acquisition Editor: Devika Battike
Content Development Editor: Athikho Sapuni Rishana
Technical Editor: Utkarsha S. Kadam
Copy Editor: Safis Editing
Project Coordinator: Kirti Pisat
Proofreader: Safis Editing
Indexer: Priyanka Dhadke
Graphics: Jisha Chirayil
Production Coordinator: Arvindkumar Gupta

First published: March 2019

Production reference: 1280319

Published by Packt Publishing Ltd.
Livery Place
35 Livery Street
Birmingham
B3 2PB, UK.

ISBN 978-1-78980-256-6

www.packtpub.com

`mapt.io`

Mapt is an online digital library that gives you full access to over 5,000 books and videos, as well as industry leading tools to help you plan your personal development and advance your career. For more information, please visit our website.

Why subscribe?

- Spend less time learning and more time coding with practical eBooks and Videos from over 4,000 industry professionals

- Improve your learning with Skill Plans built especially for you

- Get a free eBook or video every month

- Mapt is fully searchable

- Copy and paste, print, and bookmark content

Packt.com

Did you know that Packt offers eBook versions of every book published, with PDF and ePub files available? You can upgrade to the eBook version at `www.packt.com` and as a print book customer, you are entitled to a discount on the eBook copy. Get in touch with us at `customercare@packtpub.com` for more details.

At `www.packt.com`, you can also read a collection of free technical articles, sign up for a range of free newsletters, and receive exclusive discounts and offers on Packt books and eBooks.

Contributors

About the author

Francisco Juretig has worked for over a decade in a variety of industries such as retail, gambling and finance deploying data-science solutions. He has written several R packages, and is a frequent contributor to the open source community.

About the reviewer

Davor Lozic is a senior software engineer interested in a variety of subjects, in particular, computer security, algorithms, and data structures. He manages teams of more than 15 engineers and is a professor when it comes to teaching what there is to know about database systems. You can contact him at davor@warriorkitty.com. He likes cats! If you want to talk about any aspect of technology, or if you have funny pictures of cats, feel free to contact him.

Packt is searching for authors like you

If you're interested in becoming an author for Packt, please visit authors.packtpub.com and apply today. We have worked with thousands of developers and tech professionals, just like you, to help them share their insight with the global tech community. You can make a general application, apply for a specific hot topic that we are recruiting an author for, or submit your own idea.

Table of Contents

Preface

R is a popular programming language for developing statistical software. This book will be a useful guide to solving common and not-so-common challenges in statistics. With this book, you'll be equipped to confidently perform essential statistical procedures across your organization with the help of cutting-edge statistical tools.

You'll start by implementing data modeling, data analysis, and machine learning to solve real-world problems. You'll then understand how to work with nonparametric methods, mixed effects models, and hidden Markov models. This book contains recipes that will guide you in performing univariate and multivariate hypothesis tests, several regression techniques, and using robust techniques to minimize the impact of outliers in data.You'll also learn how to use the caret package for performing machine learning in R. Furthermore, this book will help you understand how to interpret charts and plots to get insights for better decision making.

By the end of this book, you will be able to apply your skills to statistical computations using R 3.5. You will also become well-versed with a wide array of statistical techniques in R that are extensively used in the data science industry.

Who this book is for

If you are a quantitative researcher, statistician, data analyst, or data scientist looking to tackle common and not-so-common challenges in statistics, then this book is what you need! A solid understanding of R programming and a basic understanding of statistics and linear algebra.

What this book covers

Chapter 1, *Getting Started with R and Statistics*, reviews a variety of techniques in R for performing data processing, data analysis, and plotting. We will also explain how to work with some basic statistical techniques, such as sampling, maximum likelihood estimation, and random number generation. In addition, we will present some useful coding techniques, such as C++ functions using Rcpp, and R6Classes. The former will allow us to add high-performance compiled code, whereas the latter will allow us to perform object-oriented programming in R.

Chapter 2, *Univariate and Multivariate Tests for Equality of Means*, explains how to answer the most basic statistical question: do two (or possibly more) populations have the same mean? This arises when we want to evaluate whether certain treatment/policy is effective compared to a baseline effect. This can naturally be extended to multiple groups, and the technique used for this is called Analysis of Variance (ANOVA). ANOVA can itself be extended to accommodate multiple effects; for example, testing whether the background color of a website and the font style drive sales up. This is known as two-way ANOVA, and leads to additional complications: not only do we have multiple effects to estimate, but also we could have interaction effects happening between these two effects (for example, a certain background color could be effective when used in conjunction with a specific font type). ANOVA can also be extended in other dimensions, such as adding random effects (effects that originate from a large population and where we don't want to estimate a parameter for each one of them), or repeated measures for each observation.

A different problem arises when we have multiple variables instead of a single variable that we want to measure across (across two or more groups). In this case, we are generalizing the t-test and ANOVA to a multi-dimensional case; for the former (two groups, the technique that we use is called Hotelling's t-test, and for the latter (more than two groups), the technique is MANOVA (multiple ANOVA). We will review how to use all these techniques in R.

Chapter 3, *Linear Regression*, deals with the most important tool in statistics. It can be used in almost any situation where we want to predict a numeric variable in terms of lots of independent ones. As its name implies, the assumption is that there is a linear relationship between the covariates and the target. In this chapter, we will review how to formulate these models with a special focus on ordinary least squares (the most widely used algorithm for linear regression).

Chapter 4, *Bayesian Regression*, explains how to work with regression in a Bayesian context. Hitherto, we have assumed that there are some fixed parameters behind the data generation process (for t-tests, we assume that there are fixed means for each group), and because of sample variability, we will observe minor deviations from them. The Bayesian approach is radically different, and founded on a different methodological and epistemological foundation. The idea is that coefficients are not fixed quantities that we want to draw inferences upon, but random variables themselves.

The idea is that given a prior density (prior belief that we have) for each coefficient, we want to augment these priors using the data, in order to arrive at a posterior density. For example, if we think a person always arrives on time (this would be a prior), and we observe that this person arrived late on 8 out of 10 occasions, we should update our initial expectation accordingly. Unfortunately, Bayesian models do not generate closed formed expressions (in most practical cases), so they can't be solved easily. We will need to use sophisticated techniques to estimate these posterior densities: the tool that is used most frequently for this purpose is MCMC (Markov chain Monte Carlo). We will review how to formulate models using the best packages available: JAGS and STAN.

Chapter 5, *Nonparametric Methods*, explains how classical methods rely on the assumption that there is an underlying distribution (usually a Gaussian one), and derive tests for each case. For instance, the underlying assumption in t-tests is that the data originates from two Gaussian populations with the same variance. In general, these assumptions do make sense, and even when they are not met, in large samples, the violations to those assumptions become less relevant: (for example, the t-test works well for large sample even when the normality assumption is violated). But what can we do when we are working with small samples, or cases where normality is absolutely needed? Non-parametric methods are designed to work with no distributional assumptions by using a series of smart tricks that depend on each particular case. When the data follows the same distribution that we need (for example normality for t-tests), they work almost as well as the parametric ones, and when the data does not follow that distribution, they still work anyway. We will use a variety of non-parametric tools for regression, ANOVA, and many more.

Chapter 6, *Robust Methods*, explains why classical methods don't work well in the presence of outliers. On the other hand, robust methods are designed to intelligently flag abnormal observations, and estimate the appropriate coefficients in the presence of contamination. In this chapter, we will review some of the most frequently used robust techniques for regression, classification, ANOVA, and clustering.

Chapter 7, *Time Series Analysis*, describes how to work with time series (sequences of observations indexed by time). Although there are several ways of modeling them, the most widely used framework is called ARIMA. The idea is to decompose the series into the sum of deterministic and stochastic components in such a way that the past is used to predict the future of the series. It has been established that these techniques work really well with actual data but, unfortunately, they do require a lot of manual work. In this chapter, we will present several ARIMA techniques, demonstrating how to extend them to multivariate data, how to impute missing values on the series, how to detect outliers, and how to use several automatic packages that build the best model for us.

Chapter 8, *Mixed Effects Models*, introduces mixed effects models. These models arise when we mix fixed and random effects. Fixed effects (the ones we have used so far except for Chapter 4, *Bayesian Regression*) are treated as fixed parameters that are estimated. For example, if we model the sales of a product in terms of a particular month, each month will have a distinct parameter (this would be a fixed effect). On the other hand, if we were measuring whether a drug is useful for certain patients, and we had multiple observations per patient, we might want to keep a patient effect but not a coefficient for each patient. If we had 2,000 patients, those coefficients would be unmanageable and at the same time, would be introducing a lot of imprecision to our model. A neater approach would be to treat the patient effect as random: we would assume that each patient receives a random shock, and all observations belonging to the same patient will be correlated.

In this chapter, we will work with these models using the lme4 and lmer packages, and we will extend these models to non-linear mixed effects models (when the response is non-linear). The main problem for these models (both linear and non-linear) is that the degrees of freedom are unknown, rendering the usual tests useless.

Chapter 9, *Predictive Models Using the Caret Package*, describes how to use the caret package, which is the fundamental workhorse for (some of them have already been presented in previous chapters). It provides a consistent syntax and a unified approach for building a variety of models. In addition, it has great tools for performing preprocessing and feature selection. In this chapter, we present several models in caret, such as random forests, gradient boosting, and LASSO.

Chapter 10, *Bayesian Networks and Hidden Markov Models*, describes how, in some cases, we might want to model a network of relationships in such a way that we can understand how the variables are connected. For example, the office location might make employees happier, and also make them arrive earlier to work: the two combined effects might make them perform better. If they perform better, they will receive better bonuses; actually, the bonuses will be dependent on those two variables directly, and also on the office location indirectly. Bayesian networks allow us to perform complex network modeling, and the main tool used for this is the bnlearn package. Another advanced statistical tool is hidden Markov models: they allow us to estimate the state of unobserved variables by using a very complex computational machinery. In this chapter we will work with two examples using Hidden Markov Models.

To get the most out of this book

Users should have some familiarity with statistics and programming. Some general knowledge of probability, regression, and data analysis is recommended.

R is required for this book, and RStudio is highly recommended. All the packages used throughout this book can be installed following the instructions for each recipe.

Download the example code files

You can download the example code files for this book from your account at www.packt.com. If you purchased this book elsewhere, you can visit www.packt.com/support and register to have the files emailed directly to you.

You can download the code files by following these steps:

1. Log in or register at www.packt.com.
2. Select the **SUPPORT** tab.
3. Click on **Code Downloads & Errata**.
4. Enter the name of the book in the **Search** box and follow the onscreen instructions.

Once the file is downloaded, please make sure that you unzip or extract the folder using the latest version of:

- WinRAR/7-Zip for Windows
- Zipeg/iZip/UnRarX for Mac
- 7-Zip/PeaZip for Linux

The code bundle for the book is also hosted on GitHub at https://github.com/PacktPublishing/R_Statistics_Cookbook. In case there's an update to the code, it will be updated on the existing GitHub repository.

We also have other code bundles from our rich catalog of books and videos available at https://github.com/PacktPublishing/. Check them out!

Download the color images

We also provide a PDF file that has color images of the screenshots/diagrams used in this book. You can download it here: https://www.packtpub.com/sites/default/files/downloads/9781789802566_ColorImages.pdf.

Conventions used

There are a number of text conventions used throughout this book.

CodeInText: Indicates code words in text, database table names, folder names, filenames, file extensions, pathnames, dummy URLs, user input, and Twitter handles. Here is an example: "Import the ggplot2 and reshape libraries."

A block of code is set as follows:

```
library(bbmle)
N <- 1000
xx <- rgamma(N, shape=20,rate=2)
```

Any command-line input or output is written as follows:

```
> install.packages("tscount")
```

Bold: Indicates a new term, an important word, or words that you see on screen. For example, words in menus or dialog boxes appear in the text like this. Here is an example: "The **cumulative density function (CDF)** returns the cumulative probability mass for each value of X."

Warnings or important notes appear like this.

Tips and tricks appear like this.

Sections

In this book, you will find several headings that appear frequently (*Getting ready, How to do it..., How it works..., There's more...,* and *See also*).

To give clear instructions on how to complete a recipe, use these sections as follows:

Getting ready

This section tells you what to expect in the recipe and describes how to set up any software or any preliminary settings required for the recipe.

How to do it...

This section contains the steps required to follow the recipe.

How it works...

This section usually consists of a detailed explanation of what happened in the previous section.

There's more...

This section consists of additional information about the recipe in order to make you more knowledgeable about the recipe.

See also

This section provides helpful links to other useful information for the recipe.

Get in touch

Feedback from our readers is always welcome.

General feedback: If you have questions about any aspect of this book, mention the book title in the subject of your message and email us at customercare@packtpub.com.

Errata: Although we have taken every care to ensure the accuracy of our content, mistakes do happen. If you have found a mistake in this book, we would be grateful if you would report this to us. Please visit www.packt.com/submit-errata, selecting your book, clicking on the Errata Submission Form link, and entering the details.

Piracy: If you come across any illegal copies of our works in any form on the internet, we would be grateful if you would provide us with the location address or website name. Please contact us at copyright@packt.com with a link to the material.

If you are interested in becoming an author: If there is a topic that you have expertise in, and you are interested in either writing or contributing to a book, please visit authors.packtpub.com.

Reviews

Please leave a review. Once you have read and used this book, why not leave a review on the site that you purchased it from? Potential readers can then see and use your unbiased opinion to make purchase decisions, we at Packt can understand what you think about our products, and our authors can see your feedback on their book. Thank you!

For more information about Packt, please visit packt.com.

Getting Started with R and Statistics

1

In this chapter, we will cover the following recipes:

- Maximum likelihood estimation
- Calculation densities, quantiles, and CDFs
- Creating barplots using `ggplot`
- Generating random numbers from multiple distributions
- Complex data processing with `dplyr`
- 3D visualization with the `plot3d` package
- Formatting tabular data with the `formattable` package
- Simple random sampling
- Creating plots via the `DiagrammeR` package
- C++ in R via the `Rcpp` package
- Interactive plots with the `ggplot GUI` package
- Animations with the `gganimate` package
- Using `R6` classes
- Modelling sequences with the `TraMineR` package
- Clustering sequences with the `TraMineR` package
- Displaying geographical data with the `leaflet` package

Introduction

In this chapter, we will introduce a wide array of topics regarding statistics and data analysis in R. We will use quite a diverse set of packages, most of which have been released over recent years.

We'll start by generating random numbers, fitting distributions to data, and using several packages to plot data. We will then move onto sampling, creating diagrams with the `DiagrammeR` package, and analyzing sequence data with the `TraMineR` package. We also present several techniques, not strictly related to statistics, but important for dealing with advanced methods in R—we introduce the `Rcpp` package (used for embedding highly efficient C++ code into your R scripts) and the `R6` package (used for operating with `R6` classes, allowing you to code using an object-oriented approach in R).

Technical requirements

We will use R and its packages, that can be installed via the `install.packages()` command, and we will indicate which ones are necessary for each recipe in the corresponding *Getting ready* section.

Maximum likelihood estimation

Suppose we observe a hundred roulette spins, and we get red 30 times and black 70 times. We can start by assuming that the probability of getting red is 0.5 (and black is obviously 0.5). This is certainly not a very good idea, because if that was the case, we should have seen nearly red 50 times and black 50 times, but we did not. It is thus evident that a more reasonable assumption would have been a probability of 0.3 for red (and thus 0.7 for black).

The principle of maximum likelihood establishes that, given the data, we can formulate a model and tweak its parameters to maximize the probability (likelihood) of having observed what we did observe. Additionally, maximum likelihood allows us to calculate the precision (standard error) of each estimated coefficient easily. They are obtained by finding the curvature of the log-likelihood with respect to each parameter; this is obtained by finding the second-order derivatives of the log-likelihood with respect to each parameter.

The likelihood is essentially a probability composed of the multiplication of several probabilities. Multiplying lots of probabilities is never a good idea, because if the probabilities are small, we would very likely end up with a very small number. If that number is too small, then the computer won't be able to represent it accurately. Therefore, what we end up using is the log-likelihood, which is the sum of the logarithms of those probabilities.

In many situations, we also want to know if the coefficients are statistically different from zero. Imagine we have a sample of growth rates for many companies for a particular year, and we want to use the average as an indicator of whether the economy is growing or not. In other words, we want to test whether the mean is equal to zero or not. We could fit that distribution of growth rates to a Gaussian distribution (which has two parameters, μ, σ), and test whether $\hat{\mu}$ (estimated μ) is statistically equal to zero. In a Gaussian distribution, the mean is μ. When doing hypothesis testing, we need to specify a null hypothesis and an alternative one. For this case, the null hypothesis is that this parameter is equal to zero. Intuition would tell us that if an estimated parameter is large, we can reject the null hypothesis. The problem is that we need to define what large is. This is why we don't use the estimated coefficients, but a statistic called the **Z value**—this is defined as the value that we observed divided by the standard error. It can be proven that these are distributed according to a Gaussian distribution.

So, once we have the Z value statistic, how can we reject or not reject the null hypothesis? Assuming that the null hypothesis is true (that the coefficient is equal to zero), we can compute the probability that we get a test statistic as large or larger than the one we got (these are known as p-values). Remember that we assume that the coefficients have fixed values, but we will observe random deviations from them in our samples (we actually have one sample). If the probability of finding them to be as large as the ones that we observed is small, assuming that the true ones are zero, then that implies that luck alone can't explain the coefficients that we got. The final conclusion in that case is to reject the null hypothesis and conclude that the coefficient is different from zero.

Getting ready

The `bbmle` package can be installed using the `install.packages("bbmle")` function in R.

How to do it...

In this exercise, we will generate a 1000 random gamma deviates with its two parameters set to `shape=20` and `rate=2`. We will then estimate the two parameters by using the `mle2` function in the `bbmle` package. This function will also return the Z values, and the p-values. Note that we need to assume a distribution that we will use to fit the parameters (in general we will receive data, and we will need to assume which distribution is reasonable). In this case, since we are generating the data, we already know that the data comes from a gamma distribution.

We will use the `bbmle` package, which will allow us to maximize the log-likelihood. This package essentially wraps an appropriate numerical maximization routine; we only need to pass a function that computes the sum of the log-likelihood across the whole dataset.

1. Generate `1000` random gamma deviations with its parameters set to `shape=20` and `rate=2` as follows:

   ```
   library(bbmle)
   N <- 1000
   xx <- rgamma(N, shape=20, rate=2)
   ```

2. Pass a function that computes the sum of the log-likelihood across the whole dataset as follows:

   ```
   LL <- function(shape, rate) {
   R = suppressWarnings(dgamma(xx, shape=shape, rate=rate))
         return(-sum(log(R)))
   }
   ```

3. Estimate the two parameters by using the `mle2` function in the `bbmle` package as follows:

   ```
   P_1000 = mle2(LL, start = list(shape = 1, rate=1))
   summary(P_1000)
   ```

The estimated coefficients, standard errors, and p-values (*N*=10) are as follows:

	Estimate	Std. error	Z value	p-value
Shape	19.04	0.84	22.54	<2.2e-16***
Rate	1.89	0.08	22.68	<2.2e-16***

The standard errors are very small relative to the estimated coefficients, which is to be expected as we have a large sample (1,000 observations). The p-values are consequently extremely small (the asterisks mark that these values are smaller than 0.001). When the p-values are small we say that they are significative (choosing a threshold is somewhat debatable, but most people use 0.05—in this case, we would say that they are highly significative).

How it works...

The `LL` function wraps the log-likelihood computation, and is called by the `mle2` function sequentially. This function will use a derivative-based algorithm to find the maximum of the log-likelihood.

There's more...

Within a maximum likelihood context, the standard errors depend on the number of observations—the more observations we have, the smaller the standard errors will be (greater precision). As we can see in the following results, we get standard errors that are almost 50% of the estimated coefficients:

```
N <- 10
x <- rgamma(N, shape=20,rate=2)
LL <- function(shape, rate) {
  R = suppressWarnings(dgamma(x, shape=shape, rate=rate))
  return(-sum(log(R)))
}

P_10 = mle2(LL, start = list(shape = 1, rate=1))
summary(P_10)
```

The estimated coefficients and standard errors (*N*=10) are as follows:

	Estimate	Std. error	Z value	p-value
Shape	13.76	6.08	2.24	0.02*
Rate	1.36	0.61	2.22	0.02*

The standard errors are much larger than before, almost 50% of their estimated coefficients. Consequently, the p-values are much larger than before, but still significative at the 0.05 level (which is why we get an asterisk). We still conclude that the coefficients are different from zero.

We can also compute confidence intervals using the confint function (in this case, we will use 95% intervals). These intervals can be inverted to get hypothesis tests. For example, we can test whether the shape is equal to 18 with a 95% confidence for our 1,000-sample example, by assessing if 18 is between the upper and lower boundaries; since 18 is between 17.30 and 20.59, we can't reject that the shape is equal to 18. Note that the confidence intervals are much tighter for the 1,000-sample case than for the 10-sample one. This is to be expected, as the precision depends on the sample size (we have already seen that the standard deviation for each estimated parameter depends on the sample size).

This is done via the following command:

```
confint(P_1000)
confint(P_10)
```

The confidence intervals are as follows:

Parameter	Sample size	2.5%	97.5%
Shape	10	13.64	81.08
Shape	1,000	17.30	20.59
Rate	10	1.48	8.93
Rate	1,000	1.71	2.04

See also

Maximum likelihood estimators converge in probability to the true values (are consistent) as long as certain regularity conditions hold (see `https://en.wikipedia.org/wiki/Maximum_likelihood_estimation`).

Calculating densities, quantiles, and CDFs

R provides a vast number of functions for working with statistical distributions. These can be either discrete or continuous. Statistical functions are important, because in statistics we generally need to assume that the data is distributed to some distribution.

Let's assume we have an X variable distributed according to a specific distribution. The **density function** is a function that maps every value in the domain in the distribution of the variable with a probability. The **cumulative density function** (CDF) returns the cumulative probability mass for each value of X. The **quantile function** expects a probability p_0 (between 0 and 1) and returns the value of X that has a probability mass of p_0 to the left. For most distributions, we can use specific R functions to calculate these. On the other hand, if we want to generate random numbers according to a distribution, we can use R's random number generators **random number generators** (RNGs).

Getting ready

No specific package is needed for this recipe.

How to do it...

In this recipe we will first generate some Gaussian numbers and then, using the `pnorm()` and `qnorm()` functions, we will calculate the area to the left and to the right of x=2, and get the 90th quantile to plot the density.

1. Generate `10000` Gaussian random numbers:

    ```
    vals = rnorm(10000,0,1)
    ```

2. Plot the `density` and draw a red line at x=2:

    ```
    plot(density(vals))
    abline(v=2,col="red")
    ```

3. Calculate the area to the left and to the right of x=2, using the `pnorm()` function and use the `qnorm()` quantile function to get the 97.7th quantile:

    ```
    print(paste("Area to the left of x=2",pnorm(2,0,1)))
    print(paste("Area to the right of x=2",1-pnorm(2,0,1)))
    print(paste("90th Quantile: x value that has 97.72% to the
    left",qnorm(0.9772,0,1)))
    ```

    After running the preceding code, we get the following output:

```
> print(paste("Area to the left of x=2",pnorm(2,0,1)))
[1] "Area to the left of x=2 0.977249868051821"
> print(paste("Area to the right of x=2",1-pnorm(2,0,1)))
[1] "Area to the right of x=2 0.0227501319481792"
> print(paste("90th Quantile: x value that has 90% to the left",qnorm(0.9772,0,1)))
[1] "90th Quantile: x value that has 90% to the left 1.99907721497177"
```

The following screenshot shows the density with a vertical line at 2:

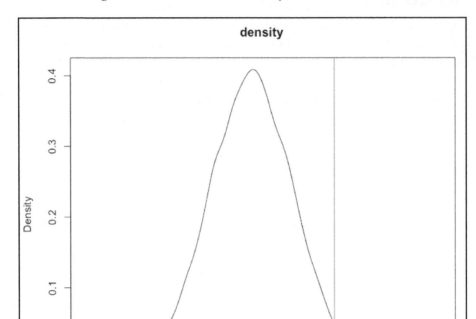

How it works...

Most distributions in R have densities, cumulative densities, quantiles, and RNGs. They are generally called in R using the same approach (**d** for densities, **q** for quantiles, **r** for random numbers, and **p** for the cumulative density function) combined with the distribution name.

For example, `qnorm` returns the quantile function for a normal-Gaussian distribution, and `qchisq` returns the quantile function for the chi-squared distribution. `pnorm` returns the cumulative distribution function for a Gaussian distribution; `pt` returns it for a Student's t-distribution.

As can be seen in the diagram immediately previous, when we get the 97.7% quantile, we get 1.99, which coincides with the accumulated probability we get when we do `pnorm()` for x=2.

There's more...

We can use the same approach for other distributions. For example, we can get the area to the left of x=3 for a chi-squared distribution with 33 degrees of freedom:

```
print(paste("Area to the left of x=3",pchisq(3,33)))
```

After running the preceding code we get the following output:

```
> print(paste("Area to the left of x=3",pchisq(3,33)))
[1] "Area to the left of x=3 2.2915465503982e-12"
```

Creating barplots using ggplot

The `ggplot2` package has become the dominant R package for creating serious plots, mainly due to its beautiful aesthetics. The `ggplot` package allows the user to define the plots in a sequential (or additive) way, and this great syntax has contributed to its enormous success. As you would expect, this package can handle a wide variety of plots.

Getting ready

In order to run this example, you will need the `ggplot2` and the `reshape` packages. Both can be installed using the `install.packages()` command.

How to do it...

In this example, we will use a dataset in a wide format (multiple columns for each record), and we will do the appropriate data manipulation in order to transform it into a long format. Finally, we will use the `ggplot2` package to make a stacked plot with that transformed data. In particular, we have data for certain companies. The adjusted sales are sales where the taxes have been removed and the unadjusted sales are the raw sales. Naturally, the unadjusted sales will always be greater than the adjusted ones, as shown in the following table:

Company	Adjusted sales	Unadjusted sales
Company1	298	394
Company2	392	454
Company3	453	499
Company4	541	598
Company5	674	762

1. Import the `ggplot2` and `reshape` libraries as follows:

```
library(ggplot2)
library(reshape)
```

2. Then load the dataset:

```
datag = read.csv("./ctgs.csv")
```

3. Transform the data into a long format:

```
transformed_data = melt(datag,id.vars = "Company")
```

4. Use the `ggplot` function to create the plot:

```
ggplot(transformed_data, aes(x = Company, y = value, fill =
variable)) + geom_bar(stat = "identity")
```

This results in the following output:

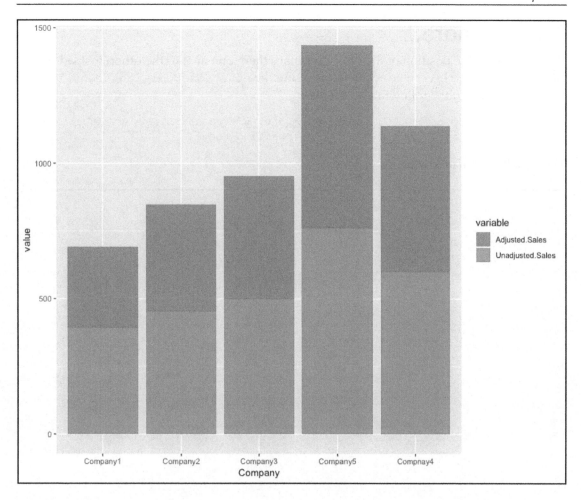

How it works...

In order to build a stacked plot, we need to supply three arguments to the aes() function. The x variable is the *x*-axis, y is the bar height, and fill is the color.
The geom_var variable specifies the type of bar that will be used. The stat=identity value tells ggplot that we don't want to apply any transformation, and leave the data as it is. We will use the reshape package for transforming the data into the format that we need.

The result has one bar for each company, with two colors. The red color corresponds to the **Adjusted Sales** and the green color corresponds to the **Unadjusted Sales**.

There's more...

We can change the position of the bars, and place them one next to the other, instead of stacking them up. This can be achieved by using the `position=position_dodge()` option as shown in the following code block:

```
ggplot(transformed_data, aes(x = Company, y = value, fill = variable)) +
geom_bar(stat = "identity",position=position_dodge())
```

This results in the following output:

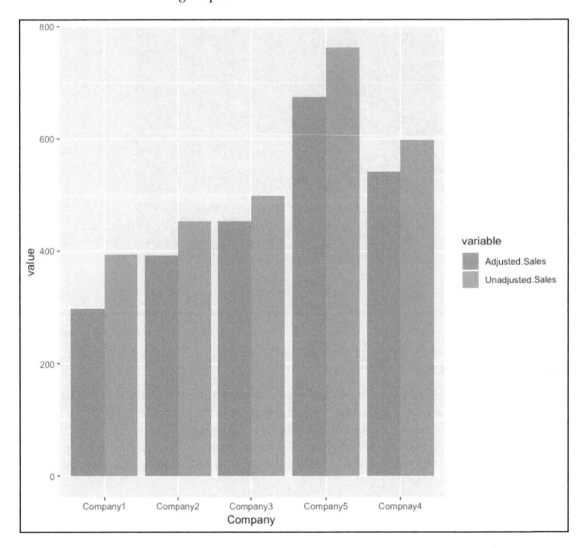

See also

An excellent `ggplot2` tutorial can be found at `http://r-statistics.co/Complete-Ggplot2-Tutorial-Part2-Customizing-Theme-With-R-Code.html`.

Generating random numbers from multiple distributions

R includes routines to generate random numbers from many distributions. Different distributions require different algorithms to generate random numbers. In essence, all random number generation routines rely on a uniform random number generator that generates an output between (0,1), and then some procedure that transform this number according to the density that we need.

There are several ways of doing this, depending on which distribution we want to generate. A very simple one, which works for a large amount of cases is the inverse transformation method. The idea is to generate uniform random numbers, and find the corresponding quantile for the distribution that we want to sample from.

Getting ready

We need to install the `ggplot2`, and `tidyr` packages which can be installed via `install.packages()`.

How to do it...

We will generate two samples of 10,000 random numbers, the first one via the `rnorm` function, and the second one using the inverse transformation method.

1. Generate two samples of `10000` random numbers:

```
rnorm_result = data.frame(rnorm = rnorm(10000,0,1))
inverse_way = data.frame(inverse = qnorm(runif(10000),0,1))
```

2. We concatenate the two datasets. Note that we are transposing it using the `gather` function. We need to transpose the data for plotting both histograms later via `ggplot`:

```
total_table = cbind(rnorm_result,inverse_way)
transp_table = gather(total_table)
colnames(transp_table) = c("method","value")
```

3. We will then plot the histogram:

```
ggplot(transp_table, aes(x=value,fill=method)) +
geom_density(alpha=0.25)
```

How it works...

We are generating two samples, then joining them together and transposing them (from a wide format into a long format). For this, we use the `gather` function from the `tidyr` package. After that, we use the `ggplot` function to plot the two densities on the same plot. Evidently, both methods yield very similar distributions as seen in the following screenshot:

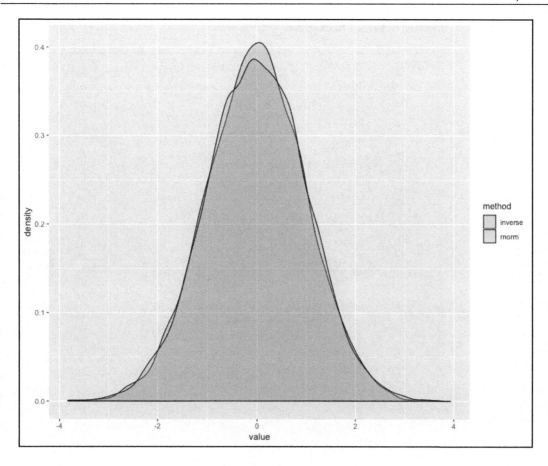

There's more...

The method can also be used to generate random numbers for discrete distributions as well. For example, we can generate random numbers according to a Poisson distribution with a value $\lambda = 5$. As you can see in the histogram, we are generating a very similar amount of counts for each possible value that the random variable can take:

```
rpois_result = data.frame(rpois = rpois(10000,5))
inverse_way = data.frame(inverse = qpois(runif(10000),5))
total_table = cbind(rpois_result,inverse_way)
transp_table = gather(total_table)
colnames(transp_table) = c("method","value")
ggplot(transp_table, aes(x=value,fill=method)) +
geom_histogram(alpha=0.8,binwidth=1)
```

This yields the following overlaid histogram:

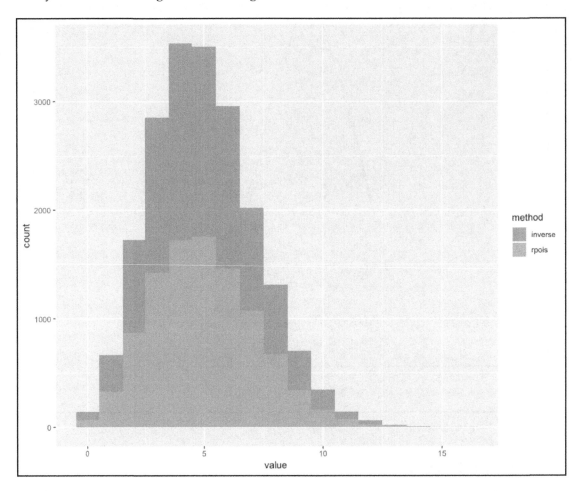

Complex data processing with dplyr

The `plyr` function has started a small revolution within the R community, due to its fantastic functions for data manipulation/wrangling. Its creators released an improved package, called `dplyr`, which is essentially a `plyr` on steroids: some of its machinery has been rebuilt via the `Rcpp` package (this allows the inclusion of C++ functions in R) achieving a much better performance.

The `dplyr` function is tightly connected to the `maggrittr` package, which allows us to use the `%>%` notation to chain operations one after the other. For instance, we could do something like `sort %>% filter %>% summarize`, wherein the output of each operation will be sent as an input for the next one. This becomes really powerful when writing a lot of code for data manipulation.

Getting ready

The `dplyr` package can be installed via `install.packages()` as usual.

How to do it...

We will use it to do data wrangling with the very famous `mtcars` dataset. This dataset contains several attributes (both numeric and categorical) for several car models. We will combine several of the `dplyr` functions to compute the mean horsepower and mean miles per gallon for each gear type. We will finally sort the result by the mean horsepower.

1. Import the `dplyr` library:

   ```
   library(dplyr)
   ```

2. The main step is grouping the data by gear; we calculate the mean horsepower, and the sum of the miles per gallon by gear. We then destroy the group structure and we sort the results by mean horsepower using the following code block:

   ```
   mtcars %>% group_by(am,gear) %>% summarise(mean_hp =
   mean(hp),sum_mpg = sum(mpg)) %>% ungroup %>% arrange(mean_hp)
   ```

How it works...

The beauty of the `dplyr` package is that it allows us to chain several operations together one after the other. This greatly reduces the complexity of our code, generating very simple and readable code. The `ungroup` statement is not strictly needed, but it destroys the grouped structure that we have had up to that point. In certain situations, this is necessary, because we might need to work on the ungrouped data after some grouping or summarizing is done.

There's more...

The `dplyr` function can be used to do dozens of interesting things, as it allows us to summarize, sort, group, compute ranks, arrange accumulators by group, and so on.

See also

The `dplyr` function's official website (`https://dplyr.tidyverse.org`) is an excellent reference source for learning it.

3D visualization with the plot3d package

The `plot3d` package can be used to generate stunning 3-D plots in R. It can generate an interesting array of plots, but in this recipe we will focus on creating 3-D scatterplots. These arise in situations where we have three variables, and we want to plot the triplets of values on the *x-y-z* space.

We will generate a dataset containing random Gaussian numbers for three variables, and we will plot them into the same plot using the `plot3d` package.

Getting ready

This package can be installed in the usual way via `install.packages("plot3D")`.

How to do it...

We will generate a dataset containing random gaussian numbers for three variables, and we will plot them into the same plot using the plot3d package.

1. Import the `plot3D` library:

```
library(plot3D)
```

2. Generate a dataset containing random Gaussian numbers for three variables:

```
x = rnorm(100)
y = rnorm(100)
z = x + y + rnorm(100,0,0.3)
idrow = 1:100
```

3. Plot the variable in the same plot:

```
scatter3D(x, y, z, bty = "g", colkey = TRUE, main ="x-y-z plot",phi
= 10,theta=50)
text3D(x, y, z, labels = idrow, add = TRUE, colkey = FALSE, cex =
0.5)
```

The following screenshot is the resulting 3D plot:

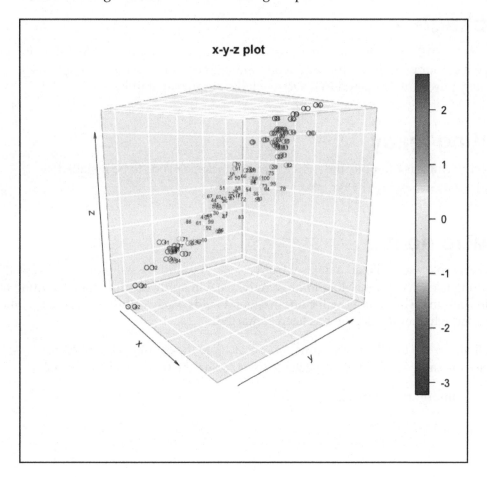

How it works...

The `scatter3D` function draws the scatterplot, and we have an interesting set of options for it. We can turn the color key on/off using the `colkey` parameter. `phi` and `theta` control the angles that will be used to show the plot. The color key is quite useful as it helps to highlight the observations that have higher Z values. This is useful because in 3-D plots it is sometimes difficult to understand a single image without rotating it. We are also using the `text3D` function to print the values for Z for each point. This step could certainly be omitted, but it is generally useful for isolating individual observations.

Formatting tabular data with the formattable package

The `formattable` package provides an excellent way of formatting tables, allowing us to change the color of each column, add icons, and add conditional formatting. This is extremely powerful compared to R's native table output capabilities.

Getting ready

In order to run this example, the `formattable` package needs to be installed using `install.packages("formattable")`.

How to do it...

In this example, we will load a dataset from a `.csv` file, and we will apply different formatting to each column. More interestingly, we will apply conditional formatting to certain columns. This dataset will contain several fields, such as the career, the age, the salary, and whether the person has been contacted.

After that, we can use the `table` function to calculate the counts using two variables. We then use the same `formattable` package for coloring the frequencies in this table.

1. Import the libraries:

   ```
   library(expss)
   library(formattable)
   ```

2. Load the data and specify the format for each column. For the `Person` column, we do basic formatting (specifying the color and font weight), and for the `Salary` column, we use a color scale ranging between two different green colors. For the `Contacted` column, we define a conditional formatting (green or red) with an appropriate icon:

```
data = read.csv("/Users/admin/Documents/R_book/person_salary.csv",
stringsAsFactors = FALSE)
Green = "#71CA97"
Green2 = "#DeF7E9"
table__out = data.frame(table(data$Career, data$Age))
colnames(table__out) = c("Career", "Age", "Freq")
formattable(table__out, align =c("c", "c", "c"), list("Freq"=
color_tile(Green, Green2)))
```

This results in the following output:

Career	Age	Freq
Egineer	+45	0
Engineer	+45	2
Lawyer	+45	0
Pilot	+45	0
Sales	+45	0
Teacher	+45	1
Egineer	20-30	0
Engineer	20-30	0
Lawyer	20-30	2
Pilot	20-30	0
Sales	20-30	1
Teacher	20-30	1
Egineer	30-45	1
Engineer	30-45	0
Lawyer	30-45	0
Pilot	30-45	1
Sales	30-45	2
Teacher	30-45	1

How it works...

The `formattable` package requires a data frame to work. We then have lots of options for each column that we want to format. Before specifying the format for each column, we are setting the alignment for each column (in this case we want to center each column, using the `c` option for each one).

There's more...

This package is particularly interesting when calculating tables using the `tables()` function. For example, we might want to calculate the number of cases that we have for all the combinations of career and age, and then paint that column on a green color scale:

```
formattable(data,align =c("c","c","c","c"), list("Person" =
formatter("span", style = ~ style(color = "grey",font.weight = "bold")),
"Salary"= color_tile(Green, Green2),
"Contacted" = formatter("span", style = x ~ style(color = ifelse(x,
"green", "red")),
  x ~ icontext(ifelse(x, "ok", "remove"), ifelse(x, "Yes", "No")))))
```

The following screenshot shows the output (the contacted column now contains ticks and crosses):

Person	Career	Age	Salary	Contacted
John	Engineer	+45	10	✔ Yes
Mike	Engineer	+45	13	✘ No
Lisa	Teacher	30-45	12	✔ Yes
Marcel	Sales	30-45	18	✔ Yes
Max	Sales	30-45	12	✔ Yes
Paul	Teacher	+45	13	✘ No
Paul	Egineer	30-45	18	✘ No
Anthony	Sales	20-30	13	✘ No
Tom	Lawyer	20-30	19	✘ No
Lisa	Lawyer	20-30	18	✔ Yes
Alex	Teacher	20-30	21	✔ Yes
Tom	Pilot	30-45	23	✔ Yes

Simple random sampling

In many situations, we are interested in taking a sample of the data. There could be multiple reasons for doing this, but in most practical considerations this happens due to budget constraints. For example, what if we have a certain amount people in a neighborhood, and we want to estimate what proportion of them is supporting Candidates A or B in an election? Visiting each one of them would be prohibitively expensive, so we might decide to find a smaller subset that we can visit and ask them who they are going to vote for.

The `sample` function in R can be used to take a sample with or without the replacement of any arbitrary size. Once a sample is defined, we can sample those units. An interesting question is estimating the variability of that sample with respect to a given sample size. In order to do that, we will build a thousand replications of our sampling exercise, and we will get the upper and lower boundaries that enclose 95% of the cases. Nevertheless, we could also compute approximate confidence intervals for the proportion of people voting for Candidate A, using the well known Gaussian approximation to an estimated proportion.

When the sample size is not very small, the estimated proportion is distributed approximately as a Gaussian distribution:

$$\hat{p} \sim \mathcal{N}(\hat{p}, \sqrt{\frac{\hat{p}(1-\hat{p})}{n}})$$

This can be used to compute an approximate confidence interval, where we need to choose Z in order to achieve an interval of $1 - \alpha$ as implemented in the following formula:

$$\hat{p} \pm Z_{\alpha/2}\sqrt{\frac{\hat{p}(1-\hat{p})}{n}}$$

Both methods will be in agreement for reasonably large samples (>100), but will differ when the sample sizes are very small. Still, the method that uses the sample function can be used for more complex situations, such as cases when we use sample weights.

Getting ready

In order to run this exercise, we need to install the `dplyr` and the `ggplot2` packages via the `install.packages()` function.

How to do it...

In this recipe, we have the number of people in a town, and whether they vote for Candidate A or Candidate B – these are flagged by 1s and 0s. We want to study the variability of several sample sizes, and ultimately we want to define which sample size is appropriate. Intuition would suggest that the error decreases nonlinearly as we increase the sample size: when the sample size is small, the error should decrease slowly as we increase the sample size. On the other hand, it should decrease quickly when the sample is large.

1. Import the libraries:

```
library(dplyr)
library(ggplot2)
```

2. Load the dataset:

```
voters_data = read.csv("./voters_.csv")
```

3. Take 1,000 samples of size 10 and calculate the proportion of people voting for Candidate A:

```
proportions_10sample = c()
for (q in 2:1000){
  sample_data = mean(sample(voters_data$Vote, 10, replace = FALSE))
  proportions_10sample = c(proportions_10sample, sample_data)
}
```

4. Take 1,000 samples of size 50 and calculate the proportion of people voting for Candidate A:

```
proportions_50sample = c()
for (q in 2:1000){
  sample_data = mean(sample(voters_data$Vote, 50, replace = FALSE))
  proportions_50sample = c(proportions_50sample, sample_data)
}
```

5. Take 1,000 samples of size 100 and calculate the proportion of people voting for Candidate A:

```
proportions_100sample = c()
for (q in 2:1000){
  sample_data = mean(sample(voters_data$Vote, 100, replace = FALSE))
  proportions_100sample = c(proportions_100sample, sample_data)
}
```

6. Take 1,000 samples of size 500 and calculate the proportion of people voting for Candidate A:

```
proportions_500sample = c()
for (q in 2:1000){
  sample_data = mean(sample(voters_data$Vote,500,replace = FALSE))
  proportions_500sample = c(proportions_500sample,sample_data)
}
```

7. We combine all the DataFrames, and calculate the 2.5% and 97.5% quantiles:

```
joined_data50 =
data.frame("sample_size"=50,"mean"=mean(proportions_50sample),
"q2.5"=quantile(proportions_50sample,0.025),"q97.5"=quantile(propor
tions_50sample,0.975))
joined_data10 =
data.frame("sample_size"=10,"mean"=mean(proportions_10sample),
"q2.5"=quantile(proportions_10sample,0.025),"q97.5"=quantile(propor
tions_10sample,0.975))
joined_data100 =
data.frame("sample_size"=100,"mean"=mean(proportions_100sample),
"q2.5"=quantile(proportions_100sample,0.025),"q97.5"=quantile(propo
rtions_100sample,0.975))
joined_data500 =
data.frame("sample_size"=500,"mean"=mean(proportions_500sample),
"q2.5"=quantile(proportions_500sample,0.025),"q97.5"=quantile(propo
rtions_500sample,0.975))
```

8. After combining them, we use the Gaussian approximation to get the 2.5% and 97.5% quantiles. Note that we use 1.96, which is the associated 97.5% quantile (and -1.96 for the associated 2.5% quantile, due to the symmetry of the Gaussian distribution):

```
data_sim =
rbind(joined_data10,joined_data50,joined_data100,joined_data500)
data_sim = data_sim %>% mutate(Nq2.5 = mean - 1.96*sqrt(mean*(1-
mean)/sample_size),N97.5 = mean + 1.96*sqrt(mean*(1-
mean)/sample_size))
data_sim$sample_size = as.factor(data_sim$sample_size)
```

9. Plot the previous DataFrame using the ggplot function:

```
ggplot(data_sim, aes(x=sample_size, y=mean, group=1)) +
  geom_point(aes(size=2), alpha=0.52) +
theme(legend.position="none") +
  geom_errorbar(width=.1, aes(ymin=q2.5, ymax=q97.5),
colour="darkred") + labs(x="Sample Size",y= "Candidate A ratio",
```

```
title="Candidate A ratio by sample size", subtitle="Proportion of
people voting for candidate A, assuming 50-50 chance",
caption="Circle is mean / Bands are 95% Confidence bands")
```

This provides the following result:

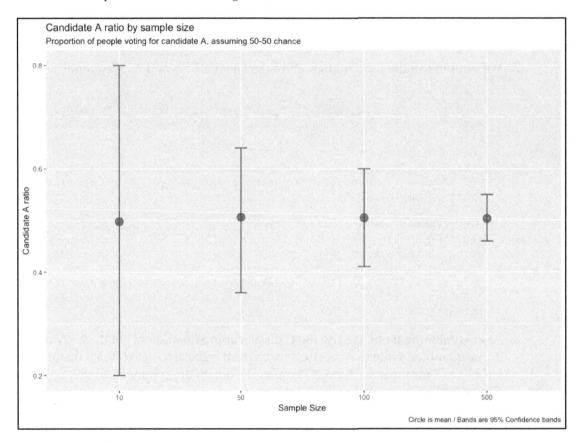

How it works...

We run several simulations, using different sample sizes. For each sample size, we take 1,000 samples and we get the mean, and 97.5% and 2.5% percentiles. We use them to construct a 95% confidence interval. It is evident that the greater the sample sizes are, the narrower these bands will be. We can see that when taking just 10 elements the bands are extremely wide, and they get narrower quite quickly when we jump to a larger sample size.

In the following table you can see why, when elections are tight (nearly 50% of voters choosing A), they are so difficult to predict. Since the election is won by whoever has the majority of the votes, and our confidence interval ranges from 0.45 to 0.55 (even when taking a sample size of 500 elements), we can't be certain of who the winner will be.

Take a look at the following results—95% intervals—left simulated ones; right Gaussian approximation:

sample_size	mean	2.5% quantile (sampling)	97.5% quantile (sampling)	Gaussian 2.5% quantile	Gaussian 97.5%
10	0.507	0.20	0.80	0.19	0.81
50	0.504	0.38	0.64	0.36	0.64
100	0.505	0.41	0.60	0.40	0.60
500	0.505	0.45	0.55	0.46	0.54

Creating diagrams via the DiagrammeR package

The `ggplot` package greatly enhances R's plotting capabilities, but in some situations, this is not sufficient. In situations whenever we want to plot relationships between entities or elements, we need a different tool. Diagrams are well suited for this, but drawing them manually is very hard (since we need to draw each square or circle, plus the text, plus the relationships between the elements).

The `DiagrammeR` package allows us to create powerful diagrams, supporting the Graphviz syntax. Using it is actually simple. We will essentially define nodes, and we will then tell `DiagrammeR` how we want to connect those nodes. Of course, we can control the format of those diagrams (color, shapes, arrow types, themes, and so on).

Getting ready

In order to run this example, you need to install the `DiagrammeR` package using `install.packages("DiagrammeR")`.

How to do it...

In this recipe, we will draw a diagram depicting a company structure. The company is split into three groups, and within each group we will draw the sales in blue and the market share in green.

1. Import the library:

```
library('DiagrammeR')
```

2. We define the diagram using Graphviz's dot syntax. Essentially, it needs three parts—the `graph` part controls the global elements of the diagram, the `node` part defines the nodes, and the `edge` part defines the edges:

```
grViz("
digraph dot {

graph [layout = dot]

node [shape = circle,
style = filled,
color = grey,
label = '']

node [fillcolor = white, fixedsize = true, width = 2]
a[label = 'Company A']

node [fillcolor = white]
b[label = 'IT+RD Consulting'] c[label = 'General Consulting']
d[label = 'Other Activities']

node [fillcolor = white]

edge [color = grey]
a -> {b c d}
b -> {e[label = '254';color=blue] f[label = '83%';color=green]}
c -> {k[label = '132';color=blue] l[label = '61%';color=green]}
d -> {q[label = '192';color=blue] r[label = '47%';color=green]}
}")
```

How it works...

Inside our diagram, we define two main objects, nodes and edges. We define two nodes, and we define multiple edges that specify how everything will be connected. For each element, we can define the label that will be shown, and the color. The `label` and `color` arguments are used to specify the text and color that will be displayed for each node.

We use the `fixedsize` and the `width` parameters to force the elements in the corresponding node to have the same size. Had we not, then the circles for those nodes would be of different sizes.

The `grViz()` function is used to build the Graphviz diagram, as shown in the following screenshot:

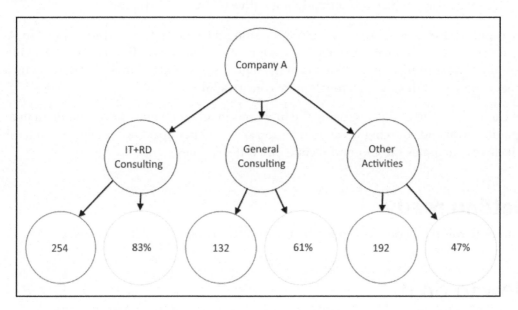

See also

The `DiagrammeR` package's homepage can be found at `http://rich-iannone.github.io/DiagrammeR/`.

C++ in R via the Rcpp package

The Rcpp package has become one of the most important packages for R. Essentially, it allows us to integrate C++ code into our R scripts seamlessly. The main advantage of this, is that we can achieve major efficiency gains, especially if our code needs to use lots of loops. A second advantage, is that C++ has a library called the **standard template library** (STL) that has very efficient containers (for example, vectors and linked lists) that are extremely fast and well suited for many programming tasks. Depending on the case, you could expect to see improvements anywhere from 2x to 50x. This is why many of the most widely used packages have been rewritten to leverage Rcpp. In Rcpp, we can code in C++ using the typical C++ syntax, but we also have specific containers that are well suited to store R-specific elements. For example, we can use the Rcpp::NumericVector or the Rcpp::DataFrame, which are certainly not native C++ variable types.

The traditional way of using Rcpp involves writing the code in C++ and sourcing it in R. Since Rcpp 0.8.3, we can also use the Rcpp sugar style, which is a different way of coding in C++. Rcpp sugar brings some elements of the high-level R syntax into C++, allowing us to achieve the same things with a much more concise syntax.

We can use Rcpp in two ways, using the functions in an inline way, or coding them in a separate script and sourcing it via sourcecpp(). The latter approach is slightly preferable as it clearly separates the C++ and R code into different files.

Getting ready

In order to run this code, Rcpp needs to be installed using install.packages ("Rcpp").

How to do it...

In this case, we will compare R against Rcpp (C++) for the following task. We will load a vector and a matrix. Our function will loop through each element of the vector, through each row, and through each row and column of that matrix, counting the number of instances where the elements of the matrix are greater than the ones in the vector.

1. Save the C++ code into a file named rcpp_example.cpp and we will source it from an R script:

   ```
   #include <Rcpp.h>
   using namespace Rcpp;
   // [[Rcpp::export]]
   ```

```
int bring_element (NumericVector rand_vector, NumericMatrix
rand_matrix) {
Rcout << "Process starting" << std::endl;
int mcounter = 0;
for (int q = 0; q < rand_vector.size();q++){
    for (int x = 0; x < rand_matrix.rows();x++){
        for (int y = 0; y < rand_matrix.cols();y++){
            double v1 = rand_matrix.at(x,y);
            double v2 = rand_vector[q];
            if ( v1 < v2){
                mcounter++;
            }
        }
    }
}
Rcout << "Process ended" << std::endl;
return mcounter;
}
```

2. In the corresponding R script, we need the following code:

```
library(Rcpp)
sourceCpp("./rcpp_example.cpp")
Rfunc <- function(rand__vector,rand_matrix){
 mcounter = 0
 for (q in 1:length(rand__vector)){
     for (x in 1:dim(rand_matrix)[1]){
         for (y in 1:dim(rand_matrix)[2]){
             v1 = rand_matrix[x,y];
             v2 = rand__vector[q];
             if ( v1 < v2){
                 mcounter = mcounter+1
             }
         }
     }
 }
 return (mcounter)
}
```

3. Generate a vector and a matrix of random Gaussian numbers:

```
some__matrix = replicate(500, rnorm(20))
some__vector = rnorm(100)
```

4. Save the starting and end times for the `Rcpp` function, and subtract the starting time from the end time:

```
start_time <- Sys.time()
bring_element(some__vector,some__matrix)
end_time <- Sys.time()
print(end_time - start_time)
```

5. Do the same as we did in the previous step, but for the R function:

```
start_time <- Sys.time()
Rfunc(some__vector,some__matrix)
end_time <- Sys.time()
print(end_time - start_time)
```

The C++ function takes 0.10 seconds to complete, whereas the R one takes 0.21 seconds. This is to be expected, as R loops are generally slow, but they are extremely fast in C++:

```
> start_time <- Sys.time()
> bring_element(some__vector,some__matrix)
Process starting
Process ended
[1] 522081
> end_time <- Sys.time()
> print(end_time - start_time)
Time difference of 0.106581 secs
>
>
> start_time <- Sys.time()
> Rfunc(some__vector,some__matrix)
[1] 522081
> end_time <- Sys.time()
> print(end_time - start_time)
Time difference of 0.2182128 secs
```

How it works...

The `sourcecpp` function loads the C++ or `Rcpp` code from an external script and compiles it. In this C++ file, we first include the `Rcpp` headers that will allow us to add R functionality to our C++ script. We use `using namespace Rcpp` to tell the compiler that we want to work with that namespace (so we avoid the need to type `Rcpp::` when using `Rcpp` functionality). The `Rcpp::export` declaration tells the compiler that we want to export this function to R.

Our `bring_element` function will return an integer (so that is why we have an `int` in its declaration). The arguments will be `NumericVector` and `NumericMatrix`, which are not C++ native variable types but `Rcpp` ones. These allow us to use vectors and matrices that operate with numbers without needing to declare explicitly if we will be working with integers, large integers, or float numbers. The `Rcout` function allows us to print output from C++ to the R console. We then loop through the columns and rows from the vector and the matrix, using standard C++ syntax. What is not standard here is the way we can get the number of columns and rows in these elements (using `.rows()` and `.cols()`), since these attributes are available through `Rcpp`. The R code is quite straightforward, and we then run it using a standard timer.

See also

The homepage for `Rcpp` is hosted at `http://www.rcpp.org`.

`Rcpp` is deeply connected to the `Armadillo` library (used for very high-performance algebra). This allows us to include this excellent library in our `Rcpp` projects.

The `Rinside` package (`http://dirk.eddelbuettel.com/code/rinside.html`), built by the creators of `Rcpp`, allows us to embed R code easily inside our C++ projects. These C++ projects can be compiled and run without requiring R. The implications of the `Rinside` package are enormous, since we can code highly performant statistical applications in C++ that we can distribute as standalone executable programs.

Interactive plots with the ggplot GUI package

The `ggplot GUI` package is excellent for making quick plots using the `ggplot` package, using a drag-and-drop approach. It will allow us to export the plots easily, and it will generate the corresponding `ggplot` code that creates the plots. It uses the excellent `Shiny` package to create a fully interactive approach for creating plots.

Most interestingly, the package has several different types of plots such as violin plots, histograms, scatterplots, and many more.

Getting ready

In order to install this package, we can use the `install.packages("ggplotgui")` command.

How to do it...

In this example, we will first create a histogram for the miles per gallon of vehicles from a dataset, and then produce a scatterplot showing the relationship between the miles per gallon and the horsepower of those vehicles.

1. We call the `ggplot_shiny()` function with an argument specifying that we want to work with the `mtcars` dataset:

```
library("ggplotgui")
ggplot_shiny(mtcars)
```

The following screenshot shows the `ggplot` GUI interface :

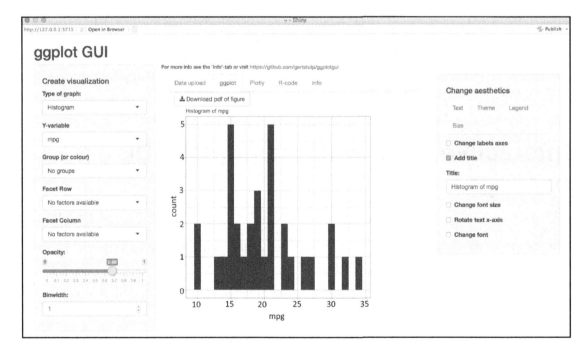

2. Doing a scatterplot is equally simple—we need to just choose the Scatter option and then the X-variables and Y-variables. We could also choose a grouping variable if we wanted to incorporate an extra dimension into this plot:

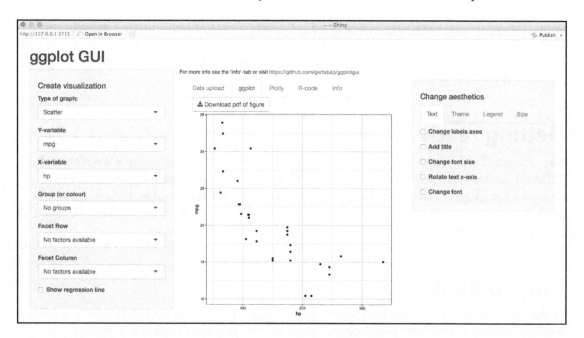

How it works...

This function will launch an interactive interface that we can use very easily. We just select the variables, the type of plot, and the format that we want. Finally, we can save the output as an image. The **R code** tab can be used to obtain the corresponding R code.

There's more...

We can do this instead, and we will be able to use a drag-and-drop approach to load datasets, instead of passing one as an argument:

```
ggplot_shiny()
```

Animations with the gganimate package

The `ggplot` package is great for creating static plots, but it can't handle animations. These are used when we have data indexed by time, and we want to show an evolution of that data. The `gganimate` package is designed following a similar logic, but for animations. It will construct plots for every time period and it will then interpolate between the frames in order to construct a smooth animation. This animation can also be exported as a GIF, then embedded later on any website or in any report.

Getting ready

The `gganimate` package is not yet available on the **Comprehensive R Archive Network (CRAN)**, so it needs to be downloaded from GitHub. In order to do that, we need the `devtools` package. It can be installed in the usual way and after that is done, we can call `install_github` to get the package from GitHub. In order to use this function, we need the `devtools` package.

How to do it...

In this exercise, we have sales and profits for several companies across multiple years. We want to create a scatterplot (which shows pairs of values between sales and profit) animated through time.

1. Start by installing the library:

```
install.packages('devtools')
devtools::install_github('thomasp85/gganimate')
```

2. Load the necessary libraries:

```
# Load required package
library(gapminder)
library(ggplot2)
library(gganimate)
# Basic scatter plot
```

3. Load the data and set the colors that will be used later:

```
data = read.csv("./companies.csv",stringsAsFactors = FALSE)
colors =
c("A"="#AB5406","B"="#EC9936","C"="#BE1826","D"="#9B4A06","E"="#FDD
6A2","F"="#9ACD62")
```

4. Execute the ggplot function. Note that labs(), transition_time(), and ease_aes() are specific to the gganimate function, and are not ggplot elements:

```
p = ggplot(data, aes(Sales, Profit, size = Profit,colour=Company))
+
 geom_point(alpha = 0.7, show.legend = FALSE) +
 scale_colour_manual(values = colors) +
 scale_size(range = c(2, 12)) +
 labs(title = 'Year: {frame_time}', x = 'GDP per capita', y = 'life
expectancy') +
 transition_time(Year) +
 ease_aes('linear')
```

5. Animate, and save the output into a .gif file:

```
animate(p, nframes = 48, renderer =
gifski_renderer("./gganim.gif"))
```

Here, we pick just two frames at random out of the total of 48:

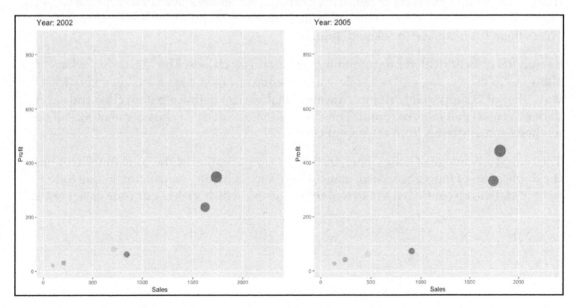

How it works...

The core of our script is the `animate` function, which will make repeated calls to the `ggplot` part, which is included in *p*. The `ggplot` function is just creating a regular scatterplot, and most of the code there defines the formatting and colors that we want. The only different part from a regular `ggplot` statement are these two parts: `transition_time(Year)` and `ease_aes("linear")`. The former specifies the variable that indicates the time steps, while the latter specifies the type of interpolation used to generate all the frames that we need. The `animate` function will make repeated calls to this, for purposes such as changing the year and using a linear interpolation.

See also

The package's website (`https://github.com/thomasp85/gganimate`) contains several other examples, such as animated boxplots.

Using R6 classes

Object-oriented programming allows us to organize our code in classes, encapsulating similar functionality together, and also allowing us clearly to separate internal from external methods. For example, we can design a class that has a method for reading data from a file, another method for removing outliers, and another one for selecting a subset of the columns. We can decide to keep all of these methods as public, meaning that we can access them from outside the class definition.

R supports object-oriented programming via `S3` and `S4` classes. The `R6Class` package, allows us to use `R6` classes. These allow us to define our own classes in R in a very easy way. They also support inheritance, meaning that we can define a parent class and several derived classes that inherit from it. This implies that the derived classes can access all the methods and attributes from the parent class.

The central advantage of using inheritance is its simplification of the code (thus avoiding the duplication of functions). Also, using inheritance generates a structure in our code (where classes are connected via base/parent classes), which makes our code easier to read.

Getting ready

In order to run this example, we need to install the R6 package. It can be installed using `install.packages("R6")`

How to do it...

We will load data from a `.csv` file containing records customers, and we will instantiate a new class instance for each record. These records will be added to a list.

1. Import the R6 library:

   ```
   library(R6)
   ```

2. Load the data from a `.csv` file:

   ```
   customers = read.csv("./Customers_data.csv")
   ```

3. We will now begin defining the R6Class structure. Note that we have two lists, one for the public attributes or methods, and another one for the private (these methods or attributes can only be accessed by other methods from this class). The `initialize` method is called whenever we create a new instance of this class. Note that we refer to the internal elements from this class using the `self$` notation:

   ```
   Customer = R6Class(public=list(Customer_id = NULL,Name = NULL,City
   = NULL,
   initialize =
   function(customer_id,name,city,Missing_product,Missing_since){
     self$Customer_id <- customer_id
     self$Name <- name
     self$City <- city
   },
   is_city_in_america = function(){
     return (upper_(self$City) %in% c("NEW
   YORK","LONDON","MIAMI","BARCELONA"))
   },
   full_print = function(){
     print("-------------------------------------")
     print(paste("Customer name ->",self$Name))
     print(paste("Customer city ->",self$City))
     print("-------------------------------------")
   }
   ),private=list(
   upper_ = function(x){
   ```

```
    return (toupper(x))
  }
))
```

4. We loop through our DataFrame and create a new `Customer` instance, passing three arguments. These are passed to the `initialize` method that we defined previously:

```
list_of_customers = list()
for (row in 1:nrow(customers)){
  row_read = customers[row,]
  customer =
Customer$new(row_read$Customer_id,row_read$Name,row_read$City)
  list_of_customers[[row]] <- (customer)
}
```

5. We call our `print` method:

```
list_of_customers[[1]]$full_print()
```

The following screenshot prints the customer name and city:

```
> list_of_customers[[1]]$full_print()
[1] "------------------------------------"
[1] "Customer name -> Michaela"
[1] "Customer city -> London"
[1] "------------------------------------"
>
```

How it works...

Let's assume we want to process clients' data from a CSV file. The R6 classes support public and private components. Each one of them will be defined as a list containing both methods or attributes. For example, we will store the `customer_id`, the `name`, and the `city` as public attributes. We need to initialize them to NULL. We also need an `initialize` method that will be called whenever the class is instantiated. This is the equivalent of a constructor in other programming languages. Inside the initializer or constructor, we typically want to store the variables provided by the user. We need to use the `self` keyword to refer to the class variables. We then define a method that will return either TRUE or FALSE if the city belongs is in America or not. Another method, called `full_print()`, will print the contents of the class.

The `lock_objects` method is not usually very important; it indicates whether we want to lock the elements in the class. If we set `lock=FALSE`, that means that we can add more attributes later, if we want to.

Here, we only have one private method. Since it is private, it can only be called within the class, but not externally. This method, called `upper_`, will be used to transform the text into uppercase.

After the class is defined, we loop through the DataFrame and select each row sequentially. We instantiate the class for each row, and then we add each one of these into a list.

The convenience of using classes is that we now have a list containing each instance. We can call the specific methods or attributes for each element in this list. For example, we can get a specific element and then call the `is_city_in_america` method; and finally we call the `full_print` method.

There's more...

The `R6` package also supports inheritance, meaning that we can define a base class (that will act as a parent), and a derived class (that will act as a child). The derived class will be able to access all the methods and attributes defined in the parent class, reducing code duplication, and simplifying its maintainability. In this example, we will create a derived class called `Customer_missprod`, which will store data for clients who haven't yet received a product they were expecting. Note that the way we achieve this is by using the `inherit` parameter.

Note that we are overriding the `full_print` method, and we are printing some extra variables. It is important to understand the difference between the `super` and `self` methods—the former is used to refer to attributes or methods present in the base class. We evidently need to override the constructor (already defined in the base class) because we have more variables now:

```
library(R6)
customers = read.csv("./Customers_data_missing_products.csv")
Customer_missprod = R6Class(inherit = Customer,
                     public=list(Missing_prod = NULL,Missing_since =
NULL,
initialize = function(customer_id,name,city,Missing_product,Missing_since){
  super$Customer_id <- customer_id
  super$Name <- name
  super$City <- city
  self$Missing_prod <- Missing_product
  self$Missing_since <- Missing_since
```

```
  },
  full_print = function(){
    print("----------------------------------")
    print(paste("Customer name ->",super$Name))
    print(paste("Customer city ->",super$City))
    print(paste("Missing prod ->",self$Missing_prod))
    print(paste("Missing since ->",self$Missing_since))
    print("----------------------------------")
  }
 )
 )

list_of_customers = list()
for (row in 1:nrow(customers)){
  row_read = customers[row,]
  customer =
Customer_missprod$new(row_read$Customer_id,row_read$Name,row_read$City,row_
read$Missing_product,row_read$Missing_since)
  list_of_customers[[row]] <- (customer)
}

list_of_customers[[1]]$full_print()
```

Take a look at the following screenshot:

```
> list_of_customers[[1]]$full_print()
[1] "----------------------------------"
[1] "Customer name -> Michaela"
[1] "Customer city -> London"
[1] "Missing prod  -> TV"
[1] "Missing since -> 01/01/2018"
[1] "----------------------------------"
>
```

Modeling sequences with the TraMineR package

The TraMineR package allows us to work with categorical sequences, to characterize them, and to plot them in very useful ways. These sequences arise in a multiplicity of situations, such as describing professional careers: university→Company A→unemployed→Company B, or for example when describing what some clients are doing—opening account→buying→closing account.

In order to work with this package, we typically want one record per unit or person. We should have multiple columns—one for each time step. For each time step, we should have a label that indicates to which category that unit or person belongs to, at that particular time. In general, we are interested in doing some of the following—plotting the frequency of units at each category for each time step, analyzing how homogeneous the data is for each time step, and finding representative sequences. We will generally be interested in carrying these analyses by certain cohorts.

Getting ready

The `TraMineR` package can be installed via `install.packages("TraMineR")` function.

How to do it...

In this example, we will use the `TraMineR` package to analyze data from a club membership. The clients can choose from three membership levels/tiers—**L1** (cheap membership), **L2** (general membership), or **L3** (VIP membership), and they can obviously cancel their membership. We want to characterize these levels further by age and sex tiers. We have four cohorts defined by the intersection between two age groups (**18-25** and **26-45**) and sex (**F** or **M**).

This club offers a discount after 12 weeks, in order to entice clients to jump into either the **L2** or **L3** membership (which are obviously more premium, and thus more expensive). We should expect to see the majority of customers on the **L1** membership initially, and then observe them jumping to **L2** or **L3**.

1. Import the library:

   ```
   library(TraMineR)
   ```

2. Load the data and set the labels and the short labels for the plots:

   ```
   datax       <- read.csv("./data_model.csv",stringsAsFactors =
   FALSE)
   mvad.labels <- c("CLOSED","L1", "L2", "L3")
   mvad.scode  <- c("CLD","L1", "L2", "L3")
   mvad.seq    <- seqdef(datax, 3:22, states = mvad.scode,labels =
   mvad.labels)
   group_      <- paste0(datax$Sex,"-",datax$Age)
   ```

3. The `seqfplot` function can be used to plot the most frequent sequences:

```
seqfplot(mvad.seq, with.legend = T, border = NA, title = "Sequence
frequency plot")
```

This results in the following output:

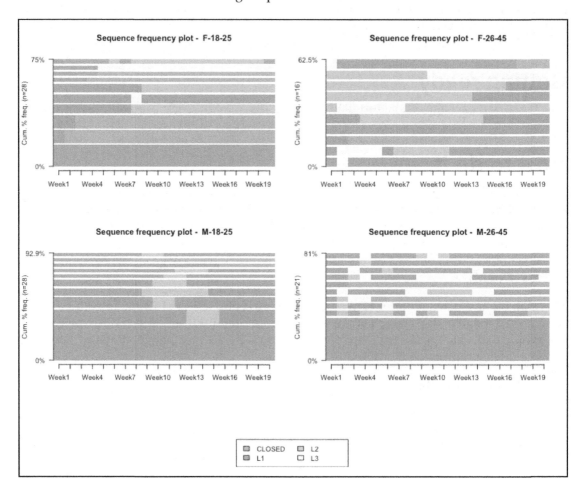

How it works...

These plots represent the most typical sequences for each cohort. We have one color for each class (level). The height represents the proportion of cases. The number of the upper-left part indicates the proportion of the data represented in this plot.

As we can see, there are obvious patterns by age group-sex combination. Let's direct our attention towards the ones in the lower part (male plots). Evidently, the majority of them stay in the Level-1 group forever (lower tall bars); a substantial amount spend most of their time in Level 1, although they sometimes switch to either group **L2** (orange) or close their accounts (green). Clearly, the **18-25** age range is much more stable and less prone to jumping into other memberships. Indirectly, we could conclude that most of them are quite happy with **L1** membership.

We could extend the same analysis for the females, although it is quite interesting that the ones from **18-25** are quite prone to closing their accounts in the first 2-3 weeks. Interestingly, the females in the **26-45** grouping are more prone to enrolling directly in the **L2** or **L3** memberships, which is quite a distinctive characteristic of this cohort.

In general, we observe that clients enrolled in **L1** are more likely to cancel their subscriptions than those in **L2** or **L3**. This makes sense, as clients paying more (**L2** or **L3**) should be, in principle, more happy with the club.

There's more...

The `TraMineR` package allows us to plot histograms for the sequences. The interpretation is analogous to a regular histogram, with the obvious difference that the histogram is indexed by time:

```
seqdplot(mvad.seq, with.legend = T, group=group__, border = NA, title =
"State distribution plot")
```

The following screenshot shows the `TraMineR` histograms:

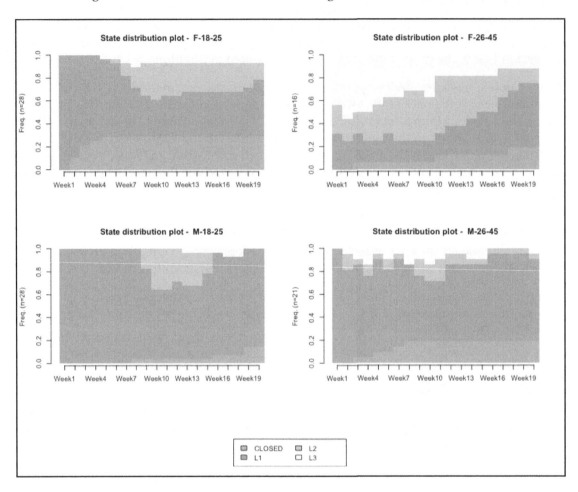

For every case, **L1** is the most frequent tier, maybe except for females **F-26-45**. In this case, **L3** and **L2** are quite important. It seems that for both groups between 18 and 25, there are no clients moving to groups **L2/L3** until **Week 10**, and even when they do, they don't seem to stay much time in either one compared to both groups in the **26-45** range. We can also confirm that females **F-18-25** are generally more likely to close their accounts.

Clustering sequences with the TraMineR package

When dealing with sequences of events it might even be more interesting to find clusters of sequences. This will always be necessary as the number of possible sequences will be very large.

Getting ready

In order to run this example, you will need to install the TraMineR package with the install.packages("TraMineR") command.

How to do it...

We will reuse the same example from the previous recipe, and we will find the most representative clusters.

1. Import the library:

   ```
   library(TraMineR)
   ```

2. This step is exactly the same as we did for the previous exercise. We are just assigning the labels and the short labels for each sequence:

   ```
   datax <- read.csv("./data__model.csv",stringsAsFactors = FALSE)
   mvad.labels <- c("CLOSED","L1", "L2", "L3")
   mvad.scode <- c("CLD","L1", "L2", "L3")
   mvad.seq <- seqdef(datax, 3:22, states = mvad.scode,labels =
   mvad.labels)
   group__ <- paste0(datax$Sex,"-",datax$Age)
   ```

3. Calculate the clusters:

   ```
   dist.om1 <- seqdist(mvad.seq, method = "OM", indel = 1, sm =
   "TRATE")
   library(cluster)
   clusterward1 <- agnes(dist.om1, diss = TRUE, method = "ward")
   plot(clusterward1, which.plot = 2)
   cl1.4 <- cutree(clusterward1, k = 4)
   cl1.4fac <- factor(cl1.4, labels = paste("Type", 1:4))
   seqrplot(mvad.seq, diss = dist.om1, group = cl1.4fac,border = NA)
   ```

The following screenshot shows the clusters using TraMiner:

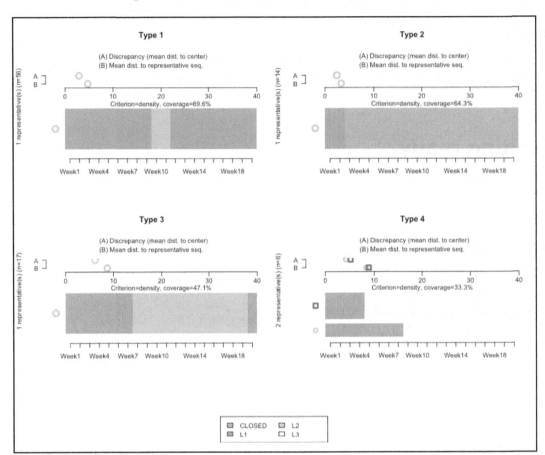

How it works...

This algorithm finds representative clusters for our dataset. Note that here, we don't want to do this by cohort (if we wanted to, we would first need to subset the data). The horizontal bars reflect the clusters, and the **A-B** parts on top are used to calculate the discrepancies between the data and the cluster.

Type 1 and **Type 3** refer to sequences starting at **L1**, then moving to **L2** at around **Week 9**, and then remaining for either a few weeks or for many weeks. Both are quite homogeneous, reflecting that the sequences don't diverge much with respect to the representative ones.

Type 2 relates to sequences starting at **L1**, and then those accounts closing almost immediately. Here, the mean differences with respect to that sequence are even smaller, which is to be expected: once an account is closed, it is not reopened, so we should expect closed accounts to be quite homogeneous.

Type 4 is interesting. It reflects that after opening an **L1** account, those clients jump directly to **L3**. We have two bars, which reflects that the algorithm is finding two large groups—people jumping to **L3** in **Week 9**, and people jumping to **L3** in **Week 4**.

There's more...

Entropy is a measure of how much disorder exists within a system (its interpretation is similar to entropy in physics). We will calculate it by cohort:

```
seqHtplot(mvad.seq,group=group__, title = "Entropy index")
```

The following screenshot shows the entropy for each group/week:

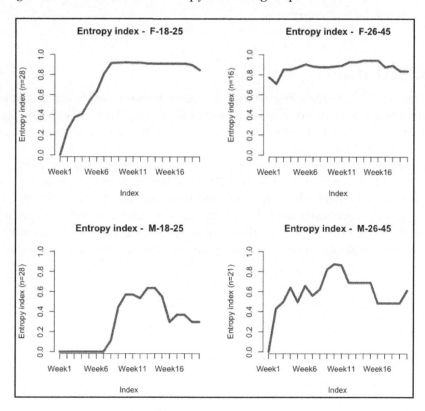

Evidently, the entropy should be **low** at the beginning as most people are enrolled at **L1**. We should expect it to go up dramatically after Weeks 7-10, since this company is offering a discount at around that stage, so people might then jump into **L2** or **L3**.

Displaying geographical data with the leaflet package

The `leaflet` package is the de facto package for creating interactive maps in R. Part of its success is due to the fact that it works really well in conjunction with `Shiny`. Shiny is used to create interactive web interfaces in R, that can be accessed from any browser.

Getting ready

In order to run this recipe, you need to install the `leaflet` and `dplyr` packages using the `install.packages()` command.

How to do it...

On November 15, 2017, a submarine from the Argentine Navy was lost in the South Atlantic Ocean along with its crew. It is suspected that a catastrophic accident occurred, that caused an explosion and later an implosion. The submarine departed from Ushuaia (South Argentina) and was expected to arrive at its headquarters in Mar del Plata (Central Argentina) navigating on a south-north trajectory. Its last contact was recorded circa -46.7333, -60.133 (when around 50% of its route had been covered), and a sound anomaly was later detected by hydrophones and triangulated at -46.12, -59.69. This anomaly happened a few hours after the submarine's last contact, and was consistent with an explosion. In November 2018, the submarine was found using several remotely operated underwater vehicles (ROVs) very near to the sound anomaly's position at around 900 meters depth.

In this recipe, we will first plot a line connecting its departure and destination ports. We will then add two markers—one for its last known position, and another one for the sound anomaly position. We will finally add a circle around this anomaly's position, indicating the area where most of the search efforts were concentrated.

1. Load the libraries:

```
library(dplyr)
library(leaflet)
```

2. We use two DataFrames—one for the line, and another one for the markers:

```
line = data.frame(lat =
c(-54.777255,-38.038561),long=c(-64.936853,-57.529756),mag="start")
sub_data = data.frame(lat =
c(-54.777255,-38.038561,-46.12,-46.73333333333333),long=c(-64.93685
3,-57.529756,-59.69,-60.13333333333333),mag=c("start","end","sound
anomaly","last known position"))
area_search = data.frame(lat=-46.12,long=-59.69)
```

3. Plot the map with the line, the markers, and also a circle:

```
leaflet(data = sub_data) %>% addTiles() %>%
  addMarkers(~long, ~lat, popup = ~as.character(mag), label =
~as.character(mag)) %>%
  addPolylines(data = line, lng = ~long, lat = ~lat) %>%
addCircles(lng = -59.69, lat = -46.12, weight = 1,radius = 120000)
```

The following screenshot shows the map and trajectory:

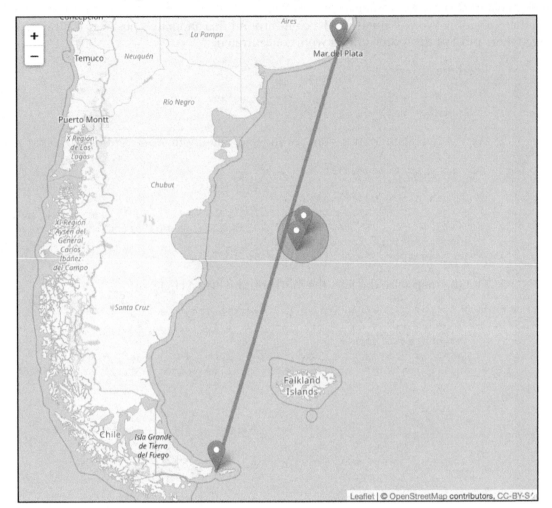

How it works...

The `leaflet` package renders the map, along with the markers that we are passing through the `sub_data` DataFrame. The line is drawn using the `addPolylines` function. And the circle is drawn using the `addCircles` function.

2
Univariate and Multivariate Tests for Equality of Means

We will cover the following recipes in this chapter:

- The univariate t-test
- The Fisher-Behrens problem
- Paired t-test
- Calculating ANOVA sum of squares and F tests
- Two-way ANOVA
- Type I, Type II, and Type III sum of Squares
- Random effects
- Repeated measures
- Multivariate t-test
- MANOVA

Introduction

One of the most basic problems that we need to solve in statistics is comparing the means from two (or more) groups. It's tempting to just take those means and compare them while ignoring all of the statistical theory. The central problem is that, if we did that, we would not have a reference level that we can compare that difference against (we wouldn't know whether that difference is large or small).

The statistical approach provides a foundation for this comparison, providing us with critical values that we should do this comparison against. In essence, this comparison depends on the variability in the data (the noisier the data is, the greater this difference needs to be to be deemed significative) and on how certain we want to be that a non-significative difference is considered significative (this is called the α value, which is also known as type 1 error).

This test can be extended to more complex scenarios, such as comparisons between paired observations (that is, measurements before and after treatment is applied to certain subjects), multiple groups (this is called **ANOVA**), or multivariate data. In this chapter, we will review certain techniques that are relevant for these situations.

The univariate t-test

The t-test is a basic tool in statistics used to compare the means of two samples. Its most strict version assumes that both samples are distributed according to a Gaussian distribution and have the same (unknown) variance.

In statistics, we refer to the null hypothesis as the hypothesis we want to test, and the alternative hypothesis as the one we use when the null is rejected. They are usually referred to as H_0 and H_1.

The t-test tests the equality of means from two populations, and it can be formulated in three possible ways:

- H_0: The means of the two populations are the same versus H_1: in that the means of the populations are different.
- H_0: The mean of population 1 is greater or equal than the one from population 2 versus H_1: the mean of population 1 is smaller than population 2.
- H_0: The mean of population 1 is smaller or equal than the one from population 2 versus H_1: the mean of population 1 is greater than population 2.

The user needs to define which one should be used, according to what needs to be tested. Each one will return a different p-value; in particular, the first one will be a two-sided test, and the other ones will be one-sided. What this means is that if we test (1), the p-value will be equivalent to the area to the right of the test statistic, plus the area to the left of the negative value of the test statistic (this is because the p-values reflect the probability that we get a test statistic as extreme or more extreme than the one we got, and since we are testing whether the means of both groups are equal, that difference could be positive or negative).

The following screenshot shows the two sided test:

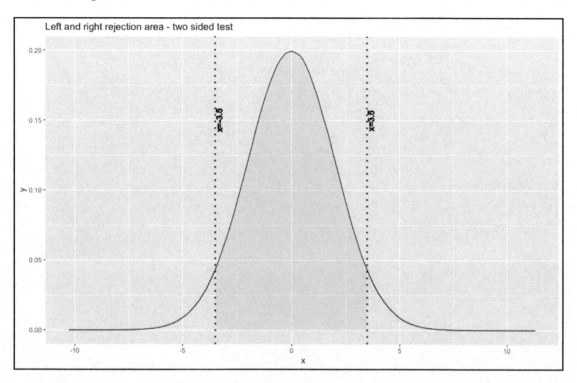

The following screenshot shows the left rejection area:

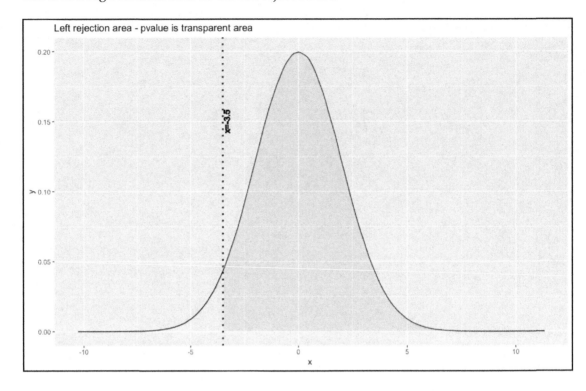

The following screenshot shows the right rejection area:

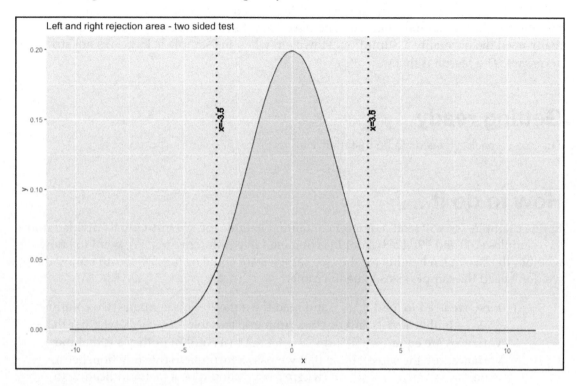

The test statistic for this case is as follows:

$$t = \frac{\bar{X}_1 - \bar{X}_2}{S_p \sqrt{(\frac{1}{n_1} + \frac{1}{n_2})}}$$

S_p is the pooled standard deviation estimator (note that we are assuming that the variances are the same between the two groups):

$$S_p = \sqrt{\frac{(n_1 - 1)S_{p^1}^2 + (n_2 - 1)S_{p^2}^2}{n_1 + n_2 - 2}}$$

This is distributed according to a t-Student distribution with n_1+n_2-2 degrees of freedom. So far, we have assumed that both samples are distributed according to a Gaussian distribution, but sometimes that won't be the case. When the sample is small (<30), we really need the normality assumption. However, when the sample is large, it's not strictly necessary. The reason is that.

Getting ready

The `dplyr` package needs to be installed via `install.packages("dplyr")`.

How to do it...

In this example, we will load a dataset containing heights for 199 individuals divided into two samples (100 and 99). Each sample is obtained in a different area. We want to know whether the two mean heights for the two samples are equal or not. It's worth noting that we don't need the sample sizes to be the same:

1. First, we need to load `dplyr` and read the dataset. This contains two columns: `Sample` (either 1 or 2) and `Height` (numeric variable). To check whether the variances are equal, we first do `LeveneTest` (its null hypothesis is that the variances are the same). Note that we pass a formula to this function, because it expects `variable ~ group` (where `group` should be a factor indicating to which sample each observation belongs). This is why we transformed the `Sample` variable into a factor (it was numeric). Because we get a p-value of 0.42, we don't reject the null hypothesis and conclude that the variances are equal. Now, we may continue with our t-test:

    ```
    library(dplyr)
    library(car)
     data = read.csv("./heights.csv")
     data$Sample = as.factor(data$Sample)
     leveneTest(Height ~ Sample.data)
    ```

The preceding code displays the following output of `leveneTest` results:

```
> leveneTest(Height ~ Sample,data)
Levene's Test for Homogeneity of Variance (center = median)
       Df F value Pr(>F)
group   1  0.6526 0.4201
      197
```

2. Now, we create two DataFrames containing the respective samples using `dplyr`, as follows:

```
sample1 = data %>% filter(Sample==1) %>% select(Height)
sample2 = data %>% filter(Sample==2) %>% select(Height)
```

3. We are now ready to do our analysis using the `t.test` function. We pass the two samples with `var.equal=TRUE` (we have already tested the equality of the variances). We can also pass the confidence level that we want for the test, which in this case is 95%. The statistic is equal to -0.141 with 197 degrees of freedom (=199 - 2) yielding a p-value of 0.88. Consequently, we do not reject the null hypothesis, and conclude that there is no statistical evidence to conclude that the means are different. As expected, the 95% confidence interval (from -3.09 to 2.68) does include the zero:

```
t.test(sample1,sample2,var.equal=TRUE,conf.level =
.95,alternative="two.sided")
```

The preceding code displays the following output of the two sample t-test. The null hypothesis is not rejected:

```
> t.test(sample1,sample2,var.equal=TRUE,conf.level = .95,alternative="two.sided")

        Two Sample t-test

data:  sample1 and sample2
t = -0.14195, df = 197, p-value = 0.8873
alternative hypothesis: true difference in means is not equal to 0
95 percent confidence interval:
 -3.096543  2.680704
sample estimates:
mean of x mean of y
 179.5081  179.7160
```

How it works...

R calculates the statistic using the two samples, and then calculates the p-value according to the hypothesis that we specified (in this case, we are testing hypothesis 1, so we are testing the two-sided version).

There's more...

Confidence intervals and hypothesis tests are tightly related, as the former can be inverted to yield the latter and vice versa. Given a fixed type 1 error equal to C (usually 5%), if a hypothesis test rejects the null hypothesis (that a statistic is equal to zero), then the 1-C (95%) confidence intervals won't include the zero. Notice that the pooled standard deviation estimate is obtained by pooling the variability for the two samples. In the next recipe, we will discuss what happens when this assumption is violated.

The Fisher-Behrens problem

The original t-test is designed for two Gaussian samples with equal unknown variance. When the variances are not the same, the degrees of freedom for the test are not the usual ones (the equality of variances is known as homocedasticity). Consequently, we can't calculate the p-values and, by extension, we can't test our hypothesis. This is known as the **Fisher-Behrens problem**.

It has been found that the t-test (with its usual degrees of freedom) can still be used with moderate departures from the homocedasticity (equality of variances) assumption. But this does not take us very far: translating the idea that the test is robust to departures from this assumption is difficult to operationalize (the impact depends on the sample sizes, the relative differences in the variances, and so on).

If the sample is large enough, we can ignore the problem altogether and get the p-values using a Gaussian distribution (a t-Student distribution converges to a Gaussian distribution as the degrees of freedom go to infinity). If the sample is small, we need a different technique. The preferred one is the **Welch t-test**, which finds the appropriate degrees of freedom using the so-called **Welch-Satterwhite approximation**.

To use Welch's test, we can simply use the `t.test` function with the `var.equal=FALSE` option. Even when the variances are the same, it works quite well compared to the standard t-test:

```
t.test(.....,var.equal=FALSE,....)
```

How to do it...

In the following exercise, we will generate two samples with the same mean and different variances, and we will calculate the effective error I rates for the t-test. In general, this is a futile exercise, since statistical tests are designed to yield the very same error I rate as they promise. However, in this case, we are introducing a violation to the assumptions in the test, namely that the variances are different (so the effective α rates will differ from the nominal ones).

If the variances were the same, we would expect to see that 5% of them have a p-value less than 0.05 ((in this case, even though the null hypothesis is true, 5% of them should be rejected just because of random chance). But in our case, the variances won't be the same, so the effective type I errors won't match the theoretical ones:

1. This will be our main function here. Note how we extract the p-values from the t-test:

```
calc_effective_alphas <- function(n,sd1,sd2,equalvar){
  rejected <- 0
  for (x in 1:100000){
  data1 <- rnorm(n,10,sd1)
  data2 <- rnorm(n,10,sd2)
  result <- t.test(data1,data2,var.equal=equalvar)$p.value
  if (result < 0.05){
  rejected <- rejected + 1
  }
  }
  return (rejected/100000)
  }
```

2. We will print four cases here. The first and third cases will be done simulating two samples with standard deviations of 2 | 5 respectively); the second and fourth cases will be done assuming that the standard deviations are 5 | 20. The first two cases are estimated using the standard t-test, whereas the other two are estimated using Welch's correction. The intention is to compare 1 vs 3, and 2 vs 4 in order to gauge how well Welch's test works relative to the standard t-test:

```
print(paste("n=10 / sd1=2 / sd2=5 / effective
alpha=",calc_effective_alphas(10,2,5,TRUE)))
print(paste("n=10 / sd1=2 / sd2=20/ effective
alpha=",calc_effective_alphas(10,2,20,TRUE)))
print(paste("n=10 / sd1=2 / sd2=5 / effective
alpha=",calc_effective_alphas(10,2,5,FALSE)))
print(paste("n=10 / sd1=2 / sd2=20/ effective
alpha=",calc_effective_alphas(10,2,20,FALSE)))
```

The preceding code generates the following output of `effective alpha` rates:

```
> print(paste("n=10 / sd1=2 / sd2=5 / effective alpha=",calc_effective_alphas(10,2,5,TRUE)))
[1] "n=10 / sd1=2 / sd2=5 / effective alpha= 0.05647"
> print(paste("n=10 / sd1=2 / sd2=20/ effective alpha=",calc_effective_alphas(10,2,20,TRUE)))
[1] "n=10 / sd1=2 / sd2=20/ effective alpha= 0.06595"
> print(paste("n=10 / sd1=2 / sd2=5 / effective alpha=",calc_effective_alphas(10,2,5,FALSE)))
[1] "n=10 / sd1=2 / sd2=5 / effective alpha= 0.04978"
> print(paste("n=10 / sd1=2 / sd2=20/ effective alpha=",calc_effective_alphas(10,2,20,FALSE)))
[1] "n=10 / sd1=2 / sd2=20/ effective alpha= 0.05031"
```

These results confirm our following suspicions:

- The first two cases (the ones using the standard t-test) yield effective alpha rates are larger than the effective ones (we would be rejecting the null hypothesis more than we should—5%).
- By comparing the first case vs the second one, we realize that the greater the variance difference is, the larger the actual alpha values are (for the t-test).
- The effective alpha rates are almost 5% when we use Welch's correction (the third and fourth cases). This indicates that Welch's correction is working really well.

How it works...

We run this simulation multiple times, compute the t-tests/Welch tests, and accumulate them into a `rejected` variable. As we explained previously, we should expect to get 5% of cases rejected (this works as an accumulator when using a critical 0.05 p-value.

There's more...

A valid question is whether we are losing power due to Welch's correction when the variances are the same. Intuition would suggest that Welch's should be worse than the standard t-test, even when the variances are the same. The t-test (its standard version) is a uniform that's very powerful to test, meaning that, for any possible alternative, it has the greatest power. How can we assess the loss in statistical power when we use Welch's test?

In this case, we will study what happens when we have two samples with different means (12 versus 10) and the same variance:

```
calc_power <- function(n,sd1,sd2,equalvar){
  rejected <- 0
  for (x in 1:100000){
```

```
data1 <- rnorm(n,12,sd1)
data2 <- rnorm(n,10,sd2)
result <- t.test(data1,data2,var.equal=equalvar)$p.value
if (result < 0.05){
rejected <- rejected + 1
}
}
return (rejected/100000)
}
print(paste("n=10 / sd1=2 / sd2=20/ effective
power=",calc_power(10,2,2,TRUE)))
print(paste("n=10 / sd1=2 / sd2=20/ effective
power=",calc_power(10,2,2,FALSE)))
```

The preceding code generates the following output of effective power:

```
> print(paste("n=10 / sd1=2 / sd2=20/ effective power=",calc_power(10,2,2,TRUE)))
[1] "n=10 / sd1=2 / sd2=20/ effective power= 0.5658"
> print(paste("n=10 / sd1=2 / sd2=20/ effective power=",calc_power(10,2,2,FALSE)))
[1] "n=10 / sd1=2 / sd2=20/ effective power= 0.55787"
```

The power here is the proportion of cases that have been rejected (we know that, since the means are different, we should be rejecting 100% of them). As we can see, the power is almost the same (for this alternative at least) when we use Welch's test with equal variances.

We can conclude that Welch's test works well when the variances are different, and almost as good as the t-test when the variances are the same.

Paired t-test

There is a variant of the t-test that can be used when the data is paired (this usually happens when we have two observations for each subject). For example, this may occur if we use a specific program and we want to evaluate its effectiveness by taking one measurement before and after the program is executed. The advantage of this is that the difference (after-before) truly represents the impact of the program that we are evaluating (we are making sure that any possible external variable has been filtered out).

This is much better than having just two samples, where one is taken before the policy was executed and another is one (with different individuals) taken after. If there are differences between those two samples, they might bring trouble to our test. For example, let's suppose that sample1 contains individuals that perform better at work, while sample2 contains individuals that don't perform so well. We choose sample2, and we give them a bonus. The problem is that, if we test whether those means are the same, we won't be able to separate the initial difference from the bonus' effect.

The underlying idea of the paired t-test is to subtract the old value from the new, and test whether that difference is equal to zero. As in the standard t-test, we have three hypotheses (smaller or equal to zero versus greater than zero; equal to zero or different; equal or greater than zero versus smaller). The greater power of this test is derived from the fact that, when we subtract newer-previous, we are effectively removing all of the variability between subjects, and only keeping whatever is caused due to the policy/treatment that we are evaluating.

In this case, we are actually subtracting a set of values minus the other ones, and testing whether that mean difference is equal to zero. Consequently, the test statistic is as follows:

$$t = \frac{\bar{d}}{\sqrt{\frac{S^2}{n}}}$$

Here, the numerator is the mean difference, and in the denominator, we have the sum of squares divided by the sample size. The degrees of freedom are *n-1*.

How to do it...

In the following example, we will load performance indexes from 80 employees (before and after a new bonus scheme was announced). We want to test whether the bonus has produced an improvement in performance. In this case, the null hypothesis will be that the performance change is smaller than zero or equal to zero, versus greater than zero:

1. Load the data, as follows:

```
data = read.csv("./paired_scores.csv")
```

2. Perform the `paired` t-test:

```
t.test(data$post_bonus,data$pre_bonus,conf.level =
.95,alternative="greater",paired=TRUE)
```

The preceding code generates the following output:

```
> t.test(data$post_bonus,data$pre_bonus,conf.level = .95,alternative="greater",paired=TRUE)

        Paired t-test

data:  data$post_bonus and data$pre_bonus
t = 3.676, df = 79, p-value = 0.0002151
alternative hypothesis: true difference in means is greater than 0
95 percent confidence interval:
 1.265567      Inf
sample estimates:
mean of the differences
          2.312674
```

3. The mean of the differences is 2.31, which generates a t statistic of 3.67 with 79 degrees of freedom (80-1), yielding a p-value < 0.01. We then conclude that the true difference is greater than 0. Consequently, the bonus program was effective in generating an increase in employee performance.

How it works...

R calculates the differences and computes the mean and the sum of squares. It then uses the appropriate degrees of freedom and gets the final test statistic. The p-value is obtained in this case as the area to the right of the test statistic (because it's so small, it implies that, if the difference was actually 0, it would be very rare to have seen a value as extreme as the one we got).

There's more...

If we had used a different hypothesis, the p-values would have been different. For example, if we had tested whether the difference was greater than zero versus smaller than zero, we would have got a very big p-value. The test-statistic would still be the same (3.67), but the way we compute the p-value would be different. In this case, we would take the area to the left of the test statistic (we would be looking at values as small or smaller than the one we got):

```
t.test (data$Score2,data$Score1,conf.level =
.95,alternative="less",paired=TRUE)
```

The preceding code generates the following output for the t-test result. We don't reject the null hypothesis:

```
> t.test(data$post_bonus,data$pre_bonus,conf.level = .95,alternative="less",paired=TRUE)


        Paired t-test

data:  data$post_bonus and data$pre_bonus
t = 3.676, df = 79, p-value = 0.9998
alternative hypothesis: true difference in means is less than 0
95 percent confidence interval:
     -Inf 3.359781
sample estimates:
mean of the differences
            2.312674
```

Calculating ANOVA sum of squares and F tests

Analysis of Variance (**ANOVA**) is a technique that's used for analyzing the differences between the means from several groups (it is essentially an extension of the t-test to multiple samples). It is deeply tied to a statistical discipline known as **experimental design**, a discipline that analyzes how to collect the data, how to layout an experiment, and which variables should be measured.

In statistics, **correlation** is not the same as **causality**: two phenomena might be correlated, but deducing causality out of that correlation is usually wrong. For example, most animals wake up just before dawn, but we can't deduce that waking up causes the sunlight to appear.

A very important question then, is: how can we determine causality within a statistical framework? The way we identify causality in statistics is by first laying out an experiment in a structured way. We identify the relevant factors that we think cause a response in a target variable, we identify blocking factors (factors that we are not interested in per se, but could explain part of the variability of the data), and we collect the data in accordance to the framework and budget that we defined.

The most important part is that we define one factor to be a baseline/placebo that we can compare all of the treatments against. We do this because we usually want to test using a treatment/action versus not doing anything. Because using the treatment will always be more expensive than not doing anything, we want to be sure that there is a measurable effect (a statistically significative effect-causality).

For example, if we have a website, we can change the background color to red, green, or blue. We will be interested in evaluating whether the background color has any impact on the purchases that people make through the website. In statistical terms, our null hypothesis is that there is no difference that's attributable to the colors.
Our alternative hypothesis is that there is at least one color that induces a different response from the rest of them.

If we find evidence that rejects that hypothesis, we will then obviously be interested in finding which colors cause a statistically different amount of purchases. Most websites are currently built using this data-driven approach; in fact, this is known as **A/B testing**. Of course, ANOVA can actually be used in any context, for any imaginable industry. The central assumption is that the data is distributed according to a Gaussian distribution, which is a lax assumption that applies to most situations.

This is achieved by decomposing the variability in the data into two parts: one part that is related to the group variability (color, in our example), and another part that is related to the internal variability within each group. The former is usually referred to as **explained variability** (because we can attribute it to a group, such as color effect), while the latter is referred to as **unexplained variability** (we can't explain why the data deviates from the group means). If the null hypothesis was true (the color type is not related to the sales), we would expect both variabilities to be quite similar. This would imply that the fluctuations of the data around the group means is similar to the fluctuations of the data with respect to the global mean of the data. If there was a color effect, we should see that the between effects variability is substantially greater than the within variability. Operationally, this is achieved by computing the sum of the squared deviations for the within and between effects components. If the relevant statistic is large (meaning that the between sum of squares is larger than the within sum of squares), we can conclude that the factor (in this case, the color) is statistically significative.

The following screenshot shows the ANOVA same means:

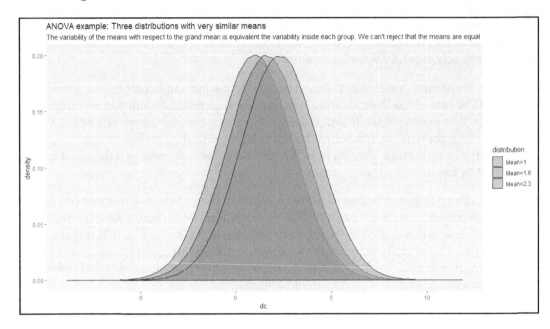

The following screenshot shows the ANOVA different means:

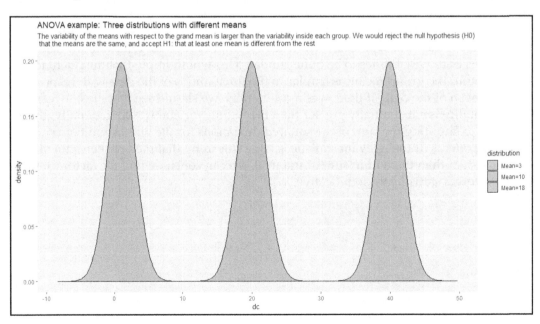

How to do it...

In this exercise, we will focus on a simple ANOVA example and show the mechanics of the sum of squares and F-tests. We will use a balanced dataset and calculate the sum of squares and the F-tests manually. The dataset will contain weight measurements for animals, and these will depend on which food type they were fed on and which lot the animals were assigned.

In R, we can compute the `anova` table using the `anova` function on a linear model that we can estimate via the `lm` or `aov` functions:

1. Load the dataset, as follows:

```
data = read.csv("./anova__lot_type.csv")
```

2. We need to compute the sum of squares for the first factor. This is defined as the sum of squared deviations between the predictions and the target variable:

```
result = lm(Result ~ Lot,data=data)
SS_LOT = sum((predict(result)-mean(data$Result))**2)
```

3. Now, we will compute the sum of squares for the second factor. Regarding the LOT factor, we just added it and computed the sum of squares. However, we are adding the Lot effect and then adding the food type effect. We are calculating the sum of squares for the food type after we have controlled the Lot effect. This is called the sequential sum of squares and will be the default that R will report when we use the automatic ANOVA functions. In the ANOVA terminology, this is called the Type I sum of squares: it has a major drawback in that it depends on the order that we are specifying the factors in. The first factor was tested in isolation, and the second factor was tested after the first factor was added. In this case, we purposely added the block/control factor first, and we then added the main effect. We usually just want to test the main effect conditional on the block effects (blocking just means adding an extra nuisance factor to get more precision - in our case the Lot); we really don't care much about the block effect, per se. But what would have happened if we had two main effects; how should they have been added? Take a look at the following code:

```
result = lm(Result ~ Lot + Food.Type,data=data)
SS_FOODTYPE = sum((predict(result)-mean(data$Result))**2) - SS_LOT
```

4. Now, we will compute the residual sum of squares. It is defined as the sum of the squared differences between the predictions and the target variable. Note that this is the variability of the model that we can't explain:

```
SS_ERROR = sum((predict(result)-data$Result)**2)
```

5. We now compute the F statistics. They are defined as the ratio between the sum of squares and the residual sum of squares (each one of them respectively divided by their degrees of freedom). The degrees of freedom for the LOT effect is equal to 1, and the degrees of freedom for the food type is equal to 2 (they are equal to the number of levels minus one). The residual degrees of freedom are equal to the number of observations minus the number of parameters that were estimated (in this case we have 60 observations and 4 parameters that were estimated - an intercept, a coefficient for the south lot, and two coefficients for the food type). Note that the p-values are calculated as the area to the right of the test statistic (according to an F distribution). It can be proven that since the F statistic involves the division of two sum of squares (that are distributed according to Chi Square distributions) divided by their respective degrees of freedom, it is distributed as an F distribution.

```
FF_LOT       = (SS_LOT/1)/(SS_ERROR/56)
FF_FOODTYPE  = (SS_FOODTYPE/2)/(SS_ERROR/56)
pval_LOT     = 1-pf(FF_LOT,1,56)
pval_FOODTYPE = 1-pf(FF_FOODTYPE,2,56)
```

6. Let's print all of the values that we have calculated, as follows:

```
print(paste("SS(ERROR) = ",SS_ERROR))
print(paste("SS(LOT) =",SS_LOT,"/F(LOT) = ",FF_LOT,"pvalue =
",pval_LOT))
print(paste("SS(FOODTYPE) =",SS_FOODTYPE,"/F(FOODTYPE) =
",FF_FOODTYPE,"pvalue = ",pval_FOODTYPE))
```

The following screenshot shows the mean squares, F values, and p-values :

```
> print(paste("SS(ERROR) = ",SS_ERROR))
[1] "SS(ERROR) =  5124.39647632035"
> print(paste("SS(LOT) =",SS_LOT,"/F(LOT) = ",FF_LOT,"pvalue = ",pval_LOT))
[1] "SS(LOT) = 573.680971022944 /F(LOT) =  6.2692522964877 pvalue =  0.0152258042235658"
> print(paste("SS(FOODTYPE) =",SS_FOODTYPE,"/F(FOODTYPE) = ",FF_FOODTYPE,"pvalue = ",pval_FOODTYPE))
[1] "SS(FOODTYPE) = 4038.80007335211 /F(FOODTYPE) =  22.0682381967178 pvalue =  8.56406995319858e-08"
```

7. The ANOVA table can be printed using the following syntax. Obviously, this matches our calculations:

```
anova(result)
```

The preceding code shows the ANOVA table:

```
> anova(result)
Analysis of Variance Table

Response: Result
          Df Sum Sq Mean Sq F value    Pr(>F)
Lot        1  573.7  573.68  6.2693   0.01523 *
Food.Type  2 4038.8 2019.40 22.0682 8.564e-08 ***
Residuals 56 5124.4   91.51
---
Signif. codes:  0 '***' 0.001 '**' 0.01 '*' 0.05 '.' 0.1 ' ' 1
```

Two-way ANOVA

We could extend our initial example (a website with different color palettes) to something slightly more complex: instead of having just one factor (color), we could have another one (actually, we could have even more than two). For example, we could add the font type that was used on the website and study how those two factors (color and font type) impact the number of purchases that are made. Unfortunately, this adds an extra complication, because one effect might depend on the levels for the other one: for example, the font type might be relevant to explain the number of purchases, but only when the color is red.

The effects for the color and website are usually referred to as main effects, and the interaction between them is referred to as the interaction effect. Before analyzing the main effects, we should always study the interaction effect first: if it is found to be significant, we can't really look at the main effects, since the factors involved in the interaction won't have an effect when taken in isolation.

There are actually three ways of calculating the sum of squares, which are usually referred to as Type1, Type2, and Type3 sum of squares. If the underlying design is balanced, the three ways are equivalent and yield the same results. When it is unbalanced, the three of them will differ. A balanced design is one where the number of observations for each combination of effects is the same.

How to do it...

In this example, we will use a dataset that contains several days of data for a website selling furniture. On each day, 50% of the website users are exposed to each background color (red or blue). Also, within each group, 50% of them are exposed to a classic font type, and 50% of them to a modern font type. The objective is to understand whether these two factors cause any impact on the sales for this website. Finally, if there are differences, we want to characterize them:

1. Load the data, as follows:

```
library(dplyr)
r = read.csv("./2wayanova.csv")
```

2. We need to prepare the ANOVA table via the `aov()` function. The formula that we will use is `Sales ~ Colour + Font + Font*Colour`, meaning that we want to model `Sales` as a function of two factors: the color and the font type. The `Font*Colour` term is the interaction: we want to test it and proceed only if it is found to be nonsignificative. Then, we do a quantile-quantile plot to determine whether the residuals are Gaussian (ANOVA needs the residuals to be Gaussian and have the same variance in each group):

```
d = aov(Sales ~ Colour + Font + Font*Colour,data=r )
plot(d, 2)
shapiro.test(residuals(d))
```

The preceding code generates the following output of `qqplot`—normality doesn't seem reasonable here as the residuals don't lie over a line:

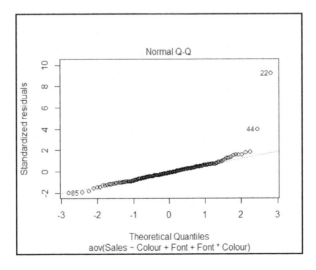

The `shapiro-wilk` test rejects the null hypothesis of normality:

```
> shapiro.test(residuals(d))

            Shapiro-Wilk normality test

data:   residuals(d)
W = 0.7372, p-value < 2.2e-16
```

3. Evidently, the quantile-quantile plot indicates that the data is not Gaussian, mainly because of a few observations on the left. We can identify them by clicking on them and pressing *Esc*. Hopefully, after removing them, we can rerun our analysis and get correct estimates. Another way of testing the normality of the data is by using the **Shapiro-Wilk statistic**; it tests the null hypothesis that the data is Gaussian (in this case, we reject it since we get a p-value of 8.624e-05, confirming our analysis using qqplot). So, we remove observations 22 and 44:

```
r = r[-c(22,44),]
d = aov(Sales ~ Colour + Font + Font*Colour,data=r )
plot(d, 2)
shapiro.test(residuals(d))
```

The preceding code generate the following output of qqplot—the residuals are all over the line once we remove the two abnormal values:

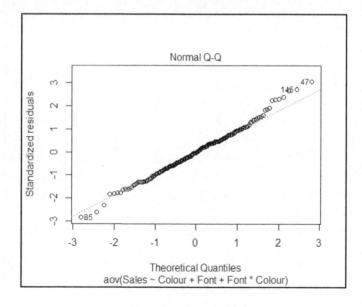

The following screenshot shows that the `shapiro-wilk` test looks much better now; we do not reject the normality of `residuals`:

```
> shapiro.test(residuals(d))

          Shapiro-Wilk normality test

data:  residuals(d)
W = 0.9926, p-value = 0.4141
```

4. This looks much better since most of the points lie near the line. This is confirmed by `shapiro-Wilk p-value=0.8688` (we don't reject the null hypothesis of normality). Once we are satisfied with the normality of the residuals, we can evaluate whether the variance is similar across the different groups. In this case, we can conclude that, except for a few cases, the spread of the data is fairly similar:

```
plot(d, 1)
```

The preceding code generates the following output of residuals versus fitted. There is no obvious structure in the residuals, and the variance seems to be constant as we move through the *X* axis:

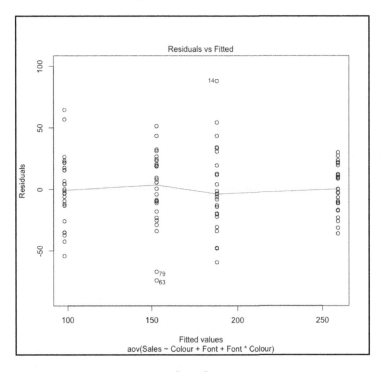

5. Finally, we get the `anova` table using the following code. The interaction is obviously not significative:

```
anova(d)
```

This is the resulting ANOVA table:

```
> anova(d)
Analysis of Variance Table

Response: Sales
            Df Sum Sq Mean Sq  F value    Pr(>F)
Colour       1  67573   67573 173.9832 < 2.2e-16 ***
Font         1  18751   18751  48.2786 5.399e-11 ***
Colour:Font  1    280     280   0.7209    0.3969
Residuals  195  75735     388
---
Signif. codes:  0 '***' 0.001 '**' 0.01 '*' 0.05 '.' 0.1 ' ' 1
```

How it works...

The ANOVA table shows the degrees of freedom, the sum of squares, the mean squares (sum of squares divided by the degrees of freedom), the F statistic value, and the p-values. As we stated previously, we need to focus our attention on the interaction: it can be seen that it is not significative at the 0.05 level. Once it is rejected, we can proceed with our analysis: both the color and the font are highly significant. We can then conclude that `Colour` and the `Font` type explain a substantial part of the variability. This implies that, for both effects, at least one of the levels (one of the colors or one of the font types) has a mean that is different from the rest. Some statisticians prefer to re-estimate the model without the interaction in case it has been found to be non-significative.

There's more...

In general, once we have determined that a factor is significative (at least one of its levels has a mean that's different from the rest), we want to plot the differences between the levels, along with their 95% confidence intervals. This can be achieved via the **Tukey Honest Differences** function (`TukeyHSD` in R), as follows:

```
rbind(TukeyHSD(d)$Colour,TukeyHSD(d)$Font)
```

The preceding code generates the following output:

```
> rbind(TukeyHSD(d)$Colour,TukeyHSD(d)$Font)
                   diff       lwr       upr        p adj
Red-Blue       -36.85853 -42.36961 -31.34746 0.000000e+00
Modern-Classic  19.42561  13.91175  24.93947 5.391809e-11
```

This prints all of the mean differences between each pair of factors, along with the lower and upper 95% confidence intervals (this can be changed via the `conf.level` parameter). Finally, the p-value is printed (the null hypothesis is that the difference is equal to zero) with an adjustment. This adjustment is necessary because, when we do multiple comparisons, it is likely that some of them will appear to be significative just because of random chance.

We can conclude that the `Blue` background colour provides a statistically significative difference with respect to the `Red` colour (it is actually between 31 and 42). For the font type, we can conclude that the modern font type yields an extra average of 19.42 over the classic one.

Type I, Type II, and Type III sum of squares

In a one-way ANOVA, the sum of squares can be obtained in a straightforward manner. However, in a two-way ANOVA, things get much more complicated because we have at least three possibilities for computing them. For the following examples, let's assume that we have two factors (A and B), each one with their respective levels.

Type I

The first possibility is the Type I sum of squares, which can be computed by first calculating the sum of squares for factor A, then the sum of squares of B conditional on A, and finally the sum of squares of the interaction (AB) after including the factors, A and B. This is why this is called the **sequential sum of squares**. Consequently, the order is as follows:

$$SS(A)$$
$$SS(B|A)$$
$$SS(AB|A, B)$$

The main problem here is that these calculations depend on the order in which we specified the model. So, $Y = A + B + A*B$ will be different from $Y = B + A + A*B$, which makes it very hard to justify (and hence to use in certain cases). Nevertheless, the interaction part is fine, since it is tested after we consider A and B. This is why Type I is generally used for testing the interaction, and not the main effects (when the design is unbalanced; if it was balanced, then we could test the main effects as well because $SS(B) = SS(B|A)$).

Type II

The second possibility is the Type II sum of squares, which are computed by calculating the sum of squares given one factor, and then doing the reverse. However, we can't test any interaction here (we first need to test whether AB is significative and only use Type II when it is not):

$$SS(A|B)$$
$$SS(B|A)$$

Type III

The final possibility is to calculate the sum of squares conditional on the interaction. This is uncommon, as we typically aren't interested in the main effects given that a significant interaction exists. If the interaction is not significative, then Type II has more power:

$$SS(A|B, AB)$$
$$SS(B|A, AB)$$

If the underlying design is balanced (the same amount of observations for each factor combination), the three of them will be equivalent. If they are not, they will differ. In general, Type II is preferred since we want to test an effect after controlling the other one, but we can't test the interaction using it. So, we generally prefer Type I initially to test the interaction, and if it is found to be nonsignificative, we continue with Type II. On the other hand, if it is found to be significative, we can proceed with Type III, but whether it makes sense to make inferences on a main effect after an interaction is detected is questionable.

The `anova` and `aov` functions in R will work with the Type I sum of squares. To get Type II or Type III, we can use the `anova` function in the `car` package.

Getting ready

We will need the `car` package in R. If it's missing, it can be installed via `install.packages("car")`.

How to do it...

We will use the following steps to perform ANOVA:

1. In the previous example, we loaded a balanced dataset that had two outliers. These had to be removed to get a model that had Gaussian residuals. The problem that we ignored in the previous chapter is that the design is no longer balanced:

    ```
    library(dplyr)
    r = read.csv("./2wayanova.csv")
    r = r[-c(22,44),]
    ```

2. Let's use the ANOVA Type I sum of squares. The interaction is clearly not significative:

    ```
    type1 = aov(Sales ~ Colour + Font + Font*Colour,data=r )
    summary(type1)
    ```

    This results in the following output:

    ```
    > summary(type1)
                 Df Sum Sq Mean Sq F value  Pr(>F)
    Colour        1  67573   67573 173.983 < 2e-16 ***
    Font          1  18751   18751  48.279 5.4e-11 ***
    Colour:Font   1    280     280   0.721   0.397
    Residuals   195  75735     388
    ---
    Signif. codes:  0 '***' 0.001 '**' 0.01 '*' 0.05 '.' 0.1 ' ' 1
    ```

3. Since the interaction is not significative, we can use the Type II sum of squares. Both are significative (same as with Type1), so the conclusions remain the same:

    ```
    type2 = Anova(aov(Sales ~ Colour + Font + Font*Colour,data=r
    ),type=c("II"))
    type2
    ```

The following screenshot shows the output of the Anova table:

```
> type2
Anova Table (Type II tests)

Response: Sales
           Sum Sq  Df F value     Pr(>F)
Colour      67967   1 175.248 < 2.2e-16 ***
Font        18751   1  48.347 5.187e-11 ***
Residuals   76015 196
---
Signif. codes:  0 '***' 0.001 '**' 0.01 '*' 0.05 '.' 0.1 ' ' 1
```

4. We could have obtained the Type3 sum of squares using the type=III option. The numbers do change slightly, but the same conclusions hold for the main effects:

```
options(contrasts = c("contr.sum","contr.poly"))
 f = Anova(aov(Sales ~ Colour + Font + Font*Colour,data=r
),type=c("III"))
 f
```

The following screenshot shows the output of the Anova table:

```
> type3
Anova Table (Type III tests)

Response: Sales
               Sum Sq  Df   F value     Pr(>F)
(Intercept) 2105397    1 5420.8923 < 2.2e-16 ***
Colour        68190    1  175.5741 < 2.2e-16 ***
Font          18817    1   48.4498 5.034e-11 ***
Colour:Font     280    1    0.7209    0.3969
Residuals     75735 195
---
Signif. codes:  0 '***' 0.001 '**' 0.01 '*' 0.05 '.' 0.1 ' ' 1
```

How it works...

As we explained at the beginning of this recipe, if the interaction is not significative, Type II sum of squares are preferred. Because in our case the interaction's p-value is 0.39 > 0.05, we should use Type II sum of squares. If the interaction had been significative, we should have used Type III or I instead.

The inconsistency of Type III is reflected in the following example. If we had two effects (A,B), and an interaction (AB), Type III would compare a model with (A,B,AB) versus a model with (B,AB). This is not intuitive, why our baseline model has an interaction but not both terms of that interaction?

If we are interested in the interaction, then the distinction between Type I, II, and III is irrelevant as the sum of squares will be the same for that term.

Random effects

So far, we have explored models where we have different fixed levels for each effect. This makes a lot of sense when we have a set of possible levels for an effect that we control and are interested in measuring. It also makes sense when we have a blocking effect that has a finite (and small) set values (for example, the sex or occupation of a person). In some cases, we will have a huge amount of levels that will be generally unimportant, for example, if we want to measure whether a drug is effective, and we are dealing with multiple observations per person, we want to add a blocking effect for a person. In these cases, we are not interested in the effect per se, but we certainly want to use it as a control variable for our model. A model that uses proper blocks, will be more efficient: think of ANOVA as a method of attributing variability to factors. If we have the right factors in place, we can be sure that we are putting the variance in the right buckets.

The first issue is that, if we have lots of levels (people, in our example), our model will require lots of parameters. If the number of observations for some people is small, that will imply that those parameters won't be accurately estimated. The second issue is that estimating a parameter for each person is generally not very useful, since we will use this effect just to control the variability in the model. As it usually happens in statistics, we tend to prefer models that are as simple as possible, since more complex models have a natural tendency to overfit (instead of fitting to the structure of the data, the model starts to capture the noise).

These models/examples (that we have used so far in ANOVA) are fixed effects models (we have k-1 parameters for each effect/factor). Random effects models are different: in this case, we assume that all observations belonging to the same subject are correlated (they all share a random shock). We then need to estimate a single parameter: the variance of the random effect. When all of the effects are random (this is an unusual situation), we say that the model is a random effects model. If all of the effects are fixed, we say that the model is a fixed effects model. And if we have fixed and random effects, we say that the model is a **mixed effects model**.

How can we decide whether an effect should be fixed or random? In most cases, this is solved by looking at whether the levels for the effect are a sample of a larger population. This is natural when working with people, companies, or animals.

Getting ready

To run this recipe, we will need the lme4, lsmeans, and lmerTest packages.

How to do it...

In the following example, we will work with a mixed effects model, containing data for some clients. We have 100 observations with 50 subjects and several replications per subject. Each client is contacted each time by a salesman using a variety of communication strategies (this is the fixed effect we are interested in).

The target variable is the amount sold, and we want to understand whether there are differences that are attributable to the different communication strategies. If that is the case, we want to implement the best communication strategy as the main one for the entirety of the sales team:

1. First, we need to load the necessary libraries and dataset, as follows:

```
library(lme4)
library(lmerTest)
library(lsmeans)
clients <- read.csv("./clients.csv")
```

2. We will use the lmer function from the lme4 package. We want to model Sales in terms of Strategy, Client, and Salesman. The notation for this model will be different from a model where the effects are fixed. The (1|Client) term means that we want to add a random intercept (mean) effect for each client. This implies that all of the observations belonging to the same client will be correlated (they will share a common shock). We use the same approach for the Salesman effect:

```
E = lmer(Sales ~ Strategy + (1|Client) + (1|Salesman),data=clients)
summary(E)
```

Note that all of the fixed effects coefficients are statistically significative. Regarding the random effects, we can see that most of the variability of the model is explained by the salesman (it's almost as big as the combined client variability and the unexplained variability – residual).

The preceding code generates the following output of mixed effects model results:

```
> summary(E)
Linear mixed model fit by REML. t-tests use Satterthwaite's method ['lmerModLmerTest']
Formula: Sales ~ -1 + Strategy + (1 | Client) + (1 | Salesman)
   Data: clients

REML criterion at convergence: 1627.8

Scaled residuals:
     Min       1Q    Median       3Q      Max
-2.33945 -0.49886 -0.07755  0.65161  2.40887

Random effects:
 Groups    Name         Variance Std.Dev.
 Client    (Intercept)   61.47    7.840
 Salesman  (Intercept)  243.51   15.605
 Residual                73.90    8.596
Number of obs: 212, groups:  Client, 80; Salesman, 10

Fixed effects:
                        Estimate Std. Error      df t value Pr(>|t|)
StrategyDiscount_driven   83.712      5.236 10.812   15.99 7.22e-09 ***
StrategyModern            57.135      5.257 10.974   10.87 3.26e-07 ***
StrategyTraditional       98.612      5.131  9.978   19.22 3.27e-09 ***
---
Signif. codes:  0 '***' 0.001 '**' 0.01 '*' 0.05 '.' 0.1 ' ' 1

Correlation of Fixed Effects:
           StrtD_ StrtgM
StratgyMdrn 0.885
StrtgyTrdtn 0.952  0.903
```

3. The ANOVA table can be obtained as usual, and obviously the fixed effect is highly significative:

```
anova(E)
```

The following screenshot shows ANOVA table:

```
> anova(E)
Type III Analysis of Variance Table with Satterthwaite's method
         Sum Sq Mean Sq NumDF  DenDF F value    Pr(>F)
Strategy  45775   15258     3 21.537  206.48 5.101e-16 ***
---
Signif. codes:  0 '***' 0.001 '**' 0.01 '*' 0.05 '.' 0.1 ' ' 1
```

How it works...

The `lmer` function can estimate a model using **Maximum Likelihood (ML)** or **Restricted Maximum Likelihood (REML)**. ML yields biased estimates for the variance components (the variances for our random effects) but can be used for comparing results between different models that contain different fixed effects formulations (the usual case). REML provides unbiased estimates for the variance components, but can't be used for comparing between different models. By default, `lmer` uses REML, which can be changed via `REML = FALSE`.

ML estimates have a lower variance than REML but are, of course, biased. Nevertheless, the bias disappears as the sample size rises to infinity. That is why ML is preferred when *n* is large, and REML is preferred for small samples.

The REML criterion is the **restricted maximum likelihood (REML)** values at the end of the iterations, and the scaled residuals shows that they are symmetric here. These models can be estimated by either REML or ML: REML provides unbiased estimates for the (random effects) variance components, but the REML value cannot be compared between models having different fixed effects. ML provides biased variance components, but the ML values can be used to compare between different models having different fixed effects. For large samples, ML is preferred since the bias disappears. Let's direct our attention to the random effects: the standard errors are 8.59 for the residual, 15.6 for the salesman effect, and 7.8 for the client effect. Thus, the salesman effect explains roughly 50% of the variability in the model. We can conclude that the salesman is very important, and the client variability is not very relevant. A correct sales strategy would then be to focus the attention on having the right salesmen, and don't invest much time on picking the right clients to target.

The fixed effects part looks slightly different from our previous ANOVA tables, since we now have a coefficient for each level of our fixed effects. Remember that we are not estimating an intercept here, and we are getting one coefficient per level.

The p-values require some special comments: they are not printed when you use the `lmer` function, but are obtained when you load the `lmerTest` package. By default, the `lmer` function does not print them since the degrees of freedom that should be used for them is debatable. The interpretation is still the same: if the number is small, it implies that the coefficient is statistically significative.

There's more...

After we are satisfied with our model, we can jump into the most interesting part: obtaining confidence intervals for the means of the fixed effects that we estimated. This can be achieved using the following function (note that we are indicating the `lsmeans` function, which we want to use to get the analysis for the `Strategy` effect):

```
result_lsmeans = lsmeans(E,pairwise ~ Strategy)
print(result_lsmeans)
```

The preceding code generate the following output of `lsmeans` results:

```
> print(result_lsmeans)
$`lsmeans`
 Strategy         lsmean  SE   df lower.CL upper.CL
 Discount_driven   83.7 5.24 10.9    72.2     95.3
 Modern            57.1 5.26 11.0    45.6     68.7
 Traditional       98.6 5.13 10.0    87.2    110.0

Degrees-of-freedom method: kenward-roger
Confidence level used: 0.95

$contrasts
 contrast                       estimate  SE    df t.ratio p.value
 Discount_driven - Modern          26.6 2.52 110.5  10.539 <.0001
 Discount_driven - Traditional    -14.9 1.61 148.4  -9.266 <.0001
 Modern - Traditional             -41.5 2.29  86.1 -18.084 <.0001

P value adjustment: tukey method for comparing a family of 3 estimates
```

This prints two parts. The first part part has the least-squares means for the mean effects for each level (along with the 95% confidence intervals), while the second part has the estimated differences for all possible contrasts. Contrasts are just differences between all levels. We can see that all of the contrasts are statistically significative.

Repeated measures

Repeated measures designs contain several measurements for the same experimental unit. This generally occurs when we assign different doses of a treatment to a unit and want to evaluate the response through time.

We now have a fixed effect for time, which is typically coded as 1, 2, 3 . . , k that needs to be added. We would expect that this variable/effect will have an impact on the response.

These designs raise four major points, and we need to decide how to solve them:

- Do we think that time has the same impact for all of the experimental units? We have two options for this:
    - If yes, we will just add the time variable as a fixed effect.
    - If no, we will still add the time variable as a fixed effect, plus a random effect for time by subject. What this means is that the time effect can be obtained as the sum of the fixed effect (average for all units) plus the random effect. This is a way of adding heterogeneity in the effect, ensuring that the total effects are pulled toward the mean effect (fixed effect).
- Should the time effect be linear or nonlinear? Or should each timestep have a distinct effect? There are two options:
    - If we assume linearity, we will just treat the time variable as numeric
    - If we assume that each time step has a distinct effect, we should add the time variable as a factor (it will have k levels)
- Do we need a special covariance structure? By default, once we set up a random effect (typically by experimental unit), all of the observations for that unit will be correlated (will share a common shock). This is usually questionable, as it implies that the covariance between a pair of any two observations will be constant. Observations that are further away in time should be less correlated than observations for consecutive time steps.
- Since we are including the time effect, should we consider an interaction between the main effect and time? This implies that the response to the treatment changes according to the time step we are in. In general, this interaction is initially added, and discarded if not significative.

Getting ready

We will use the `ggplot2`, `nlme`, and `lsmeans` packages in this recipe. These can be installed via the usual `install.packages()` command.

How to do it...

In the following example, we will load a dataset containing performance scores for employees. We will observe four records for each employee. For each time step, each employee will receive either the traditional or the boost compensation package. We want to find out whether there are differences between the two compensation packages:

1. First, we need to load the necessary libraries and the dataset that we will use:

```
library(ggplot2)
library(nlme)
data_company = read.csv("./repeated_measures.csv")
```

2. We will plot the responses for each employee. Here, we want to determine whether the Time/Performance slopes are the same between employees or not. We can see that the slopes (`Performance-Time`) are similar, so it doesn't seem necessary to add a different time response for each employee:

```
ggplot(data_company,aes(x=Time,y=Performance)) + geom_line() +
geom_point(data=data_company,aes(x=Time,y=Performance)) +
facet_wrap(~Employee,nrow=3)
```

The preceding code generates the following output:

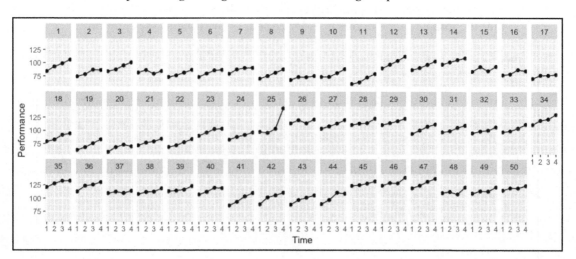

3. The fixed effects part will consist of the Bonus type, Sector (company department), Time, and a Time:Bonus type interaction. For the random effects part, we will only have a random intercept by Employee. We are also specifying an **autoregressive order 1 (AR1)** lag structure. This will cause every pair of consecutive observations for the same experimental unit to be correlated. The first thing we notice is the **Akaike information criterion (AIC)** number, which can be used to among different models. The random effects part contains the variance for the random effects, plus the variance for the residual. It can be seen that the Employee variance contributes 80% more variability than the residual. The Phi coefficient is the autoregressive coefficient for the residual. We then get the estimated coefficients for the fixed effects, along with the standard errors and the p-values:

```
fit <- lme(Performance ~ Bonus + Sector + Time + Time:Bonus ,
random = list( ~1 |Employee) , correlation = corAR1(form=
~Time|Employee), data = data_company)
 summary(fit)
```

The following screenshot shows the model results. We are testing whether there is an interaction between time and bonus. It is slightly non-significative, meaning that the impact of the bonus is independent of the time in the company:

```
Linear mixed-effects model fit by REML
 Data: data_company
       AIC      BIC      logLik
 1175.053 1204.464 -578.5266

Random effects:
 Formula: ~1 | Employee
         (Intercept) Residual
StdDev:     8.121308 4.708467

Correlation Structure: AR(1)
 Formula: ~Time | Employee
 Parameter estimate(s):
      Phi
0.7055112
Fixed effects: Performance ~ x_Bonus + x_Sector + Time + Time:x_Bonus
                  Value Std.Error  DF  t-value p-value
(Intercept)    84.84882 1.4303763 145 59.31923  0.0000
x_Bonus1        9.82991 1.1033073 145  8.90949  0.0000
x_Sector1     -10.04146 1.8167875 145 -5.52704  0.0000
x_Sector2       0.17172 1.1674012 145  0.14710  0.8833
Time            5.04404 0.2592823 145 19.45387  0.0000
x_Bonus1:Time   0.43554 0.2527656 145  1.72310  0.0870
 Correlation:
               (Intr) x_Bns1 x_Sct1 x_Sct2 Time
x_Bonus1       -0.085
x_Sector1       0.021  0.044
x_Sector2       0.043 -0.027 -0.783
Time           -0.455  0.065  0.001 -0.119
x_Bonus1:Time   0.051 -0.573  0.000 -0.010 -0.113

Standardized Within-Group Residuals:
        Min          Q1         Med          Q3         Max
-3.40845899 -0.36621574 -0.01625146  0.42886226  1.70236869

Number of Observations: 200
Number of Groups: 50
```

4. The ANOVA table can be built using the following code. These F tests are consistent with what we have already seen in the fixed effects coefficients. All of the effects are significative, except for the `TimexBonus` interaction:

```
anova(fit)
```

The preceding code generates the following output for the `anova` table:

```
> anova(fit)
              numDF denDF  F-value p-value
(Intercept)       1   145 6079.059  <.0001
x_Bonus           1   145  154.109  <.0001
x_Sector          2   145   19.749  <.0001
Time              1   145  391.135  <.0001
x_Bonus:Time      1   145    2.969   0.087
```

5. But do we really need the AR1 error term? The issue is that the more irrelevant terms we have in our model, the greater the imprecision will be for our main effects. So, we only want to keep the necessary parts of our model:

```
fit <- lme(Performance ~ Bonus + Sector + Time + Time:Bonus ,
random = list( ~1 |Employee) , data = data_company)
 summary(fit)
 anova(fit)
```

The following screenshot shows the simplified model with no autoregressive structure:

```
Linear mixed-effects model fit by REML
 Data: data_company
       AIC      BIC    logLik
 1195.103 1221.246 -589.5517

Random effects:
 Formula: ~1 | Employee
         (Intercept) Residual
StdDev:     8.580379 3.071642

Fixed effects: Performance ~ x_Bonus + x_Sector + Time + Time:x_Bonus
                 Value Std.Error  DF  t-value p-value
(Intercept)   84.97143 1.3371508 145 63.54663  0.0000
x_Bonus1      10.24409 1.0169992 145 10.07286  0.0000
x_Sector1    -10.00198 1.7639710 145 -5.67015  0.0000
x_Sector2      0.47204 1.1025057 145  0.42815  0.6692
Time           5.02791 0.2023747 145 24.84454  0.0000
x_Bonus1:Time  0.21025 0.1973925 145  1.06514  0.2886
 Correlation:
              (Intr) x_Bns1 x_Sct1 x_Sct2 Time
x_Bonus1      -0.077
x_Sector1      0.022  0.043
x_Sector2      0.046 -0.028 -0.804
Time          -0.381  0.052  0.002 -0.154
x_Bonus1:Time  0.040 -0.485  0.000 -0.014 -0.107

Standardized Within-Group Residuals:
       Min          Q1         Med          Q3         Max
-5.39626213 -0.46356930  0.02759754  0.55655047  2.84400914

Number of Observations: 200
Number of Groups: 50
```

6. The AIC criterion can be used to choose the best model among a set of competing ones. The likelihood always increases with the more parameters we add because a more complex model always fits the data better. So, the likelihood itself cannot be used to determine which model should be used (it would just tell us to always use the more complex model). The AIC penalizes the log-likelihood by the number of parameters. Operationally, we just pick the model with the lowest AIC. As we can see, the model that does not include the AR1 coefficient has a lower AIC.

7. Consequently, we decide to use our starting model.

8. We finally calculate `lsmeans`. We can conclude that the `boost_bonus` pack provides a statistically significative increase in the performance score of 108.4 (note that, in this model formulation, we have removed the interaction). The contrast between `boost_bonus` and the standard bonus is highly significative as well, as we would expect:

```
library(lsmeans)
fit <- lme(Performance ~ Bonus + Sector + Time , random = list( ~1
|Employee) , data = data_company)
print(lsmeans(fit,pairwise ~ Bonus))
```

The preceding code generates the following output of the `lsmeans` results:

```
$`lsmeans`
 x_Bonus      lsmean   SE df lower.CL upper.CL
 boost_bonus  108.4 1.50 49    105.4    111.4
 standard      86.6 1.62 49     83.3     89.8

Results are averaged over the levels of: x_Sector
d.f. method: containment
Confidence level used: 0.95

$contrasts
 contrast                  estimate   SE  df t.ratio p.value
 boost_bonus - standard        21.8 1.81 146  12.049  <.0001

Results are averaged over the levels of: x_Sector
```

How it works...

The presence of the time dimension does not really alter the way the model is estimated, and the process ends up being almost identical to what we did in the other ANOVA models.

There's more...

If we wanted to add varying time-response slopes (by `Employee`), we should have used the following formulation, which indicates that we want both a random intercept and a time response by employee.

What this would imply is that each employee's performance will change through time in a different way. Some employees will have an upward performance, some of them will have a flat one, and so on.

In either case, doing this in `lme` is rather easy:

```
fit <- lme(Performance ~ Bonus + Sector + Time + Time:Bonus , random =
list( ~1 + Time |Employee) , correlation = corAR1(form= ~Time|Employee),
data = data_company)
```

Take a look at the following screenshot:

```
Linear mixed-effects model fit by REML
 Data: data_company
       AIC      BIC    logLik
 1176.371 1212.317 -577.1855

Random effects:
 Formula: ~1 + Time | Employee
 Structure: General positive-definite, Log-Cholesky parametrization
            StdDev   Corr
(Intercept) 9.893662 (Intr)
Time        1.090883 -0.609
Residual    3.493198

Correlation Structure: AR(1)
 Formula: ~Time | Employee
 Parameter estimate(s):
      Phi
0.5151983
Fixed effects: Performance ~ x_Bonus + x_Sector + Time + Time:x_Bonus
                  Value Std.Error  DF  t-value p-value
(Intercept)    84.87072 1.5530358 145 54.64827  0.0000
x_Bonus1        9.55327 1.1877900 145  8.04289  0.0000
x_Sector1      -9.69168 1.7532483 145 -5.52784  0.0000
x_Sector2      -0.25139 1.1217456 145 -0.22411  0.8230
Time            5.04330 0.2719045 145 18.54805  0.0000
x_Bonus1:Time   0.56062 0.2613440 145  2.14516  0.0336
 Correlation:
               (Intr) x_Bns1 x_Sct1 x_Sct2 Time
x_Bonus1       -0.083
x_Sector1       0.022  0.033
x_Sector2       0.041 -0.020 -0.768
Time           -0.611  0.074 -0.005 -0.115
x_Bonus1:Time   0.058 -0.664  0.009 -0.016 -0.112

Standardized Within-Group Residuals:
        Min          Q1         Med          Q3         Max
-3.126789886 -0.395687859  0.004531282  0.459027846  2.082166827

Number of Observations: 200
Number of Groups: 50
```

Multivariate t-test

So far, we have worked with univariate data (one variable measured across two samples), and we wanted to test whether the means are equal or not. In certain cases, we might work with multivariate data (for example, measurements of height and weight for certain individuals), and we will be interested in testing the multivariate hypothesis, which is that the means for all of the variables are equal between two groups or not. This is usually formulated as follows:

$$H_0 : \bar{x}_1 = \bar{x}_2$$
$$H_1 : \bar{x}_1 \neq \bar{x}_2$$

The difference is that each element is a vector, and we are testing whether all of the elements in a vector are the same between groups. The main assumption here (similar to the univariate t-test) is that the data comes from a multivariate Gaussian distribution.

A relevant question at this stage is whether we can ignore the multi-dimensionality of the problem, and just do univariate t-tests. This would be fine if the variables were not correlated, but in general this won't be the case. Taking the correlation into account will imply that the data points that lie within the main axis of variation (in the simplest case of *correlation=1*, that would imply that most of the data will lie over a 45 degree line) will be considered closer than the points that are above or below that axis of variation. For example, in the weight-height example, a point of 100kg-2.00mts will be considered closer to another point of 110kg-2.10mts than to 100kg-2.10mts, just because there is a positive relationship between height and weight.

The tool that is used for this is the **Hotelling T2 statistic**, which can be interpreted as a multivariate extension to the t-Student test. It is defined as follows:

$$t^2 = \frac{n_1 n_2}{n_1 + n_2}(\bar{x} - \bar{y})^T \hat{\sum}^{-1}(\bar{x} - \bar{y}) \sim T^2(p, n_1 + n_2 - 2)$$

Here, $\hat{\sum}$ is the pooled variance estimator (note that we are assuming that the covariance matrices are the same between the samples—this is analogous to our homocedasticity assumption for the standard t-test):

$$\hat{\sum} = \frac{(n_1 - 1)\hat{\sum}_1 + (n_2 - 1)\hat{\sum}_2}{n_1 + n_2 - 2}$$

Note that this formula is actually a multivariate extension of the t-Student test. If we had just one variable, $\Sigma = \sigma$, we would get the following formula:

$$t^2 = \frac{(\bar{x}_1 - \bar{x}_2)^2}{\sigma^2 \left(\frac{1}{n_1} + \frac{1}{n_2} \right)}$$

If we take the square root, we will end up with the usual t-Student statistic.

Getting ready...

To run this example, you will need to install both the `Hotelling` and `heplots` packages, which can be obtained via the usual `install.packages()` function.

How to do it...

In the following example, we will load scores (`Math`, `History`, and `Physics`) for two classes and we will be interested in assessing whether the means are the same or not between them:

1. First, we will load the `Hotelling` library and the two datasets that we will work with:

```
library(Hotelling)
data1 = read.csv("./class1.csv")
data2 = read.csv("./class2.csv")
sapply(data1,mean)
sapply(data2,mean)
```

The preceding code generate the following output:

```
> sapply(class1,mean)
    Math  History  Physics
6.824406 5.000136 4.893103
> sapply(class2,mean)
    Math  History  Physics
5.949069 5.873906 5.754169
```

2. There is a clear difference between the two groups, `Math` between `Physics`, and a negligible one for `History`. We still need to do a formal test to determine whether the scores differ by group. As we can see, the p-value is <0.01. We then decide to reject the null hypothesis that states that the three means are the same for the two groups:

```
test_hotelling = hotelling.test(class1,class2)
print(test_hotelling)
```

The preceding code generate the following output for the `hotelling` T2 test results:

```
> print(test_hotelling)
Test stat:  9.0882
Numerator df:  3
Denominator df:  96
P-value:  2.358e-05
```

How it works...

R calculates the T2 statistic and then computes the appropriate p-value. All of the attributes from this result can be extracted using the `$` symbol on the `test_hotelling` object.

There's more...

As it happens with the univariate case, we should also check whether the covariance matrices are the same between the two samples. This obviously requires a more sophisticated test (compared to the univariate test), because we are now working with matrices. There are several possible strategies, although a simple one is to use **Box's M** test, which can be obtained via the `heplots` package.

We need to create a combined dataset and a grouping variable to use `boxM`:

```
library(heplots)
class1$group = "1"
class2$group = "2"
combined = rbind(class1,class2)
combined$group = as.factor(combined$group)
boxM(cbind(combined$Math,combined$History,combined$Sociology)~group,data =
combined)
```

The preceding code generate the following output for testing the homogeneity of the covariance matrices. We don't reject the homogeneity assumption:

```
> boxM(cbind(combined$Math,combined$History,combined$Sociology)~group,data = combined)

        Box's M-test for Homogeneity of Covariance Matrices

data:   Y
Chi-Sq (approx.) = 5.9204, df = 3, p-value = 0.1155
```

Because the p-value is larger (much larger than 5%), we decide to accept the null hypothesis that the covariance matrices are the same between the two groups.

MANOVA

We have already explained that ANOVA is the generalization of the t-test for multiple samples. On the other hand, the t-test is designed to work with just one variable, and in case we have multiple variables, we need to use Hotelling T2. Is it possible to extend ANOVA to work with multiple variables? The answer is yes, and the technique for doing so is called MANOVA (Multiple ANOVA). The assumptions for MANOVA are similar to the ones we have when using Hotelling T2 for two samples: equality of covariance matrices between the groups, the data should come from a multivariate Gaussian distribution for each group, and there should not be outliers.

In this example, we will generate data from a multivariate Gaussian distribution (with three variables) with an arbitrary covariance matrix. We will assign the columns' names to represent the History, Math, and Biology scores for three classes (in each class, we will have 50 students). Of course, in real exercises, we will receive our data and we won't be generating any data ourselves. The reason we choose to work this simulated dataset here is because we want to do our MANOVA tests in a controlled environment where we know the true parameters.

Getting ready

We will use the MASS package in this recipe. It can be installed via the usual `install.packages()` command.

How to do it...

In this example, we will generate data from a multivariate Gaussian distribution (with three variables) with an arbitrary covariance matrix. We will assume that these are History, Math and Biology scores, so we will code the matrices accordingly. In a real example, we would load this data from a file, and the column names would obviously be already defined. We will have 50 (observations-students) in each class. The reason we have chosen to work with this simulated dataset is to carry our MANOVA tests in a controlled environment where we know the true parameters:

1. First, we load the MASS library and generate a 3x3 covariance matrix object, as follows:

```
library(MASS)
f = matrix(c(2,1,1,1,2,1,1,1,2),3,3)
```

2. We generate three datasets via the mvrnorm function, all sharing the same covariance matrix object. The first argument is the number of samples that we want to generate, the second argument is the vector of means, and the third argument is the covariance matrix object:

```
x1 = mvrnorm(50,c(10,10,10),f)
x1 = cbind(x1,1)
x2 = mvrnorm(50,c(10,10,10),f)
x2 = cbind(x2,2)
x3 = mvrnorm(50,c(30,10,10),f)
x3 = cbind(x3,3)
```

Let's assume that this was data coming from a school. We assign names to the variables (this is just for simplifying how we refer to them later—let's imagine they come from schools and that we have three classes: History, Math and Biology):

```
total_data = data.frame(rbind(x1,x2,x3))
colnames(total_data) = c("History","Math","Biology","class")
```

4. We then call the manova function from the MASS package:

```
result = manova(cbind(History,Math,Biology) ~
class,data=total_data)
summary(result)
```

The preceding code generates the following output of MANOVA test statistics:

```
> summary(result)
          Df  Pillai approx F num Df den Df    Pr(>F)
class      1 0.73891   137.74      3    146 < 2.2e-16 ***
Residuals 148
---
Signif. codes:  0 '***' 0.001 '**' 0.01 '*' 0.05 '.' 0.1 ' ' 1
```

The p-value is very small, so we reject the null hypothesis that the mean vectors for the three groups are the same (we already knew this, since we generated the data ourselves—the first group has means (10,10,10), the second one (10,10,10), and the third one (30,10,10)).

5. Using the summary.aov function, we can find which component of our vector is the one that's driving the differences (of course, we know it's the first one, History):

```
summary.aov(result)
```

The preceding code generates the following output of ANOVA results:

```
> summary.aov(result)
 Response History :
             Df  Sum Sq Mean Sq F value    Pr(>F)
class         1 10118.4 10118.4  396.98 < 2.2e-16 ***
Residuals   148  3772.3    25.5
---
Signif. codes:  0 '***' 0.001 '**' 0.01 '*' 0.05 '.' 0.1 ' ' 1

 Response Math :
             Df  Sum Sq Mean Sq F value Pr(>F)
class         1   4.488  4.4879  2.3414 0.1281
Residuals   148 283.685  1.9168

 Response Biology :
             Df  Sum Sq Mean Sq F value Pr(>F)
class         1   0.064 0.06407  0.0323 0.8576
Residuals   148 293.421 1.98258
```

We can see that History is the only one to be significative.

How it works...

There are actually four statistics that are used for MANOVA: Pillai's trace, Hotelling-Lawley's trace, Wilks' lambda, and Roy's largest root. In general, the four of them will differ, and Pillai's trace is considered to be the best. All of these tests work with the sum of squares (we have two sum of squares terms: the model one and the error one). In our case, these two will be 3 x 3 matrices and, under the null hypothesis, the means are the same (no group effect); in consequence, the model sum of squares should be close to the error one. If that is not the case, and the model sum of squares is larger than the error one, we may conclude that the group effect is significative:

```
SS = summary(result)$SS
print(SS)
```

The preceding code generate the following output:

```
> print(SS)
$class
             History          Math        Biology
History 10118.41365 213.0971610 -25.46234256
Math       213.09716   4.4878972  -0.53624541
Biology    -25.46234  -0.5362454   0.06407436

$Residuals
             History       Math  Biology
History 3772.2972 230.4865 229.5842
Math       230.4865 283.6854 160.5399
Biology    229.5842 160.5399 293.4213
```

In particular, Pillai's test uses the following statistic (where H is the model SS and E is the error SS):

$$V = trace(H(H + E)^{-1})$$

The idea is that under the null hypothesis, H will be roughly similar to $H + E$, because H should be small (the sum of squares explained by the model). The other tests use different test statistics, but the general idea remains the same.

There's more...

What happens to this test when the covariance matrices are different? In theory, the results should not be reliable, but in practice, it has been found that this is fairly robust:

```
library(MASS)
f1 = matrix(c(2,1,1,1,2,1,1,1,2),3,3)
f2 = matrix(c(3,2,1,2,3,1,1,1,3),3,3)
f3 = matrix(c(2,1,-0.5,1,2,1,-0.5,1,2),3,3)
x1 = mvrnorm(50,c(10,10,10),f1)
x1 = cbind(x1,1)
x2 = mvrnorm(50,c(10,10,10),f2)
x2 = cbind(x2,2)
x3 = mvrnorm(50,c(30,10,10),f3)
x3 = cbind(x3,3)
total_data = data.frame(rbind(x1,x2,x3))
colnames(total_data) = c("History","Math","Biology","class")
result = manova(cbind(History,Math,Biology) ~ class,data=total_data)
summary(result)
```

The preceding code generate the following output of MANOVA tests:

```
> summary(result)
             Df  Pillai approx F num Df den Df    Pr(>F)
class         1 0.73891   137.74      3    146 < 2.2e-16 ***
Residuals 148
---
Signif. codes:  0 '***' 0.001 '**' 0.01 '*' 0.05 '.' 0.1 ' ' 1
```

We still reject the null with a very low p-value, suggesting that differences in covariance matrices don't have a major impact on our MANOVA results.

3
Linear Regression

We will cover the following recipes in this chapter:

- Computing ordinary least squares estimates
- Reporting results with the sjPlot package
- Finding correlation between the features
- Testing hypothesis
- Testing homoscedasticity
- Implementing sandwich estimators
- Variable selection
- Ridge regression
- Working with LASSO
- Leverage, residuals, and influence

Introduction

Linear regression is perhaps the most important tool in statistics. It can be used in a wide array of situations and can be easily extended to work in those cases where it can't work in principle. Conceptually, the idea is to model a dependent variable in terms of a set of independent variables and capture coefficients that relate each independent variable to the dependent one. The usual formula here is as follows (assuming that we have one variable and an intercept):

$$y_i = \beta * x_i + intercept + u_i$$

Here, the beta and the *intercept* are coefficients that we need to find. x_i is the independent variable, u_i is an unobserved residual, and y_i is the target variable. The previous formula can naturally be extended to multiple variables. In that case we would have multiple /beta coefficients.

Maybe the most important aspect of linear regression is that we can do very simple yet powerful interpretations from it. For example, in a model relating prices to quantities, we would be able to calculate the increase in sales that a reduction in prices causes. In the preceding equation, the beta coefficient has an easy interpretation: it's the marginal increase that x_i causes on y_i. For example, if beta = 0.9, an increase of x of 1 unit would produce an increase of *0.9 x 1 = 0.9* in the target variable (*y*).

The main technique for fitting linear regression models is **ordinary least squares (OLS)**. The idea is to minimize the sum of the squared residuals (defined as our predictions minus the observed values). This minimization will operate by finding the best weights (coefficients) that we should be multiplying our variables by (we also have an intercept that is not multiplied by any variable).

It's worth noting that OLS needs certain assumptions in order to work properly. In this chapter, we will review what the necessary ones are, how to test them, and how to fix them in case they are not satisfied.

Computing ordinary least squares estimates

Ordinary least squares estimates are derived from minimizing the sum of the squared residuals. It can be proven that this minimisation leads to $\beta = (X^t X)^{-1}(X^t Y)$. It should be noted that we need to compute an inverse, and that can only be done if the determinant is different from zero. The determinant will be zero if there is a linear dependency between the variables.

It can also be proven that the beta coefficients are distributed according to a Gaussian distribution with variances equal to the diagonal elements of $\sigma^2 (X^t X)^{-1}$ where σ is the estimated residual standard error.

How to do it...

In this exercise, we will simulate some data, and compute the β estimates using both the `lm` function and doing the matrix calculations ourselves. This is very useful for understanding the inner mechanics behind the `lm` function:

1. We first generate some data, and do a simple linear regression using `lm`:

```
library(sjPlot)
clients <- read.csv("./clients.csv")
model1 <- lm(Sales ~ Strategy + (Client) + (Salesman),data=clients)
tab_model(model1)
```

The `lm` output reports an intercept and two coefficients that are very close to the ones we used (40,1,1). The standard errors can be interpreted as the (im)precision of each estimate, and the t-values are just the coefficients divided by the standard errors. The p-values on the right are derived from a t-distribution, using the t-values presented before: these p-values represent the probability that we get as extreme (or more extreme) values for each t-value, under the null hypothesis that each coefficient is equal to zero. This is known as a significance test, because it tests whether each coefficient is significative or not (different from zero or not):

```
Call:
lm(formula = depvar ~ sim_data1 + sim_data2, data = model_data)

Residuals:
    Min      1Q  Median      3Q     Max
-58.429 -13.158   0.645  13.329  64.036

Coefficients:
            Estimate Std. Error t value Pr(>|t|)
(Intercept) 38.21207    1.59951   23.89   <2e-16 ***
sim_data1    0.99035    0.03020   32.79   <2e-16 ***
sim_data2    1.01592    0.02082   48.79   <2e-16 ***
---
Signif. codes:  0 '***' 0.001 '**' 0.01 '*' 0.05 '.' 0.1 ' ' 1

Residual standard error: 19.08 on 997 degrees of freedom
Multiple R-squared:  0.9158,    Adjusted R-squared:  0.9157
F-statistic:  5424 on 2 and 997 DF,  p-value: < 2.2e-16
```

2. We are now going to create an X matrix containing one column with ones (this is because we want to add an intercept) and then the two variables that we want. We also need another matrix, Y, containing the variable that we want to model:

```
X = as.matrix(model_data[c("sim_data1","sim_data2")])
X = cbind(rep(1,1000),X)
colnames(X)[1] = "intercept"
Y = as.matrix(model_data["depvar"])
```

3. The β coefficients can be computed by doing the following:

```
beta =  solve(t(X) %*% X) %*% (t(X) %*% Y)
beta
```

The following screenshot shows the estimated beta coefficients:

```
> beta
                 depvar
intercept 41.0854952
sim_data1  0.9928917
sim_data2  0.9958641
```

4. The predictions are obtained by multiplying the coefficients by the independent variables:

```
predictions = X %*%  beta
```

The following screenshot shows the predictions:

```
> head(predictions)
          depvar
[1,] 222.4471
[2,] 172.8185
[3,] 150.7092
[4,] 229.6940
[5,] 114.6576
[6,] 118.9390
```

5. Finally, we compute the covariance matrix for the beta coefficients. Note that the diagonal elements contain the variances, and the off-diagonal elements contain the covariances. If the variables are correlated, the off-diagonal elements will get larger—and if they get too big, then the matrix won't be invertible:

```
residuals = predictions - Y
sd_c = var(residuals)[1]
cov_matrix = solve(t(X) %*% X ) * sd_c
diag(cov_matrix) = sqrt(diag(cov_matrix))
print(paste("Std Error:",diag(cov_matrix)))
```

The standard errors for our coefficients are the following (note that these obviously match the ones reported by the `lm` function):

```
> print(paste("Std Error:",diag(cov_matrix)))
[1] "Std Error: 1.78487972893079"    "Std Error: 0.0316733298440072" "Std Error: 0.023208226271635"
```

How it works...

When we call `lm()` in R, it uses ordinary least squares to find the coefficients for our model. Internally, it uses a similar approach to what we used here (there are some computational tricks that can be used to ensure that the matrix inversion is more robust to correlation).

We have already explained how the t-values are computed and how they are used to calculate p-values. For the p-values, R uses numerical routines to calculate the area to the right of the test statistic, and to the left of its negative value. In other words, the total probability that we get values more extreme than the one we got assuming the coefficients are equal to 0 (null hypothesis). If that p-value is small, it means that, if the coefficient was 0, it would have been extremely unlikely to have observed a t-value so large.

Reporting results with the sjPlot package

Exporting our linear regression results for publication is usually a cumbersome task, because there is a lot of important content in them (p-values, coefficients, other fit metrics) and R does not print particularly nice tables.

One option is to export these numbers and create a new table in any text-editing software. But that takes a lot of effort, and it never looks that great.

The `sjPlot` package can be used for creating publication-grade output values such as tables and plots, and it's not just restricted to operate with linear models, it can also work with a wide array of techniques (such as principal components and clustering).

Getting ready

The `sjPlot` package needs to be installed from GitHub (the `devtools` package needs to be installed first) via `devtools: install_github("strengejacke/strengejacke")`.

How to do it...

In this recipe, we will use the `sjPlot` package to generate tables for `lm` and `lmer` outputs, and we will explore some of its basic capabilities:

1. Let's start by creating a table for a linear model estimated via `lm`. The `tab_model` function creates the output that we need based on a fitted model:

```
library(sjPlot)
clients <- read.csv("./clients.csv")
model1 <- lm(Sales ~ Strategy + (Client) + (Salesman),data=clients)
tab_model(model1)
```

The following screenshot shows the estimated coefficients (the **<0.001** are highly significative):

	Sales		
Predictors	*Estimates*	*CI*	*p*
(Intercept)	22.92	19.87 – 25.97	**<0.001**
Offer_discount	-0.73	-2.77 – 1.31	0.485
Client	-0.28	-1.01 – 0.46	0.465
Michael	7.19	4.69 – 9.69	**<0.001**
Tom	13.76	11.26 – 16.26	**<0.001**
Observations	51		
R^2 / adjusted R^2	0.720 / 0.696		

2. The `tab_model` function can be used with mixed effects models (the ones that include both fixed and random effects). Random effects are used when we want to model an effect as originating from a large (and possibly infinite) sample. For each random effect, we get a variance component, instead of getting one coefficient for each factor level in the effect (this is what happens for fixed effects):

```
model2 <- lmer(Sales ~ Strategy + (1|Client) +
(1|Salesman),data=clients)
tab_model(model2)
```

The following screenshot shows the estimated coefficients for a mixed model:

Predictors	Estimates	CI	p
	Sales		
(Intercept)	29.90	21.74 – 38.07	**<0.001**
Offer_discount	-0.74	-2.78 – 1.30	0.476
Client	-0.28	-1.01 – 0.46	0.463
Random Effects			
σ^2	13.77		
τ_{00} Salesman	46.56		
ICC Salesman	0.77		
Observations	51		
Marginal R^2 / Conditional R^2	0.005 / 0.773		

How it works...

The `tab_model` function only needs a fitted model, and it builds the appropriate table. It accepts lots of parameters to specify the format that we want for the table.

There's more...

Th `sjPlot` package also allows us to print tables properly formatted for books and other publications. This is done via the following:

```
tab_df(clients,title="Clients dataset",alternate.rows = TRUE)
```

The following screenshot shows the printing of a table:

Clients dataset			
Client	*Salesman*	*Strategy*	*Sales*
1	John	Classic	21.2901894915695
2	John	Classic	28.0594553276812
2	John	Classic	21.1247966461804
3	John	Classic	22.7955063753133
3	John	Classic	12.8519131030086
4	John	Classic	22.1577007145641
4	John	Classic	24.3990014648445
5	John	Classic	27.4734552070313
1	Michael	Classic	28.0201688368905
1	Michael	Classic	30.4597384141886
2	Michael	Classic	30.4698635798089
2	Michael	Classic	28.7626171676902

Finding correlation between the features

In a linear model, the correlation between the features increases the variance for the associated parameters (the parameters related to those variables). The more correlation we have, the worse it is. The situation is even worse when we have almost perfect correlation between a subset of variables: in that case, the algorithm that we use to fit linear models doesn't even work. The intuition is the following: if we want to model the impact of a discount (yes-no) and the weather (rain–not rain) on the ice cream sales for a restaurant, and we only have promotions on every rainy day, we would have the following design matrix (where **Promotion=1** is **yes** and **Weather=1** is **rain**):

Promotion	Weather
1	1
1	1
0	0
0	0

This is problematic, because every time one of them is 1, the other is 1 as well. The model cannot identify which variable is driving the sales. The correlation here is actually 1, and if we want to invert the matrix $X^t X$, we wouldn't be able to do so. The only possible solution is to remove one of these variables.

The correlation problem might not appear just between two variables but between a linear combination of variables and a variable. For example, imagine we now have two promotion types and either one of them is executed if and only if the day is rainy. The design matrix then would be as follows:

Promotion A	Promotion B	Weather
1	0	1
0	1	1
0	0	0
0	0	0

The correlation between *Promotion A-Promotion B* and the *Weather* is *1*. This is an equivalent situation to what we had before. In practice, this is slightly worse because the inverse is computed numerically: even if the correlation is not 100% between the variables (or a linear combination of variables and a variable), this can bring numerical instability up to the point that the inverse won't be properly calculated. The previous paragraphs describe the degenerate situation where the inverse cannot be even computed. For instance, if we model the prices of the properties in terms of the size of the property and the number of bathrooms, we will find out that these two variables will be naturally correlated (larger properties will have more bathrooms, just because they are expected to accommodate more people). Without any loss of generality, we will have models with the following structure:

$$Y = B_1 * V_1 + B_2 * V_2 + B_3 * V_3 + \cdots + B_k * V_k$$

If V_2 is correlated (that is 70%) to with $V_3 + V_4$, the standard errors for V_2, V_3, and V_4 will be larger than what they would be in the absence of such a correlation. What this means is that the model won't be very sure of which variable the effect should be attributed to. It is tempting to just exclude, the V2 variable, but that brings other problems (maybe even worse ones). By using asymptotic statistical theory, it can be shown that excluding a variable from the model that is correlated with a variable that we are keeping in the model biases the coefficient for the variable we are keeping. Why? Imagine we model the sales of a product in terms of the day of the week (so we have a dummy variable for each day 1-7), and a variable that stores the information of whether we did a discount on a specific day. Imagine discounts are done on a Friday, and we exclude this variable (the one that flags whether a discount was done) from the model. What would happen with the Friday dummy variable?

It would get inflated, because it will not only capture the Friday effect, but also part of the discount effect (since most of it is concentrated on Fridays). So, we have a delicate balance: if the variable is relevant and correlated, removing it biases our estimates. If we keep this variable in our model, it inflates our variances for the estimated coefficients (that are correlated). Both problems are quite serious: biased coefficients mean that the coefficient will never reach its true value 0.8, and inflated variances means that, if we get more data, the estimated coefficient will change dramatically. In practice, coefficients are removed if the correlation is between 0.7 and 1, or between -0.70 and -1. Usually, combining them is slightly preferred (if the new group makes sense)—for example, if we have two promotion types, and they are correlated, we can group them inside a `combined_promotion` variable. This avoids the remove/keep variable dilemma but makes the interpretation much more difficult than before.

Getting ready...

The `caret` and the `car` package will be used here. Both can be installed via `install.packages()`.

How to do it...

In this exercise we will detect variables that are correlated using a dataset containing prices for several apparel categories. The target variable will be the sales, but we will need to make sure that we treat all the correlations accordingly.We will first load our dataset. It contains the following variables:

```
"Sales", "women_apparel_price", "male_apparel_price", "shoes_female_price",
"shoes_male_price", "shoes_kids_prices", "shoes_male_price.1" and
"prices_shoes".
```

What we want to model are `Sales` in terms of all the other variables: female/male apparel price, female/male shoes price, female/kids/male shoes price, and shoe prices in general (we will explain in step 2, the significance of this last variable). The problem is that there are several variables in this model that are highly correlated. Hence, we need to filter those variables out:

1. We first load our data and the `caret` library. We use `findLinearCombos` from the caret package to find the correlated ones:

    ```
    data = read.csv("./sales__shop.cs")
    library(caret)
    X = data[-1]
     findLinearCombos(X)
    ```

The following screenshot shows linear combinations:

```
> findLinearCombos(X)
$linearCombos
$linearCombos[[1]]
[1] 6 4

$linearCombos[[2]]
[1] 7 3 4 5


$remove
[1] 6 7
```

2. This is detecting two linear combinations that need to be removed: first, variables 6 and 4 are the same thing (`shoes_male_price` and `shoes_male_price.1`). Second, `shoes_male_price` + `shoes_female_price` + `shoes_kids_price` s = prices_shoes. Before removing them, check what happens with $X^t X$ which needs to be inverted:

```
X = as.matrix(X)
det(t(X) %*% X)
```

The determinant is zero, because there are obvious linear dependencies. This matrix is very important, because (if you recall the first recipe of this chapter) we need it for the OLS formulas. If the determinant of matrix is zero, then the inverse cannot be computed, therefore we can't get the OLS estimates:

```
> det(t(X) %*% X)
[1] 0
```

3. This determinant is equal to zero, meaning that there are linear combinations. If the determinant is zero, the matrix cannot be inverted, so we can't really recover the coefficients. We can execute our model using the following code:

```
model = lm(data=data,Sales ~ women_apparel_price +
male_apparel_price+ shoes_female_price + shoes_male_price
+shoes_kids_prices+shoes_male_price.1+prices_shoes)
summary(model)
```

Note the NAs in our following results:

```
Call:
lm(formula = Sales ~ women_apparel_price + male_apparel_price +
    shoes_female_price + shoes_male_price + shoes_kids_prices +
    shoes_male_price_b + prices_shoes, data = data)

Residuals:
    Min      1Q  Median      3Q     Max
-44.066 -11.621  -0.917  13.037  32.518

Coefficients: (2 not defined because of singularities)
                    Estimate Std. Error t value Pr(>|t|)
(Intercept)         -14.6255    14.9773  -0.977  0.33208
women_apparel_price   0.8027     0.3428   2.342  0.02197 *
male_apparel_price    1.2161     0.3420   3.556  0.00067 ***
shoes_female_price    5.5924     1.0756   5.199  1.8e-06 ***
shoes_male_price     11.3961     0.3525  32.332  < 2e-16 ***
shoes_kids_prices     6.2991     1.0405   6.054  5.8e-08 ***
shoes_male_price_b        NA         NA      NA       NA
prices_shoes              NA         NA      NA       NA
---
Signif. codes:  0 '***' 0.001 '**' 0.01 '*' 0.05 '.' 0.1 ' ' 1

Residual standard error: 17.74 on 72 degrees of freedom
Multiple R-squared:  0.9818,    Adjusted R-squared:  0.9805
F-statistic: 775.3 on 5 and 72 DF,  p-value: < 2.2e-16
```

4. We get missing values for one coefficient for each linear combination. Now, let's remove the coefficients and check the determinant:

```
det(t(X[,c(-6,-7)]) %*% X[,c(-6,-7)])
```

Take a look at the following screenshot:

```
> det(t(X[,c(-6,-7)]) %*% X[,c(-6,-7)])
[1] 2.182987e+19
```

5. And this determinant is equal to *3.023922e+32 > 0*. The new model:

```
fixedmodel = lm(data=data, Sales ~ women_apparel_price +
male_apparel_price+ shoes_female_price +   shoes_male_price
+shoes_kids_prices)
summary(fixedmodel)
```

The following screenshot shows the model results:

```
Residuals:
    Min      1Q  Median      3Q     Max
-85.359 -25.993  -3.738  20.830  88.742

Coefficients:
                     Estimate Std. Error t value Pr(>|t|)
(Intercept)          37.82833   15.48058   2.444   0.0164 *
women_apparel_price   0.27156    0.15078   1.801   0.0749 .
male_apparel_price    0.08271    0.14102   0.587   0.5589
shoes_female_price    0.09460    0.01341   7.052 3.07e-10 ***
shoes_male_price      0.07854    0.01358   5.782 9.81e-08 ***
shoes_kids_prices     0.11604    0.01611   7.203 1.51e-10 ***
---
Signif. codes:  0 '***' 0.001 '**' 0.01 '*' 0.05 '.' 0.1 ' ' 1

Residual standard error: 37.66 on 93 degrees of freedom
Multiple R-squared:  0.712,     Adjusted R-squared:  0.6965
F-statistic: 45.98 on 5 and 93 DF,  p-value: < 2.2e-16
```

6. The previous output looks much better than the one in step 3. We have removed the perfect correlations that didn't allow us to properly invert a matrix and get the co-efficient, and consequently we were unable to get the coefficients. R is able to do some tricks to get get some of those coefficients anyway, but we still get those NA values (it's always best to get clean output). We are, Nevertheless, we are omitting the fact that some of the correlations might still be large, and we might want to remove them. There are several ways of doing this: one option is to use the so-called **variance inflation factors** (**VIFs**); these values are ratios showing how much larger the standard errors get between a model containing just one variable versus a model containing all of them.

   If a VIF is large, it means that we won't get a precise estimate of the effect, and if we got more data, then the estimate would change a lot. It is evident here that we have two pairs of variables that are very correlated (women_apparel_price, male_apparel_price and shoes_female_price – shoes_kids_prices):

```
> vif(fixedmodel)
women_apparel_price male_apparel_price shoes_female_price    shoes_male_price  shoes_kids_prices
          26.375024          26.358965          10.229845            1.065036          10.287159
```

7. This means that the first two coefficients are 26 times larger just because they are in a model with other variables (the same argument holds for the other pair). We can either remove one of them or aggregate them in the same variable:

```
aggregated_apparel    = data$women_apparel_price +
data$male_apparel_price
aggregated_femalekids = data$shoes_female_price +
data$shoes_kids_prices
finalmodel = lm(data=data,Sales ~ aggregated_apparel +
shoes_male_price + aggregated_femalekids)
summary(finalmodel)
vif(finalmodel)
```

The model looks better than before, as all variables are significative (except for the intercept):

```
Call:
lm(formula = Sales ~ aggregated_apparel + shoes_male_price +
    aggregated_femalekids, data = data)

Residuals:
    Min      1Q  Median      3Q     Max
-43.195 -12.076  -0.985  12.703  33.518

Coefficients:
                      Estimate Std. Error t value Pr(>|t|)
(Intercept)           -8.36624   11.73747  -0.713    0.478
aggregated_apparel     1.01046    0.03316  30.472   <2e-16 ***
shoes_male_price      11.39867    0.34866  32.692   <2e-16 ***
aggregated_femalekids  5.94341    0.17072  34.813   <2e-16 ***
---
Signif. codes:  0 '***' 0.001 '**' 0.01 '*' 0.05 '.' 0.1 ' ' 1

Residual standard error: 17.56 on 74 degrees of freedom
Multiple R-squared:  0.9816,    Adjusted R-squared:  0.9809
F-statistic:  1319 on 3 and 74 DF,  p-value: < 2.2e-16
```

8. As we can see, we get small standard errors now, and the VIFs do look much better:

```
vif(finalmodel)
```

The following screenshot shows the variance inflation factors for the aggregated model:

```
> vif(finalmodel)
  aggregated_apparel      shoes_male_price aggregated_femalekids
           1.000553              1.064195              1.064043
```

Testing hypothesis

After a model is fitted, we get coefficients for each variable. In general, the relevant test is whether a coefficient is zero or not. If it is zero, it can be safely removed from the model. But sometimes we want to do more complex tests, involving possibly several variables, for example, testing whether the combined coefficients of variable1 and variable2 are equal to variable3.

The way this works is that we will define a contrast, and we will then estimate the significance for that contrast. We will do this using the multcomp package, which allows us to test linear hypotheses for lots of models.

Getting ready

In order to run this recipe, you will need to install the multcomp package via the command install.packages("multcomp").

How to do it...

In this exercise, we will load a dataset containing house prices. The independent variables are size, number.bathrooms, number.bedrooms, number.entrances, size_balcony, and size_entrance. We will then do a few complex hypothesis tests:

1. We first load the dataset and do our model:

```
library(multcomp)
data  = read.csv("./house_prices.csv")
model = lm(Property_price ~ size + number.bathrooms +
number.bedrooms + number.entrances +  size_balcony  +
size_entrance,data=data)
```

Take a look at the following screenshot:

```
Call:
lm(formula = Property_price ~ size + number.bathrooms + number.bedrooms +
    number.entrances + size_balcony + size_entrance, data = data)

Residuals:
    Min      1Q   Median      3Q      Max
-18.4347  -4.6414  -0.0136   4.4449  23.6712

Coefficients:
                  Estimate Std. Error t value Pr(>|t|)
(Intercept)       -16.7063     2.5520  -6.546 1.54e-10 ***
size                5.6270     0.1068  52.666  < 2e-16 ***
number.bathrooms    1.1513     0.1457   7.904 1.91e-14 ***
number.bedrooms     1.4115     0.1758   8.028 7.86e-15 ***
number.entrances    0.6621     0.2079   3.186  0.00154 **
size_balcony        1.3693     0.2137   6.408 3.56e-10 ***
size_entrance       0.4055     0.0906   4.476 9.54e-06 ***
---
Signif. codes:  0 '***' 0.001 '**' 0.01 '*' 0.05 '.' 0.1 ' ' 1

Residual standard error: 6.491 on 474 degrees of freedom
Multiple R-squared:  0.8612,    Adjusted R-squared:  0.8594
F-statistic: 490.1 on 6 and 474 DF,  p-value: < 2.2e-16
```

2. We could ask the following question: since the size has a coefficient of 5.6, and the sum of the coefficients
   for `number_bedrooms + number_bathrooms + number_entrances + size_balcony + size_entrance` is roughly 5, can we say that the sum of all of those effects is similar to the sole effect of the size? This is represented in the following:

```
summary(glht(model,linfct = c("number.bathrooms + number.entrances
+ number.bedrooms + size_balcony +  size_entrance - size  = 0")))
```

The following screenshot shows the estimated contrast; we don't reject the null hypothesis that the combined effect of those variables is the same as the effect for the size:

```
> summary(glht(model,linfct = c("number.bathrooms + number.entrances + number.bedrooms + size_balcony + size_entrance - size  = 0")))

        Simultaneous Tests for General Linear Hypotheses

Fit: lm(formula = Property_price ~ size + number.bathrooms + number.bedrooms +
    number.entrances + size_balcony + size_entrance, data = data)

Linear Hypotheses:
                                                                               Estimate Std. Error t value Pr(>|t|)
number.bathrooms + number.entrances + number.bedrooms + size_balcony + size_entrance - size == 0  -0.6272    0.3845  -1.631    0.104
(Adjusted p values reported -- single-step method)
```

3. Let's now test whether `number.entrances + number.bathrooms` is equal to effect of `size_balcony + size_entrance`. The p-value here is very large, so we also conclude that the contrast is not statistically significative (we don't reject the null hypothesis that the contrast is zero):

```
summary(glht(model,linfct = c("size_balcony - size = 0")))
```

The following screenshot shows test results:

```
> summary(glht(model,linfct = c("number.entrances + number.bathrooms - size_balcony - size_entrance = 0")))

        Simultaneous Tests for General Linear Hypotheses

Fit: lm(formula = Property_price ~ size + number.bathrooms + number.bedrooms +
    number.entrances + size_balcony + size_entrance, data = data)

Linear Hypotheses:
                                                                       Estimate Std. Error t value Pr(>|t|)
number.entrances + number.bathrooms - size_balcony - size_entrance == 0   0.03864    0.33817   0.114    0.909
(Adjusted p values reported -- single-step method)
```

How it works...

The `glht` function needs a contrast (or a matrix of contrasts) to be estimated. It then reports the point estimate and a confidence interval for it. A contrast is a linear combination of terms that should be equal to something (we are not restricted to having a zero on the right-hand side of the contrast).

Testing homoscedasticity

The ordinary least squares algorithm generates estimates that are unbiased (the expected values are equal to the true values), consistent (converge in probability to the true estimates), and with the minimal variance among unbiased estimates (when we get more data, the estimates don't change much, compared to other techniques). Also, the estimates are distributed according to a Gaussian distribution. But all of this occurs when certain conditions are met, in particular the following ones:

- The residuals should be homoscedastic (same variance).
- The residuals should not be correlated, which generally occurs with temporal data.
- There is no perfect correlation between variables (or linear combinations of variables).
- Exogeneity—the regressors are not correlated with the error term.
- The model is linear and is correctly specified.
- There should not be outliers: abnormal values, typically generated due to errors in the data collection step.

If the first or the second rule is violated, the distribution of the parameters is no longer gaussian, but the estimates still converge to their true values. This means that we can't do any inference on the model (for example, we can't interpret either the t-values or the F-tests). Nevertheless, we can still use the point estimates. If the third rule is violated, we can't even compute the estimates. 4, 5, and 6 are worse, as they break the consistency of the estimates—the estimates are biased. In practice, 5 is not tested, and the model is formulated in such a way that the modeler is happy with the formulation. There are statistical tests for 1 and 2, and if those assumptions are violated, they can be fixed using special techniques. Violations to item 4 are complicated, and usually happen whenever. 4 is complicated, and usually happens when we exclude a relevant variable that is correlated with one of the regressors. For example, if we model the house prices in terms of the size of the property and the number of bathrooms and we exclude the number of bathrooms, our property size estimate will be biased because the residual will now contain this variable (the number of bathrooms). Consequently, the property size estimate will be correlated with the residual—larger properties will have more bathrooms). So, our estimated property size coefficient will be biased upward (it will be capturing both its effect + the number of bathrooms effect). There is a special technique designed to work in these cases called instrumental variables.

Getting ready

We need to install the `lmtest` package that can be installed via `install.packages()`.

How to do it...

In the following example, we will load a dataset containing house prices and several variables. We will direct our attention towards the first assumption we have previously defined (that the residuals should be homoscedastic: in other words, have the same variance):

1. We'll start by loading our dataset and estimating our model:

   ```
   data = read.csv("./people_shopping.csv")
   model = lm(sales ~ people_in + discount,data=data)
   ```

2. We can direct our attention towards the first plot. It is evident that the variability gets larger as the fitted values increase. This is a violation of our homoscedasticity assumption:

   ```
   plot(model)
   ```

   The following screenshot shows the `Residuals vs Fitted`. The variance is non-constant:

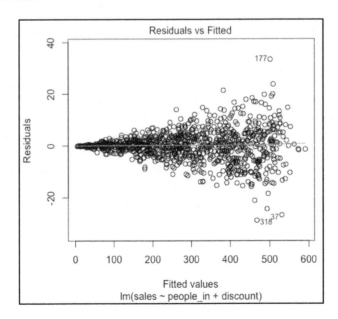

3. We can use another tool for this: the Breusch-Pagan test can be used to test the null hypothesis that the variance is constant. We use the `lmtest` library with the `bptest` function:

   ```
   library(lmtest)
   bptest(model)
   ```

   The following screenshot shows the Breusch-Pagan test: we reject the null hypothesis of homoscedasticity:

   ```
   > bptest(model)

                   studentized Breusch-Pagan test

   data:   model
   BP = 149.49, df = 2, p-value < 2.2e-16
   ```

   We get a p-value that is very small: we reject the null hypothesis that the residuals are homoscedastic.

How it works...

The Breusch-Pagan test works by regressing the squared residuals on the regressors used in the model. Under the null hypothesis, these regressors should not be relevant for explaining these squared values. If they are not, it means that the squared residuals depend on the regressor values; and what's the relationship between the squared residuals and the variance of the residuals? They are the same thing, because the expected value of the residuals is zero.

Implementing sandwich estimators

We have seen that the residuals should be **homoscedastic** (the variance should be the same), and in case that doesn't happen, the distribution of the t-values is no longer t-Student. The relevant question is naturally how we can fix this. The so-called sandwich estimators from the `sandwich` package allow us to use heteroscedasticity-robust standard errors. With this correction, we can still use the t-tests as usual. The best thing is that this is easy to implement.

Getting ready

The sandwich and the `lmtest` packages need to be installed via `install.packages()`.

How to do it...

We will work with the same dataset that we used for the previous chapter, which contains the sales in a shop, and two features (the number of people that entered the shop and the discount that was done to all clients on each day):

1. We first load the data and start with our model:

   ```
   data = read.csv("./people_shopping.csv")
   model = lm(sales ~ people_in + discount,data=data)
   library("lmtest")
   bptest(model)
   ```

2. As we did on the previous recipe, we can test whether the residuals are homoscedastic:

   ```
   summary(model)
   ```

   We reject the null hypothesis of homoscedasticity:

   ```
   > bptest(model)

               studentized Breusch-Pagan test

   data:  model
   BP = 149.49, df = 2, p-value < 2.2e-16
   ```

3. Let's see how the estimated model looks like (the `p-value` will not be correct as the residuals are not homoscedastic). The resulting model can't be used for inference as the heteroscedasticity needs to be corrected:

```
Call:
lm(formula = sales ~ people_in + discount, data = data)

Residuals:
    Min      1Q  Median      3Q     Max
-28.885  -2.557   0.108   2.635  33.422

Coefficients:
              Estimate Std. Error t value Pr(>|t|)
(Intercept)    0.13544    0.43329   0.313    0.755
people_in     10.00003    0.01281 780.793   <2e-16 ***
discount     179.33456    1.31497 136.379   <2e-16 ***
---
Signif. codes:  0 '***' 0.001 '**' 0.01 '*' 0.05 '.' 0.1 ' ' 1

Residual standard error: 5.876 on 997 degrees of freedom
Multiple R-squared:  0.9984,    Adjusted R-squared:  0.9984
F-statistic: 3.129e+05 on 2 and 997 DF,  p-value: < 2.2e-16
```

4. We now print the heteroscedasticity robust errors. As we can see, our conclusions don't change by much:

```
library(sandwich)
coeftest(model, vcov=sandwich)
```

The sandwich estimators are robust to heteroscedasticity. Both variables are still highly significative, and the change in the intercept's p-value does not alter our conclusions. In many cases, when we correct for heteroscedasticity, the p-values can change substantially, hence altering our conclusions:

```
t test of coefficients:

              Estimate Std. Error t value Pr(>|t|)
(Intercept)   0.135440   0.313656  0.4318    0.666
people_in    10.000028   0.014173 705.5933   <2e-16 ***
discount    179.334557   1.324899 135.3571   <2e-16 ***
---
Signif. codes:  0 '***' 0.001 '**' 0.01 '*' 0.05 '.' 0.1 ' ' 1
```

How it works...

Instead of using the usual calculations for the variance components of our model, we use a method that is robust to heteroscedasticity and serial correlation. The usual estimate for the variance-covariance matrix is as follows:

$$\hat{\sigma}^2 (X^T X)^{-1}$$
$$(X^T X)^{-1} X^T \Omega X (X^T X)^{-1}$$

Variable selection

A fundamental question when doing linear regression is how to choose the best subset of variables that we have already included. Every variable that is added to a model changes the standard errors of the other variables already included. Consequently, the p-values also change, and the order is relevant. This happens because in general the variables are correlated, causing the coefficients' covariance matrix to change (hence changing the standard errors). Sandwich estimators use a different formula for the standard errors. Note the Ω which is the new element here. This matrix is estimated by the sandwich package. This formula also explicits why this is called the **sandwich method** (the Ω gets sandwiched between two equal expressions). Sandwich estimators use a different formula for the standard errors. Note the Ω which is the new element here. This matrix is estimated by the sandwich package. This formula also explicits why this is called the sandwich method (the Ω gets sandwiched between two equal expressions). There are two major metrics that can be used for this: the AIC (Akaike criterion) and the p-values for each variable. There are four possible ways of doing variable selection:

- Compute all possible models and choose the one that maximizes the adjusted R square or AIC. This is the best approach, but usually not practical, since the combinations grow exponentially with respect to the number of variables.
- Start with an empty model and add the `best` variable sequentially.
- Start with a saturated model (containing all possible regressors) and remove the `worst` variable sequentially.
- Start with an empty model and add one variable at a time. We add the `best` variable, and we then remove the `worst` variable. We iterate over all variables doing this.

Getting ready

In order to run this example, we need to install the `olsrr` and `dplyr` package via `install.packages()`.

How to do it...

In the following exercise, we will work with the famous Boston dataset, which is included in R. The idea is to model the median property value in Boston, in terms of several numeric indicators such as environmental and crime factors:

1. First, we have to load the data:

```
library("olsrr")
library(dplyr)
model = lm(data=Boston, medv ~ .)
```

2. The first option is to run all possible models. Of course, this method can only be used for small datasets. When we have more than 15–20 variables, it becomes computationally unfeasible, as all possible subsets are used. This approach will always give us the best model, as all of the models are evaluated. Here, we can sort the tibble object by the metric we are interested in (for example, the adjusted R square) and get the largest value. All possible regression can be done using the following command. The predictors column is the regression column; it tells us which variable should be included:

```
head(ols_step_all_possible(model) %>% arrange(desc(adjr)))
```

The following screenshot prints all the model:

mindex	n	predictors	rsquare	adjr	predrsq	cp	aic	sbic	sbc	msep
1	8100 11	crim zn chas nox rm dis rad tax ptratio black lstat	0.7405823	0.7348058	0.7214716	10.11455	3023.726	1588.436	3078.671	22.97774
2	8178 12	crim zn indus chas nox rm dis rad tax ptratio black lstat	0.7406412	0.7343282	0.7207760	12.00275	3025.611	1590.384	3084.783	23.06590
3	8179 12	crim zn chas nox rm age dis rad tax ptratio black lstat	0.7405837	0.7342694	0.7196558	12.11176	3025.724	1590.490	3084.895	23.07102
4	8191 13	crim zn indus chas nox rm age dis rad tax ptratio black lstat	0.7406427	0.7337897	0.7189544	14.00000	3027.609	1592.438	3091.007	23.15973
5	7814 10	crim zn nox rm dis rad tax ptratio black lstat	0.7352631	0.7299149	0.7187463	18.20493	3031.997	1596.197	3082.715	23.35414
6	8101 11	crim zn indus nox rm dis rad tax ptratio black lstat	0.7354930	0.7296032	0.7181603	19.76882	3033.557	1597.793	3088.502	23.42852

	fpe	apc	hsp
1	22.96389	0.2720210	0.04550083
2	23.04966	0.2730369	0.04567542
3	23.05476	0.2730974	0.04568554
4	23.14088	0.2741175	0.04586121
5	23.34226	0.2765029	0.04624618
6	23.41440	0.2773575	0.04639347

3. The `ols_step_forward_p` function can be used to do forward selection based on p-values. This starts with a model containing no variables and adds them sequentially. We get three tables: the first one describes a model summary for the best model, the second one prints the estimates for the final model, and the third one provides a summary of each model (after each term is added):

```
ols_step_forward_p(model)
```

The following screenshot shows forward selection based on p-values:

Model Summary			
R	0.861	RMSE	4.736
R-Squared	0.741	Coef. Var	21.019
Adj. R-Squared	0.735	MSE	22.432
Pred R-Squared	0.721	MAE	3.272

RMSE: Root Mean Square Error
MSE: Mean Square Error
MAE: Mean Absolute Error

The following screenshot shows the result:

```
                              Parameter Estimates
--------------------------------------------------------------------------------
      model       Beta    Std. Error   Std. Beta      t      Sig     lower     upper
--------------------------------------------------------------------------------
(Intercept)     36.341      5.067                    7.171   0.000   26.385    46.298
      lstat      -0.523      0.047      -0.406      -11.019   0.000   -0.616    -0.429
         rm       3.802      0.406       0.290        9.356   0.000    3.003     4.600
    ptratio      -0.947      0.129      -0.223       -7.334   0.000   -1.200    -0.693
        dis      -1.493      0.186      -0.342       -8.037   0.000   -1.858    -1.128
        nox     -17.376      3.535      -0.219       -4.915   0.000  -24.322   -10.430
       chas       2.719      0.854       0.075        3.183   0.002    1.040     4.397
      black       0.009      0.003       0.092        3.475   0.001    0.004     0.015
         zn       0.046      0.014       0.116        3.390   0.001    0.019     0.072
       crim      -0.108      0.033      -0.101       -3.307   0.001   -0.173    -0.044
        rad       0.300      0.063       0.284        4.726   0.000    0.175     0.424
        tax      -0.012      0.003      -0.216       -3.493   0.001   -0.018    -0.005
--------------------------------------------------------------------------------


                              Selection Summary
--------------------------------------------------------------------------------
        Variable                   Adj.
Step    Entered    R-Square    R-Square     C(p)        AIC        RMSE
--------------------------------------------------------------------------------
  1     lstat       0.5441      0.5432    362.7530    3288.9750    6.2158
  2     rm          0.6386      0.6371    185.6474    3173.5423    5.5403
  3     ptratio     0.6786      0.6767    111.6489    3116.0973    5.2294
  4     dis         0.6903      0.6878     91.4853    3099.3590    5.1386
  5     nox         0.7081      0.7052     59.7536    3071.4386    4.9939
  6     chas        0.7158      0.7124     47.1754    3059.9390    4.9326
  7     black       0.7222      0.7183     37.0589    3050.4384    4.8818
  8     zn          0.7266      0.7222     30.6240    3044.2750    4.8474
  9     crim        0.7288      0.7239     28.4179    3042.1546    4.8326
 10     rad         0.7342      0.7288     20.2658    3034.0687    4.7895
 11     tax         0.7406      0.7348     10.1145    3023.7264    4.7362
--------------------------------------------------------------------------------
```

4. Stepwise backward regression (using p-values) can be done with the following command. In a similar vein to the previous command, we get three tables. The first two are the same ones we got before, and the third one shows the model metrics for each variable that was removed (starting with a model containing all of the variables):

```
ols_step_backward_p(model)
```

The following screenshot shows backward elimination result:

```
Final Model Output
------------------

                        Model Summary
-----------------------------------------------------------
R                        0.861    RMSE              4.736
R-Squared                0.741    Coef. Var        21.019
Adj. R-Squared           0.735    MSE              22.432
Pred R-Squared           0.721    MAE               3.272
-----------------------------------------------------------
RMSE: Root Mean Square Error
MSE: Mean Square Error
MAE: Mean Absolute Error
```

The following screenshot shows final results and elimination summary:

model	Beta	Std. Error	Std. Beta	t	Sig	lower	upper
(Intercept)	36.341	5.067		7.171	0.000	26.385	46.298
crim	-0.108	0.033	-0.101	-3.307	0.001	-0.173	-0.044
zn	0.046	0.014	0.116	3.390	0.001	0.019	0.072
chas	2.719	0.854	0.075	3.183	0.002	1.040	4.397
nox	-17.376	3.535	-0.219	-4.915	0.000	-24.322	-10.430
rm	3.802	0.406	0.290	9.356	0.000	3.003	4.600
dis	-1.493	0.186	-0.342	-8.037	0.000	-1.858	-1.128
rad	0.300	0.063	0.284	4.726	0.000	0.175	0.424
tax	-0.012	0.003	-0.216	-3.493	0.001	-0.018	-0.005
ptratio	-0.947	0.129	-0.223	-7.334	0.000	-1.200	-0.693
black	0.009	0.003	0.092	3.475	0.001	0.004	0.015
lstat	-0.523	0.047	-0.406	-11.019	0.000	-0.616	-0.429

Parameter Estimates

Elimination Summary

Step	Variable Removed	R-Square	Adj. R-Square	C(p)	AIC	RMSE
1	age	0.7406	0.7343	12.0027	3025.6114	4.7405
2	indus	0.7406	0.7348	10.1145	3023.7264	4.7362

5. Stepwise regression (using p-values) can be implemented with the following command. It starts with an empty model, adds the variable with the lowest p-value, and then attempts to remove any non-significative variable. This process is repeated multiple times until all variables are tested. It is important to realize that when we add a new variable, because of correlation, some of the already included variables p-values can change quite dramatically (maybe even become non-significative). In this case, all of the steps involved adding, and no variable was dropped:

```
ols_step_both_p(model)
```

The following screenshot shows final model output:

```
Final Model Output
------------------


                         Model Summary
-----------------------------------------------------------
R                        0.861    RMSE                4.736
R-Squared                0.741    Coef. Var          21.019
Adj. R-Squared           0.735    MSE                22.432
Pred R-Squared           0.721    MAE                 3.272
-----------------------------------------------------------
 RMSE: Root Mean Square Error
 MSE: Mean Square Error
 MAE: Mean Absolute Error
```

The following screenshot shows final estimates and stepwise summary:

```
                          Parameter Estimates
-------------------------------------------------------------------------------
      model      Beta   Std. Error   Std. Beta        t     Sig    lower     upper
-------------------------------------------------------------------------------
(Intercept)    36.341      5.067                    7.171   0.000   26.385    46.298
      lstat    -0.523      0.047      -0.406      -11.019   0.000   -0.616    -0.429
         rm     3.802      0.406       0.290        9.356   0.000    3.003     4.600
    ptratio    -0.947      0.129      -0.223       -7.334   0.000   -1.200    -0.693
        dis    -1.493      0.186      -0.342       -8.037   0.000   -1.858    -1.128
        nox   -17.376      3.535      -0.219       -4.915   0.000  -24.322   -10.430
       chas     2.719      0.854       0.075        3.183   0.002    1.040     4.397
      black     0.009      0.003       0.092        3.475   0.001    0.004     0.015
         zn     0.046      0.014       0.116        3.390   0.001    0.019     0.072
       crim    -0.108      0.033      -0.101       -3.307   0.001   -0.173    -0.044
        rad     0.300      0.063       0.284        4.726   0.000    0.175     0.424
        tax    -0.012      0.003      -0.216       -3.493   0.001   -0.018    -0.005
-------------------------------------------------------------------------------


                       Stepwise Selection Summary
-------------------------------------------------------------------------------
                  Added/              Adj.
Step  Variable   Removed  R-Square  R-Square    C(p)        AIC       RMSE
-------------------------------------------------------------------------------
  1     lstat    addition   0.544     0.543   362.7530   3288.9750   6.2158
  2        rm    addition   0.639     0.637   185.6470   3173.5423   5.5403
  3   ptratio    addition   0.679     0.677   111.6490   3116.0973   5.2294
  4       dis    addition   0.690     0.688    91.4850   3099.3590   5.1386
  5       nox    addition   0.708     0.705    59.7540   3071.4386   4.9939
  6      chas    addition   0.716     0.712    47.1750   3059.9390   4.9326
  7     black    addition   0.722     0.718    37.0590   3050.4384   4.8818
  8        zn    addition   0.727     0.722    30.6240   3044.2750   4.8474
  9      crim    addition   0.729     0.724    28.4180   3042.1546   4.8326
 10       rad    addition   0.734     0.729    20.2660   3034.0687   4.7895
 11       tax    addition   0.741     0.735    10.1150   3023.7264   4.7362
-------------------------------------------------------------------------------
```

6. Step-wise AIC forward regression can be done with the following code. This follows the same logic as with `ols_step_forward_p`, but now the AIC is used to decide instead of the p-value. In particular, the variable that produces the lowest AIC is added, as long as they reduce the AIC:

```
ols_step_forward_aic(model)
```

The following screenshot shows AIC stepwise results: variables that were added to the model:

```
No more variables to be added.
                  Selection Summary
-----------------------------------------------------------------
Variable      AIC         Sum Sq        RSS         R-Sq      Adj. R-Sq
-----------------------------------------------------------------
lstat       3288.975    23243.914    19472.381    0.54415    0.54324
rm          3173.542    27276.986    15439.309    0.63856    0.63712
ptratio     3116.097    28988.310    13727.985    0.67862    0.67670
dis         3099.359    29487.388    13228.908    0.69031    0.68784
nox         3071.439    30246.951    12469.344    0.70809    0.70517
chas        3059.939    30575.223    12141.073    0.71577    0.71236
black       3050.438    30848.060    11868.236    0.72216    0.71826
zn          3044.275    31037.996    11678.299    0.72661    0.72221
crim        3042.155    31132.708    11583.588    0.72883    0.72390
rad         3034.069    31361.312    11354.983    0.73418    0.72881
tax         3023.726    31634.931    11081.364    0.74058    0.73481
-----------------------------------------------------------------
```

7. Stepwise AIC backward regression can be done with the following code. This follows the same logic as with the `ols_step_backward_p` function but now the AIC is used to decide instead of the p-value. Starting with the model containing all of the variables, the variable that produces the highest increase in the AIC is removed. Variables are removed only if they yield an increase in the AIC:

```
ols_step_backward_aic(model)
```

The following screenshot model results—two variables were removed. The rest are not removed because they would decrease AIC:

```
Variables Removed:

* age
* indus

No more variables to be removed.

                  Backward Elimination Summary
-----------------------------------------------------------------
Variable      AIC         RSS         Sum Sq        R-Sq      Adj. R-Sq
-----------------------------------------------------------------
Full Model  3027.609    11078.785    31637.511    0.74064    0.73379
age         3025.611    11078.846    31637.449    0.74064    0.73433
indus       3023.726    11081.364    31634.931    0.74058    0.73481
-----------------------------------------------------------------
```

8. Stepwise AIC regression can be done with the following command. This follows the same logic as with the `ols_step_bot_p` function but now the AIC is used to decide instead of the p-value. As happened in the p-value case, we only ended up adding terms to the model (with no removed terms):

```
ols_step_both_aic(model)
```

The following screenshot shows stepwise AIC results—only additions were performed:

```
No more variables to be added or removed.

                          Stepwise Summary
---------------------------------------------------------------------------
Variable    Method      AIC         RSS         Sum Sq      R-Sq      Adj. R-Sq
---------------------------------------------------------------------------
lstat       addition    3288.975    19472.381   23243.914   0.54415   0.54324
rm          addition    3173.542    15439.309   27276.986   0.63856   0.63712
ptratio     addition    3116.097    13727.985   28988.310   0.67862   0.67670
dis         addition    3099.359    13228.908   29487.388   0.69031   0.68784
nox         addition    3071.439    12469.344   30246.951   0.70809   0.70517
chas        addition    3059.939    12141.073   30575.223   0.71577   0.71236
black       addition    3050.438    11868.236   30848.060   0.72216   0.71826
zn          addition    3044.275    11678.299   31037.996   0.72661   0.72221
crim        addition    3042.155    11583.588   31132.708   0.72883   0.72390
rad         addition    3034.069    11354.983   31361.312   0.73418   0.72881
tax         addition    3023.726    11081.364   31634.931   0.74058   0.73481
---------------------------------------------------------------------------
```

How it works...

Forward methods (both AIC and p-value based) start with a model with only an intercept. They then iterate over all regressors and choose the one with the lowest AIC/p-value. They keep doing this until all variables are checked. Backward methods (both AIC and p-value based) start with the full model (containing all the variables) and they iterate over each possible variable by removing it. They pick the variable with the highest AIC/p-value. This is done until all variables are checked. Stepwise methods combine both approaches. They try all of the variables and add the one causing the lowest AIC/lowest p-value. They drop the variable causing the biggest AIC increase/highest p-value. This is done until all variables are checked. These methods work well in practice.

Nevertheless, there are two main problems with these approaches:

- There is no guarantee that the models found by them make sense. Maybe there are variables that should definitely be added, but these algorithms might drop them. For example, when predicting house prices, we should always have the house size as an independent variable. A model that omitted that variable would make little sense.
- The chosen models might be good/bad in terms of the AIC and p-values, but these techniques disregard the residuals. It might be the case that a model with a good AIC has residuals with structure, or non-Gaussian, and so on.

Ridge regression

When doing linear regression, if we include a variable that is severely correlated with our regressors, we will be inflating our standard errors for those correlated variables. This happens because, if two variables are correlated, the model can't be sure to which one it should be assigning the effect/coefficient. Ridge Regression allows us to model highly correlated regressors, by introducing a bias. Our first thought in statistics is to avoid biased coefficients at all cost. But they might not be that bad after all: if the coefficients are biased but have a much smaller variance than our baseline method, we will be in a better situation. Unbiased coefficients with a high variance will change a lot between different model runs (unstable) but they will converge in probability to the right place. Biased coefficients with a low variance will be quite stable between different runs, but won't converge in probability to where they should. So, it should be evident that there is trade-off, and at the end the question is whether the variance is reduced more than the increase in the bias. What ends up happening with Ridge Regression is that the estimated coefficients will get compressed, but with a lower variance than the corresponding ordinary least squares ones.

Getting ready

We will need the following packages: `glmnet`, `ggplot2`, `tidyr`, and `MASS`. They can be installed via `install.packages()`.

How to do it...

In the following exercise, we will work with a model containing several correlated regressors:

1. We first load the MASS library, and we then build a dataset that we can later use. It will have two variables (V1, V2) that are severely correlated. And we'll have two other variables (V3-V4) that are very correlated as well. We'll have a fifth variable that is independent from V1-V4. We want to compare Ridge against ordinary least squares and see what happens with these two pairs of variables and for the independent variable. Furthermore, we will wrap everything into a function that plots a boxplot. Our preferred way of doing Ridge is using the glmnet function/package. This allows us to do something slightly more powerful than Ridge, which is called glmnet. This method is actually a mixture of Ridge and Lasso (another penalized regression technique, which we will review on the next chapter). We even have a specific parameter called alpha that controls how much Ridge/Lasso we want:

```
library(MASS)
library(tidyr)
library(ggplot2)
get_results <- function(lambda){
coeffs_total =
data.frame(V1=numeric(),V2=numeric(),V3=numeric(),V4=numeric(),V5=n
umeric())
for (q in 1:100){
V1          = runif(1000)*100
V2          = runif(1000)*10 + V1
V3          = runif(1000)*100
V4          = runif(1000)*10 + V3
V5          = runif(1000)*100
Residuals = runif(1000)*100
Y          = V1 + V2 + V3 + V4 + V5 + Residuals
coefs_lm      <- lm(Y ~ V1 + V2 + V3 + V4 + V5)$coefficients
coefs_rd      <- glmnet(cbind(V1 ,V2,V3,V4
,V5),Y,lambda=lambda,alpha=1)$beta
frame1        <- data.frame(V1= coefs_lm[2], V2= coefs_lm[3],V3=
coefs_lm[4], V4= coefs_lm[5],V5=  coefs_lm[6],method="lm")
frame2        <- data.frame(V1= coefs_rd[2], V2= coefs_rd[3],V3=
coefs_rd[4], V4= coefs_rd[5],V5=  coefs_rd[6],method="ridge")
coeffs_total <- rbind(coeffs_total,frame1,frame2)
}
transposed_data = gather(coeffs_total,"variable","value",1:5)
ggplot(transposed_data, aes(x=variable, y=value, fill=method)) +
geom_boxplot()
```

```
print(transposed_data %>% group_by(variable,method) %>%
summarise(median=median(value)))
}
```

2. We call the function using `lambda=8`. As we can see, ridge estimates are much more stable than the ordinary least squares ones. Also, the coefficients are slightly smaller (are farther away from 1, which is the correct value for them). This is the bias that is introduced by ridge regression. Note that we use `alpha=0`, meaning that we don't want any Lasso regularization here (we just want all of it to be Ridge). There are two important points here: firstly, the coefficients are much more stable than their `lm` counterparts (less variability—shorter boxes in the `boxplot`); secondly, most variables get slightly compressed (shown on the following table): this is caused by the bias introduced by Ridge. It's worth noting that the irrelevant variable got compressed quite significantly, but the result is not exactly zero:

```
get_results(8)
```

The following screenshot shows the boxplots for the coefficients:

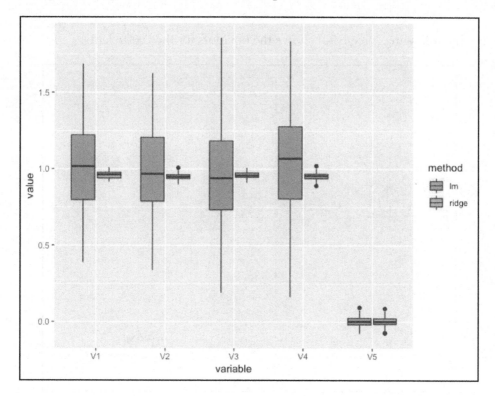

The following screenshot shows the medians for each coefficient:

	variable	method	median
	<chr>	<fct>	<dbl>
1	V1	lm	1.01
2	V1	ridge	0.962
3	V2	lm	0.966
4	V2	ridge	0.947
5	V3	lm	0.938
6	V3	ridge	0.956
7	V4	lm	1.07
8	V4	ridge	0.954
9	V5	lm	0.000713
10	V5	ridge	0.000578

3. We check our results with `lambda=0.1`. In this case, the coefficients' variability is almost the same as when using `lm` (basically, there is no ridge compression). As it happened before, the coefficients are smaller, but on a smaller scale due to the smaller lambda:

```
get_results(0.1)
```

The following screenshot shows the boxplots for the coefficients:

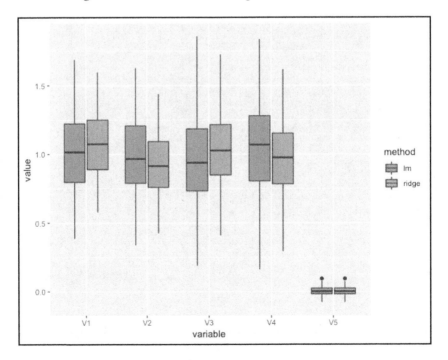

The following screenshot shows medians for each coefficient:

	variable	method	median
	<chr>	<fct>	<dbl>
1	V1	lm	1.01
2	V1	ridge	1.07
3	V2	lm	0.966
4	V2	ridge	0.914
5	V3	lm	0.938
6	V3	ridge	1.03
7	V4	lm	1.07
8	V4	ridge	0.974
9	V5	lm	0.000713
10	V5	ridge	0.000570

How it works...

Ridge is similar to ordinary least squares, with the obvious difference that there is a penalization term. The idea is to minimize the squared residuals, and at the same time have coefficients that are not big. Because the coefficients won't be as big as they would have been in the absence of the penalization term, the model won't be able to over-fit to the data. In the following equation, we have the Ridge minimization problem; note that the λ is a hyper-parameter that defines how much weight we want to place on the penalization. A large value implies that the penalization will dominate and the model will likely under-fit (not capture the structure of the data). On the other hand, a small value implies that the penalization will not be used, and the model will probably over-fit (capture even the noise in the data). The right value for λ needs to be determined via cross-validation or using training/testing data-sets:

$$\beta = argmin \sum_{i=1}^{n} (y_i - x_i^T \beta)^2 + \lambda \sum_{i=1}^{p} \beta_i^2$$

Working with LASSO

In the previous recipe, we saw that Ridge Regression gives us much more stable coefficients, at the cost of a small bias (the coefficients are compressed to a smaller size than they should). It is based on the L2 regularization norm, which is essentially the squared sum of the coefficients. In order to do that, we used the `glmnet` package, which allows us to decide how much Ridge/Lasso regularization we want.

Getting ready

Lets install same packages as in the previous recipe: `glmnet`, `ggplot2`, `tidyr`, and `MASS`. They can be installed via `install.packages()`.

How to do it...

In this example, we will follow the same logic, but we will use `alpha=1`, forcing `glmnet` to do Lasso. This will penalize the coefficients now using the L1 norm, which means that some of the coefficients (the irrelevant ones) will be pushed towards zero exactly. Therefore, some data scientists use LASSO as a variable selection tool:

1. We use the same code as before, but now with `alpha=1`:

```
library(MASS)
library(tidyr)
library(ggplot2)
library(glmnet)
get_results <- function(lambda){
coeffs_total = data.frame(V1=numeric(), V2=numeric(), V3=numeric(),
V4=numeric(), V5=numeric())
 for (q in 1:100){
 V1 = runif(1000)*100
 V2 = runif(1000)*10 + V1
 V3 = runif(1000)*100
 V4 = runif(1000)*10 + V3
 V5 = runif(1000)*100
Residuals = runif(1000)*100
Y = V1 + V2 + V3 + V4 + Residuals
coefs_lm <- lm(Y ~ V1 + V2 + V3 + V4 + V5)$coefficients
coefs_rd <- glmnet(cbind(V1 ,V2,V3,V4
,V5),Y,lambda=lambda,alpha=1)$beta
 frame1 <- data.frame(V1= coefs_lm[2], V2= coefs_lm[3],V3=
coefs_lm[4], V4=
coefs_lm[5],V5=  coefs_lm[6],method="lm")
 frame2 <- data.frame(V1= coefs_rd[1], V2= coefs_rd[2], V3=
coefs_rd[3], V4= coefs_rd[4], V5=  coefs_rd[5],method="ridge")
coeffs_total <- rbind(coeffs_total,frame1,frame2)
}
transposed_data = gather(coeffs_total,"variable","value",1:5)
ggplot(transposed_data, aes(x=variable, y=value, fill=method)) +
geom_boxplot()
print(transposed_data %>% group_by(variable,method) %>%
summarise(median=median(value)))
}
```

2. We now run the code with `lambda=8`. As you can see, the coefficients are slightly smaller than those with Ridge. But the most important part here is that the irrelevant coefficient is now equal to zero. This is slightly better than in Ridge, because it is literally telling us to discard that variable from the model:

```
get_results(8)
```

The following screenshot shows the boxplots for the (`lambda=8`) coefficients:

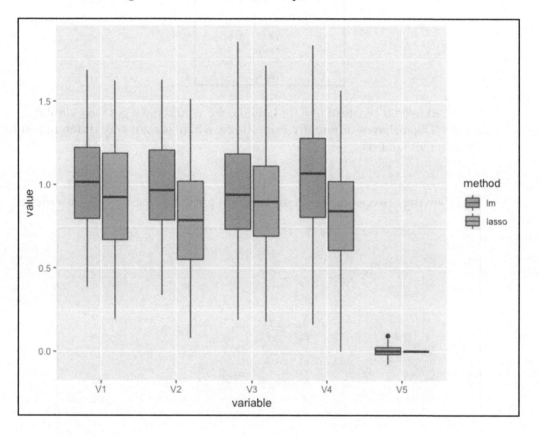

The following screenshot shows medians for each coefficient (notice that values used for the previous plot):

	variable	method	median
	<chr>	<fct>	<dbl>
1	V1	lm	1.01
2	V1	lasso	0.924
3	V2	lm	0.966
4	V2	lasso	0.786
5	V3	lm	0.938
6	V3	lasso	0.896
7	V4	lm	1.07
8	V4	lasso	0.841
9	V5	lm	0.000713
10	V5	lasso	0

3. If we had used 0.1 instead of 8 for lambda, we would have got very similar results. This behaves differently from Ridge, where we got very different results for different lambdas:

```
get_results(0.1)
```

The following screenshot shows the boxplots for the `(lambda=0.1)` coefficients:

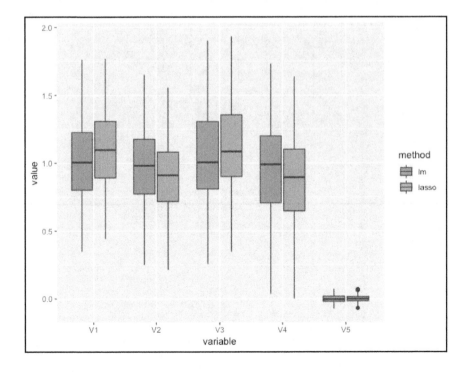

How it works...

The mechanics here are the same as in the Ridge case, with the obvious difference that we use the L1 norm here:

$$\beta = argmin \sum_{i=1}^{n} (y_i - x_i^T \beta)^2 + \lambda \sum_{i=1}^{p} |\beta_i|$$

There are some obvious differences with respect to the Ridge coefficients:

- For Lasso, we get 0 exactly for the irrelevant variables (this is a way of doing variable selection). But for Ridge, we get a smaller value (a compressed coefficient) but not exactly zero. Hence, Ridge can't be used for variable selection.
- Lasso coefficients are smaller than their Ridge counterparts (using the same lambda). In other words, the bias seems larger for Lasso.
- Ridge coefficients are more stable (measured as the height of the boxes in the boxplots).

There's more...

We haven't yet discussed how to find the optimal lambda value. This can be done using the cv.glmnet function. In this case, we won't use the loop we have used so far, but we will define a simple dataset and show you how to get the best lambda. This technique uses cross validation to determine the best value (the dataset is split into several parts, and k-1 parts are used to train, and 1 part is used to test the model—this is done several times). In the following plot, we have the log of lambda on the x axis, and on the y axis we have the **mean squared error** (MSE). The upper part of the plot shows the number of non-zero variables. There are two vertical lines: the one on the left marks where the minimum MSE is, and the one on the right marks a point that has an MSE within a standard deviation (but with a higher lambda). The latter can be used to determine a point with a higher lambda (implicitly leaving more variables equal to zero—a simpler model), with an MSE almost as good as the minimal one. The precise values can be recovered looking into the cv.lasso object; these can be seen in the following plot:

```
V1            = runif(1000)*100
V2            = runif(1000)*10 + V1
V3            = runif(1000)*100
V4            = runif(1000)*10 + V3
 V5            = runif(1000)*100
Residuals = runif(1000)*100
Y             = V1 + V2 + V3 + V4 + Residuals
```

```
cv.lasso=cv.glmnet( cbind(V1 ,V2,V3,V4 ,V5),Y, alpha=1)
plot(cv.lasso)
```

The following screenshot shows the cross-validation—mean squared error plot:

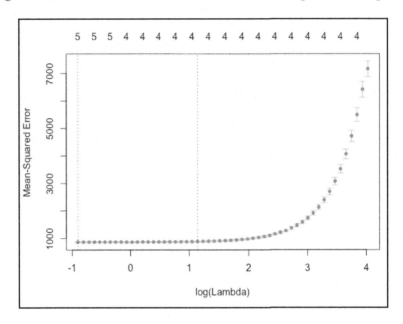

The following screenshot shows Lambda.min and lambda.1se (they are shown as vertical lines on the previous plot as logarithms) appear as vertical lines. Let's now see they actual values:

```
$lambda.min
[1] 0.4050034

$lambda.1se
[1] 3.135794
```

Once we have the best lambda (whichever we chose), we can retrain our model with that lambda and use it for prediction.

Leverage, residuals, and influence

For each observation used in a model, there are three relevant metrics that help us to understand the impact of it on the estimated coefficients. The first metric is the leverage: the potential of an observation to change the estimated coefficient. The second relevant metric is the residual, which is the difference between the prediction and the observed value. Finally, the third is the influence, which can be thought of as the product between the leverage and the residual(ness). Another way of looking at this would be to think of the leverage as the horizontal distance between an observation and the rest of the regression line and the residual as the vertical distance between the observation and the regression line. Essentially, we can have four cases, as depicted in the following graphs:

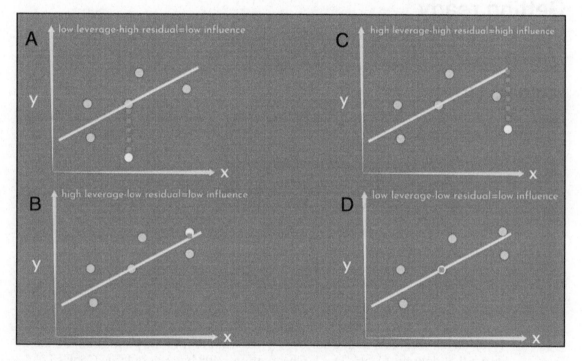

In **A**, we have an observation with a high residual, but low leverage (the regression line will not change much if we remove this observation). In **B**, we have the opposite situation: even though the leverage is large (the observation has the potential to dramatically change the coefficients), the observation lies exactly over the regression line; consequently, we end up with the same effect if we keep it or remove it—low influence. As it can be seen in **C**, when both the leverage and the residual are large, the observation has a large impact on the regression line.

In that case, the slope would be much smaller if the yellow point was included in the model. What is the relevance of identifying residuals, outliers, and influential points? Large residuals indicate a lack of fit of our model for those observations; this is not a problem per se, but could be used a starting point for investigating whether an important variable is missing. Observations carrying a high leverage indicate that they have the potential to alter our results. Again, that is not a problem per se, but could be used in the future to enhance our model. If a data point has a high leverage, we can collect more data points around that point. Finally, influential observations should be flagged and almost always removed from the model.

Getting ready

No special package is needed for this recipe.

How to do it...

In this recipe, we will work with a dataset containing house prices. The intention will be to identify influential observations:

1. We first load our dataset, and formulate our model:

```
library(car)
data = read.csv("./house_prices_aug.csv")
model = lm(Property_price ~ size + number.bathrooms +
number.bedrooms +number.entrances +size_balcony
+size_entrance,data=data)
```

2. We can build a simple plot to identify influential observations. The X axis represents the leverage, while the Y axis represents the residual size. A quick rule is to flag observations as influential if Cook's D is greater than 1. R creates two curves, one for Cook's D = 0.5 and another one for Cook's D = 1. Since we usually focus on observations with Cook's D > 1 we want to find the points outside the curve that delimits Cook's D = 1. Observation = 408 has a very large Cook's D, whereas observation = 1 has a low Cook's D, even though it has a huge leverage:

```
plot(model)
```

The following screenshot shows the residuals versus Leverage plot (observation 408 has a very large Cook's D):

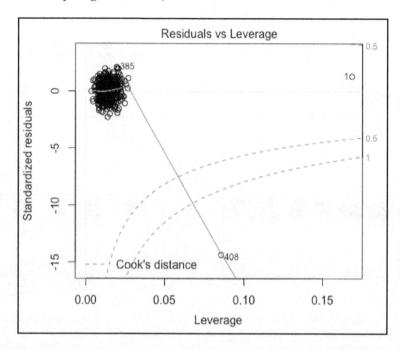

3. With the previous plot, we can't really see if the high leverage is caused by a specific variable. If we use the `leveragePlots` function, we can get that easily. This function plots the partial regression leverage plots. On the Y axis, it has the dependent variable residuals, obtained by regressing it in terms of all the variables except for the selected regressor. On the X axis, it has the selected regressor residuals obtained by regressing it in terms of all the other regressors. We can see that observation 408 has a large leverage mostly because of `size_balcony`, `size_entrance`, and `size` (this is measured along the x axis). Observation = 1 has an enormous leverage (because it has a large size variable), but because it almost falls over the regression line it has a low residual; because the residual is low, its Cook's D is small:

```
leveragePlots(model)
```

The following screenshot shows the leverage plots:

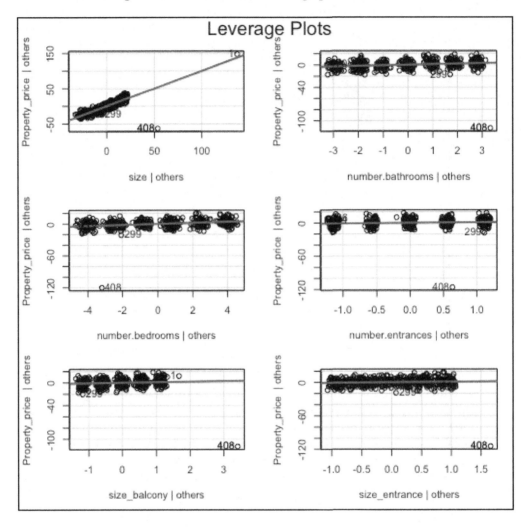

4. We can test if we have outliers using the following code. This tests whether each residual is an outlier, doing an appropriate Bonferroni correction (bear in mind that if we do multiple tests, with, for instance, an alpha of 0.05, the effective alpha for test is no longer 0.05; therefore, it needs to be corrected). Because we only have one problematic residual, the Bonferroni correction is not relevant here. We get a small p-value, so we reject the null hypothesis that there are no outliers. It's worth noting that observation=1 has a low residual (but a high leverage), so it doesn't appear here. Remember that the presence (or not) of outliers is not an indication that our model is wrong:

```
outlierTest(model)
```

The following screenshot shows outlierTest results:

```
> outlierTest(model)
        rstudent unadjusted p-value Bonferonni p
408 -19.08144          1.2928e-60     6.2183e-58
```

5. We can check the leverage with more detail. Obviously, observations 1 and 408 appear here as well:

```
plot(hatvalues(model), type = "h")
```

The following screenshot shows the another leverage plot:

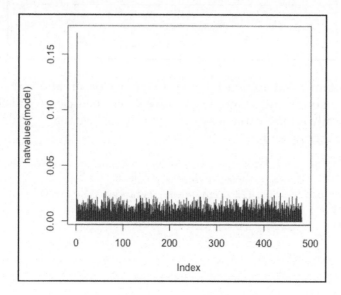

6. Let's direct our attention towards Cook's D value. We will print all the values with a Cook's D larger than 4/(n-coeffs-1). As we know, we have only one case that calls our attention (observation = 408):

```
cooksd <- sort(cooks.distance(model))
cutoff <- 4/((nrow(data)-length(model$coefficients)-1))
plot(model, which=4, cook.levels=cutoff)
```

The following screenshot shows the Cook's D plot:

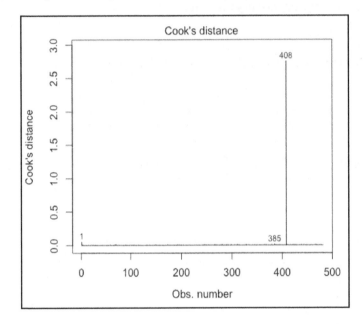

7. The recommended approach here is to remove observation 408, since it is disrupting our results. Once we remove it, the coefficients will change dramatically for the variables causing the large leverage (size_balcony and size_entrance):

```
model2 = lm(Property_price ~ size + number.bathrooms +
number.bedrooms +number.entrances
+size_balcony  +size_entrance,data=data[-c(408),])
model
model2
```

The following screenshot shows standard results (top), and corrected data results (bottom):

```
Call:
lm(formula = Property_price ~ size + number.bathrooms + number.bedrooms +
    number.entrances + size_balcony + size_entrance, data = data)

Coefficients:
    (Intercept)           size  number.bathrooms  number.bedrooms  number.entrances    size_balcony    size_entrance
        -4.8841         5.3253            0.9583           1.6219            0.5660          0.5791           0.1908

> model2

Call:
lm(formula = Property_price ~ size + number.bathrooms + number.bedrooms +
    number.entrances + size_balcony + size_entrance, data = data[-c(408),
    ])

Coefficients:
    (Intercept)           size  number.bathrooms  number.bedrooms  number.entrances    size_balcony    size_entrance
       -16.8767         5.6124            1.1817           1.4371            0.7132          1.3564           0.4043
```

How it works...

Cook's D can be obtained using the formula:

$$Cook\ D_i = \frac{\sum(\hat{Y}_j - \hat{Y}_{j(i)})^2}{(p+1)\hat{\sigma}^2}$$

This is essentially the square value of the difference between the predicted value for the full model (one with all of the observations) for observation i, and another one omitting observation i. In the denominator, we have the residual standard deviation for the full model times the number of parameters.

The leverage can be obtained by getting the diagonal elements of the so-called hat matrix. It is obtained by applying the same formula to the design matrix.

4
Bayesian Regression

We will cover the following recipes in this chapter:

- Getting the posterior density in STAN
- Formulating a linear regression model
- Assigning the priors
- Doing MCMC the manual way
- Evaluating convergence with CODA
- Bayesian variable selection
- Using a model for prediction
- GLMs in JAGS

Introduction

In this chapter, we present several Bayesian techniques in R, using either STAN or JAGS (both are the most important software packages that can be used in R). Bayesian statistics is fundamentally different from classical statistics. In the latter, parameters are fixed quantities that need to be found. In the Bayesian framework, parameters are random variables themselves that can be learned. Furthermore, Bayesian statistics allows us to incorporate prior knowledge about a distribution that we want to learn, and update it accordingly.

Getting the posterior density in STAN

STAN is the leading Bayesian engine for R, both for academia and the industry. Its performance is very good, mainly because it is written in C++.

In Bayesian statistics, and we have a very different approach than in classical statistics. Here, each coefficient will behave as a random variable, and we will use appropriate algorithms to recover the distribution of each one of them. But there is an extra element here, we will be able to incorporate prior distributions into our approach. Consequently, the idea will be the following:

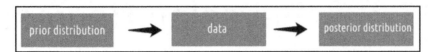

Bayesian statistics could be interpreted as an approach where we have a prior/initial idea about a coefficient, we then augment that expectation using the data, and we finally end up with a posterior distribution. This is not that different from the process humans follow when learning new things; for example, we might have an expectation that a train station is always crowded, so we then go to the station and evaluate the situation. If it is 90% crowded, that shouldn't change our initial expectation much. But if it is 10% crowded, we should then update our initial expectation in a substantial way.

There is a subtle technical point here; we generally define univariate priors, and at the end of the process, we get a joint posterior density (the density for all the parameters involved in our model). Of course, we will need to marginalize that density to get the marginal densities that only depend on one variable.

It is worth noting that in classical statistics, we usually formulate a model via maximum likelihood, and we then find the best parameters that maximize that expression. These are found using some numerical maximization routines. In the Bayesian world, things are different, because we don't want to maximize parameters, but we want to find the posterior density of them. So, if we find a technique that generates random numbers according to this posterior density, our problem would get fixed. **Markov Chain Monte Carlo (MCMC)** methods are intended to do exactly this: they are just a sophisticated way of generating random numbers. There is one issue, though: they only generate random numbers according to the target density when the stationary distribution of the chain is achieved; before then, the random numbers are not useful. Part of our job will be to identify if the stationary distribution has been achieved. It's worth reiterating that this target density is the joint posterior density (prior + data) involving all the parameters.

A slightly minor issue is that even when the convergence to the stationary distribution has been achieved, the random numbers generated via MCMC are still correlated (the nature of MCMC is based on Markov Chains). There is some discussion regarding how to fix this. Some authors recommend running the MCMC algorithm over a very large number of iterations so the auto-correlation disappears. Other authors prefer to apply thinning: only keeping every *n*th observation. We will discuss this in more detail later in this chapter.

Getting ready

In order to run this recipe, you will need to install STAN using
`install.packages("RSTAN")`.

How to do it...

In this example, we will generate 1,000 Gaussian deviates with a mean equal to five and a standard deviation equal to three. We will assign a Gaussian prior to the mean parameter, and a gamma distribution to the standard deviation. The objective will be to characterize the marginal posterior densities for mu and sigma (mean and standard deviation of a Gaussian distribution):

1. We declare our STAN model, and we will store it into a string as follows:

```
library(rstan)
values = list(y = rnorm(1000,5,3))
model ="
data {
real y[1000];
}
parameters {
real mu;
real sigma;
}
model {
mu ~ normal(0,10);sigma ~ normal(0,10);y ~ normal(mu,sigma);
}"
```

2. We call the stan function, which fits the model. The first parameter, model_code=, obviously specifies the model that we want to fit. data= specifies the data that will be used to fit model. warmup= is the amount of iterations that will be used to adjust some of the internal parameters in order to achieve a good acceptance rate for the MCMC algorithm. iter= specifies the number of iterations, and chains= specifies the number of chains that will be used.cores= specifies the number of cores that will be used and thinning= controls how many iterations will be discarded for each chain.thinning=1 means that after one iteration is accepted, we discard one:

```
fit <- stan(model_code = model, data = values, warmup = 500, iter =
1000, chains = 4, cores = 2, thin = 1)
```

3. The posterior density can actually be extracted using the `extract` function. This will return a list containing one array per parameter, as shown in the following code:

```
posterior = extract(fit)
```

4. We should always plot the posterior densities and check that they display an irregular pattern (no structure). If some structure was detected, it would imply that the convergence to the stationary distribution has not been achieved:

```
par(mfrow=c(2,1))
plot(posterior$mu, type = "l")
plot(posterior$sigma, type = "l")
```

The following screenshot shows the traceplots; ideally, they should look like this, with no apparent structure:

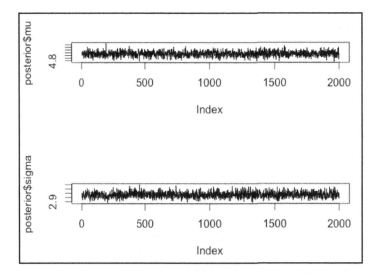

5. We can plot all the chains into the same plot. If convergence to the stationary distribution was achieved, then all the chains should wander around the same approximate value. As we can see, the chains are oscillating around similar values. As it can be seen here, the chains for mu wander around 5.1, and the ones for sigma do so around 2.9:

```
traceplot(fit)
```

The following screenshot shows the traceplot, showing each of the chains. Neither one of them should have any structure:

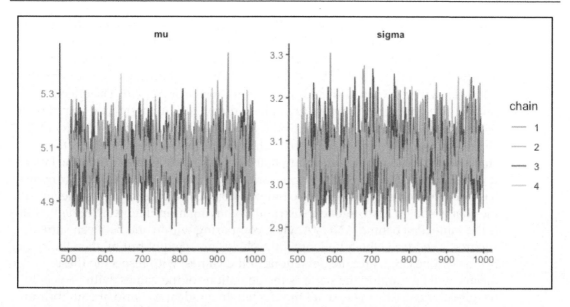

6. We can get the posterior densities using the following code. As we can see, the posteriors seem to be symmetric:

```
stan_dens(fit)
```

The following screenshot shows the posterior density for each parameter:

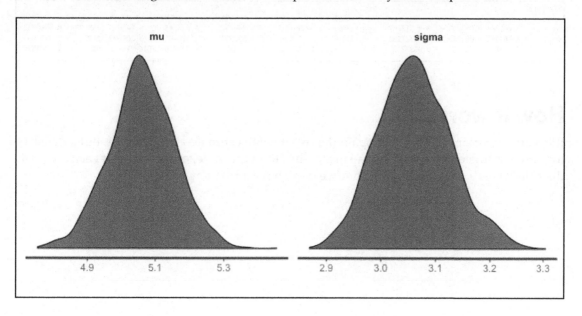

7. After we are convinced that reasonable convergence has been achieved, we can jump into proper analysis of the posterior densities. What we see in the next output is the mean, `std.error` for the mean, std. error, several quantiles, the effective sample size (`n_eff`), and the `Rhat` statistic. Note that `std.error` for the mean will go down as the number of iterations is increased. The effective sample size, (`n_eff`), is a measure of how many good/uncorrelated samples we have. The *Rhat* statistic is a metric built as a ratio involving the variability of the chains' means and the variability of each value with respect to its respective chain mean. If those differ, meaning that the former one is larger than the latter, it would imply that the chains' means are different (suggesting that convergence has not been achieved). The implicit idea is that if convergence was achieved, all the chains should converge to a distribution having a similar mean. Note that this is the same idea behind ANOVA when comparing within and between sum of squares. The idea is the following: if the chains are at equilibrium, then their means will be close, and the deviations of the values, with respect to these means, will be roughly the same as the deviations of the values, with respect to the global mean (the mean of all the chains). In an ideal scenario, if equilibrium has been achieved, `Rhat` should be very close to one:

```
summary(fit)
```

The following screenshot shows the MCMC summary statistics:

```
$summary
              mean      se_mean          sd          2.5%          25%          50%          75%        97.5%     n_eff      Rhat
mu        5.061284  0.002299197  0.09518200      4.875067     5.002210     5.060738     5.125745     5.245615 1713.7884 0.9996033
sigma     3.061439  0.001555272  0.06721101      2.937593     3.015324     3.058954     3.106601     3.204593 1867.5325 1.0012654
lp__   -1619.014663  0.031237429  0.96577384  -1621.529914 -1619.400912 -1618.724423 -1618.319770 -1618.075128  955.8733 1.0001530
```

How it works...

It is very important to highlight again that we haven't estimated a parameter, but a density for each parameter. We may use the mean, the 50th percentile, or the mode of each distribution as a reporting metric, but we don't have a true parameter.

Formulating a linear regression model

The mechanics for Bayesian linear regression follow the same logic as that which was described in the previous chapter. The only real difference is that we will specify a distribution for the residuals, which will be distributed according to a Gaussian distribution, with 0 mean and a certain variance. These residuals will originate as the subtraction of the actual values, minus the expected ones. These expected values will be equal to the sum of several coefficients times certain variables.

In a linear regression context, we want to build inferences on the coefficients. But here (as we have already mentioned), we will estimate a density for each posterior.

Getting ready

In order to run this example, we need to install STAN via `install.packages("rstan")`.

How to do it...

In the following example, we will fit a linear regression model to our house price dataset. The objective is to model the house prices in terms of several variables, such as the size of the property, the number of bathrooms, the number of bedrooms, the number of entrances, the size of the balcony, and the size of the house entrance. In this example, we won't be very specific about the priors, but we do know that all these variables should have a positive impact. One natural possibility is to use a `gamma()` distribution, which is naturally bounded by zero:

1. We first load STAN and the data as follows:

```
library(rstan)
data = read.csv("./house_prices.csv")
```

2. We then create our STAN model. This has the following three parts:
   - The data part contains two arrays, the first with one dimension and 125 elements (designed to hold our dependent variable), and a second one containing 125 rows and six columns (we will load 6 variables).
   - The parameters part declares that we will have 6 coefficients, plus an intercept (alpha) and sigma (the variance of model). The MCMC algorithm will estimate the posterior densities for these variables.

- The model part specifies the model, and the priors. In this case, we specify the prior for the beta coefficients to be gamma (3,1). We then do a loop going from one to the number of observations (125); in this loop, we specify that the dependent variable will behave as a normal variable with a mean given by a certain linear equation, and a standard error equal to sigma. The equation is the sum of each coefficient times each variable, plus an intercept:

```
model ="
data {
real y[125];
real x[125,6];
}
parameters
{
real beta[6];
real sigma;
real alpha;
}
model {
beta ~ gamma(3,1);
for (n in 1:125)
y[n] ~ normal(alpha + beta[1]*x[n,1] + beta[2]*x[n,2] +
beta[3]*x[n,3] + beta[4]*x[n,4] + beta[5]*x[n,5] + beta[6]*x[n,6],
sigma);
}
"
```

3. Just for the sake of comparison, we display the **ordinary least squares** (OLS) estimates:

```
lm(data=data, Property_price ~ size + number.bathrooms +
number.bedrooms + number.entrances + size_balcony + size_entrance)
```

The following screenshot is the linear model (estimated via OLS):

```
Call:
lm(formula = Property_price ~ size + number.bathrooms + number.bedrooms +
    number.entrances + size_balcony + size_entrance, data = data)

Coefficients:
   (Intercept)         size  number.bathrooms   number.bedrooms  number.entrances   size_balcony   size_entrance
      -16.7063       5.6270            1.1513            1.4115            0.6621         1.3693          0.4055
```

4. We pass a list containing two elements: the dependent variable, and an independent array containing six columns. Both will contain 125 rows. As can be seen here, the mean of the posterior densities is very close to the values we got just by finding the OLS estimates. This happens because the priors are quite loose, and the posteriors will be centered around those values. The situation would be quite different if the priors were tighter. The summary(fit) function returns statistics (such as mean, median, and so on) first for all the chains merged, and after that, the same statistics for each specific chain:

```
xy = list(y=data[,1],x=data[,2:7])
fit = stan(model_code = model, data = xy, warmup = 500, iter =
1000, chains = 3, cores = 2, thin = 1,verbose=FALSE)
traceplot(fit)
```

The following screenshot shows the traceplots; we have three chains for each parameter. All the chains appear to not have any structure and seem to wander around the same area. This suggests that all chains have converged to the same stationary distribution:

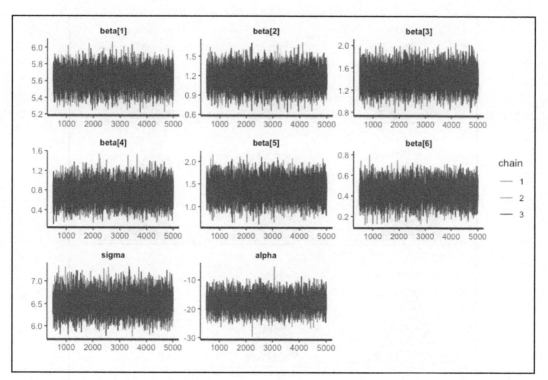

With the following code, we can see a summary for the posterior densities:

```
summary(fit)
```

The following screenshot shows the posterior density estimates:

	mean	se_mean	sd	2.5%	25%	50%	75%	97.5%	n_eff	Rhat
beta[1]	5.6225788	0.0009766837	0.10683040	5.4111115	5.5517882	5.6226907	5.6952738	5.8314363	11964.149	0.9998872
beta[2]	1.1643991	0.0012442749	0.14226817	0.8850887	1.0686641	1.1644535	1.2604379	1.4415373	13073.228	0.9999466
beta[3]	1.4262629	0.0015232267	0.17442242	1.0898667	1.3086345	1.4263075	1.5452445	1.7667870	13112.199	1.0000970
beta[4]	0.7435934	0.0015865555	0.18663472	0.3824652	0.6162078	0.7406738	0.8678405	1.1139111	13838.032	1.0000081
beta[5]	1.3852341	0.0019617951	0.21042770	0.9742840	1.2438578	1.3845633	1.5274917	1.7951890	11505.316	0.9998713
beta[6]	0.4362908	0.0007741666	0.08766455	0.2666178	0.3767417	0.4353704	0.4962245	0.6096573	12822.691	1.0000954
sigma	6.5099420	0.0018426662	0.21313951	6.1080880	6.3651862	6.5041227	6.6512168	6.9438713	13379.336	1.0000498
alpha	-17.5840560	0.0271623199	2.52921088	-22.6663692	-19.2924450	-17.5431884	-15.8754292	-12.6919085	8670.345	1.0000525
lp__	-1148.7268327	0.0254192688	2.01624282	-1153.6471968	-1149.8241523	-1148.3994550	-1147.2645835	-1145.8007536	6291.578	0.9998735

5. Actually, we can plot the posterior densities with the following code:

```
stan_dens(fit)
```

The following screenshot shows the posterior density:

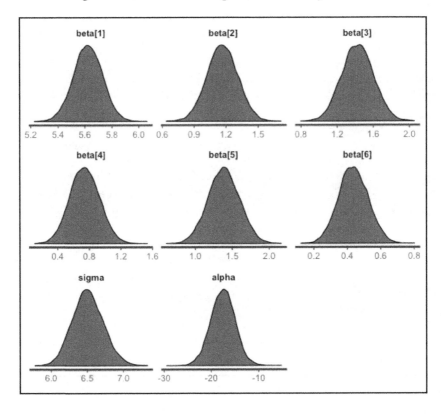

How it works...

STAN will launch the MCMC algorithm using the model that we specified. The only real difference with respect to the previous recipe is that here we are specifying a model that relates the conditional mean of the price to certain regressors. That relationship is constructed upon a series of coefficients, where we want to find out the posterior density.

There's more...

We have used gamma priors in order to force the beta coefficients to be greater than zero. But in STAN, we have a different option: we can put a boundary via real<lower=0> beta[6]. This is sufficient to ensure that the posterior densities are bounded by zero. Apart from this, we may or may not want to specify a prior density, which we can do, for example, using beta ~ normal(5,3). It is very important to note that, in these cases (when using the <lower> approach), that we are actually specifying improper priors, which are priors that have a density that doesn't sum up to one (a Gaussian density is defined from -∞ to ∞ and has an area of 1). But if the permissible range for this variable is now from 0 to ∞, that area-integral of the density will be 0.5). STAN allows us to use either improper or proper priors. The STAN code for this model is as follows:

```
model ="
data {
real y[125];
real x[125,6];
}
parameters {
real<lower=0> beta[6];
real sigma;
real alpha;
}
model {
beta ~ normal(5,3);
for (n in 1:125)
y[n] ~ normal(alpha + beta[1]*x[n,1] + beta[2]*x[n,2] +
beta[3]*x[n,3] + beta[4]*x[n,4] + beta[5]*x[n,5] + beta[6]*x[n,6],
sigma);
}"
xy = list(y=data[,1],x=data[,2:7])
fit = stan(model_code = model, data = xy, warmup = 500, iter =
1000, chains = 4, cores = 2, thin = 1,verbose=FALSE)
summary(fit)
```

The following screenshot shows a summary of the posterior densities:

	mean	se_mean	sd	2.5%	25%	50%	75%	97.5%	n_eff	Rhat
beta[1]	5.6255568	0.002820783	0.11001490	5.4159132	5.5475310	5.6279355	5.6985104	5.843097	1521.1205	1.0013970
beta[2]	1.1583504	0.004053775	0.14967539	0.8601551	1.0606004	1.1567897	1.2535384	1.448670	1363.2689	1.0007515
beta[3]	1.4199475	0.005144073	0.18548777	1.0690988	1.2909298	1.4175903	1.5455242	1.775674	1300.2186	1.0030240
beta[4]	0.6818515	0.005846059	0.20679897	0.2622836	0.5406722	0.6862651	0.8200143	1.085002	1251.3256	0.9992717
beta[5]	1.3868954	0.006095161	0.21271219	0.9596830	1.2404890	1.3883635	1.5363500	1.786665	1217.9079	1.0006140
beta[6]	0.4120919	0.002543454	0.09091023	0.2421430	0.3505592	0.4094255	0.4769115	0.591295	1277.5498	0.9998908
sigma	6.5155501	0.005030784	0.20372699	6.1263465	6.3762869	6.5130353	6.6489729	6.928737	1639.9315	1.0025792
alpha	-17.0314924	0.086909093	2.59657269	-22.2778510	-18.7123645	-17.0306260	-15.2446184	-12.158003	892.6281	0.9994337
lp__	-1144.0256355	0.074892136	2.06822589	-1148.7713547	-1145.2262920	-1143.6861299	-1142.4698515	-1140.978021	762.6469	1.0027350

We can get the posterior densities using the following code:

```
stan_dens(fit)
```

The following screenshot shows the posterior densities:

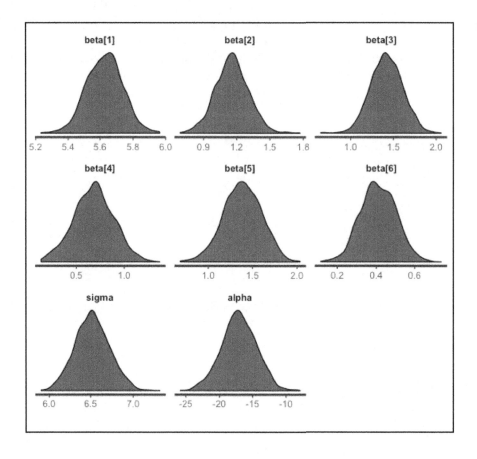

Assigning the priors

As we know, the priors are ingested by the MCMC algorithm, and are used to calculate the posterior densities. But how should the priors be assigned? Do we actually need a prior for each parameter?

Defining the support

Priors are just statistical distributions that reflect the initial expectation that the modeler has about each parameter. The very first thing we need to decide is, what is the support for the corresponding distributions? For example, for most coefficients in a linear regression model, the modeler very likely knows the correct sign for them. When modeling sales of a product in terms of its price and a promotional effect, the price effect should be negative (a higher price = less sales), and the promotional effect should be positive (more promotion = more sales). It would be natural then, to assign a distribution, bounded by zero, to both parameters. Sometimes we don't have a clear idea, and in those cases it is advisable to choose a distribution that has a support between $-\infty$ and ∞. In this fashion, we will be allowing the posterior density to take any value. Any restriction on the prior's support gets translated into the posterior's support (by support, we mean a range of permissible values).

How to decide the parameters for a prior

Once the support for the prior distribution has been determined, we need to decide what the actual shape of the prior will look like (by choosing the right parameters). For example, if we think that a certain prior should be a Gaussian distribution, it really matters whether the mean is 4 or 20. In general, these are tuned so the peak/mode of the prior is very near the value that we have in mind. For example, if we expect the promotion effect on sales to be equal to 2, we should put a prior that has a mode near 2.

However, it's not just the mode, but also the asymmetry and the variance. For example, if we think that this promotional variable has an impact around two, but we are equally unsure whether it should be 1.8 or 2.2, we should choose a symmetric distribution centered at 2 (see the left side of the following screenshot). On the other hand, if we think that large values such as four and six are quite likely, we might want to choose an asymmetric one.

The following screenshot shows two gamma options that we could use for non-negative priors:

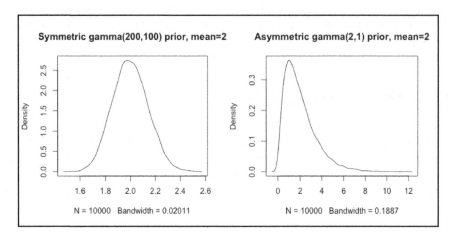

Bear in mind that when we choose a normal prior, we cannot control the asymmetry (since it is equal to zero), but we can control the variance. The way Gaussian distributions are assigned is that we first think of the expected value that we think is correct, and we put the sigma in order to reflect our certainty about it. Here we have two examples, both centered at 2: variance = 0.5, which means that we are quite certain that the parameter should be near 2 (left), and variance = 2, which means that we are not very sure about it (see the right side of the preceding screenshot).

The following screenshot shows two Gaussian distributions: one with low variance (left), and another with high variance (right):

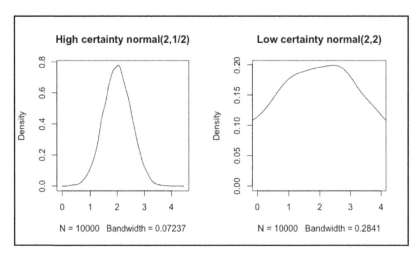

Be careful when restricting/defining density support. There should be a very robust reason justifying why a prior should have a bounded support. If you are unsure, just assign a small probability to that region, and leave the majority of the density on the likely area.

So, what's the impact of the prior?

To begin with, it will define the support for the posterior density. A prior between zero and ∞ will generate a posterior in the (zero and ∞) area. The specific shape will depend on both the data, and the prior; but in general, for small datasets, the prior will dominate, whereas in big datasets, the data will dominate. In some way, the prior gets diluted as we add more data, and that makes perfect sense.

In the following example, we will load the house price dataset that we used in the previous recipe, and we will study how different priors impact the results.

Getting ready

In order to run this example, you need to install `rstan` via `install.packages("rstan")`.

How to do it...

In the following example, we will load the house price dataset that we used in the previous recipe, and we will study how different priors impact the results:

1. We load the dataset and do our model. We will only put a prior on `beta[6]` in order to simplify our comparison. In the first case, we will put a flat prior—uniform (0,1000). We will only direct our attention toward the `beta[6]` posterior density; as we can see, the density is not very concentrated around 1:

```
data = read.csv("./house_prices.csv")
model ="
data {
real y[125];
real x[125,6];
}
parameters {
real beta[6];
real sigma;
real alpha;
}
model {
```

```
beta[1] ~ uniform(0,1000);
for (n in 1:125)
y[n] ~ normal(alpha + beta[1]*x[n,1] + beta[2]*x[n,2] +
beta[3]*x[n,3] + beta[4]*x[n,4] + beta[5]*x[n,5] + beta[6]*x[n,6],
sigma);
}"
xy = list(y=data[,1],x=data[,2:7])
fit = stan(model_code = model, data = xy, warmup = 500, iter =
1000, chains = 1, cores = 1, thin = 1,verbose=FALSE)
stan_dens(fit)
```

The following screenshot shows the posterior density:

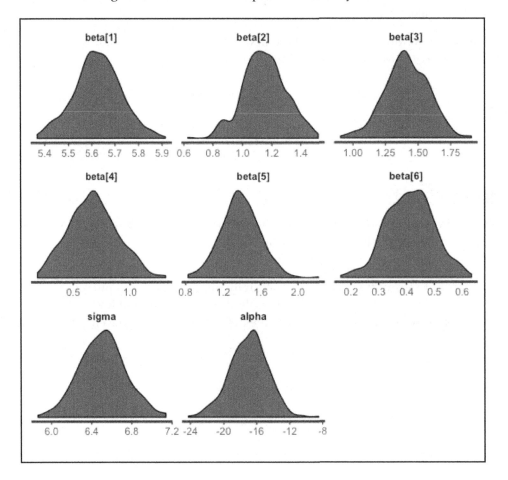

2. What would have happened if we had used different priors? We put very tight priors around one (priors so tight are seldom used). The posterior distributions are now almost centered around one (or much closer to one), as shown in the following code:

```
beta[1]   ~ uniform(0,1000);
beta[2]   ~ normal(1,0.1);
beta[3]   ~ normal(1,0.1);
beta[4]   ~ normal(1,0.1);
beta[5]   ~ normal(1,0.1);
beta[6]   ~ normal(1,0.1);
```

The following screenshot shows the posterior density:

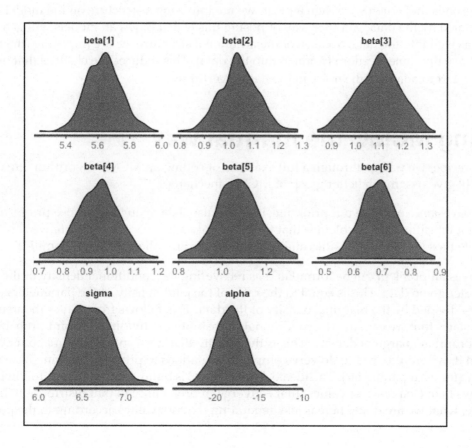

How it works...

The tighter the prior is (more concentrated around) a value is, the more concentrated the posterior is. It is always preferable to choose loose priors to avoid forcing the coefficients to be near a specific value.

 Priors should always be defined before looking at the data in order to avoid setting a prior that is almost confirmed by the data.

Bayesian models are, in general, much more robust to overfitting than classical methods. The reason is that when we assign a prior, we are imposing a structure on the model that is not dictated by the data. Another way of posing this is that Bayesian models will generally fit not as well into the data, because of the additional structure we are imposing (the model won't have the same freedom to adjust into the data). This reduces the chances that our models start to adjust to the noise in the data (overfitting).

Doing MCMC the manual way

In this recipe, we will go through a full example of coding an MCMC algorithm ourselves. This will give us a much better grasp of MCMC mechanics.

In the Bayesian world, we put prior densities and use data to augment those priors, and get posterior densities. The problem is that there are only a few occasions where we can calculate those posterior densities analytically—these are called conjugate families.

The Bayesian problem can be formulated as recovering the conditional density of the parameter given data. This is equal to the ratio of the joint density of the parameters and the data divided by the marginal density of the data. This follows from Bayes theorem, which states that we can invert a conditional probability by dividing the joint probability by the appropriate marginal density. This is the density that we want to compute, but even if we had it, we would need to do very complex calculations to properly marginalize each density (for each parameter). The idea behind MCMC is build random values following a Markov chain (sequence of values) that converge in probability to that distribution. In essence, what we are doing here is just generating random values according to the posterior density:

$$P(\theta|D) = \frac{P(\theta)P(D|\theta)}{\int P(\theta)P(D|\theta)d\theta}$$

There are several MCMC algorithms, but the simplest ones are known as **Metropolis Hastings (MH)** algorithms. The intention in MH is to generate a chain of correlated random values that eventually converges to a stationary distribution of our target (in a regression model this is the joint posterior density involving all the parameters).

In pseudocode, the algorithm works in the following way—π is the posterior density (the multiplication of the prior and the data density):

1. *Step 0* generate random starting values for each parameter. Draw random numbers for each parameter conditional on the current values using a symmetric distribution (that is, a Gaussian distribution):

$$x_{proposed} \sim q(x^i|x^{i-1})$$

2. Compute the following ratio:

$$p(x^{proposed}|x^{i-1}) = min\left[1, \frac{q(x^{i-1}|x^{proposed})\pi(x^{proposed})}{q(x^{proposed}|x^{i-1})\pi(x^{i-1})}\right]$$

Accept the values that we proposed in **1**, with probability=p. That means that we draw another random number, and if it smaller than **p**, we accept the proposed move. Note that whenever the density at the proposed values is larger than at the current ones, we always accept the proposed values (probability=1). On the other hand, when the proposed density is smaller with the proposed values, we sometimes accept the proposed values.

3. Keep running steps 1-3 until we have a necessary amount of random values.

In this example, we will generate a synthetic dataset where we already know the parameters, with the intention of estimating an MCMC model coded fully by us. Since we will be using quite simple priors, these priors should not be far away from the values used to generate the data.

Getting ready

In order to run this example, you need to install the `ggplot2` package via the usual `install.packages("ggplot2")`.

How to do it...

In this example, we will generate a synthetic dataset where we already know the parameters, with the intention of estimating an MCMC model coded fully by us. Since we are using quite simple priors, these priors should not be far away from the values used to generate the data:

1. We load the `ggplot` library, and we create our dataset. We will have six regressors, and one dependent variable. For the sake of simplicity, we will work with `coefficients=1`. The residual will be distributed according to a Gaussian distribution, with a standard `error=3`, as shown in the following code:

```
library(ggplot2)
v1_1 = rnorm(1000,10,1)
v1_2 = rnorm(1000,10,1)
v1_3 = rnorm(1000,10,1)
v2_1 = rnorm(1000,10,1)
v2_2 = rnorm(1000,10,1)
v2_3 = rnorm(1000,10,1)
U = rnorm(1000,0,3)
Y = v1_1 + v1_2 + v1_3 + v2_1 + v2_2 + v2_3 +
```

2. We need to define a function that calculates the sum of the logarithms of the priors (conceptually, the same as doing multiplication of priors). This step is shown in the following code:

```
get_prior <- function(param){
c11_prior = dnorm(param[1], 0.5,5, log = T)
c12_prior = dnorm(param[2], 0.5,5, log = T)
c13_prior = dnorm(param[3], 0.5,5, log = T)
c21_prior = dnorm(param[4], 0.5,5, log = T)
c22_prior = dnorm(param[5], 0.5,5, log = T)
c23_prior = dnorm(param[6], 0.5,5, log = T)
sdprior = dnorm(param[7], 0.5,5, log = T)
return(c11_prior+c12_prior+c13_prior+c21_prior+c22_prior+c23_prior+
sdprior)
}
```

3. Next, we define a function that gets the likelihood. This is computed for each observation, and then we sum the logarithms of all of them, as shown in the following code:

```
get_likelihood <- function(param){
pred = param[1]*v1_1 + param[2]*v1_2 + param[3]*v1_3 +
param[4]*v2_1 + param[5]*v2_2 + param[6]*v2_3
likelihood_per_observation = dnorm(Y, mean = pred, sd = param[7],
log = T)
sumll = sum(likelihood_per_observation)
return(sumll)
}
```

4. After we have functions that return the likelihood and the prior, we now need a function that gets the posterior density (which is equal to the multiplication of the prior and the likelihood, or the sum of their respective logarithms). This step is shown in the following snippet of code:

```
get_posterior <- function(param){
return_value = get_likelihood(param) + get_prior(param)
return (return_value)
}
```

5. Next, we need a proposal function that generates random numbers. We will accept or reject these numbers according to the metropolis ratio:

```
get_proposalfunction <- function(param){
return(rnorm(7,mean = param, sd=
c(.015,.015,.015,.015,.015,.015,.015)))
}
```

6. The main part of the code is the proper **Metropolis-Hastings** (**MH**) algorithm. The logic is the following: we get random values from the proposal density, and we evaluate the posterior density, both at the current values and at the proposed values. We compute the ratio between them (or the subtraction of their logarithms—let's call this Q) and we then accept the proposed move with probability Q. This step is shown in the following code:

```
MetropolisHastings_MCMC <- function(start_, iter_){
chain_values = array(dim = c(iter_+1,7))
chain_values[1,] = start_
for (i in 1:iter_){
proposal = get_proposalfunction(chain[i,])
probs = exp(get_posterior(proposal) - get_posterior(chain[i,]))
if (is.nan(probs)){
probs = 0
```

```
}
random_value = runif(1)
if (random_value < probs){
chain_values[i+1,] = proposal
}else{
chain_values[i+1,] = chain[i,]
}
}
return(chain_values)
}
```

7. We propose an initial vector used to instantiate the algorithm, and we then call our main function, as shown here:

```
startvalue = c(0.1,0.1,0.1,0.1,0.1,0.1,10)
chain_values = MetropolisHastings_MCMC(startvalue, 12000)
```

8. We then transform our matrix into a data frame, and we name the columns, accordingly. We also create a column that contains values 1 to n, which will be used for plotting:

```
data = data.frame(chain_values)
colnames(data) = c("v1_1","v1_2","v1_3","v2_1","v2_2","v2_3","sd")
data$iter = seq.int(nrow(data))
```

9. We can plot the chain for a specific variable. Let's choose v1_1 and see its trajectory. Interestingly, the initial values are quite close to the starting values, and it takes some time to reach a stationary level. Usually, these initial values are discarded because they do not correspond to the stationary distribution. This is usually referred in the MCMC literature as the burn-in:

```
ggplot(data=data,aes(x=iter, y=v1_1)) + geom_line(color="blue")
```

We get the following chain for the v1_1 variable:

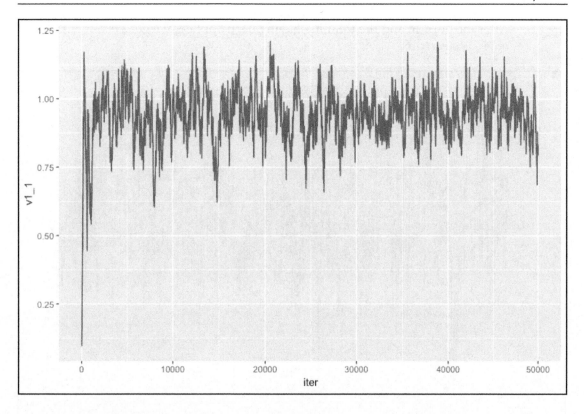

10. We apply the burn-in by dropping the first 10,000 observations. After that, we apply thinning (only keeping every nth observation—in this case, we use five). The idea is to reduce the auto-correlation of the chains. This step is shown in the following code:

```
data            = data[10000:50000,]
data            = data[seq(1, dim(data)[1], by = 5),]
ggplot(data=data,aes(x=iter, y=v1_1)) +
geom_line(color="blue")
```

After the burn-in and the thinning having been applied, we get a chain with no obvious structure:

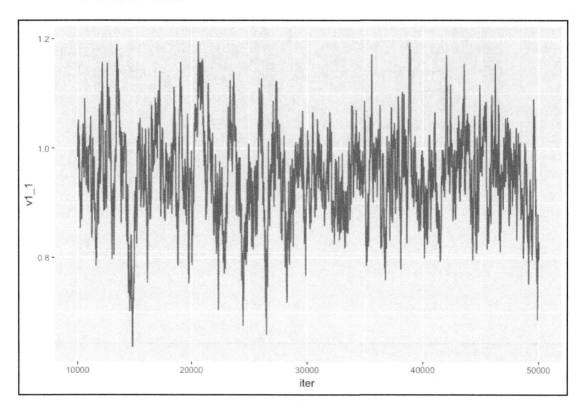

11. After the chain has no obvious structure, and looks like random noise, we can get the posterior densities, as shown in the following code:

```
seqs = seq(1, nrow(data),2)
plot(density(data[seqs,"v1_1"]), main="V1_1 posterior density")
```

We plot the posterior density for the V1_1 variable, as shown in the following screenshot:

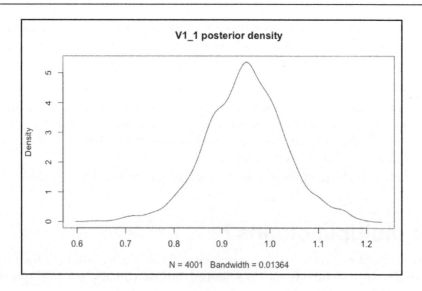

How it works...

The output that we produced here looks reasonably fine, because the posterior density seems to be oscillating slightly below 1 (this is caused because even though the coefficient is equal to 1, our priors have a mean of 0.5). It's worth noting that the proposal density (the function that proposed and generates random values) should be tuned in order to achieve a 25% acceptance rate (all Bayesian MCMC packages do this).

It's also worth noting that there is no unanimous consensus regarding how thinning should be done, to the extent that some practitioners don't even use it. They recommend running the chains for very long periods until the autocorrelation fades out, or even using the MCMC with autocorrelation.

An interesting discussion about this can be found at `https://besjournals.` `onlinelibrary.wiley.com/doi/full/10.1111/j.2041-210X.2011.00131.x.`

Evaluating convergence with CODA

The **Convergence and Diagnostics (CODA)** package is frequently used to evaluate the convergence of MCMC output. It provides several statistical tests to test whether MCMC chains have converged. Many prominent statisticians argue that convergence diagnostics should only be used to flag obvious problems with MCMC convergence, but can't be used to authoritatively tell whether MCMC chains have converged.

Remember that MCMC is an algorithm that generates correlated random numbers according to a particular distribution (in this case, our posterior distribution) only when the stationary distribution has been achieved. Consequently, we need to check the following two things:

- That the stationary distribution has been achieved. This is almost always not that simple, since we can never authoritatively tell whether that distribution has been achieved. What we can do is find obvious indicators that the stationary distribution has not been achieved.
- That the resulting random numbers are as decorrelated as possible.

One or multiple chains?

We can use one chain and the resulting numbers will behave according to the target density (the posterior density), if convergence is achieved. But we can also use multiple chains, usually one per CPU core. The advantage is that we can do additional diagnostics with multiple chains (such as the Gelman test).

Getting ready

In order to run this recipe, two packages need to be installed (coda, rstan) via the usual install.packages().

How to do it...

We will use the same house prices example that we used in the previous recipes for linear regression. We have a price variable, and several regressors, such as the number of bedrooms, bathrooms, and so on:

1. We first run our example, but with 5,000 iterations and different priors. Let's use a Gaussian prior on each beta coefficient and a lower boundary equal to 0:

```
library(rstan)
library(coda)
library(DrBats)
data =
read.csv("/Users/admin/Documents/R_book/chapter3/house_prices.csv")
model ="
data {
```

```
real y[125];
real x[125,6];
}
parameters {
real <lower=0> beta[6];
real sigma;
real alpha;
}
model {
beta ~ normal(5,20);
for (n in 1:125)
y[n] ~ normal(alpha + beta[1]*x[n,1] + beta[2]*x[n,2] +
beta[3]*x[n,3] + beta[4]*x[n,4] + beta[5]*x[n,5] + beta[6]*x[n,6],
sigma);
}"
xy = list(y=data[,1],x=data[,2:7])
fit = stan(model_code = model, data = xy, warmup = 500, iter =
5000, chains = 4, cores = 2, thin = 1,verbose=FALSE)
```

2. We will now cast our result stored in the `fit` variable into an MCMC object that can be used by the CODA library:

```
coda__obj = coda.obj(fit)
```

3. The autocorrelation plot shows the autocorrelation for different autocorrelation orders (remember that MCMC algorithms generate samples that are autocorrelated). The first column here is the autocorrelation of order zero (which will always be equal to one, so this is not analyzed), and the others refer to each autocorrelation lag. Some authors argue that even moderate autocorrelation here is not too bad. For example, a chain that has an autocorrelation of order 1 of almost 0.9 will have lots of repeated values. In this case, we say that the mixing is bad (and this would flag an obvious convergence problem). What happens when the autocorrelation here is moderate, such as the one we have here? MCMC can be ran with more iterations, or a higher number of warm-up iterations, hoping that the autocorrelation fades out, or the thinning parameter could be increased (thinning = *k* means that we keep every *k*th observation). In this example, it would be a good idea to rerun this code, with more iterations (and maybe also increase the warm-up iterations as well):

```
autocorr.plot(coda__obj)
```

Take a look at the following screenshot:

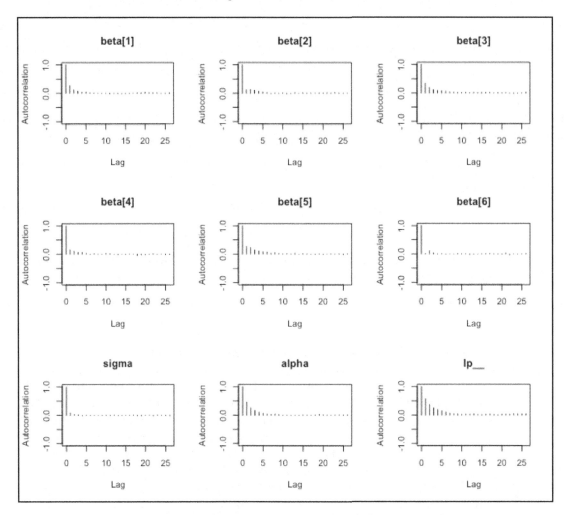

4. The cross-correlation plot shows a matrix containing the cross-correlations between the different parameters. In general, this does not flag any problem per se, unless there are pairs of variables that should not be correlated. In those cases, it could indicate poor mixing of the chain (situations where the chains get stuck in some places and do not correctly explore the posterior density). Here, we see that the intercept's posterior density (the row that contains the blue squares) is negatively correlated with the other variables. It wouldn't be unwise to rerun this model with more iterations to make sure there is no convergence problem for the intercept:

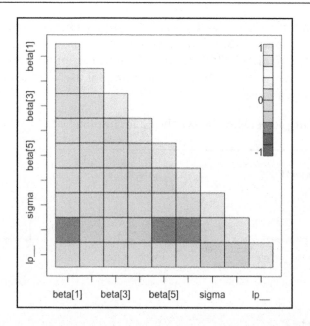

5. The `cumuplot` function plots the quantiles (*y* axis: quantiles, *x* axis: iterations). If the stationary distribution has been achieved, then this should show a very stable line at the tail of the plot (the lower and upper lines show the confidence bands). As we can see here, all of these stabilize after the first 300-500 iterations:

```
> effectiveSize(coda__obj)
   beta[1]    beta[2]    beta[3]    beta[4]    beta[5]    beta[6]     sigma      alpha       lp__
10687.791 10298.065 10233.660 12026.854  7195.862 11783.860 15356.379  6442.785  4596.752
```

6. `effectiveSize` is the sample size corrected by correlation. If the correlation is large, then `effectiveSize` goes to zero. If negligible, it will be equal to the number of iterations. As we would expect, `effectiveSize` for alpha is much lower than for the rest; this happens because there is still some big autocorrelation of order one/two for it (we have seen this in the autocorrelation plot). One way of interpreting this value is to think of it as the number of samples that effectively carry new information (autocorrelation means that information is shared between different values).

The following screenshot shows the effective sizes:

```
> effectiveSize(coda__obj)
   beta[1]    beta[2]    beta[3]    beta[4]    beta[5]    beta[6]     sigma      alpha       lp__
10687.791 10298.065 10233.660 12026.854  7195.862 11783.860 15356.379  6442.785  4596.752
```

7. The Gelman plot shows the Gelman statistic as a function of the iterations. When the stationary distribution is achieved, it should be equal to one. Most of these get close to zero after 2,000 iterations (maybe except for `beta[2]` that is taking longer to converge to 1). Since the Gelman plot uses all the chains, we only get one plot per variable.

The following screenshot shows the Gelman plots:

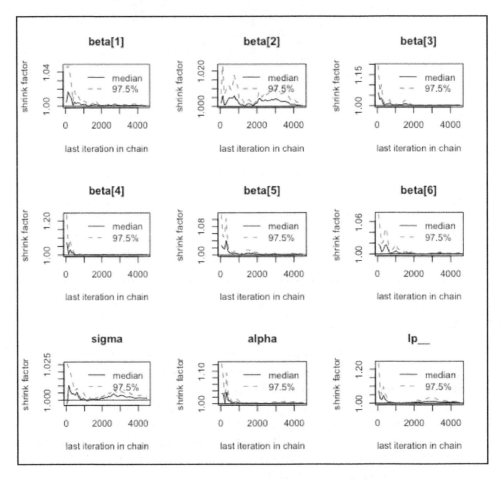

8. Geweke's statistic is rooted on the following idea: if the convergence to the stationary distribution was achieved, the last part of the chain will be correct. But the open question is whether the rest of the chain (without the last part) has converged as well.

The idea is to compare whether the mean of the chain in the first 10%, 20%, and so on. matches the mean of the chain for the last part of the data. This is useful for determining the appropriate burn-in: if we reject Geweke's test for 30% of the data, we should assign that 30% as a burn-in (discard those). The test statistic used here is the mean for each parameter/chain using a subset of the chain versus using the last part of the chain (this is essentially a Z-test).

The plot presented here shows what happens with Geweke's statistic as observations are removed. The more we move to the right over the x-axis, the more samples we are discarding from the chain. We can look at these plots and find the minimum number of samples that need to be removed in order to get Geweke's statistic between -2 and 2. It seems that here we would need to adjust our burn-in to almost 2,000. The following screenshot shows the Geweke plots :

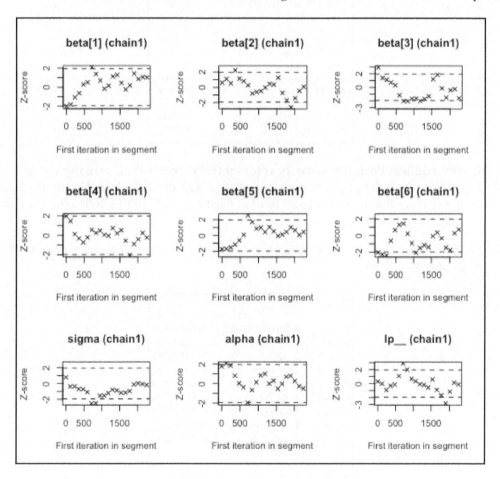

9. `heidel.diag` (Heidelberger and Welch's convergence diagnostic) is used to test whether a part of the chain comes from a stationary distribution. This is done first by using the full dataset, then by removing 10% of the initial data, then 20%, and so on, until either the null hypothesis of stationary distribution is accepted, or 50% of the sample is achieved, in which case the function returns a failure and a longer chain (more iterations) is needed. As we can see here, the p-values are all large, so there is no problem.

The following screenshot shows the Heidelberger and Welch's convergence diagnostic (printed only for the first chain):

```
[[1]]

          Stationarity start       p-value
          test          iteration
beta[1]   passed        1          0.5614
beta[2]   passed        1          0.4287
beta[3]   passed        1          0.3189
beta[4]   passed        1          0.5609
beta[5]   passed        1          0.4580
beta[6]   passed        1          0.0979
sigma     passed        1          0.2446
alpha     passed        1          0.6065
lp__      passed        1          0.5820
```

10. The **Highest Posterior Density Interval (HPD interval)** is actually not a diagnostic tool, but a summary tool that CODA can calculate. The shortest part of the density that has a probability of at least k (usually 95%). It has the property that any point inside it has a density higher than any point outside it.

The following screenshot shows `HDPintervals` for each parameter (printed only for the first chain):

```
[[1]]
                 lower              upper
beta[1]   5.251992e+00       6.00633618
beta[2]   3.408653e-01       1.41839437
beta[3]   6.126771e-01       1.87168109
beta[4]   1.178434e-03       0.83393762
beta[5]   8.508981e-02       1.54516980
beta[6]   1.377528e-02       0.55803580
sigma     5.285958e+00       6.85649074
alpha    -1.765699e+01      -0.09846626
lp__     -2.925712e+02    -283.47378452
attr(,"Probability")
[1] 0.95
```

11. `raftery.diag` (Raftery and Lewis' diagnostic) estimates the necessary amount of iterations that are needed to estimate a particular q diagnostic with a specific precision. We will get a diagnostic for each chain. `Burn-in` is the number of samples that need to be discarded (in order to avoid the initial dependence on the starting values). Total is the necessary amount of iterations needed to achieve an accuracy of 0.005 for the 0.025 quantile (this is the default quantile value for this function). `Lower bound` indicates how many samples would be needed if they were totally independent (no serial correlation). The dependence factor is a measure of how much autocorrelation we have (similar to the effective sample size). A value larger than five is considered dangerous and requires some adjustment.

The following screenshot shows the Raftery and Lewis diagnostic (printed only for the first chain):

```
[[1]]

Quantile (q) = 0.025
Accuracy (r) = +/- 0.005
Probability (s) = 0.95

          Burn-in  Total  Lower bound  Dependence
          (M)      (N)    (Nmin)       factor (I)
beta[1]   5        5557   3746         1.48
beta[2]   11       12191  3746         3.25
beta[3]   11       11890  3746         3.17
beta[4]   12       12504  3746         3.34
beta[5]   28       28460  3746         7.60
beta[6]   12       14714  3746         3.93
sigma     4        4615   3746         1.23
alpha     7        8087   3746         2.16
lp__      10       12502  3746         3.34
```

The outputs suggest that convergence to the stationary distribution has been achieved. Nevertheless, the posterior correlation between the alpha and the other variables that we saw before, suggests that re-running this with more iterations would be advisable. We have also seen that the Geweke statistic suggests increasing burn-in to around 2,000.

How it works...

All these CODA functions can't operate directly using a STAN output, so we first need to transform it (this is done using the `coda.obj` function). These CODA diagnostics are usually used in conjunction with STAN's own diagnostics. It is important to always remember that apart from these tests, some judgment and visual inspection of all the chains is necessary.

There's more...

What happens if there is substantial autocorrelation for a chain? Or posed in different terms: the effective sample size is small/or the dependence factor is too large? It could be caused by a poor choice of starting values (we could try with different starting values), or improper tuning of the MCMC algorithm (we could increase warm-up). It is always a good idea to increase the number of iterations as well.

Bayesian variable selection

Bayesian variable selection within a classical context is usually simple. It really boils down to selecting an appropriate metric (such as the AIC or p-values) and evaluating the model in a greedy way; starting with either a simple (or complex) model, and seeing what happens when we add (or remove) terms.

In a Bayesian context, things are not that easy, since we are not treating parameters as fixed values. We are estimating a posterior density, but a density itself has no significance so we can no longer remove them based on p-values. The AIC way can't be used either, as we don't have an AIC value, but a distribution of possible AICs.

Clearly, we need a different way of doing variable selection that takes into consideration that we are dealing with densities. *Kuo and Mallick* (`https://www.jstor.org/stable/25053023?seq=1#page_scan_tab_contents`) proposed a simple and powerful way of doing variable selection in a proper Bayesian context. The idea is to add an indicator variable that will be either zero or one multiplying each variable. This indicator variable will be distributed as a Bernoulli random variable with `probability = q`:

$$y \sim Normal(\mu_i, \sigma^2)$$
$$\mu_i = \theta_0 + \theta_1 x_1 + \cdots + \theta_p x_p$$
$$\theta_j = I_j \beta_j$$
$$I_j \sim Bernoulli(q)$$

Additionally, we can add a prior on this q parameter based on how many of the parameters we would expect to be relevant. If we expect most of the parameters to be relevant, we should think that, in general, q should be large. If a variable is not-relevant, then the q parameter will be estimated to be rather close to zero (meaning that the associated Bernoulli variable will generally be equal to 0). In other words, the model will assume that the variable could be multiplied by zero and nothing would change much.

Getting ready

In order to use JAGS, it needs to be installed externally (it is not an R package), and then we need the `rjags` package, which will interact with JAGS. It can be installed via `install.packages("rjags")`.

How to do it...

In the following example, we will generate a synthetic dataset containing 10 variables that are relevant and 10 variables that are irrelevant. We would expect our variable selection routine to flag those latter ones as irrelevant.

This is a good example to introduce JAGS, which is another option to using STAN. JAGS is not as sophisticated as STAN, and for some situations such as when the posterior densities are correlated, it is not as efficient. Nevertheless, JAGS is even easier to use, and can accommodate complicated models with just a few lines. It must be noted that JAGS requires a less declarative syntax where there is no necessity to declare variables and parameters:

1. We first generate our synthetic dataset. It will have three relevant features, and three irrelevant ones:

```
v1_1 = rnorm(1000,10,1)
v1_2 = rnorm(1000,10,1)
v1_3 = rnorm(1000,10,1)
v2_1 = rnorm(1000,10,1)
v2_2 = rnorm(1000,10,1)
v2_3 = rnorm(1000,10,1)
U = rnorm(1000,0,3)
Y = v1_1 + v1_2 + v1_3 + U
lista =
list(x=cbind(v1_1,v1_2,v1_3,v2_1,v2_2,v2_3),y=Y,n=length(Y))
```

2. We load JAGS, as shown in the following code snippet:

```
library('rjags')
```

3. We define our model. We loop through the dataset and do the following calculation for each variable: `index * b coefficient * variable`. The intuition behind this approach is that, if a variable is irrelevant, the posterior distribution of the index variable will be concentrated around zero. In this case, our prior distribution is a Bernoulli (0.5), meaning we think that 50% of the variables are zero:

```
mod <- " model{
for (i in 1:n){
mu[i] = id[1]*b[1]*x[i,1] + id[2]*b[2]*x[i,2] + id[3]*b[3]*x[i,3] +
id[4]*b[4]*x[i,4] + id[5]*b[5]*x[i,5] + id[6]*b[6]*x[i,6]
y[i] ~ dnorm(mu[i], prec)
}
for (i in 1:6){
b[i] ~ dnorm(0.0, 1/2)
id[i] ~ dbern(0.5)
}
prec ~ dgamma(1, 2)
}"
```

4. We compile and pass the data to our model. We are using 100 iterations as adaption, which means that JAGS will use them to tune the acceptance rate accordingly:

```
jags <- jags.model(textConnection(mod), data = lista, n.chains = 1,
n.adapt = 100)
```

5. Next, we run 5,000 iterations:

```
update(jags, 5000)
```

We extract the samples for the b and the Bernoulli indicator variables:

```
samps <- coda.samples( jags, c("b","id"), n.iter=1000 )
```

6. We do a summary. As we can see, the first three Bernoulli variables have a mean of the posterior distribution around one, which makes sense because they should be relevant. The other three variables have a mean of the posterior distribution around zero. In consequence, we should rerun this model without the variables associated to those last three Bernoulli variables (and obviously without any of the Bernoulli variables, as they were just used for variable selection):

```
summary(samps)
```

The following screenshot shows the posterior density summary. Check the first three and the last three indicator variables:

```
Iterations = 5001:6000
Thinning interval = 1
Number of chains = 1
Sample size per chain = 1000

1. Empirical mean and standard deviation for each variable,
   plus standard error of the mean:

          Mean        SD Naive SE Time-series SE
b[1]    0.988601 0.05896 0.001865       0.015826
b[2]    0.964735 0.07764 0.002455       0.025873
b[3]    1.061319 0.05691 0.001800       0.014521
b[4]    0.032153 1.38067 0.043661       0.042851
b[5]   -0.020222 1.43672 0.045433       0.048452
b[6]    0.006282 1.41533 0.044757       0.046879
id[1]   1.000000 0.00000 0.000000       0.000000
id[2]   1.000000 0.00000 0.000000       0.000000
id[3]   1.000000 0.00000 0.000000       0.000000
id[4]   0.017000 0.12934 0.004090       0.010163
id[5]   0.016000 0.12554 0.003970       0.009451
id[6]   0.019000 0.13659 0.004319       0.008653

2. Quantiles for each variable:

          2.5%      25%        50%    75% 97.5%
b[1]    0.8861   0.9458  9.851e-01 1.0349 1.101
b[2]    0.8182   0.9103  9.533e-01 1.0170 1.124
b[3]    0.9550   1.0182  1.069e+00 1.1005 1.172
b[4]   -2.6413  -0.8223  8.321e-03 0.8902 2.668
b[5]   -2.7805  -0.9974  8.653e-03 0.9164 2.826
b[6]   -2.7208  -0.9623 -4.815e-05 0.9518 2.906
id[1]   1.0000   1.0000  1.000e+00 1.0000 1.000
id[2]   1.0000   1.0000  1.000e+00 1.0000 1.000
id[3]   1.0000   1.0000  1.000e+00 1.0000 1.000
id[4]   0.0000   0.0000  0.000e+00 0.0000 0.000
id[5]   0.0000   0.0000  0.000e+00 0.0000 0.000
id[6]   0.0000   0.0000  0.000e+00 0.0000 0.000
```

How it works...

The Bernoulli indexes can be either zero or one. Of course, our prior expectation could be that they are equal to 0 50% of the time and 1 50% of the time. This is then augmented using the data, and we get different values there. Another way of interpreting this is that, for example, `id[5]` is equal to 1, 12% of the time. This variable is multiplying `b[5]`, so we could say that `b[5]` is equal to 0, 12% of the time as well.

There's more...

Putting a specific value for the Bernoulli variables can be viewed as putting a random variable with all its probability mass at 0.5. We could do something slightly more elaborate without making such a strong compromise on the specific value.

Instead of using a fixed value for the Bernoulli variables (0.5), we can use a `ka` parameter and then put a prior on `ka`. For example, we can use a beta distribution that is bounded between 0 and 1 (and can be used to generate priors for probabilities, such as our q parameter for a Bernoulli variable). Let's use beta (5,5) random variable. What this means is that, instead of saying that we think with a 100% probability that the proportion of irrelevant variables is 0.5, we are now splitting that 100% into more values. Of course, we are still concentrating them around 0.5 in this case (that obviously depends on the two beta parameters). We could choose any permissible value for those two parameters here, and we would get a different shape:

```
mod <- " model{
for (i in 1:n){
mu[i] = id[1]*b[1]*x[i,1] + id[2]*b[2]*x[i,2] + id[3]*b[3]*x[i,3] +
id[4]*b[4]*x[i,4] + id[5]*b[5]*x[i,5] + id[6]*b[6]*x[i,6]
y[i] ~ dnorm(mu[i], prec)
}
ka ~ dbeta(5,5)
for (i in 1:6){
b[i] ~ dnorm(0.0, 1/2)
id[i] ~ dbern(ka)
}
prec ~ dgamma(1, 2)
}"
jags <- jags.model(textConnection(mod), data = lista, n.chains = 1,
n.adapt = 100)
update(jags, 2000)
samps <- coda.samples( jags, c("b","id"), n.iter=1000 )
summary(samps)
```

The following screenshot shows the posterior density summary:

```
Iterations = 2001:3000
Thinning interval = 1
Number of chains = 1
Sample size per chain = 1000


1. Empirical mean and standard deviation for each variable,
    plus standard error of the mean:

          Mean       SD Naive SE Time-series SE
b[1]    1.00132 0.09977 0.003155       0.04589
b[2]    1.01713 0.10036 0.003174       0.04474
b[3]    1.05612 0.08919 0.002820       0.03660
b[4]   -0.15114 0.82688 0.026148       0.02646
b[5]    0.05981 1.09685 0.034685       0.03469
b[6]   -0.02838 1.38076 0.043663       0.04163
id[1]   1.00000 0.00000 0.000000       0.00000
id[2]   1.00000 0.00000 0.000000       0.00000
id[3]   1.00000 0.00000 0.000000       0.00000
id[4]   0.65300 0.47625 0.015060       0.34883
id[5]   0.28800 0.45306 0.014327       0.16553
id[6]   0.02700 0.16216 0.005128       0.01380


2. Quantiles for each variable:

          2.5%     25%      50%      75% 97.5%
b[1]    0.8053  0.9291  1.01673  1.06108 1.201
b[2]    0.8755  0.9436  0.99416  1.06865 1.288
b[3]    0.8850  0.9828  1.05490  1.13211 1.209
b[4]   -2.0891 -0.2335 -0.16598 -0.08432 1.918
b[5]   -2.3179 -0.4676  0.12773  0.53338 2.269
b[6]   -2.8256 -0.9137 -0.01822  0.93618 2.565
id[1]   1.0000  1.0000  1.00000  1.00000 1.000
id[2]   1.0000  1.0000  1.00000  1.00000 1.000
id[3]   1.0000  1.0000  1.00000  1.00000 1.000
id[4]   0.0000  0.0000  1.00000  1.00000 1.000
id[5]   0.0000  0.0000  0.00000  1.00000 1.000
id[6]   0.0000  0.0000  0.00000  0.00000 1.000
```

See also

The original *Variable Selection for Regression Models* paper can be accessed here: `https://www.jstor.org/stable/25053023`.

Using a model for prediction

Once we have trained a model and recovered the marginal posterior densities, we will probably want to use our model for predicting/scoring new samples. This is not as easy as in the classical approach, because our parameters are no longer fixed values, but distributions. This means that the predictions won't be point estimates/values, but a range of possible values, each one of them with an associated probability.

Getting ready

We will use STAN, which can be installed via `install.packages("rstan")`.

How to do it...

We will use the same house prices dataset that we have used previously in this chapter, and the objective will be to predict new observations:

1. We first load STAN and we load our dataset, as shown in the following code snippet:

```
library(rstan)
data = read.csv("./house_prices.csv")
```

2. We set our model as usual, with an extra block. We now specify the `generated_quantities` part, which is actually not used in the MCMC algorithm. This part is used to generate values based on the model that we are fitting. In this case, we will do this for two extra observations that we want to predict:

```
model ="
data {
real y[125];
real x[125,6];
real ns[2,6];
}
```

```
parameters {
real beta[6];
real sigma;
real alpha;
}
model {
beta ~ normal(5,10);
for (n in 1:125)
y[n] ~ normal(alpha + beta[1]*x[n,1] + beta[2]*x[n,2] +
beta[3]*x[n,3] + beta[4]*x[n,4] + beta[5]*x[n,5] + beta[6]*x[n,6],
sigma);
}
generated quantities {
vector[2] y_preds;
for (n in 1:2) {
y_preds[n] = normal_rng(alpha + beta[1]*ns[n,1] + beta[2]*ns[n,2] +
beta[3]*ns[n,3] + beta[4]*ns[n,4] + beta[5]*ns[n,5] +
beta[6]*ns[n,6], sigma);
}
}"
```

3. We then fit our model. Note that we are also passing a variable that holds the two extra observations that we want to fit. Of course, the order of the variables (columns) needs to be exactly the same as the one we used for training our model. Finally, in the model's summary we get the summary statistics for our two predictions' posterior densities:

```
topredict = rbind(c(10,3,3,3,3,20),c(7,3,3,3,3,10))
xy        = list(y=data[,1],x=data[,2:7],ns=topredict)
fit       = stan(model_code = model, data = xy, warmup = 500, iter =
5000, chains = 4, cores = 2, thin =  1, verbose=FALSE)
```

The following screenshot shows posterior summary:

	mean	se_mean	sd	2.5%	25%	50%	75%	97.5%	n_eff	Rhat
beta[1]	5.6275059	0.0009294059	0.10789966	5.4185152	5.5546606	5.6269981	5.6997151	5.8401070	13478.119	0.9998874
beta[2]	1.1518596	0.0010883722	0.14589311	0.8665166	1.0538650	1.1507702	1.2512684	1.4381903	17968.618	0.9999088
beta[3]	1.4128635	0.0013060201	0.17515826	1.0702645	1.2953674	1.4124103	1.5301027	1.7587253	17987.115	0.9999276
beta[4]	0.6676620	0.0016614802	0.21000246	0.2529046	0.5266094	0.6679713	0.8072659	1.0855280	15975.646	0.9998832
beta[5]	1.3740549	0.0018720069	0.21455924	0.9597978	1.2291736	1.3722468	1.5192225	1.7936711	13136.497	0.9999206
beta[6]	0.4056779	0.0007691102	0.09220588	0.2247098	0.3441523	0.4058902	0.4679650	0.5854535	14372.759	0.9999855
sigma	6.5077550	0.0017798626	0.21202722	6.1074628	6.3597243	6.5015079	6.6468875	6.9351702	14190.911	1.0001393
alpha	-16.7700929	0.0268396435	2.55982821	-21.8520041	-18.5110227	-16.7427922	-15.0200079	-11.8247415	9096.371	0.9999690
y_preds[1]	61.3931065	0.0492257745	6.55173940	48.6690822	56.9603209	61.4012673	65.8555620	74.2613698	17714.468	0.9998845
y_preds[2]	40.5941728	0.0498854855	6.57418160	27.4423010	36.1674000	40.6039721	45.0557747	53.3749644	17367.407	0.9999803
lp__	-1141.1022314	0.0213353678	2.02075400	-1145.8784114	-1142.2271040	-1140.7874901	-1139.6091931	-1138.1672875	8970.706	1.0001144

We now have two extra rows for `y_preds[1]` and `y_preds[2]`. The mean of the predictions can be seen under the `mean` column. The predictions make sense: the predicted mean of the first vector (which has a larger value for the first and sixth variable) is larger than the second one. Remember that the first variable is the size of the property, and the sixth one is size of the entrance.png?

4. We can naturally extract the actual predictions using the `extract` function. Here we show the first 11 iterations (of course, we have two columns, because we wanted two predictions). This is rather different from the simple predictions that we get for the classical methods (such as the `lm` function). In that case, we just get a prediction, whereas here, we get a distribution of predictions for each argument that we passed. This is because in the Bayesian realm, the coefficients are not fixed values, but random variables:

```
extract(fit)$y_preds
```

Take a look at the following screenshot:

```
> extract(fit)$y_preds

iterations        [,1]       [,2]
      [1,]  58.25559  54.86578
      [2,]  55.39696  34.32738
      [3,]  66.14404  28.76434
      [4,]  59.08469  46.10736
      [5,]  58.27192  49.48367
      [6,]  67.84411  40.79301
      [7,]  70.30991  42.59055
      [8,]  49.65133  37.09685
      [9,]  74.10806  44.17806
     [10,]  55.92604  40.12660
     [11,]  56.21416  40.60646
```

How it works...

STAN generates random numbers using the distribution that we specified in the `generated_quantities` part. It is important to stress that in OLS (the `lm` function) we do get point estimates for our predictions, but here, we will just be generating random numbers according to the posterior distribution of the predictions. Of course, for reporting purposes, we can just take the respective mean of each prediction (or any other relevant metric).

GLMs in JAGS

GLMs stand for Generalized Linear Models. It is a generalization of the linear model (that assumes normality) to other distributions of the so-called exponential family (the Gaussian one is also part of this family). This model formulation allows us to fit models using several responses for the dependent variable such as binary, categorical, count, and more. For example, logistic and Poisson regression are two models that are part of this family.

In this example, we will do Bayesian logistic regression (one type of GLM). This model is appropriate when modeling a categorical response that takes two possible values. Possible examples could be modeling whether a customer is going to buy a product or not, or a student is going to pass an exam.

Both STAN and JAGS can handle not only linear regression models, but a wide array of regression models. In this exercise, we will formulate a GLM model in STAN, although it could also be done in JAGS.

Getting ready

In order to run this example, `rstan` needs to be installed via `install.packages("rstan")`.

How to do it...

In this example, we have a variable that flags if a client has bought a special gift pack. For each client, we have several attributes, such as the age of the customer, how much the customer has already bought, and how long they have been a client:

1. We first load `rstan` and the dataset as follows:

```
library(rstan)
data    = read.csv("./clients.csv")
```

2. We formulate our model. In this case, we put loose normal priors on each coefficient. The important part is the `bernoulli_logit` line, which returns either a zero or a one:

```
model ="
data {
int<lower = 0, upper = 1> y[99];
real x[99,3];
```

```
}
parameters {
real beta[3];
real alpha;
}
model {
beta ~ normal(5,10);
for (n in 1:99)
y[n] ~ bernoulli_logit(alpha + beta[1]*x[n,1] + beta[2]*x[n,2] +
beta[3]*x[n,3]);
}"
```

3. We pass two vectors for prediction: firstly, someone young (20 years old), zero products bought before, and 1 month as a customer; and secondly, someone old (60 years old), five products bought before, and eight months as a customer. We should expect to see a low probability of buying for the first case, and a high probability for the second one:

```
topredict = rbind(c(20,0,1),c(60,5,8))
data      = read.csv("./clients.csv")
xy        = list(y=data[,1],x=data[,2:4],ns=topredict)
fit       = stan(model_code = model, data = xy, warmup =
500, iter = 5000, chains = 4, cores = 2, thin =
1,verbose=FALSE)
```

4. We can do a quick check on the quality of the convergence (we pass the parameters that we want to get the traceplot for, using the pars= argument):

```
rstan::traceplot(fit,pars=c("beta[1]","beta[2]","beta[3]","alpha"))
```

The following screenshot shows how the traceplot looks:

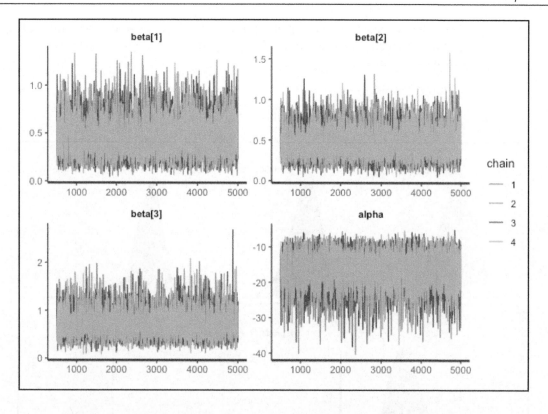

5. We can finally summarize our results and plot the posterior densities. Since we passed two vectors for making predictions, we can view the results here. We would expect that the probability for the second vector (someone older that has already bought several products, and has been a client for a while) should be close to 1. On the other hand, we should expect to see a probability equal to 0 for the first vector (someone young, who hasn't bought products before). We can confirm this by looking at the next summary:

```
summary(fit)
```

Take a look at the following screenshot:

	mean	se_mean	sd	2.5%	25%	50%	75%	97.5%	n_eff	Rhat
beta[1]	0.4756442	0.0024730002	0.18501358	0.1740971	0.3422852	0.4566114	0.5881280	0.8926634	5597.046	1.0002977
beta[2]	0.4708353	0.0019771001	0.17429737	0.1871279	0.3452296	0.4509138	0.5762759	0.8647380	7771.849	1.0003868
beta[3]	0.7399918	0.0028128931	0.25691916	0.3188437	0.5578754	0.7104427	0.8925439	1.3216234	8342.314	0.9999817
alpha	-16.5769443	0.0652489584	4.78373421	-27.2921842	-19.4677494	-16.0367246	-13.1361982	-8.7693224	5375.105	1.0001868
y_preds[1]	0.0050000	0.0005303301	0.07053564	0.0000000	0.0000000	0.0000000	0.0000000	0.0000000	17689.868	1.0000827
y_preds[2]	1.0000000		NaN	0.00000000	1.0000000	1.0000000	1.0000000	1.0000000	1.0000000	NaN	NaN
lp__	-27.3735049	0.0204878662	1.49291405	-31.2031392	-28.1092573	-27.0202943	-26.2841327	-25.5254935	5309.775	1.0005955

The following screenshot shows posterior densities. The posterior density for the first prediction is basically concentrated in 0, and for the second case it is concentrated around 1:

```
stan_dens(fit)
```

Take a look at the following screenshot:

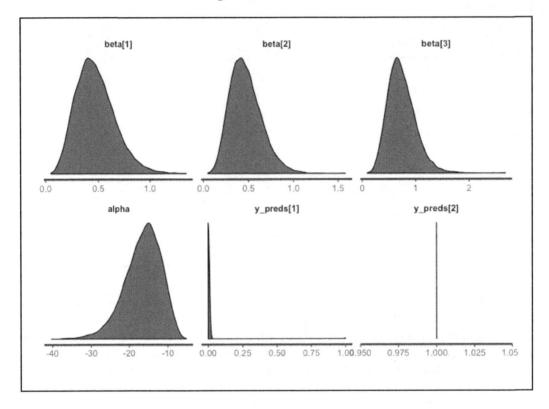

How it works...

The mechanics are actually the same as before; the priors are used in conjunction with the likelihood to compute the joint posterior distribution. The algorithm used here is the same MCMC algorithm that we have used before.

Nonparametric Methods **5**

We will cover the following recipes in this chapter:

- The Mann-Whitney test
- Estimating nonparametric ANOVA
- The Spearman's rank correlation test
- LOESS regression
- Finding the best transformations via the acepack package
- Nonparametric multivariate tests using the npmv package
- Semiparametric regression with the semiPar package

Introduction

Unfortunately, parametric methods such as the **t-test** or **ordinary least squares (OLS)**, make very strong assumptions about the distribution of the data. To some extent, they still work if the distributional assumptions are relaxed, but it really depends to which extent these assumptions are violated.

Nonparametric methods do not work with the usual parametrized distributions and are instead designed to work with any distribution. This gives them a distinct flexibility, and we are no longer required to check any distributional assumption on the data. If the data follows the same distribution that its parametric counterpart requires, they usually perform almost as well.

The Mann-Whitney test

We have already discussed how to compare the means from two groups, when both groups are distributed according to a Gaussian distribution with the same variance. However, the nonparametric test requires no distributional assumption and works well almost every time. Of course, if both distributions are Gaussian with the same variance, then the regular t-test is better—this is derived from the fact that the t-test is uniformly the most powerful one.

The **Mann-Whitney-Wilcoxon** test is a nonparametric test that tests the null hypothesis that any element chosen at random from group A is equally likely to be greater or smaller than a respective random item from group B. A different way of posing this test is to think of it as a test of whether the distributions of group A and B are the same. The only strong assumption that this test requires is that the observations from both groups are independent.

How to do it...

In this exercise, we will load the same dataset that we used for the two-sample t-test:

1. First, we load the dataset, and change the `Sample` variable to be a factor, as shown in the following code:

   ```
   data = read.csv("./heights.csv")
   data$Sample = as.factor(data$Sample)
   ```

2. Then, we call the Mann-Whitney-Wilcoxon test as follows:

   ```
   wilcox.test(Height ~ Sample,data=data)
   ```

   The preceding code displays the following output of Wilcoxon test results:

   ```
   > wilcox.test(Height ~ Sample,data=data)

           Wilcoxon rank sum test with continuity correction

   data:  Height by Sample
   W = 4868, p-value = 0.841
   alternative hypothesis: true location shift is not equal to 0
   ```

How it works...

The test is called and, as usual, we get a statistic (in this case, `W=4868`) and p-value=`0.841`. In this case, don't reject the null hypothesis that the distributions are different.

There's more...

Similarly to the paired t-test, the Mann-Whitney-Wilcoxon test can be used with paired data. In this case, we will reuse the same example we used for paired t-tests. We first load the data, and we then call `wilcox.test` with `paired=TRUE`, as shown in the following code:

```
data = read.csv("./pre_post_employee.csv")
wilcox.test(data$post_bonus, data$pre_bonus,paired=TRUE)
```

In this case, we reject the null hypothesis and we conclude that it is not equally likely for a sample taken at random from the `pre_bonus` group to be larger or smaller than one taken at random from the `post_bonus` group as follows:

```
> wilcox.test(data$pre_bonus, data$post_bonus,paired=TRUE)

        Wilcoxon signed rank test with continuity correction

data:  data$pre_bonus and data$post_bonus
V = 921, p-value = 0.0008075
alternative hypothesis: true location shift is not equal to 0
```

Estimating nonparametric ANOVA

The Mann-Whitney-Wilcoxon test that we presented in the previous recipe, can be extended to multiple groups (not just 2 was before). For one-way **Analysis Of Variance (ANOVA)**, the test that is used is called **Kruskal-Wallis**; we have the `kruskal.test()` function in base R.

For nonparametric two-way ANOVA, the **Scheirer-Ray-Hare** test can be used; however, the documentation is scarce, and it is not frequently used.

Getting ready

In order to run this script, you need to install the `FSA` and `dplyr` packages.

How to do it...

We will work with nonparametric ANOVA using the same dataset that we used in `Chapter` 2, *Univariate and Multivariate Tests for Equality of Means*, (Calculating ANOVA sum of squares and F tests). The dataset will contain weight measurements for animals, and these will depend on which food type they were fed on and which lot the animals were assigned to.

1. First, we load the necessary libraries, as in the following example:

```
library(FSA)
library(dplyr)
```

2. This dataset contains a food type variable and a numeric variable (`Result`). Because Kruskal-Wallis only accepts one-way ANOVA, we can only use one of the variables. We will need to disregard the blocking factor (`LOT`) and model just the food type. As we can see, we reject the null hypothesis that all of the food types yield the same result. This is shown in the following example:

```
t = read.csv("./anova__lot_type.csv")
kruskal.test(Result ~ Food.Type,data=t)
```

The preceding command displays the following output:

```
> kruskal.test(Result ~ Food.Type,data=t)

        Kruskal-Wallis rank sum test

data:  Result by Food.Type
Kruskal-Wallis chi-squared = 24.629, df = 2, p-value = 4.487e-06
```

3. After we have rejected the null hypothesis, we need to find which are the statistically significative comparisons. This is a multiple comparison problem, and the p-values need to be adjusted (for the same reasons we have stated in the ANOVA chapter). This can be done via Dunn's test. As it can be verified below all of the comparisons are statistically significative and A-C is actually the largest one. The most relevant difference is `A - C`, as shown in the following code:

```
dunnTest(Result ~ Food.Type,data=t)
```

The preceding command displays the following output:

```
  Comparison        Z      P.unadj        P.adj
1     A - B  3.612376  3.034039e-04  6.068078e-04
2     A - C  4.753127  2.002948e-06  6.008843e-06
3     B - C  1.140750  2.539738e-01  2.539738e-01
```

How it works...

The test works by computing ranks on all samples. The test statistic is a complex expression containing the differences between the ranks for each group and the average rank.

The Spearman's rank correlation test

The correlation coefficient between X and Y that we usually use is obtained by dividing the covariance of X, Y by the product of the variances of X and Y. It is therefore restricted to lie between -1 and 1. When the correlation is -1, it means that there is a strong negative relationship between the variables. When it is 1, it means that there is a strong positive relationship; and when it is 0, it means that there is no relationship between the variables. But there is an implicit assumption that we usually overlook: the correlation coefficient assumes that there is a linear relationship. So, it is easy to imagine lots of cases where there might be a relationship, but not a linear one.

The **Spearman rank** statistic does not test correlation in the traditional sense ((whether a greater than average value of X is associated linearly with a greater than average value of Y). But in the sense that there is a monotonic relationship between X and Y (whether this relationship is linear or nonlinear).

How to do it...

Whenever we refer to Spearman, we mean Spearman's rank statistic; and whenever we refer to Pearson, we mean the classical correlation coefficient.

In the following example, we will use a nonlinear example with no noise (in this case, Spearman's coefficient will be almost 1), and Pearson's coefficient will be high but lower. We will then introduce some noise and explain why Pearson's ends up being higher:

1. First, we generate some synthetic data. This is clearly a nonlinear relationship, as shown in the following example:

```
x = seq(1,100)
y = 20/(1+exp(x-50))
plot(x,y)
```

The preceding command displays the following output:

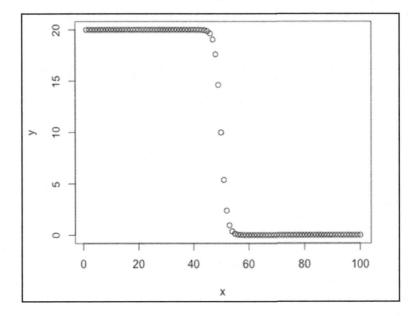

2. We now compute both the Spearman and Pearson correlation coefficients; both are negative since there is a clear negative relationship.

```
cor.test( ~ x + y, method = "spearman",conf.level = 0.95)
cor.test( ~ x + y, method = "pearson",conf.level = 0.95)
```

The preceding command displays the following output of the Spearman versus Pearson coefficients:

```
> cor.test( ~ x + y, method = "spearman",conf.level = 0.95)

        Spearman's rank correlation rho

data:   x and y
S = 333120, p-value < 2.2e-16
alternative hypothesis: true rho is not equal to 0
sample estimates:
        rho
-0.9989073

Warning message:
In cor.test.default(x = 1:100, y = c(20, 20, 20, 20, 20, 20, 20,
  Cannot compute exact p-value with ties
>
> cor.test( ~ x + y, method = "pearson",conf.level = 0.95)

        Pearson's product-moment correlation

data:   x and y
t = -18.594, df = 98, p-value < 2.2e-16
alternative hypothesis: true correlation is not equal to 0
95 percent confidence interval:
 -0.9196625 -0.8302144
sample estimates:
        cor
-0.8826926
```

Because Spearman measures if the relationship is monotone (and in this case, every single observation satisfies that with respect to the previous one), it is basically equal to -1. Of course, the relationship is not linear, and that's why Pearson is -0.88, as shown in the preceding example.

3. Now, let's add some noise, as shown in the following example:

```
x = seq(1,100)
y = sapply(x,function(x){(runif(1)-0.5)*10 + 20/(1+exp(x-50))})
plot(x,y)
```

The preceding command displays the following output:

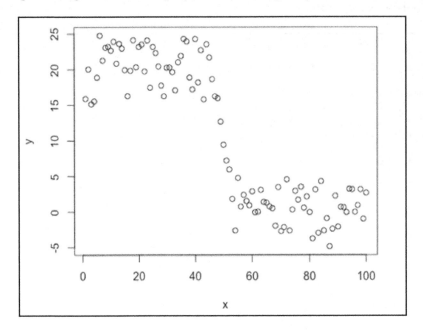

4. Now, as we can see here, Pearson's coefficient is almost the same as before, but Spearman's is reduced substantially. Intuitively, this happens because, if we had to plot a line that goes through those points, it wouldn't have changed at all due to the extra noise (so Pearson's would have stayed the same). But Spearman's coefficient is quite different, it captures how monotone the relationship is; if each variable behaves more erratically, even though the general shape is still nonlinear, we wouldn't be able to say that the relationship is monotone. This is why Spearman can be seen as how much deviation we have from a perfect case where the relationship is 100% monotone:

```
cor.test( ~ x + y, method = "spearman",conf.level = 0.95)
cor.test( ~ x + y, method = "pearson",conf.level = 0.95)
```

The preceding command displays the following output:

```
        Spearman's rank correlation rho

data:  x and y
S = 292080, p-value < 2.2e-16
alternative hypothesis: true rho is not equal to 0
sample estimates:
        rho
-0.7526793


>
> cor.test( ~ x + y, method = "pearson",conf.level = 0.95)

        Pearson's product-moment correlation

data:  x and y
t = -14.616, df = 98, p-value < 2.2e-16
alternative hypothesis: true correlation is not equal to 0
95 percent confidence interval:
 -0.8810873 -0.7541889
sample estimates:
        cor
-0.8279566
```

How it works...

Spearman's statistic is essentially constructed by taking the correlation between the ranks. The tests' results presented preceding are very questionable: Pearson's coefficient can always be calculated, but in order to derive confidence bands such as the ones that we see here, the data needs to be normal and linear (both assumptions are violated in this case). Nevertheless, Spearman does not require any distributional assumptions.

Because we take correlations just for descriptive purposes, and because we usually want to see how much linear relationship exists in the data, we usually prefer Pearson's coefficient. However, if we want to see how monotone the relationship is, we should use Spearman's rank statistic.

There's more...

There are actually two very important cases where we want to use Spearman instead of Pearson:

- We use Spearman if we have outliers; in this case, Pearson results can change a lot due to just a few abnormal values.
- The second case is if one or both variables are measured on an ordinal scale (when we can sort the variables, but can't specify their magnitude), for example, if we have education levels (these are not years of education—but education categories with an ordinal meaning: 2 means more educated than 1) and salaries. Because the ranks are used, and not the actual number, Spearman can handle these cases, whereas Pearson cannot. This is shown in the following example:

```
salary=c(10,50,45,87,69,100)
educ_level=c(1,2,3,4,5,6)
cor.test( ~ salary + educ_level, method = "spearman",conf.level =
0.95)
```

The preceding command displays the following output (note that the coefficient is 0.88):

```
          Spearman's rank correlation rho

data:   salary and educ_level
S = 4, p-value = 0.03333
alternative hypothesis: true rho is not equal to 0
sample estimates:
        rho
0.8857143
```

LOESS regression

When we have a scatterplot between two variables Y, X we usually want to present a curve that relates the two variables. Firstly, because it allows us to see if the relationship is linear (or almost linear); secondly, because interpreting scatterplots is sometimes hard; and, finally, because we might want to have a simple model that can be used to predict Y in terms of X capturing all possible nonlinear patterns.

Locally Estimated Scatterplot Smoothing (LOESS) regression works by fitting lots of local models around each point. These **local** models are then averaged out. In particular, each model (fitted around a point X_0, Y_0) is fitted using weighted least squares (each point is weighted by how close the regressors are to the point X_0). There is a parameter specified by the user, called the **bandwidth**, which specifies how much data is used in each one of these regressions. Usually, second order polynomials are used in these regressions.

Getting ready

No special library is required for this recipe.

How to do it...

In this recipe, we will use a dataset containing prices and sales. In this example, this relationship won't be linear and won't be easy to characterize:

1. First, we load the dataset, as in the following example:

   ```
   data = read.csv("./price__sales.csv")
   ```

2. Then, we create two LOESS models. We will use two different span values (bandwidth) using second degree polynomials, and Gaussian bandwidth, as shown in the following example:

   ```
   model_loess1 = loess(data$Sales~data$Price, span = 2/3, degree = 2,
   family = c("gaussian"))
   model_loess2 = loess(data$Sales~data$Price, span = 0.1, degree = 2,
   family = c("gaussian"))
   ```

3. Next, we'll create two wrapper functions, that receive a value and return the prediction for that value:

   ```
   loess1_wrapper <- function(x){
   return (predict(model_loess1,x))
   }
   loess2_wrapper <- function(x){
   return (predict(model_loess2,x))
   }
   ```

4. We now plot the scatterplot and the two LOESS curves. The first one will be painted in red, and the second one will be painted in blue. We then add the legend, and position it properly in our plot. There is a balance that needs to be achieved here, the smaller the bandwidth is, the more precise our results are (but at the same time, the more difficult they are to interpret). The bigger it is, the less precise the curve is, but the easier it is to interpret. What can be seen on the red line is that the sales decay quickly when the price is low ($0-$5), and slowly when the price is high ($10-$15):

```
plot(data$Price,data$Sales)
curve(loess1_wrapper,add=TRUE,col="red",lwd=3)
curve(loess2_wrapper,add=TRUE,col="blue",lwd=3)
legend(70, 4500, legend=c("span=0.75", "span=0.1"),col=c("red",
"blue"), lty=1:1, cex=0.8)
```

Two LOESS curves—the blue one has a very small bandwidth, and the red one has a larger one. Evidently, the red curve is preferred:

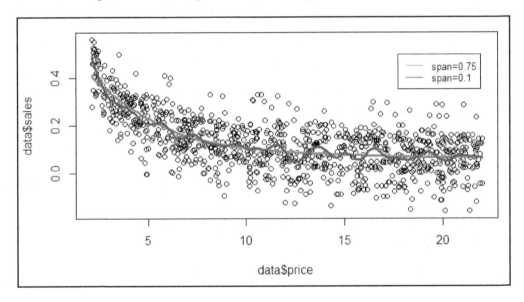

5. We can compute the predicted change of increasing the price from $5 to $10, and also from $10 to $15. The sales drop is roughly 6 times as large when the price is high (=0.12/0.02):

```
loess1_wrapper(5)  - loess1_wrapper(10)
loess1_wrapper(10) - loess1_wrapper(15)
```

The following output is displayed in the console:

```
> loess1_wrapper(5)   - loess1_wrapper(10)
[1] 0.123627
> loess1_wrapper(10)  - loess1_wrapper(15)
[1] 0.02789907
```

How it works...

LOESS works by doing lots of local regressions for each point and then averaging the predictions.

There's more...

The ggplot2 package includes an embedded method to calculate the LOESS curve. This is done using the geom_smooth() function, where we need to specify method="loess". The beauty of this method is that it can also plot the standard errors for the prediction. The two disadvantages of this, with respect to what we did previously, is that we can't use this approach to predict new observations, nor tune the parameters as much we want to (bandwidth, kernel type, and polynomial order). The bands will be wider (more imprecision), the fewer observations we have in an area or the more vertical dispersion we have. In this case, it is clear that the bands are wider at the start and at the end of the plot, as shown in the following example:

```
ggplot(data, aes(x=Price, y=Sales)) + geom_point(size=2, shape=1) +
geom_smooth(se = TRUE, method = "loess")
```

The preceding command displays the following output:

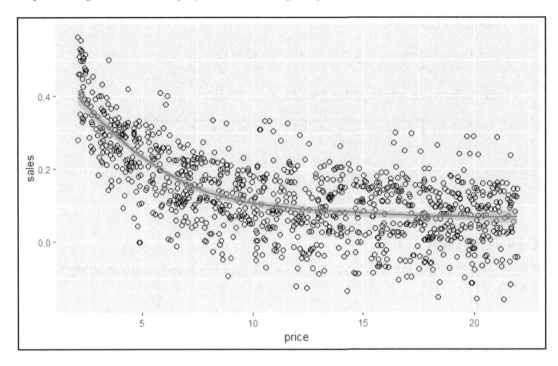

Finding the best transformations via the acepack package

When fitting linear regressions models, we always want them to fit as best as possible into the data. Sometimes, we want to transform our variables in order to get the model fit to improve as much as possible. For example, we could apply several transformations (taking logarithms, squared values, and so on) in order to improve the fit.

The `acepack` package implements the alternating conditional expectation algorithm, which finds the optimal transformations that we need to apply to our data in order to maximize the R2. Another way of looking at this would be: given the data that we have, what would be the best R2 we could get if we found the best possible transformations? In this fashion, we could get a maximum boundary on the best model that we would be able to get, assuming we can only transform the variables to capture the nonlinear relationships.

It is important to realize that whenever we transform the variables, the interpretation of the coefficient changes; so this must be done with some care.

Getting ready

In order to run this example, we will need the `acepack` package that can be installed via `install.packages("acepack")`.

How to do it...

The `house_prices` dataset that we will use here, has a dependent variable that is the house price. The independent variables are: the size, the number of bathrooms, the number of bedrooms, the number of entrances, the size of the balcony, and the size of the entrance. We will find the best transformations for the dependent and independent variables that get the best model.

1. First, we load the library, and the data. We then split the data into x (independent variables) and y (dependent variables), as shown in the following example:

    ```
    library("acepack")
    data = read.csv("./house_prices.csv")
    x = data[,2:7]
    y = data[,1]
    ```

2. Next, we run our initial ordinary least squares, because we want to see what is the standard R2 that we get there. We get an R2 of 0.86, as shown in the following example:

    ```
    lm_model = lm(data=data,Property_price~ size + number.bathrooms +
    number.bedrooms + number.entrances + size_balcony + size_entrance)
    summary(lm_model)
    ```

The preceding command displays the following output:

```
Call:
lm(formula = Property_price ~ size + number.bathrooms + number.bedrooms +
    number.entrances + size_balcony + size_entrance, data = data)

Residuals:
    Min      1Q   Median      3Q      Max
-18.4347  -4.6414  -0.0136   4.4449  23.6712

Coefficients:
                  Estimate Std. Error t value Pr(>|t|)
(Intercept)       -16.7063     2.5520  -6.546 1.54e-10 ***
size                5.6270     0.1068  52.666  < 2e-16 ***
number.bathrooms    1.1513     0.1457   7.904 1.91e-14 ***
number.bedrooms     1.4115     0.1758   8.028 7.86e-15 ***
number.entrances    0.6621     0.2079   3.186  0.00154 **
size_balcony        1.3693     0.2137   6.408 3.56e-10 ***
size_entrance       0.4055     0.0906   4.476 9.54e-06 ***
---
Signif. codes:  0 '***' 0.001 '**' 0.01 '*' 0.05 '.' 0.1 ' ' 1

Residual standard error: 6.491 on 474 degrees of freedom
Multiple R-squared:  0.8612,     Adjusted R-squared:  0.8594
F-statistic: 490.1 on 6 and 474 DF,  p-value: < 2.2e-16
```

3. We now call the `ace` function from the `acepack` package. We need two parameters: the independent variables and the dependent one. The R2 increases slightly (almost 3%) with respect to a linear model, as shown in the following example:

    ```
    ace_model = ace(x,y)
    ace_model$rsq
    ```

The following screenshot shows the best R-square via `acepack`:

```
> ace_model$rsq
[1] 0.89131
```

4. Let's check how the transformed variables look like (the untransformed variable versus the transformed variable) for two cases. The size of the entrance got transformed, but `size_balcony` was left almost untransformed:

```
par(mfrow=c(1,2))
plot(ace_model$x[1,],ace_model$tx[,1],xlab="untransformed
size_entrance",ylab="transformed size_entrance")
plot(ace_model$x[5,],ace_model$tx[,5],xlab="untransformed
size_balcony",ylab="transformed size_balcony")
```

The preceding commands display the following output of the transformed/untransformed plots for the entrance and balcony:

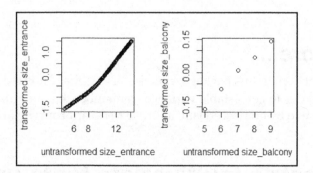

5. We can now compare how `entrance_size` relates to the dependent variable (we do this for the original variable and the transformed one) in the following way:

```
plot(ace_model$x[1,], ace_model$ty)
plot(ace_model$tx[,1], ace_model$ty)
```

The following screenshot shows the original relationship (on the left) and transformed relationship (both y and x transformed):

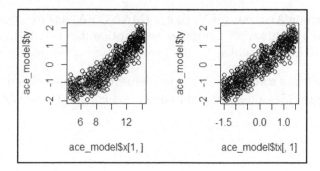

How it works...

We should probably plot the untransformed y on the left Y axis. The ace algorithm will iterate by applying appropriate transformations to both y and x, in order to maximize the R2. It is known as the alternating conditional expectations algorithm.

The algorithm works with this model and finds the appropriate Φ and θ functions that minimize the difference between the predictions and the observed values:

$$\theta(Y) = \alpha + \sum \Phi_i(X_i)$$

There is more...

There is an extra function on this package, called `avas()`, that finds the best transformations in order to get a stable variance (remember that, in ordinary least squares, we need our variance to be homoscedastic in order to do appropriate inference).

Nonparametric multivariate tests using the npmv package

In our parametric scenario, we used the t-test to compare means across two populations, and Hotelling's T2 to compare a vector of means across two populations. We then extended these cases to ANOVA and MANOVA respectively in case we were dealing with multiple populations. The underlying assumption is that the data comes from a Gaussian population in the first case and a multivariate Gaussian in the second one. In this recipe we will use the npmv package to to non-parametric MANOVA.

Traditional **Multivariate Analysis Of Variance (MANOVA)** has two main problems: firstly, it depends on a multivariate Gaussian assumption that is hard to satisfy in practice. Secondly, it is hard to identify which are the groups or variables producing the differences.

The npmv package offers a solution to both problems: it does not rely on any distributional assumption, and it provides a mechanism to detect which are the variables/groups causing the differences.

Getting ready

In order to run this recipe, the `npmv` package needs to be installed via `install.packages("npmv")`.

How to do it...

In this example, we will use the very famous iris dataset, which contains 50 observations for 3 flower species (there are three species: `Iris setosa`, `Iris virginica`, and `Iris versicolor`). There are four measurements for each observation: the length and width of the sepals and petals. Let's get started:

1. First, we do our test. The formula here needs to specify all of the variables separated by | and, after that, the group type specified by ~. Actually, this function will return four different statistics, calculated using two different p-values (the standard ones and the permutation ones—the latter are more precise). This actually leads to $4 \times 2 = 8$ p-values. In this case, all the statistics agree that there are differences between the joint distributions along the three groups. The second part of this output contains the relative treatment effects: they are very different for each flower type. These are actually probabilities, and can be interpreted as the probability of picking a random member of that group that has a greater value of that variable for all of the groups. For example, `virginica/Sepal.Length=0.75` means that there is a *0.75* probability of picking a random `Sepal.Length` virginica that is greater than any other random `Sepal.Length` value from any group (including virginica). These are known as empirical non parametric relative treatment effects:

```
nonpartest(Sepal.Length | Sepal.Width | Petal.Length | Petal.Width
~ Species, data = iris, permreps = 2000)
```

The preceding code displays the following output of nonpartest:

```
$`results`
                                                  Test Statistic   df1       df2 P-value Permutation Test p-value
ANOVA type test p-value                                  178.511 3.826 281.2335       0                        0
McKeon approx. for the Lawley Hotelling Test             316.457 8.000 203.4024       0                        0
Muller approx. for the Bartlett-Nanda-Pillai Test         67.965 8.162 293.8913       0                        0
Wilks Lambda                                             155.763 8.000 288.0000       0                        0

$releffects
            Sepal.Length Sepal.Width Petal.Length Petal.Width
setosa           0.19427     0.75307      0.16667     0.16667
versicolor       0.54767     0.30387      0.50593     0.50653
virginica        0.75807     0.44307      0.82740     0.82680
```

2. After (and if) the test is rejected, we can do a more focused analysis to identify the groups or variables causing the differences. Because we have four statistics, we need to choose one. This is done via the `test=` parameter. This should be a vector containing `0`s and a `1` for the test statistic that should be used (in this case, we chose the ANOVA one). Based on whether we specify `factors_and_variables=TRUE` or not, the analysis will use only the factors and variables. The first part starts with a global test involving all of the groups, and cascades down until the significant difference is pinpointed. What we see here is that we first reject the equality of the distributions for the three flowers, and it can actually be traced back to the fact that the `setosa-versicolor` and `setosa-virginica` pairs are different. After that, the same procedure follows for the factor levels: the four variables differ from group to group (`Petal.Width`, `Petal.Length`, `Sepal.Width`, and `Sepa.Length`), as shown in the following example:

```
ssnonpartest(Sepal.Length | Sepal.Width | Petal.Length |
Petal.Width ~ Species, data = iris, test = c(1, 0, 0, 0), alpha =
0.05,
factors.and.variables = TRUE)
```

The preceding command displays the following output:

```
The ANOVA type statistic will be used in the following test
The Global Hypothesis is significant, subset algorithm will continue

~Performing the Subset Algorithm based on Factor levels~
The Hypothesis of equality between factor levels  setosa versicolor virginica is rejected
The Hypothesis of equality between factor levels  versicolor virginica is rejected
The Hypothesis of equality between factor levels  setosa virginica is rejected
The Hypothesis of equality between factor levels  setosa versicolor is rejected
All appropriate subsets using factor levels have been checked using a closed multiple testing procedure, which controls the max
imum overall type I error rate at alpha= 0.05

~Performing the Subset Algorithm based on Response Variables~
 The Hypothesis of equality using response variables  Sepal.Length Sepal.Width Petal.Length Petal.Width is rejected
The Hypothesis of equality using response variables  Sepal.Width Petal.Length Petal.Width is rejected
The Hypothesis of equality using response variables  Sepal.Length Petal.Length Petal.Width is rejected
The Hypothesis of equality using response variables  Sepal.Length Sepal.Width Petal.Width is rejected
The Hypothesis of equality using response variables  Sepal.Length Sepal.Width Petal.Length is rejected
The Hypothesis of equality using response variables  Petal.Length Petal.Width is rejected
The Hypothesis of equality using response variables  Sepal.Width Petal.Width is rejected
The Hypothesis of equality using response variables  Sepal.Length Petal.Width is rejected
The Hypothesis of equality using response variables  Sepal.Length Petal.Length is rejected
The Hypothesis of equality using response variables  Sepal.Length Sepal.Width is rejected
The Hypothesis of equality using response variables  Petal.Width is rejected
The Hypothesis of equality using response variables  Petal.Length is rejected
The Hypothesis of equality using response variables  Sepal.Width is rejected
The Hypothesis of equality using response variables  Sepal.Length is rejected
All appropriate subsets using response variables have been checked using a multiple testing procedure, which controls the maxim
um overall type I error rate at alpha= 0.05
```

3. We finally conclude that all of the groups are different, and these differences are driven by all of the variables.

How it works...

There are two main functions here: `nonpartest()` and `ssnonpartest()`. The former provides global statistics and p-values as in MANOVA. In our case, we clearly rejected the null hypothesis of equality of means between the different groups. The latter function (`ssnonpartest`), identifies significant subsets of variables and later pinpoints which is the variable driving the differences between the groups. In our example here, the initial difference that we got using `nonpartest()` is caused by the fact that the setosa-virginica and setosa-versicolor vectors are different. We then found out that all the variables (`Petal.Width`, `Petal.Length`, `Sepal.Width`, and `Sepal.Width`) are driving that difference that we got using `nonpartest()`. The official paper describing the package's capabilities can be found here: `https://www.jstatsoft.org/article/view/v076i04`.

Semiparametric regression with the SemiPar package

Semiparametric models encompass a huge family of models that have a fully parametric (finite number of parameters) with a nonparametric part. In general, the parametric part will be linear, and the semiparametric part will be treated as nuisance; but this is not always the case. One example where a semiparametric model would be relevant, could be for example modeling the ice-cream sales in terms of the weather and the price. It's likely that the sales-weather relationship is highly nonlinear (sales are really high when the temperature is high, but low when the temperature is moderate), whereas the price-sales one could be quite linear. In that case, we would want to treat the price effect as linear and the rest as nuisance.

Getting ready

In order to run this recipe, we will need the `SemiPar` package which can be installed via `install.packages("semiPar")`.

How to do it...

We will generate synthetic data, first a fully linear model where each independent variable (two of them) will have a linear impact. Secondly, a model with one variable:

1. First, we generate some data for regression. The relationship will be linear and there is nothing new up to this point, as shown in the following example:

```
library(SemiPar)
x1 = rnorm(100,20,6)
x2 = runif(100,1,8)
y = x1 + x2 + rnorm(100,0,5)
data_sim = data.frame(x1=x1,x2=x2,y=y)
```

2. Next, we set up our semiparametric model, and we assume that there is an additive relationship between the variables. Because we generated the data, we already know that no transformation of the variables is necessary. But let's assume we didn't know this, and specify a general `f()` transformation for each variable:

```
fit <- spm(data_sim$y ~ f(data_sim$x1)+f(data_sim$x2))
summary(fit)
```

The preceding command displays the following output:

```
Summary for linear components:

                coef       se   ratio p-value
intercept 11.5000 2.31800    4.962       0
x1         0.8857 0.08716   10.160       0
x2         1.0370 0.23420    4.428       0
```

Then, run the following code:

```
par(mfrow=c(1,2))
plot(fit)
```

Estimated effect for each variable. The `SemiPar` package correctly treats them as almost linear. The gray area is the 95% confidence interval (these are slightly wider for small and large values of the independent variables, because we don't have so much data in those areas):

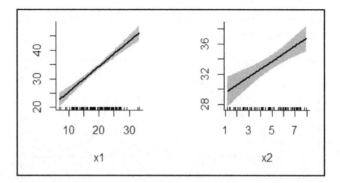

3. We can now generate a new dataset with the same structure, but now with an exponential transformation to x2. Ideally, SemiPar should identify this transformation, as shown in the following example:

```
x1 = rnorm(100,20,6)
x2 = runif(100,1,8)
y = x1 + 150*exp(-x2) + rnorm(100,0,5)
data_sim = data.frame(x1=x1,x2=x2,y=y)
```

4. We can now fit our model, with the same structure as before, as in the following code:

```
fit <- spm(data_sim$y ~ f(data_sim$x1)+f(data_sim$x2))
summary(fit)
```

Take a look at the following output:

```
Summary for non-linear components:

                 df  spar knots
f(data_sim$x1)   1 12870    24
f(data_sim$x2)   1  2592    24
```

Then, run the following code:

```
plot(fit)
```

The model correctly finds out that the correct relationship between *x2* and *x1* is via a functional relationship that resembles (`-exp(x2)`):

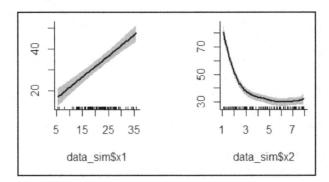

5. Both models presented before are actually fully non-parametric (we specified a general function for each of them). But we haven't yet constrained any variable to have an explicit linear effect. Let's now build a truly semiparametric model, containing a linear (parametric) and a non-linear (nonparametric) part. In this setting, we can get a coefficient for x1 that can be used for interpretation. As expected, we get a coefficient of 1 for x1, which is something we already knew, as demonstrated in the following code:

```
fit <- spm(data_sim$y ~ data_sim$x1 + f(data_sim$x2))
summary(fit)
```

The preceding code displays the following output of the linear and nonlinear components:

```
Summary for linear components:

                coef      se  ratio p-value
intercept    11.220 24.3000 0.4616  0.6454
data_sim$x1   1.012  0.1022 9.8980  0.0000




Summary for non-linear components:

                 df  spar knots
f(data_sim$x2) 5.145 2.209    24
```

How it works...

The algorithm works using penalized spline smoothing. Very detailed material on this package can be found in its official PDF documentation: `http://matt-wand.utsacademics.info/SPmanu.pdf`.

The intuition behind this technique is to find a set of knots and weights that can help in capturing the non-linear relationship. However, this is dangerous from an overfitting perspective, as more knots will produce more overfitting. Penalized splines attempt to mitigate the impact of overfitting, by intelligently penalizing the weights (not allowing them to be as big as they would be without intervention).

There's more...

The `predict.spm` function can be used to score new observations. It's also worth noting that we can effectively control the degree of smoothing that we want for the nonparametric part by using the `spar=` parameter, or alternatively by specifying the degrees of freedom using the `df=` parameter, as shown in the following example:

```
fit <- spm(data_sim$y ~ data_sim$x1 + f(data_sim$x2,spar=20))
summary(fit)
plot(fit)
fit <- spm(data_sim$y ~ data_sim$x1 + f(data_sim$x2,df=6))
summary(fit)
plot(fit)
```

6
Robust Methods

We will cover the following recipes in this chapter:

- Robust linear regression
- Estimating robust covariance matrices
- Robust logistic regression
- Robust ANOVA using the robust package
- Robust principal components
- Robust Gaussian mixture models with the `qclust` package
- Robust clustering

Introduction

Classical statistical methods don't handle outliers well. The worst part is that even the most basic methods suffer this problem: for example, the sample mean, which is the maximum likelihood estimate for the μ parameter (assuming that the distribution is Gaussian), can be wrong even with a single contaminated observation. For example, the average between the numbers: 3, 4, and 5, is 4; and if we replace that last value (=5) with a new contaminated value =100, the new average will be =107/3. Let's introduce the concept of breakdown point for an estimator. The breakdown point (of an estimator) is the proportion of values that the estimator can handle before yielding wrong results. In the case of the mean that we just explained, the breakdown is 0; meaning that even a single contaminated observation would make the estimator give wrong results. The median is much more robust than the mean, having a breakdown of 0.5 (50% of the data can be wrong and the median still be right).

Some of the most important statistical methods have their robust counterparts, which are designed to mitigate the presence of outliers. Robust methods are usually more computationally intensive than standard ones methods, but given the computational power available nowadays, this is no longer a problem.

Robust linear regression

When doing linear regression, we have seen that our estimates can change dramatically in the presence of influential points. This is usually problematic when dealing with noisy datasets. R exposes the rlm function, which offers several weighting options: Huber, and bi-square among them.

Huber weights are appropriate when we don't have many extreme cases, and bisquare weights are best for those extreme cases. In either case, the algorithm operates in the same fashion, by using **iteratively reweighted least squares (IRLS)**, which is described at the end of this recipe.

Getting ready

No special package is needed for this recipe.

How to do it...

We'll generate a synthetic dataset containing two independent variables. We will then contaminate it and see how both lm and rlm perform:

1. First, we generate a synthetic dataset, containing two independent Gaussian variables. y is equal to x1 + x2 plus a Gaussian residual:

```
set.seed(10)
x1 = rnorm(100,0,2)
x2 = rnorm(100,0,2)
y = x1 + x2 + rnorm(100,0,1)
```

2. Now, we introduce an extreme value to x1. It will certainly disrupt our estimated coefficients:

```
y[100] = 100
plot(x1,y)
```

The following screenshot shows the plot between **x1** and the dependent variable: **y** (notice the outlier on the upper-right part of the plot):

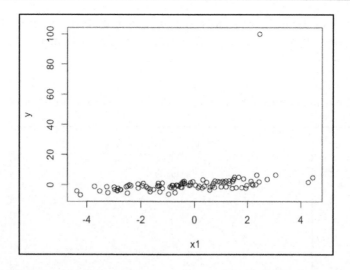

3. The coefficients are different to what they should be (both should be equal to 1):

```
e = lm(y ~ -1+ x1 + x2)
summary(e)
```

The following screenshot shows that both coefficients are now wrong (they should be close to **1**):

```
> summary(e)

Call:
lm(formula = y ~ -1 + x1 + x2)

Residuals:
    Min      1Q Median      3Q     Max
 -4.748 -1.088  0.318   1.334  96.795

Coefficients:
   Estimate Std. Error t value Pr(>|t|)
x1   1.6489     0.5270   3.129  0.00231 **
x2   0.3825     0.5146   0.743  0.45911
---
Signif. codes:  0 '***' 0.001 '**' 0.01 '*' 0.05 '.' 0.1 ' ' 1

Residual standard error: 9.966 on 98 degrees of freedom
Multiple R-squared:  0.09393,   Adjusted R-squared:  0.07544
F-statistic:  5.08 on 2 and 98 DF,  p-value: 0.00796
```

4. If we look at the influence plots, we can see that observation = 100 is clearly problematic. It has a Cook's D statistic much higher than **1**:

```
plot(e)
```

The following screenshot shows the plot of residuals versus leverage:

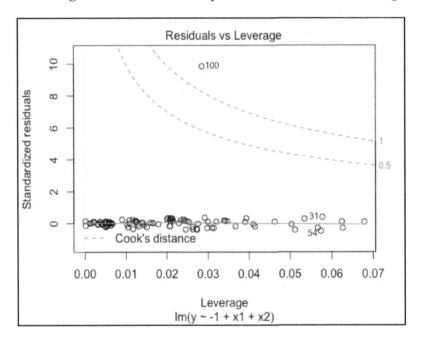

5. The `rlm` model looks much better, as both coefficients are now within 20% of their real values:

```
rlm_model = rlm(y ~ -1 + x1 + x2)
summary(rlm_model)
```

The following screenshot shows that the robust model works well: the coefficients are very close to **1**, and the standard errors are very small:

```
> summary(rlm_model)

Call: rlm(formula = y ~ -1 + x1 + x2, psi = psi.huber)
Residuals:
    Min      1Q  Median      3Q     Max
-2.6973 -0.6242  0.0971  0.6817 99.6149

Coefficients:
   Value   Std. Error t value
x1 0.9795  0.0524      18.7067
x2 0.9179  0.0511      17.9545

Residual standard error: 0.9639 on 98 degrees of freedom
```

6. We can use different weighting schemes such as the Hampel or bi-square:

```
rlm_model = rlm(y ~ -1 + x1 + x2,psi = psi.hampel)
summary(rlm_model)
```

The following screenshot shows that the Hampel weighting seems to work slightly better (both coefficients are closer to 1):

```
> summary(rlm_model)

Call: rlm(formula = y ~ -1 + x1 + x2, psi = psi.hampel)
Residuals:
     Min       1Q   Median       3Q      Max
-2.64864 -0.58826  0.09075  0.64438 99.64157

Coefficients:
   Value   Std. Error t value
x1 0.9826  0.0509      19.2935
x2 0.9335  0.0497      18.7727

Residual standard error: 0.9359 on 98 degrees of freedom
```

7. Then, run the following code:

```
rlm_model = rlm(y ~ -1 + x1 + x2,psi = psi.bisquare)
summary(rlm_model)
```

The following screenshot shows that bi-square weighting works as well as Huber but not as well as Hampel:

```
> summary(rlm_model)

Call: rlm(formula = y ~ -1 + x1 + x2, psi = psi.bisquare)
Residuals:
    Min      1Q  Median      3Q     Max
-2.6774 -0.6236  0.0923  0.6736 99.6521

Coefficients:
   Value   Std. Error t value
x1 0.9725  0.0526      18.4780
x2 0.9270  0.0514      18.0394

Residual standard error: 0.9702 on 98 degrees of freedom
```

How it works...

Conceptually, we want to minimize the sum of the residuals, but weighting them in such a way that large residuals receive a small weight (so their influence is mitigated). We can think that in OLS (ordinary least squares), every observation has a weight of 1. Huber and bi-square weighting penalize each residual by assigning a small weight. The `rlm` function works by minimizing the sum of weighted residuals. The problem is that the weights depend on the residuals, and the residuals depend on the weights. The technique that is used for this is called **iteratively reweighted least squares**. Large residuals receive a large weight, and small residuals get a small one.

The specific weight depends on which weighting scheme is used. For example, in Huber weighting, small residuals get a weight of 1 and the rest of the observations get a different weight according to how big their residuals are. In bi-square weighting, all observations get at least some weight. On the other hand, in Huber weighting, large residuals do not get a zero weight, but in bi-square weighting they do. This is why we should use bi-square weighting when we suspect that we have huge outliers. On the contrary, if we suspect that we have a few mild outliers, Huber should be preferred.

M-estimators are generalizations of maximum likelihood estimates (hence the *M*). The idea is to minimize the following expression:

$$\sum \rho(s_i) = \sum \rho(y_i - X_i'b)ca$$

The ρ is a function that is applied to each row in order to down-weight outliers. It can be Huber, bi-square, etc. Note that if ρ = 0.5 * (si)**2, then we have the usual ordinary least squares (non-robust).

An excellent introductory explanation to M-estimators can be found on the following website: `http://users.stat.umn.edu/~sandy/courses/8053/handouts/robust.pdf`.

Estimating robust covariance matrices

The standard/usual way of estimating covariance matrices involves calculating sums involving the cross products of all pairs of variables. This is obviously greatly impacted by outliers. A single outlier on variable x_k contaminates all the covariances involving x_k. In order to estimate robust covariance matrices, we will use the `robust` package.

Getting ready

In order to run this recipe, you need to install the `robust` package using `install.packages("robust")`.

How to do it...

In this recipe, we will generate random vectors according to a bivariate Gaussian distribution. We will contaminate it and see how both the standard and the robust methods work.

1. First, we will generate bivariate Gaussian numbers and then estimate the correlation matrix. Since we don't have any outliers, both the robust and non-robust methods should be roughly similar:

```
library(MASS)
library(robust)
Sigma <- matrix(c(2,1,1,2),2,2)
d <- mvrnorm(n = 1000, mu=c(5,5), Sigma)
covClassic(d,cor = TRUE)
```

The following screenshot shows the correlation matrix estimated via classic methods

```
> covClassic(d, cor = TRUE)
Call:
covClassic(data = d, corr = TRUE)

Classical Estimate of Correlation:
        V1      V2
V1 1.0000 0.4889
V2 0.4889 1.0000

Classical Estimate of Location:
   V1     V2
5.112 5.071
```

2. The robust correlation matrix looks perfect as well. This is interesting, as it proves that the robust method works very well, in the absence of any contamination:

```
cov.rob(d, cor = TRUE)
```

Robust correlation matrix estimation. We first get the centers of the distribution:

```
> cov.rob(d, cor = TRUE)
$center
[1] 5.119222 5.080008
```

The following screenshot shows estimated robust correlation matrix:

```
$cor
          [,1]      [,2]
[1,] 1.0000000 0.5371111
[2,] 0.5371111 1.0000000
```

3. We then add contamination to 5% of the data. These are quite abnormal values, having very different means (and covariance) from the data that we have used so far. The standard way starts to have issues, as the correlation matrix now has substantial deviations:

```
d[1:50,1:2] = matrix(rnorm(100,20,10),c(50,2))
covClassic(d, cor = TRUE)
```

The following screenshot shows the estimated correlation matrix with 5% of contamination:

```
Call:
covClassic(data = d, corr = TRUE)

Classical Estimate of Correlation:
        V1      V2
V1 1.0000 0.5341
V2 0.5341 1.0000

Classical Estimate of Location:
   V1      V2
5.733  5.811
```

4. The robust way has no problem. Both the centers and the correlation matrix are still very close to where they should be. It seems like the contamination did not occur at all. The centers and the correlation matrix are still very close to their true values:

```
cov.rob(d,cor = TRUE)
```

The following screenshot shows the estimated robust center of the distribution with 5% contamination:

```
$center
[1] 5.095713 5.066022
```

The following screenshot shows the estimated robust correlation matrix with 5% correlation:

```
$cor
           [,1]       [,2]
[1,] 1.0000000 0.5278468
[2,] 0.5278468 1.0000000
```

5. Finally, we add a contamination to 20% of the data (200 observations), and use the classical approach:

```
d[1:200,1:2] = matrix(rnorm(400,20,10),c(50,2))
covClassic(d,cor = TRUE)
```

The following screenshot shows the estimated classical correlation matrix with 20% contamination:

```
> covClassic(d,cor = TRUE)
Call:
covClassic(data = d, corr = TRUE)

Classical Estimate of Correlation:
        V1      V2
V1 1.0000 0.6128
V2 0.6128 1.0000

Classical Estimate of Location:
   V1     V2
7.883 7.874
```

6. The robust approach is again much better, yielding estimates within 10% of their true values:

```
cov.rob(d,cor = TRUE)
```

The following screenshot shows the estimated robust centers with 20% contamination:

```
> cov.rob(d,cor = TRUE)
$center
[1] 5.097614 5.062966
```

The following output shows the Estimated robust correlation matrix with 20% contamination:

```
$cor
          [,1]      [,2]
[1,] 1.0000000 0.5056711
[2,] 0.5056711 1.0000000
```

How it works...

Standard estimation of covariance matrices is quite simple, as it relies on simple covariance and variance estimates for each variable. The usual formula for the covariance matrix does not discriminate whether the values are outliers or not (it involves taking the sums of the cross products between the observed vectors):

$$Q = \frac{1}{n-1} \sum_{i=1}^{n} (x_i - \bar{x})(x_i - \bar{x})^T$$

Robust estimation using `covRob` employs either the Donoho-Stahel or the orthogonalized quadrant correlation depending on the problem size. More algorithmic details can be found in the package's documentation: `http://ftp.auckland.ac.nz/software/CRAN/doc/packages/robust.pdf`.

Robust logistic regression

Logistic regression is used for modeling a categorical variable (for example yes/no) in terms of a set of covariates. The intention is to assess the impact of these covariates on the conditional probabilities estimated by the model.
The problem is that this technique is not robust to outliers, and even minor ones can greatly impact our estimation. This is the same problem that we had for linear regression.

The robust package offers functionality to estimate robust logistic regression models. These are relevant for the same reasons as for robust regression.

Getting ready

In order to run this recipe, you need to install the `robust` package using `install.packages("robust")`.

How to do it...

In this recipe, we will investigate how robust logistic regression handles extreme observations. The mechanics will be the same that we implemented for robust linear regression (we will generate data, contaminate it, and see how our estimates change).

1. First, load the `robust` package:

   ```
   library(robust)
   ```

2. We first generate `1000` observations for logistic regression, and we try both logistic regression and robust logistic regression. Of course, both methods yield correct results in the absence of contamination:

   ```
   set.seed(1000)
   x1 = rnorm(1000)
   x2 = rnorm(1000)
   link_val = 2 + 2*x1 + 5*x2
   pr = 1/(1+exp(-link_val))
   y = rbinom(1000,1,pr)
   df = data.frame(y=y,x1=x1,x2=x2)
   glm(y~x1+x2,data=df,family="binomial")
   robust::glmRob(y~x1+x2,data=df,family="binomial")
   ```

   Estimated results. Non-robust (top) and robust (below). Because we don't have any contamination here, both will yield similar results:

   ```
   > glm( y~x1+x2,data=df,family="binomial")

   Call:  glm(formula = y ~ x1 + x2, family = "binomial", data = df)

   Coefficients:
   (Intercept)            x1            x2
         1.767         1.927         4.990

   Degrees of Freedom: 999 Total (i.e. Null);  997 Residual
   Null Deviance:      1307
   Residual Deviance: 440.5         AIC: 446.5
   > robust::glmRob(y~x1+x2,data=df,family="binomial")
   Call:
   robust::glmRob(formula = y ~ x1 + x2, family = "binomial", data = df)

   Coefficients:
   (Intercept)            x1            x2
         1.764         1.923         4.981

   Degrees of Freedom: 1000 Total; 997 Residual
   Residual Deviance: 440.5
   ```

3. We now contaminate 5% of the results and repeat the procedure. The standard logistic regression model is not working properly: x1 has an estimated coefficient that equal to 0.08, which is very far away from the correct value (-1). x2 is also wrong, with an estimated coefficient of 3.26 instead of 5. The robust method is much better here: x1 is 0.63 instead of 1, and x2 is 3.65:

```
x1 = rnorm(1000)
x2 = rnorm(1000)
link_val = 2 + 2*x1 + 5*x2
pr = 1/(1+exp(-link_val))
y = rbinom(1000,1,pr)
x1[1:100] = 10*rnorm(100)
df = data.frame(y=y,x1=x1,x2=x2)
glm(y~x1+x2,data=df,family="binomial")
robust::glmRob(y~x1+x2,mthod="cubif",data=df,family="binomial")
```

Standard and robust results. Standard ones are greatly impacted by the outliers:

```
> glm( y~x1+x2,data=df,family="binomial")

Call:  glm(formula = y ~ x1 + x2, family = "binomial", data = df)

Coefficients:
(Intercept)            x1            x2
      1.767         1.927         4.990

Degrees of Freedom: 999 Total (i.e. Null);  997 Residual
Null Deviance:       1307
Residual Deviance: 440.5        AIC: 446.5
> robust::glmRob(y~x1+x2,data=df,family="binomial")
Call:
robust::glmRob(formula = y ~ x1 + x2, family = "binomial", data = df)

Coefficients:
(Intercept)            x1            x2
      1.764         1.923         4.981

Degrees of Freedom: 1000 Total; 997 Residual
Residual Deviance: 440.5
```

4. We now repeat the same exercise, but contaminating 10% of the data. The conclusions are quite similar: the classical GLM has serious problems, whereas the robust one works well:

```
x1 = rnorm(1000)
x2 = rnorm(1000)
link_val = 2 + 2*x1 + 5*x2
pr = 1/(1+exp(-link_val))
y = rbinom(1000,1,pr)
x1[1:200] = 10*rnorm(200)
df = data.frame(y=y,x1=x1,x2=x2)
```

Classical and robust GLM results with a 10% contamination:

```
> glm( y~x1+x2,data=df,family="binomial")

Call:  glm(formula = y ~ x1 + x2, family = "binomial", data = df)

Coefficients:
(Intercept)           x1           x2
    1.36236      0.09564      3.46004

Degrees of Freedom: 999 Total (i.e. Null);  997 Residual
Null Deviance:       1320
Residual Deviance: 602.9           AIC: 608.9
> robust::glmRob(y~x1+x2,mthod="cubif",data=df,family="binomial")
Call:
robust::glmRob(formula = y ~ x1 + x2, family = "binomial", data = df,
    mthod = "cubif")

Coefficients:
(Intercept)           x1           x2
     1.3982       0.2321       3.4954

Degrees of Freedom: 1000 Total; 997 Residual
Residual Deviance: 630.7
```

How it works...

Logistic regression is usually fitted via maximum likelihood, but it can be used here. We need to adjust the ML technique in order to get robust estimates. The `robust` package implements several algorithms that can be chosen using the `method=` option, such as: Mallows, cubif, and misclass. Essentially, Mallows downweights the observations that have covariates with a high leverage and misclass assumes that there are certain observations that will be missclassified.

Detailed algorithms can be found on the following websites: `https://www.jstor.org/stable/2345763?seq=1#page_scan_tab_contents` and `https://pdfs.semanticscholar.org/0687/32a9fb924a9360254e6ed9384707c8ee92bf.pdf`.

Robust ANOVA using the robust package

After fitting a linear regression model using `lm`, we can feed that into the `anova` function. Thus, we get the corresponding sum of squares and F-tests. But since analysis of variance (ANOVA) relies on a sum of squares (or linear regression residuals) it also suffers from the presence of outliers.

The mechanics here are quite similar to the non-robust/standard way: first, we do the robust regression model, and then we pass the estimated model into the `anova.lmrob` function.

Getting ready

In order to run this example, the `robust` package needs to be installed using `install.packages("robust")`.

How to do it...

We will work with the `PlantGrowth` dataset, which is already included in R. It contains the weights of certain plants and a variable flagging whether the plant is in the control, treatment1, or treatment2 groups.

1. First, we load the `robust` package and the dataset:

```
library(robust)
r = PlantGrowth
```

2. Let's model this using standard ANOVA. Because there are no obvious outliers, the standard ANOVA table should match the robust one reasonably well:

```
d = aov(weight ~ group,data=r )
summary(d)
```

The following screenshot shows the classical ANOVA table for the standard model:

```
> summary(d)
            Df Sum Sq Mean Sq F value Pr(>F)
group        2  3.766  1.8832   4.846 0.0159 *
Residuals   27 10.492  0.3886
---
Signif. codes:  0 '***' 0.001 '**' 0.01 '*' 0.05 '.' 0.1 ' ' 1
```

Then, type the following code:

```
plot(d, 2)
```

The following screenshot shows the **Q-Q** plot – a few observations are slightly off, but we could still assume normality:

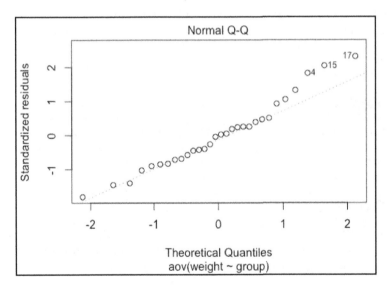

3. As we can see, the F-sum of squares, and p-values are very similar in the robust model and the standard one (presented in the previous recipe):

```
robanova = robust::lmRob(weight ~ group,data=r )
robust::anova.lmRob(robanova)
```

The following screenshot shows the ANOVA table for the robust model: it's very close to the standard ANOVA one:

```
> robust::anova.lmRob(robanova)

Terms added sequentially (first to last)

             Chisq Df RobustF    Pr(F)
(Intercept)        1
group              2   9.3139 0.001871 **
---
Signif. codes:  0 '***' 0.001 '**' 0.01 '*' 0.05 '.' 0.1 ' ' 1
```

4. Let's contaminate just two observations with a 50. Even though this is a minor contamination, it still causes major problems.

```
r[1,1] = 50
r[2,1] = 50
d = aov(weight ~ group,data=r )
plot(d, 2)
```

The following screenshot shows that even with two contaminated observations, the effects on the standard (non-robust) ANOVA model are major: we cannot support the normality hypothesis:

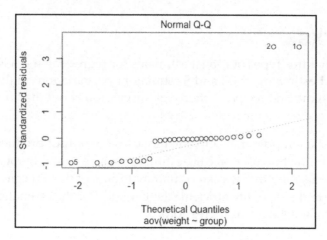

Then, type the following code:

```
summary(d)
```

The following screenshot shows that, the p-value is obviously wrong: it's almost eight times larger now:

```
> summary(d)
            Df Sum Sq Mean Sq F value Pr(>F)
group        2    539   269.7   2.248  0.125
Residuals   27   3239   120.0
```

5. The robust method has no problem, and the F statistic and p-values are almost the same ones we had before the contamination happened:

```
robanova = robust::lmRob(weight ~ group,data=r )
robust::anova.lmRob(robanova)
```

The following screenshot shows, the robust ANOVA p-values and F statistics very close to the original ones:

```
> robust::anova.lmRob(robanova)

Terms added sequentially (first to last)

            Chisq Df RobustF    Pr(F)
(Intercept)        1
group              2  7.9748 0.004006 **
---
Signif. codes:  0 '***' 0.001 '**' 0.01 '*' 0.05 '.' 0.1 ' ' 1
```

How it works...

There are essentially three types of robust estimates for regression models: M-estimators, S-estimators, and MM-estimators. MM and S estimators are variations of the M estimators that we presented in the first recipe. A thorough discussion about the three of them can be found here: https://ijpam.eu/contents/2014-91-3/7/7.pdf.

Anova.lmrob is just a wrapper that conveniently uses the output produced by lm.rob models. The lm.rob function uses an MM-estimator, which is highly robust (it has a 50% breakdown point – meaning that we can contaminate 50% of the data and still get reasonable results), and it is highly efficient (the variance for the estimated coefficients is as large as the one obtained via linear regression).

Robust principal components

In this recipe, we will work with robust principal components. Principal components are used to project data into a smaller subspace that is easier to work with. It is probably the most important dimensionality reduction technique.

Analyzing and working with lots of features is usually complicated for two main reasons:

- It's difficult to find patterns between them, because combinations of them might be relatively correlated.
- Modeling variables to predict another variable sometimes carries a significant amount of noise. Ideally, we would like to compress some of the information contained in the data in order to have a simpler model.

In order to introduce principal components, let's review a basic example. Let's assume we have a football and rugby score for some students:

Person	Football	Rugby
John	10	8
Michael	3	5

It would actually be best if we found a single variable that collapsed the information from both variables. We could for example do: *0.5 x 10 + 0.5 x 8 = 9* for the first student. And we would get *0.5 x 3 + 0.5 x 5 = 4* for the second one. This would be useful, because we can now work with a single metric. But a natural question arises: can we multiply them by another set of weights different from *(0.5, 0.5)* in order to capture more of the variability that exists between those two variables?

Principal components are just linear combinations of variables that capture the main directions of variability in our datasets. They have an interesting property: each one of them is orthogonal to the other ones. This property means, in layman's terms, , intuitively, that the variability that each one of them captures is not contained in the other ones.

Mathematically, principal components are extracted by computing the eigenvalues—that is, the eigenvectors from the covariance matrix. Each eigenvector will have as many elements as variables that we have. Each eigenvector will be associated with an eigenvalue, and the size of the eigenvalue will determine how much variability is explained by the eigenvector. Going back to our example, we would have two principal components. Each one of them would have two entries and each one of them should be multiplied by each column in order to project the data.

Principal component analysis is usually used in two ways:

- To project features into a smaller subspace that is more robust and provides more stable predictions.
- To find groups of variables that are related. This can be determined by finding variables that have high loadings into some principal components.

A separate question is how many principal components should be kept. Usually, a scree plot is used, which shows the eigenvalues for each principal component; a strategy is usually adopted to keep all of them that are greater than 1.

Getting ready

In order to run this example, you need to install the `robust` package using `install.packages("robust")`.

How to do it...

We will follow a similar to the one as we have used so far. We will generate a dataset, contaminate it, and then extract both regular principal components and robust ones. Because principal components are calculated using the covariance matrix, they suffer from serious sensitivity to outliers:

1. First, we generate a synthetic multivariate Gaussian dataset:

```
library(MASS)
library(rospca)
set.seed(100)
matrix = diag(10)
matrix[2,1] = 0.8
matrix[1,2] = 0.8
matrix[4,3] = 0.8
matrix[3,4] = 0.8
matrix[5,6] = 0.8
matrix[6,5] = 0.8
```

2. We now fit both principal component analysis and robust principal component analysis models:

```
d <- mvrnorm(n = 1000, mu=rep(0,10), matrix)
prcomp(d, scale=TRUE, center=TRUE)
```

These eigenvalues can be interpreted as size of each principal component (if we divide each value by the sum of these values, we get the proportion of variability explained by each principal component). We usually keep all the principal components which have eigenvalues greater than 1:

```
Standard deviations (1, .., p=10):
 [1] 1.4164259 1.3425988 1.2985310 1.0337184 0.9984854 0.9763466 0.9583313 0.4550208 0.4264126 0.4229815
```

Then, we run the following code:

```
x1 = rospca::robpca(d)
x1$eigenvalues
```

The following screenshot shows the Robust principal components (no contamination):

```
> x1$eigenvalues
      PC1       PC2       PC3       PC4       PC5       PC6
2.1628126 1.8364713 1.6630791 1.0449954 0.9669290 0.9306331
```

3. We now contaminate a single observation for all the variables:

```
d[1:1,1:10] <- -400
```

4. The same two models are estimated again. The impact on the standard principal component analysis is massive, as all the eigenvalues are wrong now. If we were to follow these results, we would only keep the first eigenvalue (it's the only one that is >1). However, the robust principal component analysis works really well reporting essentially the same principal component as before:

```
Standard deviations (1, .., p=10):
 [1] 3.15375504 0.11429621 0.10610480 0.09134895 0.08006696 0.07545510 0.07356575 0.03584887 0.03512249 0.03358356
```

The following screenshot Robust principal components (with contamination):

```
> x1$eigenvalues
      PC1       PC2       PC3       PC4       PC5       PC6
2.1675611 1.8456676 1.6573998 1.0494377 0.9724306 0.9306576
```

How it works...

A simple and possible approach for doing robust principal component analysis could be to replace the covariance matrix with its robust counterpart. We could then extract the eigenvalues/eigenvectors out of it and get the principal components, but this was found not to work too well.

The robust principal component analysis algorithm used for this is quite complex. A good reference on the computational details used for robust covariance matrix estimation can be found on https://arxiv.org/pdf/1506.00691.pdf.

Robust Gaussian mixture models with the qclust package

Clustering is usually done via the k-means algorithm. It works by assigning each observation to the closest centroid (vector of means for each group), then recalculating the centroid, and then iterating across all observations. The algorithm stops when no observation changes from cluster. But k-means has a major flaw. Because each observation is assigned to the closest centroid, we are implicitly assuming that the clusters are spherical (no correlation between the variables). In many cases this is not a realistic assumption.

A different approach is to assume that each observation comes from one out of three possible distributions. These distributions are assumed to be multivariate Gaussian, with possibly different covariance matrices. Of course, since the algorithm relies on estimating covariance matrices using standard techniques (maximum likelihood), it can be severely impacted by outliers. A robust alternative to this method can be used, using the `qclust` package.

After these are estimated, we are usually interested in plotting the densities. This is useful to understand what the areas of high density for each cluster are.

Getting ready

In order to run this recipe, the `qclust` package needs to be installed using `install.packages("qclust")`.

How to do it...

We will work with the `geyser2` dataset, which contains two features (eruption length and previous eruption length). The objective is to cluster the data into three groups, taking care of the fact that there is a distinct covariance pattern in each cluster.

1. First, we load the library, which includes the `geyser2` dataset:

   ```
   library(qclust)
   data ("geyser2")
   ```

2. We estimate our clusters, using the `qclust` function. We want to get three clusters, and we set the `q` (robust parameter) to 0.99. We plot the clusters and the densities:

   ```
   result_robust_mixture <- qclust::Qclust (geyser2,K=3,q=0.9999)
   plot (result_robust_mixture)
   ```

   Estimated clusters—these covariance matrices are not very robust. The blue cluster seems to be suffering from the small group of blue members on the lower left part:

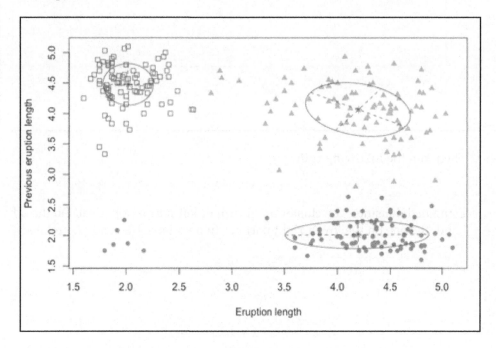

Then, type the following code:

```
plot(result_robust_mixture,what="density",type="persp")
```

The following screenshot shows the covariance and the precision for each assigned observation. The large ones refer to those cases where the algorithm is unsure to which cluster they belong:

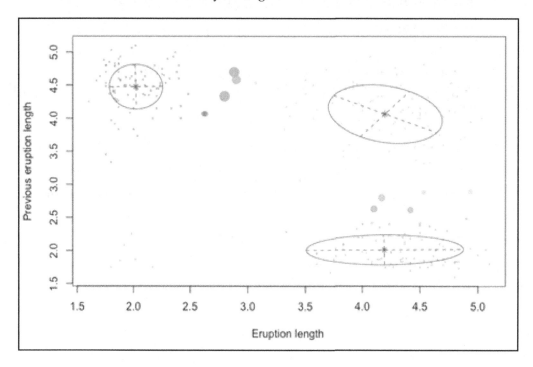

Then, run the following code:

```
plot(result_robust_mixture,what="boundaries",ngrid=200)
```

Estimated densities: the cluster on the upper left part is spherical. On the other hand, the one on the lower right part has two variables severely correlated:

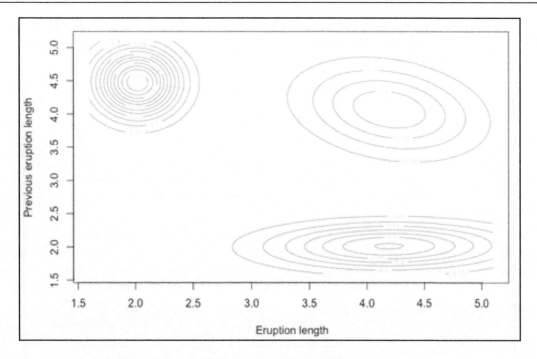

The following screenshot shows the **Density** 3D plot:

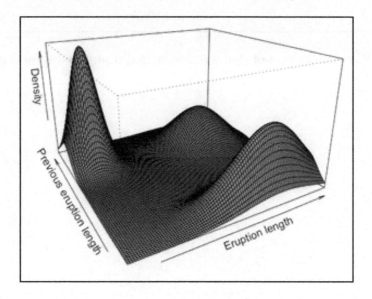

3. We now repeat the procedure, with a *q=0.10*. The covariance matrix looks much better than before. The three of them are less elongated, and this is particularly true for the blue cluster:

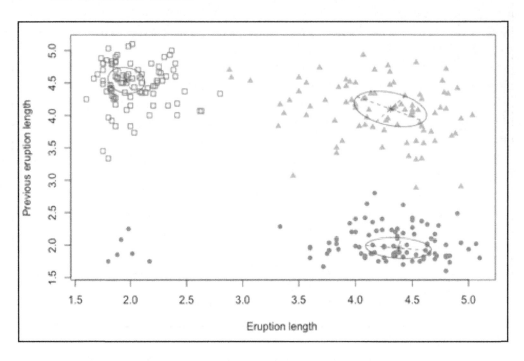

The following screenshot shows the estimated contour plots for each density cluster:

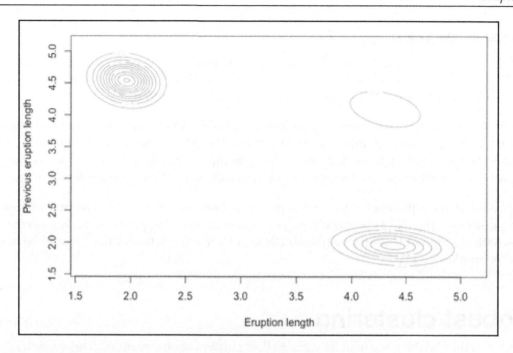

The following screenshot shows the 3D density:

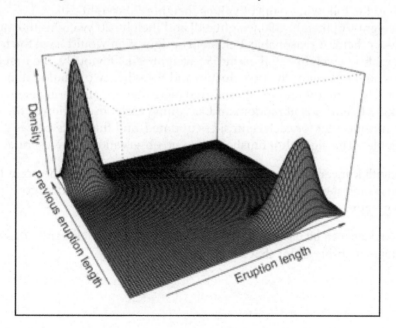

How it works...

The results are not as good as the ones we got in the previous recipe. The group of outliers on the lower-left part of the plot are now assigned to a cluster, instead of being flagged as outliers. Moreover, tuning the q parameter seems quite challenging.

Nevertheless, the covariance matrix is adjusted according to the q parameter, which means that the estimated densities differ in the two cases. The smaller the q parameter is, the smaller the impact of each (outlier) observation on the covariance estimation. As we can see, we get densities that are obviously more concentrated as this q parameter decreases.

Regardless of the q parameter, the nice aspect about this model is that it also provides an estimate of uncertainty. As we would expect, observations lying between classes are the ones with the highest uncertainty (the model is not very sure whether they should be in one class or another).

Robust clustering

Given certain variables, we usually want to find clusters of observations. These clusters should be as different as possible, and should contain "similar" observations inside. Suppose we had the following pairs of values [height=170,weight=50], [height=180,weight=70],[height=190,weight=90] and [height=200,weight=100] and we wanted to cluster them. A reasonable 2-cluster configuration would have the following centroids: [height=175,weight=60],[height=195,weight=95]. Obviously, the first two observations would fall under the first cluster, and the other two should fall under the second cluster. The simplest and most preferred algorithm for clustering is k-means. It works by picking *k* centroids at random and assigning each observation to the nearest centroid. The mean/center for each centroid is updated, and the procedure is repeated for the other variables. The algorithm finishes when no observation changes for a cluster.

The problem with k-means is that it uses the mean of each cluster as the point that is used to identify the center of each cluster. But means are non-robust, so this algorithm will suffer from outliers greatly.

The `tclust` package can be used to fix this issue: it works by intelligently discarding a small percentage of observations that are extreme.

Getting ready

The `tclust` and `ggplot2` packages need to be installed using `install.packages()`.

How to do it...

We will work with the `geyser2` dataset, which contains two features (eruption length and previous eruption length). The objective is to cluster the data into three groups, taking care of the fact that there are some outliers that shouldn't be included in any group. It is worth noting that the number of clusters is usually decided by the modeler. In general, we don't want too many clusters, as interpreting more than 5-8 clusters is very hard.

1. We first load the `tclust` library and the `geyser` dataset. This contains two features:

   ```
   library(tclust)
   data ("geyser2")
   ```

2. Now, we try the standard `kmeans` and `tkmeans`, and we set up `alpha=0.05`. We add an extra variable to the `geyser` dataset, which we will then use in `ggplot`:

   ```
   clus_kmeans <- kmeans (geyser2, centers = 3)
   clus_tkmeans <- tkmeans (geyser2, k = 3, alpha = 0.05)
   geyser2$cluster <- as.factor(clus_kmeans$cluster)
   ```

3. We now plot the `kmeans` results and `tkmeans`:

   ```
   plot (clus,main="Standard k-means",xlab="X-axis label", ylab="y-
   axix label")
   ggplot(geyser2, aes(x=geyser2$`Eruption length`,
   y=geyser2$`Previous eruption  length`,color=geyser2$cluster))   +
   labs(x = "Eruption length", y = "Previous eruption length")+
   theme(legend.position="none") +  geom_point(aes(size=3,alpha =
   0.2))
   ```

The following screenshot shows the standard k-means: the green observations near (2,2) should have probably been flagged as outliers. Instead, they were assigned to the green cluster:

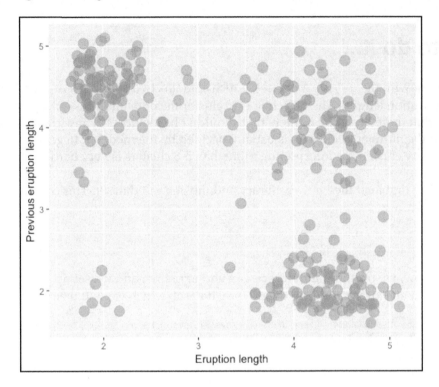

The following screenshot shows the **Robust k-means** plots: the observations on the lower-left part of the plot were correctly flagged as outliers. There are obviously a few other extra outliers that fall in between the clusters:

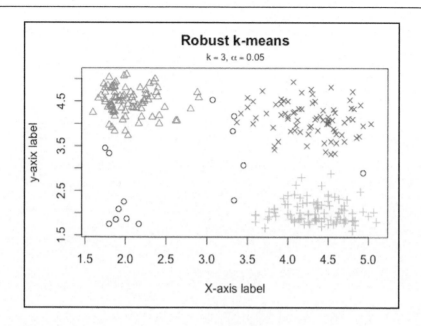

How it works...

The `tkmeans` package implements the trimmed k-means algorithm. More information about this can be found on the following paper: `https://www.jstor.org/stable/2242558?seq=1#page_scan_tab_contents`.

7
Time Series Analysis

We will cover the following recipes in this chapter:

- The general ARIMA model
- Seasonality and SARIMAX models
- Choosing the best model with the forecast package
- Vector autoregressions (VARs)
- Facebook's automatic Prophet forecasting
- Modeling count temporal data
- Imputing missing values in time series
- Anomaly detection
- Spectral decomposition of time series

Introduction

If we need to predict future values for, let's say oil price, we could model the price in terms of other variables (the number of rigs available, the number of companies investing in oil, and so on). These are usually referred to as cross-sectional models.

In the 1970s, many economists realized that these models were ineffective for predicting future values, and a new approach was proposed. The idea was then to use the series' past values to predict the future, in such a way that the model was chosen to mimic the temporal correlation structure as much as possible. For example, if a series had a strong serial correlation of order 1 (meaning that two consecutive values would usually be correlated), we would choose a model that generated strong autocorrelations of order 1. The new methodology was called time series analysis and it has been the dominant statistical tool for forecasting since.

All the series used in this chapter were obtained from Argentina's open data portal `https:/ /datos.gob.ar/series/api`. It contains hundreds of time series regarding finance, production, and economy.

The general ARIMA model

Time series analysis deals with several models, but **ARIMA** models are the most used ones. ARIMA means **autoregressive integrated moving average**. That implies that the model relies on two mathematical artefacts (**autoregressive (AR)** and **moving-average (MA)** processes) to model temporal phenomena. ARIMA is, thus, deeply rooted in stochastic processes, and what we will do is find a reasonable stochastic process (a combination of AR and MA processes) that matches the empirical autocovariance structure that we see in the data. AR processes are structured as *Yt = c1 Yt-1 + ... + ck Yt-k + et*, where *et* is Gaussian noise. On the other hand, MA processes are structured as *Yt = c1 et-1 +...+ck et-k + et*.

AR, MA and ARMA processes have a distinct autocorrelation structure. On the other hand, we will observe an autocorrelation structure for our data. In consequence, what we want to do is to find the AR/MA/ARMA model that generates an autocorrelation structure that is closer to the one we observe in the data. If we look at the data, and see that the we have strong autocorrelations of order 12 (usually for monthly data, where each month will tend to have similar values across different years), it won't be a good idea to use an AR(1) process. The reason is that an AR(1) process will only generate autocorrelations of order1 (because each value will be equal to the previous one plus some noise).

Both processes can obviously be combined to yield ARMA processes. Each one of the processes (AR or MA) exhibits distinctive autocorrelation patterns, and that knowledge can be used to decide which is the most appropriate model to use for an exercise/dataset. ARMA processes are somewhat more complicated and harder to identify, since they exhibit characteristics from both processes.

There are both stationary and non-stationary AR, and ARMA processes; but only stationary models are useful. Non-stationary models behave in strange ways: they don't dampen any shock to the system, so each one of these shocks causes the series to wander around different values constantly. Another way of stating this, is that non-stationary models do not revert to the mean. It can be proven that a non-stationary time series can be made stationary by differencing it as many times as necessary.

The number of AR lags that we have is usually referred to as the **p order**. The number of MA lags that we have is referred as the **q order**, and the number of times that we need to differentiate the series (until it is stationary) is the **I order**. So, for example a (2,1,2) model means that we have 2 AR lags, 1 differentiating, and 2 MA lags.

Chapter 7 *Chapter 7*

Getting ready

No special package is needed for this recipe.

How to do it...

In this recipe, we will generate two ARIMA models, (0,1,0) and (1,0,0), and we will see how to work with them:

1. We first create a function that will generate the time series. It will receive a parameter that will govern the AR coefficient:

```
set.seed(95)
build_series = function(coef){
start_value = 90
values = c(start_value)
previous_value = values
for (x in 1:200){
current_value  = coef*previous_value + rnorm(1,0,10)
values = c(values,current_value)
previous_value = current_value
}
return (values)
}
```

2. We now generate three time series with an AR coefficient = 1. We then plot the three of them, and interestingly, they all behave very differently. This is explained by the fact that the three of them are non-stationary (the AR coefficient = 1). The consequence is that the time series, is severely impacted by the shocks (after each large residual, the following values of the time series stay around that value, instead of converging toward the mean of the time series). Non-stationary time series do not exhibit mean-reversion:

```
ss1 = build_series(1)
ss2 = build_series(1)
ss3 = build_series(1)
plot(ss1,type="l",ylim=c(-200,300))
lines(ss2,col="red")
lines(ss3,col="green")
```

[265]

[265]

The following output shows the three non-stationary time series. They diverge after receiving a shock:

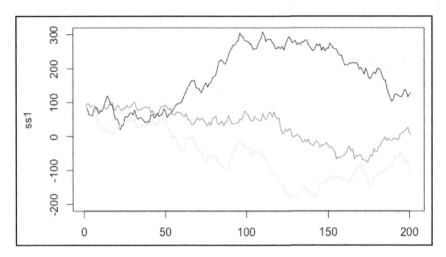

3. We now do the same exercise, but for a stationary time series (the coefficient is now smaller than 1 in modulus). The three time series wander around a similar value—actually they converge around the time series mean, which is equal to 90/(1-0.2)):

```
s1 = build_series(0.2)
s2 = build_series(0.2)
s3 = build_series(0.2)
plot(s1,type="l",ylim=c(-50,50))
lines(s2,col="red")
lines(s3,col="green")
```

The following output shows the three stationary time series. They appear to wander around the same value (=0):

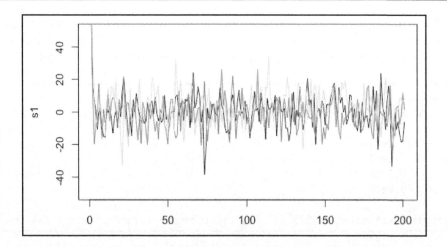

4. We now plot the **autocorrelation function** (**ACF**) for one of the stationary series, and we fit an `arima` model. As we can see, there is a fast decay in the ACF, showing that the autocorrelations fade quickly. The dotted lines show the confidence intervals and, we only have one of the correlations outside the nonsignificance area.

```
acf(s1)
arima(s1,order=c(1,0,0),include.mean = FALSE )
```

The following output shows the ACF plot for a stationary series:

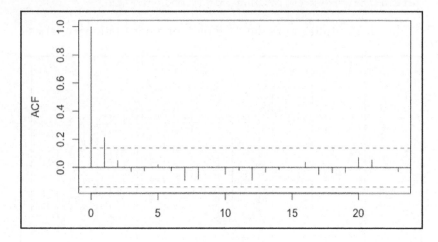

The estimated model seems fine, and the estimated coefficient for AR1 is significative. (Note that we set `include.mean=FALSE` because we don't have an intercept). The following output shows the estimated `arima` model:

```
Call:
arima(x = s1, order = c(1, 0, 0), include.mean = FALSE)

Coefficients:
         ar1
      0.2986
s.e.  0.0814

sigma^2 estimated as 125.4:  log likelihood = -770.84,  aic = 1545.69
```

5. The non-stationary model, we get autocorrelations that fade out very slowly. This means that a shock has a long-lasting impact on the series. The estimated coefficient is almost 1. This model can't be used for much, because the predictions will not match the actual values. Both the data, and our model's predictions will behave as the data that we presented in the first plot (both series will wander around random values, depending on the shocks received). Non-stationary models cannot be used in any way, and therefore they should be studied prior to modeling:

```
acf(ss1)
arima(ss1,order=c(1,0,0),include.mean = FALSE )
```

The following output shows the ACF plot for a non-stationary series:

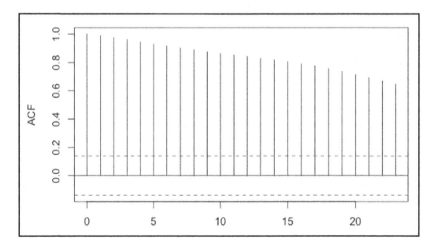

The following output shows the non-stationary `arima` model. The estimated coefficient is almost 1:

```
Call:
arima(x = ss1, order = c(1, 0, 0), include.mean = FALSE)

Coefficients:
          ar1
       0.9975
s.e.   0.0026

sigma^2 estimated as 104.6:  log likelihood = -755.24,  aic = 1514.48
```

6. When a series is non-stationary, it should be removed via differencing as many times as possible (a simpler method of nonstationarity is caused not by the AR coefficient being > 1, but because a trend is present. In these cases, the trend can be removed by first estimating it and cleaning the data, but differencing works as well here). After we difference the series, there is almost no structure left, except for something remaining at lag 14.

The following output shows the plot of differenced series. The series looks like noise, with no obvious structure.:

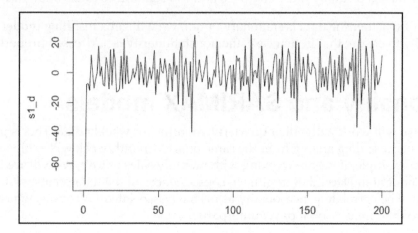

The following output shows the plot of the ACF of the differenced series:

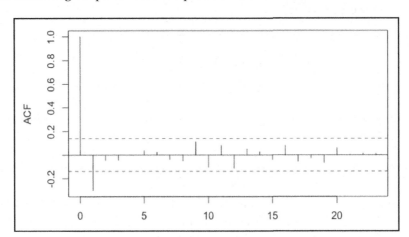

How it works...

ARIMA models cannot be estimated with the least squares method, because the moving average components are not observable. The technique that is used instead is maximum likelihood, which is certainly more complex, and can sometimes cause numerical errors.

Regardless of whether the data is stationary or not, we will get a resulting model. It is our responsibility to ensure that in that case, the nonstationarity is addressed properly.

Seasonality and SARIMAX models

In general, we will work with either quarterly, monthly, or weekly data. This is particularly interesting, because data arising from the same quarter/month/week will exhibit seasonal patterns. For example, if we are working with monthly sales of toys, we will see that they are usually bought in December as gifts. In consequence, all the data points related to December will be correlated. Seasonality terms have associated P/Q terms, which are analogous to their nonseasonal p/q counterparts.

Getting ready

In order to run this recipe, you will need to install the `forecast` package via `install.packages("forecast")`.

How to do it...

In this recipe, we will work with a time series containing data for automobiles produced in Brazil from January 1981 to December 2018. The objective will be to model this series and ultimately make predictions:

1. We first load the dataset and we transform it into a time series object:

   ```
   library(forecast)
   car_production = read.csv(".../car_production.csv")
   car_production$indice_tiempo =
   as.Date(car_production$indice_tiempo,"%Y-%m-%d")
   car_production =
   ts(car_production$produccion_automotriz_unidades,start=c(1981,1),
   frequency = 12)
   ```

2. We then plot the series, as it can be seen it is non-stationary. A complex nonlinear trend could be fitted here, but we choose to remove the nonstationarity by differencing. The ACF shows two peaks at 12 and 24 lags. We can also see that there is a significative lag of order 1:

   ```
   plot.ts(car_production)
   ```

   The following output shows the car production series for Brazil:

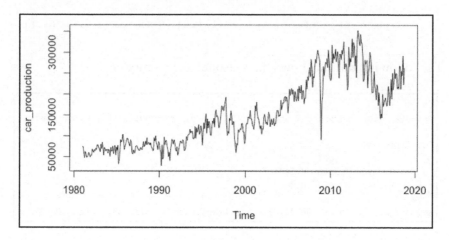

Then, run the following code:

```
acf(diff(car_production))
```

The series does not seem to be stationary because the mean of the series is very different from 1990 to 2020. This is to be expected, as Brazil's economy and population has grown substantially over the last 30 years. One way of fixing this is by taking first differences (note that we don't even need to do proper stationarity analysis—the non-stationarity is evident by looking at the series plot). The two significative lags at p=1 and 2 means that there is a strong seasonal component happening at 12 and 24 months (we should include them in our model):

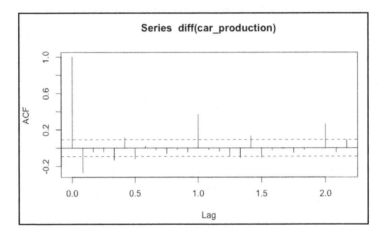

3. We then fit the model using p=1, P=2:

```
results <-
arima(car_production,order=c(1,1,0),seasonal=c(2,0,0,12))
results
```

The following output shows the seasonal `arima` model:

```
Call:
arima(x = car_production, order = c(1, 1, 0), seasonal = c(2, 0, 0, 12))

Coefficients:
          ar1     sar1     sar2
      -0.3343   0.3648   0.1494
s.e.   0.0447   0.0477   0.0482

sigma^2 estimated as 408522768:  log likelihood = -5135.38,  aic = 10278.77
```

4. Finally, we make predictions for the next two years, and then we plot them:

```
predictions <- forecast(results,24)
plot(predictions)
```

The following output shows the 24-month forecasts:

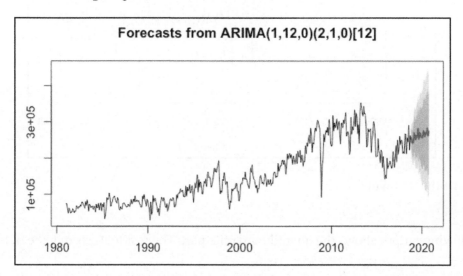

There's more...

We should always check whether the residuals are homoscedastic, whether they lack a structure, and whether they are Gaussian. In this case, there seems to be an increasing variance, and that makes us believe that the assumption of homoscedasticity is not satisfactory. The normality assumption seems plausible, a time series containing the amount of dollars sold to the market by the agricultural-export sector. though . Sometimes these problems (non-normality or heteroscedasticity) can be fixed by applying logarithsm the series:

```
plot.ts(results$residuals)
```

The following output shows the residuals:

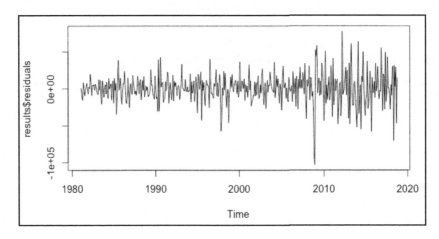

Then, type the following code:

```
qqnorm(results$residuals)
```

The following output shows the quantile-quantile plot. The residuals seem to be normal:

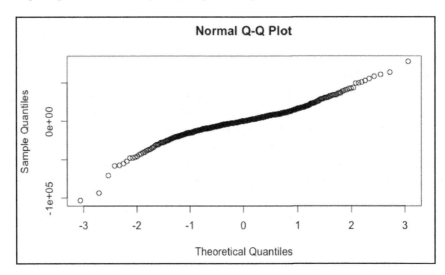

Choosing the best model with the forecast package

Based on the **partial autocorrelation function (PACF)** and ACF plots, we usually define a model that matches the data reasonably well. We can choose the best model by comparing their **Aikake information criterion (AIC)** values, and picking the model with the smallest value.

However, this is not very practical when we need to work with many time series. The forecast package offers a function that is quite often used in the industry, which is the auto.arima() function. With this function, we can specify the maximum number of p,q orders that we want to try, along with the maximum P,Q orders for the seasonal part. It has a very important parameter called stepwise, which governs how the search is done. If we want it done by searching among all possible models, we want stepwise=FALSE. It is certainly the best option when the model can be fitted quickly, but it is rather impractical for some cases. In those cases, we can specify stepwise=TRUE, and the algorithm will work similarly to the linear regression stepwise version (a variable is added, then the variable with the lowest significance is removed, and that process is repeated many times). The seasonal and stationary parameters can be used to restrict the search to nonseasonal models (or both seasonal and nonseasonal) and stationary models respectively (nonstationarity is detected by using appropriate statistical tests).

Getting ready

In order to run this recipe, you will need to install the forecast package via install.packages("forecast").

How to do it...

Temperature prediction is particularly important for electricity generation, because electricity demand is highly dependent on it. We will work with a monthly time series containing average temperatures for Buenos Aires, Argentina from January 2001 to December 2018. The objective is to use the `forecast` package to build a model automatically that can be used for prediction.

1. We load the `forecast` package, and then we load the temperature dataset, and we transform the data into a proper time series:

```
library(forecast)
average_temp = read.csv("./temperature.csv")
raverage_temp$indice_tiempo  =
as.Date(average_temp$indice_tiempo,"%Y-%m-%d")
average_temp  =
ts(average_temp$temperatura_promedio,start=c(2001,1),frequency =
12)
```

2. We plot the series, mainly to identify whether we have a trend, a seasonal component, and a nonzero mean. This series shows that no trend is discernible, and the seasonal component is very clear:

```
plot.ts(average_temp)
```

The following output shows the average temperatures for Buenos Aires, Argentina:

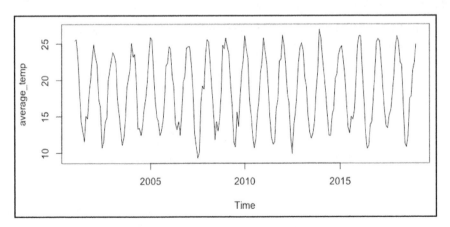

3. We run the `auto.arima` function, which will choose the best model for us. We set up a maximum AR `p order = 5`, a maximum MA `q order = 5`, a maximum seasonal `P = 2`, and a maximum seasonal `Q = 2` (we will capture up to two years of seasonal correlation). We want to search among seasonal models, because we know that temperature is, almost by definition, seasonal. Because the temperature should be nonzero on average, we will set up `allowmean=TRUE`. Because we don't think that there is a trend here, we should set up `allowdrift =FALSE`:

```
best_mode =
auto.arima(average_temp,max.p=5,max.q=5,max.Q=2,max.P=2,allowmean
= TRUE,allowdrift = FALSE)
```

The following output shows the best model found via the automatic `auto.arima` function:

```
Series: average_temp
ARIMA(0,0,1)(1,1,0)[12]

Coefficients:
          ma1      sar1
       0.1569   -0.4626
s.e.   0.0711    0.0635


sigma^2 estimated as 2.126:  log likelihood=-368.64
AIC=743.27    AICc=743.39    BIC=753.24
```

4. We now plot the series, along with the predicted values for it. Our predictions match the data very well, which should not be that surprising. The seasonal component is very large, and capturing it is usually not that hard:

```
plot.ts(average_temp)
lines(best_mode$fitted,col="red")
```

The following output shows the actual versus the predicted temperatures:

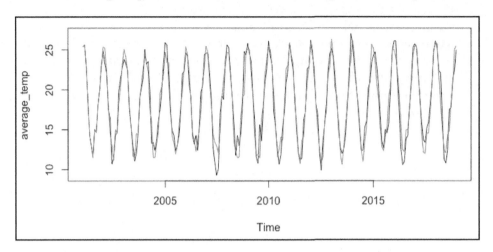

5. Finally, we plot the forecast for the next 48 months. The data is stored in the forecast table.

The following output shows the forecasts for the next 48 months:

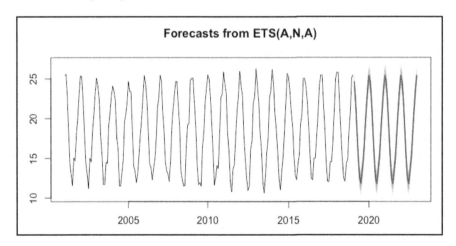

How it works...

Depending on whether `stepwise=FALSE` or `TRUE`, the `auto.arima` function will either compute either all the models up to a maximum p-q, or some of the models by iteratively adding and removing variables. Obviously, if we specify `seasonal=TRUE`, we will also consider the combinations now given by the seasonal P/Q terms.

Vector autoregressions (VARs)

Instead of working with just one time series, we could work with multiple series, exploiting the interrelationships between them. The true multivariate extension of ARIMA models are VARMA models, but they are rarely used in practice because they are very hard to fit. VAR models still offer us the possibility of modelling multiple time series, requiring rather loose assumptions, and a much simpler computational framework. This is an extension of the autoregressive (AR) models, where we model a time series in terms of its past.

These models arise when modeling related time series, where the past of a variable explains not only part of its own present, but also those of the rest of the variables. We will need essentially the same assumption that we required in terms of stationarity for ARIMA. Here, we will extend that to the multivariate case, and we will require that the roots of the inverse polynomial are outside the unit circle.

Getting ready

The `vars` package is needed for this recipe. It can be installed using `install.packages("vars")`.

How to do it...

In this recipe, we will work with multiple time series related to oil/gas in Argentina. The objective will be to model these series as a unique model, and then make predictions out of that model:

1. As usual, we first load the data:

```
library(vars)
oilgas = read.csv("./fuel_series.csv")
colnames(oilgas)    =
c("time_index","oil_processed","gasoil_prod","fueloil_prod","butane
```

```
")
joined_data = ts(oilgas[-1],start=c(1996,1),frequency=12)
```

2. Because the data is collected monthly, it is a good practice to set the lag number to 12 (this way, every month will be correlated to the same month in different years). But this is problematic in some ways, because it means that each equation will have 12 lags x 3 variables = 36 coefficients just for the endogenous part (we could also have a mean and trend for each equation, which will require more parameters).

   Many of those coefficients won't be significative, so we can use an automatic method to discard those lags/coefficients based on their t-values/p-values. If we choose to use `restrict()` and pass `method=ser`, the internal algorithm will remove all coefficients smaller than the `thresh=` value, which is 2 by default. The practical consequence of having a smaller/simpler model is that the confidence intervals for the predictions will be smaller:

   ```
   m = VAR(joined_data,p=12)
   restrict(m, method = "ser")
   ```

3. The very first thing that needs to be done here is to check that all the roots of the model are smaller than 1 in modulus. If not, the model needs to be fixed (possibly by differencing the variables). A non-stationary VAR model yields large confidence intervals and is not practical in any way. As we can see here, our model is fine:

   ```
   any(roots(m)>0.9999)
   ```

   We get the following output:

   ```
   > any(roots(m)>0.9999)
   [1] FALSE
   ```

4. The residuals should be checked. They should be homoscedastic, Gaussian, and with no structure. In our case, they almost look good, except for the fact that the Gaussian hypothesis is rejected. Fixing non-normality is much harder in VAR than in univariate AR models. One possibility is to take logs for each for each variable; nevertheless, we decide to continue with our model. We essentially get one of these plots for each variable:

   ```
   normalitytest <- normality.test(m)
   plot(normalitytest)
   ```

The following output shows the **Residuals** graph:

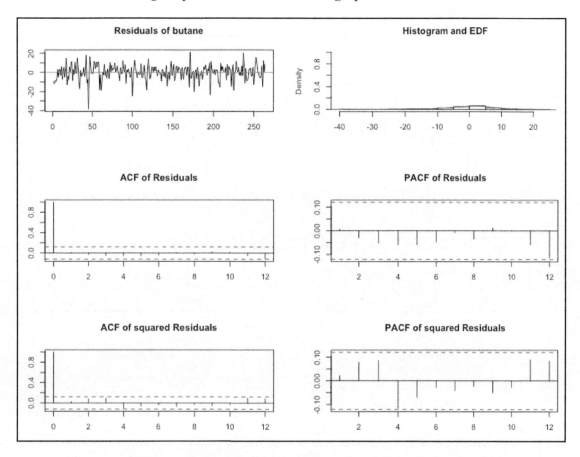

5. We can plot the actual versus the predicted values. When calling `plot`, we will get one of these plots for each variable. The model fits reasonably well, except for an obvious outlier in the first part of the series:

```
plot(m)
```

The following screenshot shows the **Diagram of fit and residuals for gasoil_prod**:

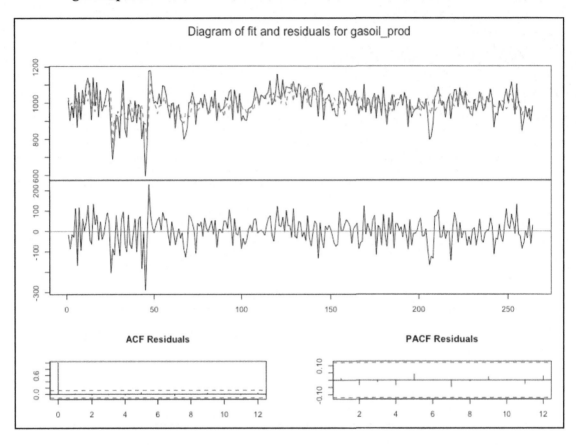

6. We then plot the forecast error decomposition: this shows how much of each variable's variability is explained by each variable. The interaction is not very relevant, and each series seems to be explained solely by itself.

The following output shows the forecast error decomposition decomposition, the processed oil explains most its variability. And it also explains a substantial amount of variability for the rest:

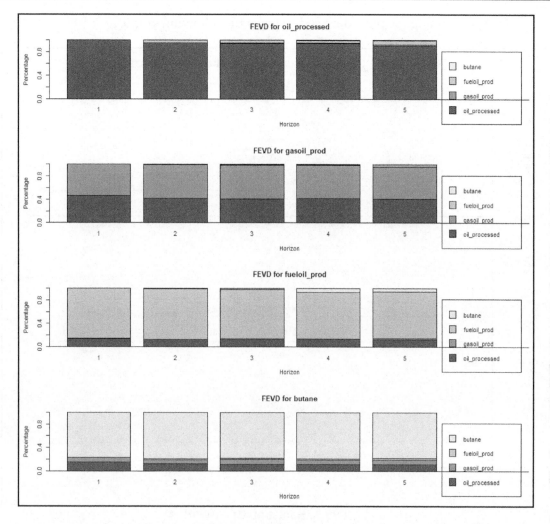

7. One usual output for VAR models are the `impulse-response` functions, which show how an impact on one variable impacts another variable. Let's see, for example, how `oil_processed` impacts the `butane`/`gasoil`/`fueloil` production: evidently, an increase in the production causes an impact on the three other series; that fades to zero after two periods (the red lines show the bootstrapped confidence intervals):

```
var.2c.irf <- irf(m, impulse = "oil_processed",
response = c("butane", "gasoil_prod", "fueloil_prod"), boot = TRUE)
plot(var.2c.irf)
```

After running the preceding code, we get the following output:

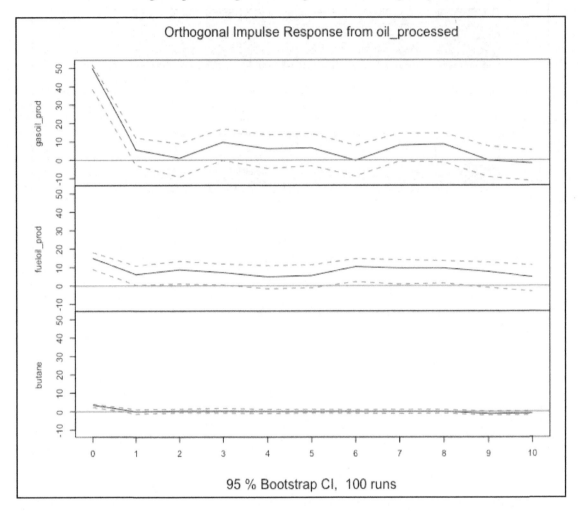

8. Finally, we predict the values for the next 2 years (24 months). The following output shows these forecasts:

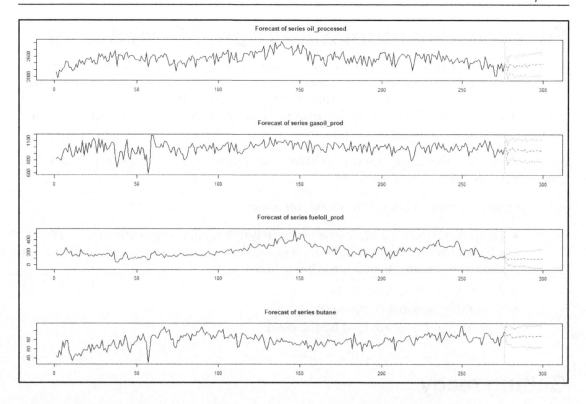

How it works...

Essentially, VAR models are the multivariate extensions of AR models. Each one of the equations is estimated via **ordinary least squares (OLS)**. Each one of these equations will contain a total amount of coefficients: `number of variables x lags + trend + mean`.

The advantage of VAR models is that we can incorporate several variables, thus increasing the predictive power of the model compared to fitting each model individually. But this should be done with some care, because the more irrelevant variables that we add, the wider the confidence intervals will be for the predictions.

Facebook's automatic Prophet forecasting

Facebook's core data science team has developed and released an automatic tool for large-scale forecasting. It does a particularly great job with highly seasonal time series, and series with complex trends. Prophet's internal algorithm for detecting trend breakpoints is particularly interesting. Even though it works with any periodicity, it works best with daily data.

Although the algorithm can be used with little to no time series knowledge, experienced users can tweak many of its parameters.

According to its documentation, it has four components:

- Trend detection via a piecewise linear trend, or nonlinear growth curves. This is relevant because some of the time series tasks that Facebook has encountered are phenomena where the data reaches saturation.
- A yearly seasonal component.
- A monthly seasonal component.
- A list of holidays (provided by the user).

Getting ready

In order to run this package, you need to install the `prophet` package using `install.packages("prophet")`.

How to do it...

In this example, we will work with a time series containing the amount of US dollars sold to the market by Argentina's agricultural-export sector from January 2003 to December 2018. We will let Prophet get the best model for us:

1. First, we load `prophet`:

```
library(prophet)
```

2. We load the dataset from Argentina's open data website. Then, we transform the date column into proper R dates:

```
currency_sales = read.csv("./sold_usd_oilseeds.csv")
```

3. We transform the names: Prophet expects two columns, one for the dates, and another one for the actual values, with the names needing to be `ds/y` respectively:

```
currency_sales$indice_tiempo =
as.Date(currency_sales$indice_tiempo,"%Y-%m-%d")
colnames(currency_sales) = c("ds","y")
```

4. After this, we fit the model. We pass three `changepoints`, reflecting the presidential elections of 2003, 2007, 2011, and 2015. Any variable that we expect will produce significant changes can be added here:

```
model <-
prophet::prophet(currency_sales,changepoints=c("2003-10-01","2007-1
0-01","2011-10-01", "2015-10-01"))
```

5. We prepare our prediction dataset using Prophet's `make_future_dataframe`. It can contain the modeling data, depending on whether or not we specify `include_history=TRUE`:

```
future <-
prophet::make_future_dataframe(model,periods=36,freq="month",includ
e_history = TRUE)
```

6. We then predict the dataset that we have just generated (it will obviously also include the predictions for the modeling dataset, as well):

```
preds <- predict(model,future)
```

7. Finally, we plot the results. This contains both the point estimates (predictions) and the appropriate confidence intervals. Even though Prophet shines with daily data, it also works quite well with monthly data. It is important to note that the dataset that we are using is not particularly large (it only has 10 years' worth of monthly data):

```
plot(model,preds)
```

The following output shows Prophet's predictions and the actual versus the observed data:

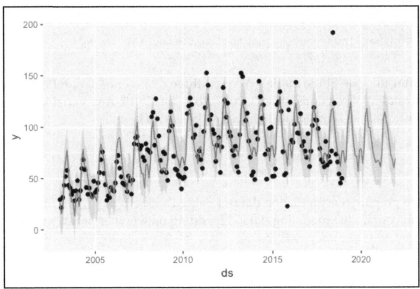

How it works...

Prophet is designed to work with business time series, which means that it can handle changes in trends, holidays, and seasonality well.

There's more...

Even though `prophet` is a very robust package, don't expect it to find extraordinary patterns in the data. Here, we are loading the beer prices for Argentina from 1994 to 2005, but will cut the data off at 2001 and will estimate our model, assuming we hadn't seen what happened after December 2001. Prophet's results look reasonable, with a variance (forecast band) that grows as we go farther into the future. The problem here, is that Argentina had a huge crisis in December 2001, which caused major economic and political upheavals. This generated a massive depreciation in its currency, which jumped around 200% over the following years. This caused the inflation rate to increase dramatically, and all prices, including beer's, more than tripled:

```
beer_prices = read.csv("beer_prices.csv")
beer_prices$indice_tiempo  = as.Date(beer_prices$indice_tiempo, "%Y-%m-%d")
```

```
colnames(beer_prices) = c("ds","y")
beer_prices1 = beer_prices[1:106,]
model <- prophet::prophet(beer_prices1)
future <-
prophet::make_future_dataframe(model,periods=48,freq="month",include_histor
y = TRUE)
preds <- predict(model,future)
plot(model,preds)
```

The following output shows Prophet's forecast:

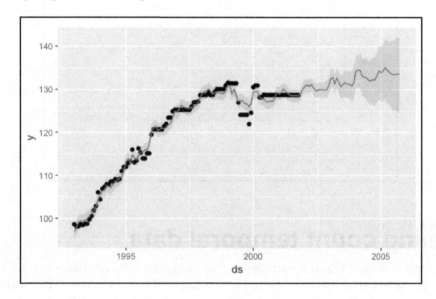

In fact, if we do `tail(preds)[,c(1,16)]`, we get that the predictions are actually 133 for Q3-2005, when the actual values (obtained by doing `tail(beer_prices)`) were around 850. In fact, the actual values can be plotted via `plot(ts(beer_prices$y, frequency=12, start=c(1993,1)))`. As we can see, there is no possible way to predict what happened after 2001 if we only have data up to 2001.

The following output shows the more complicated case—Full series after 2001. It's not possible to predict what happened after 2001:

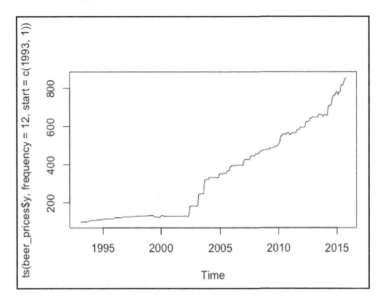

Modeling count temporal data

So far, we have assumed that the variable we are modeling behaves like a real number, taking any possible value. This is reflected in the fact that we assume that the current value of the series is equal to the previous value, plus some Gaussian noise. But this is not very useful when we modeling count data, such as the number of clients, or the number of insurance claims, and so on. When these numbers are large, the discreteness of the data is not a huge problem, but when we're modeling events that occur on a small scale, the consequences of ignoring the discreteness are much worse.

The tscount package allows us to model count time series, if the data follows a Poisson or negative binomial distribution. The framework is rooted in **generalized linear models (GLMs)**, using previous values of the series to predict the current ones.

Getting ready

In order to run this recipe, you need to install the tscount package using install.packages("tscount").

How to do it...

In this recipe, we will attempt to predict FC Barcelona's goals throughout the 2017/18 season, using some covariates and the club's previous goals. This will expose the many difficulties that exist when working with sports; even after using several important covariates, we won't be doing any better than just using the average for FC Barcelona's goals for that season (2.60):

1. First, we load the dataset and create a dummy variable for home/away. We transform the dates, so we can compute the time difference between two games (we suspect that the number of days has a positive effect on the number of goals):

    ```
    library("tscount")
    library(dummy)
    library(dplyr)
    data                = read.table("./E1.txt",sep="\t",head=T)
    data$home_away      = ifelse(data$ha == "H", 1, 0)
    data$date           = as.Date(data$date,format="%m/%d/%Y")
    data                = data %>% mutate(diff_days = as.numeric(date-
    lag(date)))
    data[is.na(data)]   = 0
    ```

2. We formulate our model, using the following variables: whether Barcelona was playing at home or away; the position in the league for the opposing team; the difference in days; and whether there was a Champions League game after that game (we suspect that the best players are not used for these games), or before that game (players can get injured after Champions League games). We specify 1,2,3 lagged values for the dependent variable—the idea is the following: after scoring lots of goals, we would expect the next game to also see lots of goals being scored (a positive autocorrelation). But these results are not encouraging: all the coefficients have large standard errors (so the confidence intervals on the last columns show that all of them include a zero). The beta coefficients relate to the lagged values for the number of goals (three lags – three coefficients). Replace by this: The eta ones relate to the regressors: for example eta_1 corresponds to whether the game was played home/away; if the 95% confidence interval did not include the zero, we would be able to say that playing home makes the team more likely to score - since the coefficient is positive. It is important to state that because neither coefficient is significative, we can't really make any inference here:

    ```
    seatbeltsfit <- tsglm(data$Goals, model = list(past_obs = c(1:3)),
    link = "log", distr = "poisson",xreg
    =   cbind(data$home_away,data$pos,data$diff_days,
    data$champions_next_days_after,data$champions_next_days_before))
    ```

The following output shows the estimated model coefficients:

```
Call:
tsglm(ts = data$Goals, model = list(past_obs = c(1:3)), xreg = cbind(data$home_away,
    data$pos, data$diff_days, data$champions_next_days_after,
    data$champions_next_days_before), link = "log", distr = "poisson")

Coefficients:
            Estimate  Std.Error  CI(lower)  CI(upper)
(Intercept)  0.74618    0.5976    -0.4251     1.9175
beta_1       0.24035    0.2854    -0.3190     0.7997
beta_2      -0.27568    0.2969    -0.8576     0.3063
beta_3      -0.03185    0.2717    -0.5644     0.5007
eta_1        0.26207    0.2425    -0.2133     0.7374
eta_2        0.01427    0.0195    -0.0239     0.0524
eta_3        0.00574    0.0330    -0.0589     0.0704
eta_4       -0.02630    0.2783    -0.5718     0.5192
eta_5       -0.18015    0.2641    -0.6978     0.3375
Standard errors and confidence intervals (level =  95 %) obtained
by normal approximation.

Link function: log
Distribution family: poisson
Number of coefficients: 9
Log-likelihood: -64.84624
AIC: 147.6925
BIC: 162.4308
QIC: 147.6925
```

3. Let's assume we want to predict the next Barcelona game, played at home against a team that ranks seventh in the domestic league, and played after a Champions League game. We get 1.86 goals, and for the same game played away we get 1.43 (which makes sense because teams always perform better when playing at home). And what happens if the next game is against that very same team, but with no Champions League game in between or after? Then, we get 1.76 goals. It is important to realize that these are the conditional mean predictions for a Poisson distribution (the lambda parameter), so these numbers should be rounded in order to present them. Here, we are just taking the prediction, but we also get confidence intervals that we can use (all of them will be bounded by zero). If we wanted to predict the next two games, we would need to pass a matrix with two rows (remember that the predicted values at $t+k$ are reused to compute the predicted ones at $t+k+1$):

```
J = matrix(c(1,7,10,1,1),c(1,5))
predict(seatbeltsfit, n.ahead = 1,  level   = 0.9, global   = TRUE,B
= 2000, newxreg = J)$pred
J = matrix(c(0,7,10,1,1),c(1,5))
```

```
predict(seatbeltsfit, n.ahead = 1,   level    = 0.9, global   = TRUE,
B        = 2000, newxreg = J)$pred
J = matrix(c(0,7,10,0,0),c(1,5))
predict(seatbeltsfit, n.ahead = 1,   level    = 0.9, global   = TRUE,
B        = 2000,   newxreg = J)$pred
```

4. Finally, we can plot the fitted versus the actual values, and as we would expect, they exhibit a very bad fit. The model is unable to predict why Barcelona scores more than two goals:

```
library(ggplot2)
frame = data.frame(true_vals = model$response, fit =
round(model$fitted.values))
ggplot(frame,aes(1:38)) + geom_line(aes(y = true_vals, colour =
"Observed goals")) + geom_line(aes(y = fit,  colour = "predicted
goals"))
```

The following output shows the predicted and observed goals for FC Barcelona:

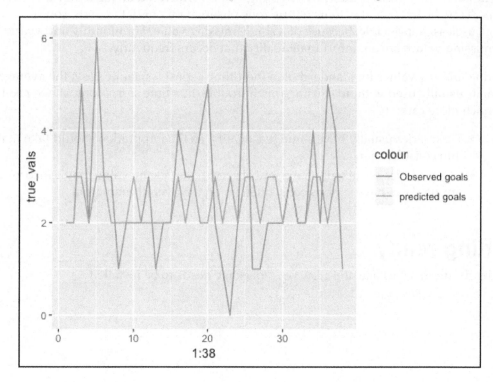

There's more...

We used a temporal model to capture the fact that teams scoring lots of goals for a game, will likely be scoring lots of goals for the next ones. This example shows the enormous complications of predicting sports events: they are impacted by psychological factors, the exact team composition, the styles of both teams, the strategy designed by the manager, and even the weather. Some of these variables can be collected, and some of them are just impossible to get.

The final complication is that we can never have too many observations, since sports seasons are limited, and each season implies very different team dynamics.

Imputing missing values in time series

Unfortunately, time series usually ave missing values, which can be caused by a variety of reasons. Time series data, due to its nature (one observation per data point), could become useless, in principle, because of a single missing value. For monthly and yearly data, missing values are an unfortunate reality that occurs frequently.

Imputing missing values for standard data (non-time series) is usually easy: the average or median is usually used without causing much trouble. In a time series context, we need to take much more care:

- Time series usually have some seasonality, so the imputation should take that into consideration
- In time series we usually have few observations, so any value that is incorrectly imputed can have serious consequences on the overall estimation

Getting ready

In order to run this package, the `imputeTS` package needs to be installed using `install.packages("imputeTS")`.

How to do it...

The `imputeTS` package is incredibly powerful and easy to use; it can be used to impute missing values for time series. In this recipe, we will load a dataset containing biodiesel production figures for Argentina (this is a monthly dataset from 2008 to 2018 containing monthly production values):

1. First, we load the `imputeTS` package and the necessary dataset:

```
library(imputeTS)
library(ggplot2)
biodisel_prod = read.csv("./biodiesel.csv")
biodisel_prod$indice_tiempo =
as.Date(biodisel_prod$indice_tiempo,"%Y-%m-%d")
```

2. We will remove six observations and use the Kalman filter approach to replace the missing values. There are multiple ways of imputing these missing values:

```
biodisel_prod$indice_tiempo =
as.Date(biodisel_prod$indice_tiempo,"%Y-%m-%d")
biodisel_prod_removed = biodisel_prod
biodisel_prod_removed[c(30,60,90,100,109,120),2] <- NA
biodisel_prod_removed = na.kalman(biodisel_prod_removed)
```

3. We now plot the results. In order to do that, we will get the dates for the missing values (those will be used to create vertical lines in the plot). We will plot two lines; a red one containing the series with the imputed values, and another one in black containing the real values. As it can be seen here, the imputation makes a lot of sense, and the imputed values are not distant from from the actual values (we are painting the points that have been removed in gray):

```
miss_lines = biodisel_prod_removed[c(30,60,90,100,109,120),1]
plot(biodisel_prod_removed,type="l",col="red",lwd=6,xlab="Time",ylab="biodiesel_production")
abline(v = miss_lines[1], untf = FALSE,col="gray")
abline(v = miss_lines[2], untf = FALSE,col="gray")
abline(v = miss_lines[3], untf = FALSE,col="gray")
abline(v = miss_lines[4], untf = FALSE,col="gray")
abline(v = miss_lines[5], untf = FALSE,col="gray")
abline(v = miss_lines[6], untf = FALSE,col="gray")
lines(biodisel_prod,type="l",pch=15)
```

The following output shows the true time series in black, and the imputed time series in red:

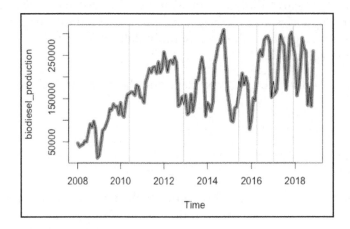

How it works...

The data is transformed into a state-space model, and the values are replaced using the Kalman filter.

The idea behind the state space representation, is to cast a time series as a set of inputs, states and outputs that evolve through time. The Kalman filter is an algorithm that allows us to operationally work with these models.

A good introduction to the Kalman filter can be found on `https://www.google.com/search?q=klaman+filterrlz=1C1GCEA_enGB822GB822oq=klaman+filteraqs=chrome..69i57j0l5.94505j0j7sourceid=chromeie=UTF-8`.

There's more...

The package has lots of functions that are quite useful, such as: `na.seadec`, which replaces the missing values by an appropriate technique after the seasonality has been removed; `na.replace`, which can be used to replace the values with a fixed value; or `na.random`, which replaces the missing values with a random value.

The package offers some nice plots, such as the following one. Both show the distribution of missing values. This is useful for understanding patterns in the not available (NA) values and helps us to investigate what caused them:

```
biodisel_prod_removed = biodisel_prod
biodisel_prod_removed[c(30,60,90,100,109,120),2] <- NA
plotNA.distribution(biodisel_prod_removed$biodisel_produccion)
plotNA.distributionBar(biodisel_prod_removed$biodisel_produccion)
```

The following output shows the **Distribution of NAs**:

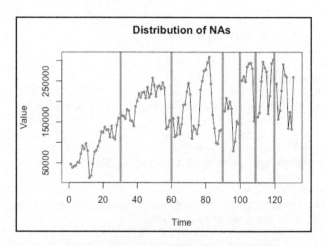

The following output shows the **Percentage Distribution of NAs**:

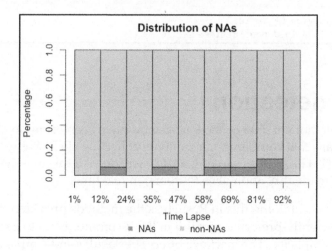

It can also generate nice metrics and outputs that are mostly useful for reporting:

```
statsNA(biodisel_prod_removed$biodisel_produccion)
```

The following output shows the missing values metrics:

```
[1] "Length of time series:"
[1] 131
[1] "------------------------"
[1] "Number of Missing Values:"
[1] 6
[1] "------------------------"
[1] "Percentage of Missing Values:"
[1] "4.58%"
[1] "------------------------"
[1] "Stats for Bins"
[1] "  Bin 1 (33 values from 1 to 33) :       1 NAs (3.03%)"
[1] "  Bin 2 (33 values from 34 to 66) :      1 NAs (3.03%)"
[1] "  Bin 3 (33 values from 67 to 99) :      1 NAs (3.03%)"
[1] "  Bin 4 (32 values from 100 to 131) :     3 NAs (9.38%)"
[1] "------------------------"
[1] "Longest NA gap (series of consecutive NAs)"
[1] "1 in a row"
[1] "------------------------"
[1] "Most frequent gap size (series of consecutive NA series)"
[1] "1 NA in a row (occuring 6 times)"
[1] "------------------------"
[1] "Gap size accounting for most NAs"
[1] "1 NA in a row (occuring 6 times, making up for overall 6 NAs)"
[1] "------------------------"
[1] "Overview NA series"
[1] "  1 NA in a row: 6 times"
```

Anomaly detection

In recent years, a plethora of data collection systems have been set up in almost every company. This means that companies are not only collecting clicks/views/logins, but they are also gathering IT data such as server load/IoT sensors. All this massive influx of data has created a need to identify anomalies (outliers) in real time.

There are several ways of doing this in R, such as the methods provided in the `tsoutliers` package, but the currently-preferred method in the R community is to use the `anomalize` package due to its simplicity. This package offers spectacular and simple plots, separating out seasonality, outliers, trends, and residuals/remainders.

Getting ready

The `anomalize` package needs to be installed using `install.packages("anomalize")`.

How to do it...

We will use the `anomalize` package to detect outliers for a time series containing the amount of dollars sold to the market by the agricultural-export sector.

1. First, we load the necessary libraries:

   ```
   library(anomalize)
   library(dplyr)
   library(tibbletime)
   ```

2. We load the time series for US dollars sold by farmers in Argentina:

   ```
   currency_sales = read.csv("./sold_usd_oilseeds.csv")
   currency_sales$indice_tiempo =
   as.Date(currency_sales$indice_tiempo,"%Y-%m-%d")
   ```

3. We then do the anomaly detection, which has several components. First, we transform the dataset into a `tibbletime` object, and then we decompose the time series into trend, seasonality, and remainder components. Second, we detect the anomalies using the remainder, and we finally join everything back together using `time_recompose()`. After that, we can plot the result using `plot_anomaly_decomposition`:

   ```
   results_anomalies =
   tibbletime::as_tbl_time(currency_sales,indice_tiempo)
   %>%time_decompose
   (promedio_diario,
   merge = TRUE) %>%
   anomalize(remainder) %>% time_recompose()
   results_anomalies %>%
   plot_anomaly_decomposition(ncol=3,alpha_dots = 0.3)
   ```

The following output shows the decomposition of the series into seasons, trend, and remainders, with anomalies painted in red:

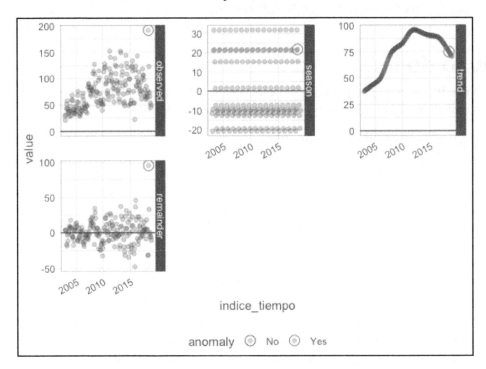

How it works...

The idea is first to remove the trend and the seasonality using the underlying `stl()` function in R. After that is done, the remainder is obtained, and the anomaly detection algorithm runs using that series of residuals.

There's more...

The number of anomalies can be adjusted using two parameters: the alpha that controls the amplitude of what is considered normal. If a value is outside those normal values (for the remainder, this is after the trend and seasonality have been removed), it is then considered to be an anomaly.

If the alpha is reduced to 0.1, we will be lowering the threshold, and more anomalies will appear. On the other hand, we can set `max_anoms=0.02` meaning that, at most, 2% of the data could be considered to be anomalies:

```
results_anomalies = tibbletime::as_tbl_time(currency_sales,indice_tiempo)
%>%time_decompose(promedio_diario, merge = TRUE) %>%
anomalize(remainder,alpha=0.10,max_anoms=0.02) %>% time_recompose()
results_anomalies %>% plot_anomaly_decomposition(ncol=3,alpha_dots = 0.3)
```

The following screenshot shows the detected anomalies in red:

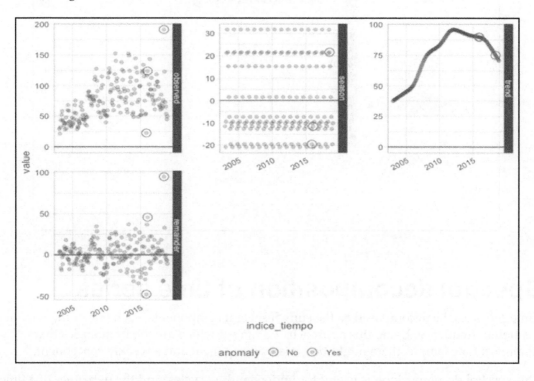

We can use a different algorithm to detect the trend. The `method="twitter"` overrides the default **interquartile range (IQR)** and yields multiple pieces of linear trends. The selection of the best algorithm depends on the actual data. If the data appears to have a piecewise linear structure, the twitter is more appropriate:

```
results_anomalies = tibbletime::as_tbl_time(currency_sales,indice_tiempo)
%>% time_decompose(promedio_diario, merge = TRUE,method="twitter") %>%
anomalize(remainder,alpha=0.10,max_anoms=0.02) %>% time_recompose()
results_anomalies %>% plot_anomaly_decomposition(ncol=3,alpha_dots = 0.3)
```

Take a look at the following screenshot:

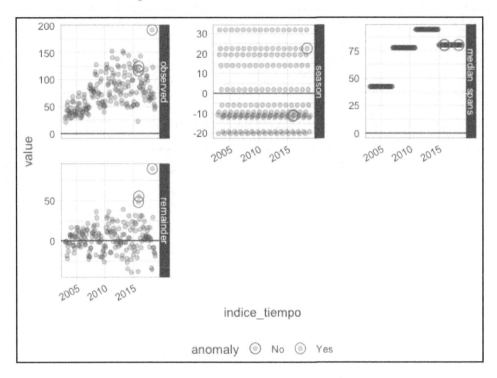

Spectral decomposition of time series

Time series can be decomposed as the sum of several components, each one of them having a different frequency. Using this approach, we can see which are the frequencies that dominate: for example, there might be a yearly component and a weekly component.

This spectral decomposition is useful for understanding cycles, and the dynamics of a time series. It can also be used as a preliminary tool for studying seasonality in detail. This knowledge can then be used to choose the right seasonality structure for removal from the series.

Getting ready

In order to run this recipe, the `timesboot` package needs to be installed using `install.packages()`.

How to do it...

We will work with the steel production for Argentina. This is a monthly series collected from January 1993 to December 2018. We will analyze this time series according to its spectral density:

1. First, we load the dataset and we plot it. The evident problem here is that the series has a trend. Spectral analysis cannot be carried out with a trend, because low-frequency components will dominate (think of the trend as a component transmitting information between data points, separated through time). The more linear the trend is, the more profound this effect will be. Note that this trend is nonlinear:

```
library(imputeTS)
library(timesboot)
butane =  read.csv("./steel.csv")
butane = ts(butane$valor,start=c(1993,1),frequency = 12)
plot.ts(butane)
spectrum(butane, spans = c(5, 7),lty = 1)
```

The following output shows the steel time series:

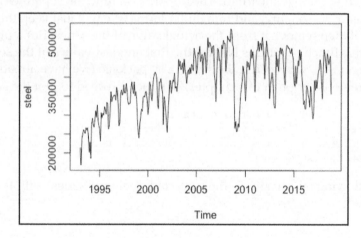

The impact of not removing the trend can be seen here, and essentially the whole spectrum is governed by the low-frequency components:

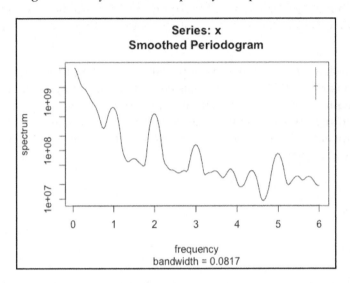

2. We need to remove the trend. The `decompose` function separates a time series into trend, seasonality, and remainder terms. We will just keep the trend part, but will then remove it from the actual value of the series. But a problem arises here: this function returns NA for the first and last values of the series. In order to correct that, we will use the `imputeTS` package (we have already introduced it in a previous recipe in this chapter). We then proceed to plot the series:

```
steel_trend  = decompose(steel)
corrected = steel - steel_trend$trend
corrected = imputeTS::na.kalman(corrected)
plot.ts(corrected)
```

The following output shows the corrected steel time series, with the trend removed:

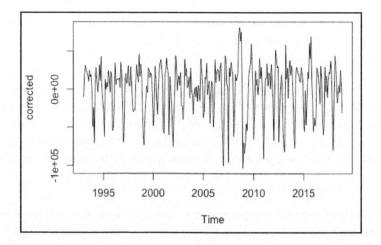

3. The spectrum option can be used to plot the smoothed spectrum. We need to define a window in order to get the smoothing done. See how the low frequencies have disappeared after the trend was removed? But the question is whether the peaks at **1** and **2** are statistically significative (the blue bar represents the 95% confidence bands. What this plot is telling us is that the frequencies at 12 months and 24 months are important:

```
spectrum(corrected, spans = c(5, 7),lty = 1)
```

The smoothed periodogram shows the importance for each frequency:

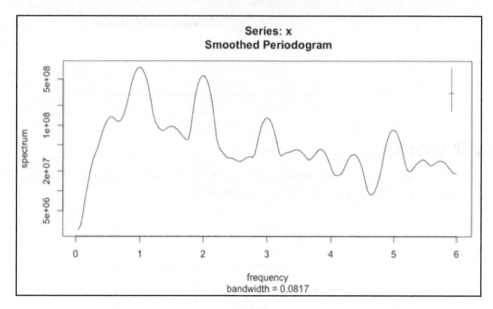

4. A similar approach uses the `timesboot` package to get a similar plot, with 95% confidence intervals. intervals. Note that in this case, we get the bands for each frequency (and not global bands as we had before). Both of the peaks at **1** and **2** are clearly significant (here, we are interested in how much the lower line is above **0**). We can see that for frequencies above 2.5, the lower band seems to be almost **0**. What this means is that we have statistical evidence that there are two cycles on this series, at 12 months and 24 months, that are very important, and not much more. This is probably caused by a strong seasonality pattern—the demand for steel is typically similar for the same months across different years:

```
td = timesboot::boot_spec(corrected, de_trend = FALSE)
```

The bootstrapped periodogram shows the precision for each frequency (wider is less precise):

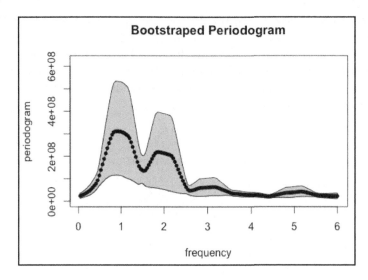

How it works...

The `timesboot` package works by bootstrapping the time series (essentially splitting it into pieces and resampling those pieces with replacements).

8

Mixed Effects Models

We will cover the following recipes in this chapter:

- The standard model and ANOVA
- Some useful plots for mixed effects models
- Nonlinear mixed effects models
- Crossed and nested designs
- Robust mixed effects models with `robustlmm`
- Choosing the best linear mixed model
- Mixed generalized linear models

Introduction

In `Chapter 2`, *Univariate and Multivariate Tests for Equality of Means,* we discussed mixed effects models in the context of the **analysis of variance (ANOVA)**. These models arise when we have a mixture of fixed and random effects. Fixed effects are associated to standard coefficients that appear in every regression problem, and random effects are variance components that govern shocks that are shared by members of the same groups. For example, the grades of any student can be thought of as the sum of how many hours the student spent studying (this would be the fixed effect) and a random shock that is shared across all students from the same school. The idea is to capture that students belonging to the same school to have correlated grades.

The standard model and ANOVA

In this recipe, we will be more interested in the regression part of it, instead of the ANOVA part. In the previous ANOVA chapter, we only used random effects for the intercepts, and this is usually not the price only way that random effects are introduced. Imagine that we model the sales in terms of price for certain customers, where we have several observations for each one of them. The **ordinary least squares (OLS)** standard approach would be to ignore this heterogeneity and pool all the observations together.

Naturally, this would introduce a problem, because the residuals would then be correlated (observations belonging to the same individual will produce similar residuals). The correct approach would be to introduce a random effect per individual, but there is a subtle point here: we are not expecting the response to differ in terms of an intercept, but in terms of the coefficient that relates prices to sales. More formally, we would expect that the coefficient relating prices to sales, would be equal to a fixed coefficient (an average/standard effect) plus an individual effect. Of course, if we look at the aggregate picture, the random effect does not really change our price-sales relationship, we will be more interested in the regression part of it, instead of the ANOVA part..

Getting ready

The `lme4` package is needed for this recipe, and it can be installed using `install.packages("lme4")`.

How to do it...

In the following exercise, we will model the amount deposited by clients, based on just two variables:

- The amount of time that each salesperson spent on the client
- The number of salespeople involved with the specific client

1. We first load our dataset:

```
data = read.csv("./sample_random_regression.csv")
data$clientid = as.factor(data$clientid)
library("lme4")
```

2. In order to practice with different formulations, let's start with the most complex one. Here, we have an intercept and two coefficients (one for each fixed effect). We then have a random effect for both the salespeople involved and the time spent on the deal. Because we added two terms for the parts involving the client IDs, we assume that the shocks impacting each variable will not be correlated:

```
lmer(data=data, deal_size ~ salespeople_involved + time_spent_deal +
(-1 + salespeople_involved|clientid)
+ (-1 + time_spent_deal|clientid) )
```

The following screenshot shows the estimated mixed model:

```
Linear mixed model fit by REML ['lmerMod']
Formula: deal_size ~ salespeople_involved + time_spent_deal + (-1 + salespeople_involved |
    clientid) + (-1 + time_spent_deal | clientid)
   Data: data
REML criterion at convergence: 774.8291
Random effects:
 Groups      Name                   Std.Dev.
 clientid    salespeople_involved   2.297
 clientid.1  time_spent_deal        1.266
 Residual                          10.244
Number of obs: 100, groups:  clientid, 10
Fixed Effects:
         (Intercept)   salespeople_involved        time_spent_deal
          48.833                 1.956                  2.759
```

3. This is a similar model, now with an intercept, two fixed effects, and a random slope for only the salespeople involved. A subtle detail here is that we assume that the shocks impacting the slope and the intercept might be correlated:

```
lmer(data=data, deal_size ~ salespeople_involved + time_spent_deal +
(1  + salespeople_involved|clientid))
```

The following screenshot shows the estimated model:

```
Linear mixed model fit by REML ['lmerMod']
Formula: deal_size ~ salespeople_involved + time_spent_deal + (1 + salespeople_involved |        clientid)
   Data: data
REML criterion at convergence: 773.9846
Random effects:
 Groups    Name                   Std.Dev. Corr
 clientid (Intercept)              7.816
          salespeople_involved    1.980    0.49
 Residual                        10.350
Number of obs: 100, groups:  clientid, 10
Fixed Effects:
         (Intercept)  salespeople_involved       time_spent_deal
              50.295                  1.627                 2.739
```

4. Another model could have these three random effects: one for the intercept,
   another one for the time spent, and a final one for the salespeople involved. Here,
   we allow for nonzero correlation between the three of them:

```
lmer(data=data, deal_size ~ salespeople_involved + time_spent_deal +
(1  + time_spent_deal
+   salespeople_involved|clientid))
```

Mixed model result—allowing for correlation between the variables and
intercept:

```
Linear mixed model fit by REML ['lmerMod']
Formula: deal_size ~ salespeople_involved + time_spent_deal + (1 + time_spent_deal +        salespeople_involved | clientid)
   Data: data
REML criterion at convergence: 768.192
Random effects:
 Groups    Name                 Std.Dev. Corr
 clientid (Intercept)            6.624
          time_spent_deal        1.046    -0.24
          salespeople_involved  2.057    -0.31 1.00
 Residual                        9.959
Number of obs: 100, groups:  clientid, 10
Fixed Effects:
         (Intercept)  salespeople_involved       time_spent_deal
              49.50                  1.86                  2.71
convergence code 0; 1 optimizer warnings; 0 lme4 warnings
```

5. Finally, let's suppose we choose the initial formulation, and we want to predict the differences (predictions) for each group, for each random effect. We can do this with the `ranef` function. For example, `client_id=1`, has a predicted smaller `salespeople_involved`–`deal_size` relationship than the average client. A very similar interpretation follows for same client for the `time_spent_deal`. `Client = 8` has a positive and abnormally large response to the `salespeople_involved` variable: each extra person involved in dealing with this client yields a much larger response in the deal size than for the other groups:

```
model = lmer(data=data,deal_size ~ salespeople_involved +
time_spent_deal + (-1
+  salespeople_involved|clientid) + (-1 + time_spent_deal|clientid)
)
ranef(model)
```

Take a look at the following screenshot:

```
$clientid
     salespeople_involved time_spent_deal
1             -1.2168381      -1.2586696
2             -0.9524152      -1.0154345
3             -0.5808371       0.7857888
4             -1.9134247      -0.4041685
5              2.2273657       0.4613553
6              1.5211412       1.1708320
7             -2.8446889      -1.3699988
8              2.6419682       1.5660341
9              2.5395813       0.6396795
10            -1.4218524      -0.5754181

with conditional variances for "clientid"
```

How it works...

Linear mixed effects models can be estimated using different techniques. The `lmer` function uses penalized weighted-least squares. A very detailed discussion on the algorithm can be found at `https://cran.r-project.org/web/packages/lme4/vignettes/Theory.pdf`.

Some useful plots for mixed effects models

In this recipe, we will explore some interesting plots that are for presenting and analyzing the results from mixed effects models. In the simplest formulation of mixed effects models, we have a random intercept by group. Every observation belonging to the same group will share that very same shock, rendering all of them correlated. But this can be extended to other coefficients (not just the intercept). We could have yet another coefficient, that is, beta would be the sum of `beta1` (which would be fixed) and `beta_random` (this would be a random effect). What this would imply is that the slope relating to the regressor and the response, would have two parts: a part that is the same for all the observations, and another part that depends on each group.

Getting ready

The `dplyr`, `lme4`, and `ggplot2` packages are required for this recipe. They can be installed using `install.packages()`.

How to do it...

In this recipe, we will work with the same dataset that we used before. It contains `clientid`, `deal_size`, `salespeople_involved`, and `time_spent_deal`. `deal_size` is the target variable, and the two variables that we have are the number of salespeople involved and the time spent on each deal. Both are expected to have a positive effect on the deal size.

1. We first load the necessary dataset and libraries:

```
library(dplyr)
library("lme4")
library(ggplot2)
data = read.csv("/sample_random_regression.csv")
data$clientid = as.factor(data$clientid)
```

2. A useful initial plot, which is usually used in the context of mixed models, is one that shows the dependent variable versus each independent variable faceted by subject. This can be used to understand if there are different responses for each independent variable by subject:

```
ggplot(data=data, aes(x=salespeople_involved, y=deal_size,
col=clientid))+
geom_point(size=.7, alpha=.8, position = "jitter")+
```

```
geom_smooth(method=lm,se=FALSE, size=0.6,
alpha=.5)+theme_minimal()+labs(title="Linrved",
subtitle="The  lsses", col= "Yeance")
```

The following output shows the **sales_people involved/deal_size** for each group. This plot is used to understand if the slopes change by group. If they do, we probably want to add a random slope by client:

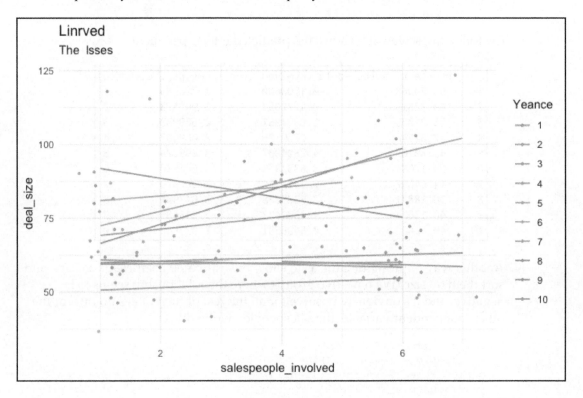

3. We now estimate a model containing a random intercept and a random effect for the salespeople variable, and another one for the `time_spent_deal`. We allow for a possible correlation between them. We also get the predicted effects (fixed and random) for each client:

```
model = lmer(data=data,deal_size ~ salespeople_involved +
time_spent_deal
(1+salespeople_involved+time_spent_deal|clientid) )
```

The following screenshot shows the predicted effects per client:

	(Intercept)	salespeople_involved	time_spent_deal	clientid
1	52.20568	-0.1303600	1.708985	1
2	49.72813	0.4777053	1.995823	2
3	53.21839	1.6994957	2.669033	3
4	47.22548	0.6760296	2.069997	4
5	43.80163	4.2804007	3.899074	5
6	50.17681	3.6832969	3.662500	6
7	44.84697	-0.2417718	1.567070	7
8	56.18871	3.5225308	3.647934	8
9	48.13624	4.0871472	3.848485	9
10	49.42407	0.5496581	2.029642	10

4. Another way of presenting this is to show the estimated coefficients as bars, and sort them by size. We have two groups where the relationship seems to be negative, and it's obviously positive for all the rest of them. Let's do this for the other independent variable: the salespeople involved:

```
F = coef(model)$clientid
F$clientid = row.names(F)
ggplot(F,aes(x=reorder(clientid, -salespeople_involved),
y=salespeople_involved)) + geom_bar(stat="identity", color="blue",
fill="white") + labs(x = "Clientid",y = "Fixed + Random
effect",title = "Sales people involved / Deal size slope")
```

Take a look at the following screenshot:

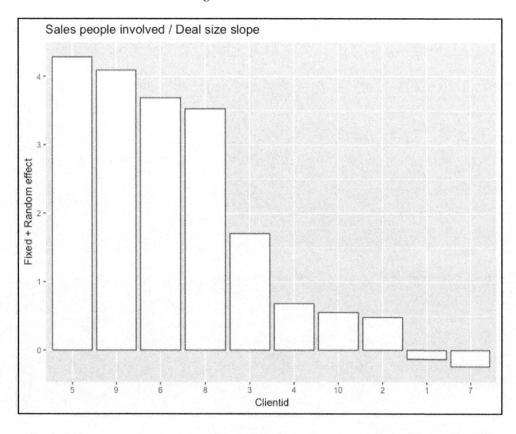

5. Another way of presenting this is by using the sjp package, and calling the sjp.lmer function. This prints the random effects part only for each clientid:

```
plot_model(model,type="re")
```

The following screenshot shows the results for each client:

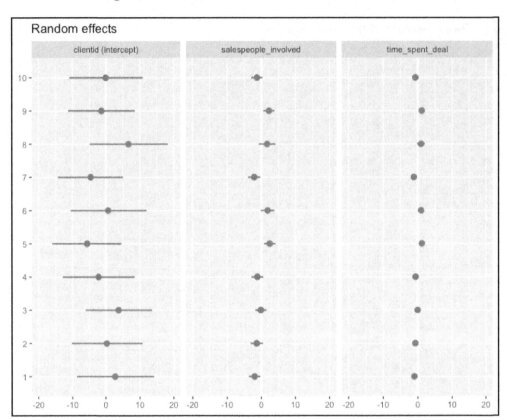

There's more...

After a model has been fitted, it is important to analyze the residuals. We need to take some extra care because the data will belong to groups. Thus, we need to do a separate analysis for each group:

```
plot(model, resid(., scaled=TRUE) ~ fitted(.) | clientid, abline = 0)
```

The following output shows the fitted versus the residuals. These look good, and there is no obvious traces of structure here:

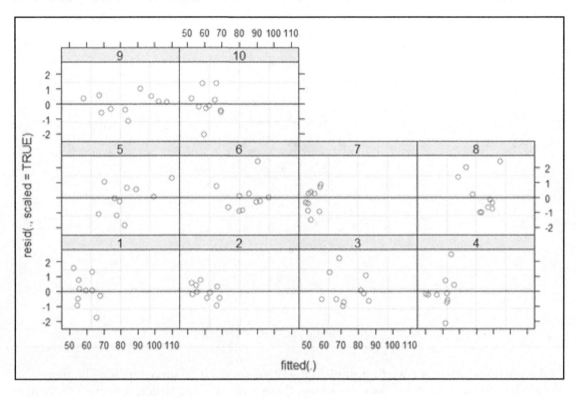

Then, type the following code:

```
plot(model, clientid ~ resid(., scaled=TRUE))
```

The following output shows the scaled residuals for each group:

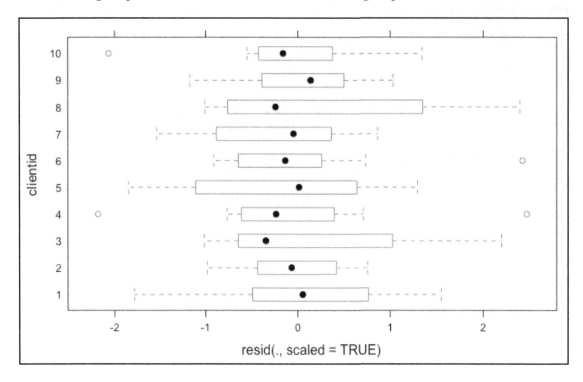

In the previous two plots, we first showed the fitted-residual relationship; ideally, there should be no structure there. As you can see, there is no obvious structure there. We then plotted `boxplots` for the residuals in each group. Again, there is nothing particularly interesting.

Now, let's plot the fitted versus the actuals. There should be a positive linear relationship here. If this weren't the case, it would imply that we were missing some structure in the model:

```
plot (model, deal_size ~ fitted(.) | clientid, abline = c (0,1))
```

The following screenshot shows that the fitted versus the actuals doesn't present any obvious problems:

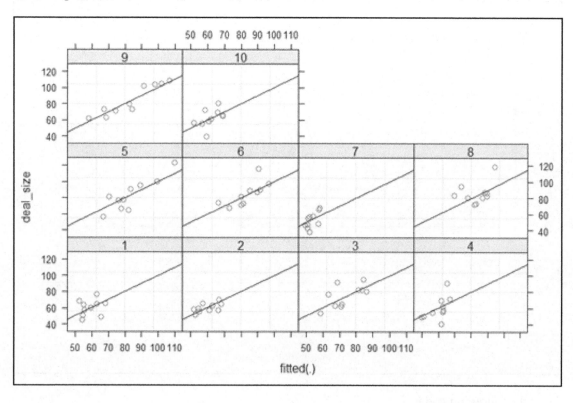

Finally, we can print both the sales people-residuals and time spent-residuals. The same concept should be applied here—there should not be any structure appearing here:

```
plot(model, resid(., scaled=TRUE) ~ salespeople_involved | clientid, abline
= 0)
```

Take a look at the following screenshot:

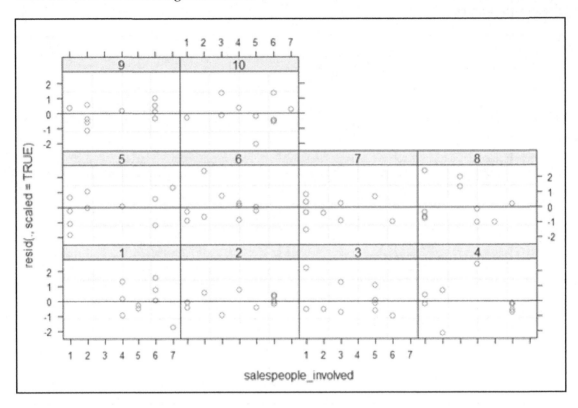

Type the following code:

```
plot(model, resid(., scaled=TRUE) ~ time_spent_deal | clientid, abline = 0)
```

Take a look at the following screenshot:

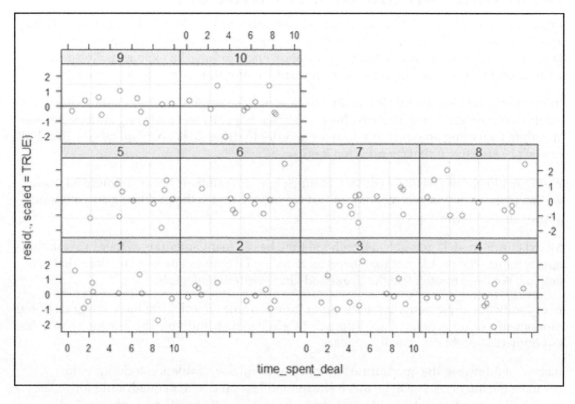

A model should essentially leave no missing structure in the residuals, and this is actually the same thing we should check for in a simple OLS model. The only difference here is that we have done our analysis for each subject.

Even though we haven't tested whether the residuals are Gaussian, it needs to be checked as well. This should be checked both for the residuals, and the residuals within each group.

Nonlinear mixed effects models

Linear mixed effects models assume that a linear relationship exists between the predictors and the target variable. In many cases, this is a problematic assumption; whenever the target is expected to show any kind of saturation effect or have an exponential response with respect to any of the regressors, the linearity assumption needs to be removed.

In medicine and biology, this is usually the case, as dose response studies almost always exhibit a certain kind of saturation effect. The same happens for marketing studies, because spending increasing amounts of resources in order to drive sales up might be effective, but it won't be effective if that spend is too large.

Fitting nonlinear mixed effects models is much harder than their linear counterpart. Here, we can't rely on any matrix techniques and we need to attack the problem using numerical approximation techniques.

Mixed effects models generate a likelihood that, has as many integrals as there are random effects for us. The problem is that, here, there are no OLS and matrix calculations that can help us. We need to calculate the likelihood along with the integrals.

Every software implementation uses quadrature formulas to calculate these integrals (if the random effects are generated according to a Gaussian distribution). This is usually very fast but numerical problems usually appear.

Instead of following the quadrature approach, we will use simulation techniques to calculate the integrals. It will be much slower and less precise than quadrature formulas, but it will be much simpler to illustrate how the mechanics of nonlinear mixed effects models work (the other advantage is that this approach can be extended to nonlinear mixed effects involving other distributions, such as Student's t-distributions).

Getting ready

No special package is needed for this recipe.

How to do it...

In this recipe, we will generate a synthetic dataset using R techniques. This will contain just one independent variable and one random effect. We will have 100 groups with 10 members each. We will choose a nonlinear relationship that exhibits saturation effects. As it has been stated previously, this is usually, this is usually fitted using quadrature methods, which are slightly more involved. Instead, we will approximate the integrals using standard Monte Carlo simulation; this will be much slower, but it will be easier to understand.

1. First, we create a dataset:

```
set.seed(10)
X = 7*runif(1000)
G = c()
for (x in 1:100){
   G = c(G,rep(x,10))
}
pre____frame          = cbind(X=X,G=G,NOISE = rnorm(1000,0,0.03))
shocks_frame          = cbind(G = 1:100,shocks = rnorm(100,0,1))
merged_frame          = merge(pre____frame,shocks_frame,by="G")
merged_frame$Y        = 1/(1+exp(-merged_frame$X +
merged_frame$shocks)) + merged_frame$NOISE
XYG = merged_frame[,c(1,2,5)]
```

2. We then build a function that computes the log-likelihood. The idea is the following: we can sum the likelihood terms for each group. Each one of these will entail an integral over all the possible random effects values (imagine an opposite and more simplistic case: if we had only two random effects, we would just sum over two possible values, but here, we have an infinite amount of them dictated by the support of the Gaussian distribution). In order to approximate those integrals for each group, we simulate 500 values and average the value that we obtain. We multiply the likelihood by –1 at the end, because the optimizer that we will use in the next step performs minimization:

```
get__loglikelihood = function(params){
  BETA1  = params[1]
  SIGMAG = params[2]
  SIGMA  = params[3]
  GROUP_LIK = 0
  IS_ERROR = FALSE
  for (q in 1:100){
  group_data      = XYG[XYG$G==q,]
  average = 0;
  for (sim in 1:500){
```

```
group_data$shock= rnorm(10,0,SIGMAG)
group_data$pred = 1/(1+exp(-BETA1*group_data$X +
group_data$shock))
mult            = 1
for (x in 1:10){
mult = mult * dnorm(group_data$pred[x]-group_data$Y[x],0,SIGMA)
}
average = average + mult
}
average = average/500
average = log(average)
GROUP_LIK = GROUP_LIK + average
}
if (is.na(GROUP_LIK) | GROUP_LIK == -Inf){
GROUP_LIK = -1000000000
}
return(-GROUP_LIK)
}
```

3. Finally, we call the optimizer. We need to pass a set of initial values, a function to be minimized, and some control parameters. Here, we just want to print the current value for each iteration in order to monitor what is happening:

```
Sys.time()
optim(c(1,1,0.03),get__loglikelihood,method="BFGS",control=list(tra
ce=1,REPORT=1))
Sys.time()
```

On the upper part we have the log-likelihood. After that, in $par we have the estimated coefficients:

```
> optim(c(1,1,0.03),get__loglikelihood,method="BFGS",control=list(trace=1,REPORT=1))
initial  value -778.940438
iter    2 value -1150.292479
iter    3 value -1161.257702
iter    4 value -1175.141029
iter    5 value -1175.588396
iter    5 value -1168.403484
final   value -1175.588396
converged
$par
[1] 1.01401561 0.96580905 0.05792872

$value
[1] -1175.588

$counts
function gradient
      68        5

$convergence
[1] 0

$message
NULL
```

How it works...

We are approximating the integrals inside each group via simulation (we draw multiple instances of Gaussian random numbers and we average them). This is done for each group and the logarithms of those values are then summed. Ideally, we would like to use as many simulations as possible, but the more we use, the slower the algorithm is. As it can be seen at the end, we get almost the same values as we should: 1,1, and 0.03; the reasons these results are not the same is, firstly, because we are using a small number of simulations per integral, and secondly, because there is always some sample variability.

A very important point, worth clarifying, is that the functional relationship that we choose for our models needs to be defined before fitting the model. In many biological datasets, this is trivial, but in many cases (for example, price-sales or marketing-sales) this is a very delicate and difficult decision. In these cases, there is no mathematical rationale for why a specific formula should be chosen over another.

There's more...

Mixed effects packages/software do not solve these integrals by using simulation, but use other techniques instead, based on Gaussian quadrature. The idea is to evaluate the integrals at some specific points and then average them. In practice, these methods are much faster and more precise than the one we presented here.

Crossed and nested designs

Whenever we collect data of a model with the intention of testing something, we are implicitly working with an experimental design. Experimental design refers to the setup that defines which experimental units are used, and how they are allocated to each treatment. For example, if we want to measure whether clients are more likely to buy a product after receiving a discount, we need to define which clients will be in the control or test group. Furthermore, we need to define how many of them will fall in each group. All these decisions will have implications regarding the effects and contrasts that we can estimate, and what the precision will be for each one. This is why experimental design has transcendental consequences for our ANOVA and regression models.

Understanding the underlying design for an experiment is of prime importance. The design type has consequences not only for the efficiency of the estimations, but also for how we should set up the model. The difference between nested and crossed designs is a good example of this, because both designs require a specific formulation.

Crossed design

In a crossed design, every factor level appears once for each replication of the parent factor (if it appears at least once it is called a fully crossed design, and if it doesn't, it is called a partially crossed design). For example, if we had three veterinarians and cows, every veterinarian could do a treatment on each of two cows. For example, Veterinary A applies a certain treatment to both cows, and the other veterinarians. This crossed design is what R assumes if we do (1|Veterinary) + (2|Cow): we have two random effects that are unrelated in some way:

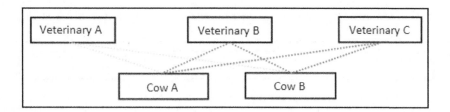

Nested design

Let's suppose we want to measure a policy on the workforce at a particular company. Each employee naturally belongs to a particular area of the company. So, each employee is actually nested within a sector. We could assign a distinct letter to each employee within the same area. The model could now get confused, because every time Employee A is encountered, it won't be clear to which Employee A we are referring. This confusion can be avoided by telling R that this is a nested design. This is done by doing: (1 | Employee/Area)

The following screenshot shows how the employees are nested in an area/department:

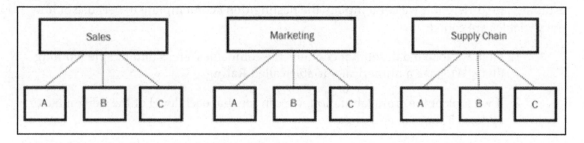

The key element here is to understand how things are coded: if we code each employee as a unique letter, then there can't be any confusion when we load this into the model: whenever an **A** is detected, it will clearly refer to a distinct person rather than any other employee designated with that letter. In this case, treating the effect as crossed or nested does yield the exact same estimates. The reason is that this is equivalent to the person effect being crossed against the area (since there is no real crossing happening, as the area-person mapping is unique).

The following screenshot shows that the employees are not nested in an area/department:

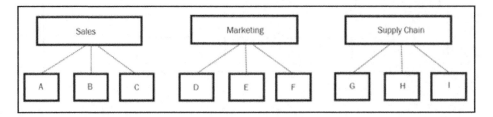

Getting ready

The lmer package needs to be installed using install.packages("lmer").

How to do it...

In the following exercise, we will set up a simple nested model, and we will show that the estimates are different if we contemplate the nesting/don't contemplate it, because of how the variables are coded:

1. First, we load a dataset that contains the companies' areas and people working there. We have a numerical variable called **Rating**.

2. If we look at the cross tabulation, we can see that each level of the **Person** factor appears **5** times in each area:

   ```
   xtabs(~ Group + Person, data)
   ```

   ```
   > xtabs(~ Group + Person, data)
                 Person
   Group        A B C D
     Marketing  5 5 5 5
     Sales      5 5 5 5
   ```

3. Let's look at the results if we treat the results as nested versus crossed. Clearly, the results are different, as the names are the same across both groups:

   ```
   data = read.csv("./company_areas.csv")
    lmer(Rating ~ -1 + (1 | Group/Person), data = data)
    lmer(Rating ~ -1 + (1 | Group) + (1 | Person), data = data)
   ```

Take a look at the following screenshot:

```
> lmer(Rating ~ -1 + (1 | Group/Person)        , data = data)
Linear mixed model fit by maximum likelihood  ['lmerMod']
Formula: Rating ~ -1 + (1 | Group/Person)
   Data: data
      AIC       BIC    logLik  deviance  df.resid
  223.0909  228.1576 -108.5455  217.0909        37
Random effects:
 Groups        Name        Std.Dev.
 Person:Group (Intercept)   3.001
 Group        (Intercept)  26.755
 Residual                   2.584
Number of obs: 40, groups:  Person:Group, 8; Group, 2
No fixed effect coefficients
>
> lmer(Rating ~ -1 + (1 | Group) + (1 | Person), data = data)
Linear mixed model fit by maximum likelihood  ['lmerMod']
Formula: Rating ~ -1 + (1 | Group) + (1 | Person)
   Data: data
      AIC       BIC    logLik  deviance  df.resid
  217.4469  222.5135 -105.7234  211.4469        37
Random effects:
 Groups  Name        Std.Dev.
 Person  (Intercept)   3.061
 Group   (Intercept)  26.688
 Residual              2.530
Number of obs: 40, groups:  Person, 4; Group, 2
No fixed effect coefficients
```

4. Let's look the cross-tabulation for the same dataset, which has been re-coded in order to have unique levels for each group. As can be seen here, all AA, BB, CC, and DD people appear only for the Sales group:

```
xtabs(~ Group + Person, data2)
```

Take a look at the following screenshot:

```
> xtabs(~ Group + Person, data2)
           Person
Group       A AA B BB C CC D DD
  Marketing 5  0 5  0 5  0 5  0
  Sales     0  5 0  5 0  5 0  5
```

5. We now load a dataset that contains unique IDs. Here, both the nested and crossed formulations yield the same results:

```
data2 = read.csv("./company_areas2.csv")
lmer(Rating ~ -1 + (1 | Group/Person), data = data2)
lmer(Rating ~ -1 + (1 | Group) + (1 | Person), data = data2)
```

Take a look at the following screenshot:

```
> lmer(Rating ~ -1 + (1 | Group/Person)         , data = data2)
Linear mixed model fit by maximum likelihood   ['lmerMod']
Formula: Rating ~ -1 + (1 | Group/Person)
   Data: data2
      AIC        BIC    logLik  deviance  df.resid
 223.0909   228.1576 -108.5455  217.0909        37
Random effects:
 Groups       Name        Std.Dev.
 Person:Group (Intercept)  3.001
 Group        (Intercept) 26.755
 Residual                  2.584
Number of obs: 40, groups:  Person:Group, 8; Group, 2
No fixed effect coefficients
>
> lmer(Rating ~ -1 + (1 | Group) + (1 | Person), data = data2)
Linear mixed model fit by maximum likelihood   ['lmerMod']
Formula: Rating ~ -1 + (1 | Group) + (1 | Person)
   Data: data2
      AIC        BIC    logLik  deviance  df.resid
 223.0909   228.1576 -108.5455  217.0909        37
Random effects:
 Groups   Name        Std.Dev.
 Person   (Intercept)  3.001
 Group    (Intercept) 26.755
 Residual              2.584
Number of obs: 40, groups:  Person, 8; Group, 2
No fixed effect coefficients
```

How it works..

Both nested and crossed designs are estimated using the same techniques. The only difference is how they are treated internally before the algorithm starts.

Robust mixed effects models with robustlmm

The `lme4` package is the `de facto` package for linear mixed models. Its syntax has become a standard in the industry and most researchers working with applied linear models use it. As we have seen with many techniques so far, the problem with it is that it can be impacted greatly by outliers. Even a minor contamination causes major estimation problems.

Getting ready

The `lme4` and `robustlmm` packages are needed for this recipe. They can be installed using `install.packages()`.

How to do it...

In this recipe, we will use the `robustlmm` package to estimate **robust linear mixed effects models**. Its biggest advantage is that it uses the exact same syntax (and outputs) that the `lmer` function uses. We will evaluate what happens when we contaminate 5% of the data with abnormal values. As we will see, the `lmer` function suffers enormously with even a 5% contamination. The `robustlmm` package, on the contrary, does a great job, reporting coefficients almost as if no contamination had happened.

1. First, we generate data for 100 groups, containing 10 members each. Then, we generate random Gaussian deviates that are pasted to the dataset. Each group will share a common random shock that will render all the observations from that group to be correlated:

```
library(lme4)
library(robustlmm)
set.seed(10)
X = 7*runif(1000)
G = c()
for (x in 1:100){
G = c(G,rep(x,10))
}
pre____frame           = cbind(X=X,G=G,NOISE = rnorm(1000,0,0.03))
shocks_frame           = cbind(G = 1:100,shocks = rnorm(100,0,1))
merged_frame           = merge(pre____frame,shocks_frame,by="G")
merged_frame$Y         = 10 + merged_frame$shocks +
merged_frame$NOISE
```

```
XYG                      = merged_frame[,c(1,2,5)]
lmer(data=XYG, Y ~ 1 + (1|G))
rlmer(data=XYG, Y ~ 1 + (1|G))
```

As expected, both methods work well and yield similar results:

```
> lmer(data=XYG, Y ~ (1|G))
Linear mixed model fit by REML ['lmerMod']
Formula: Y ~ 1 + (1 | G)
   Data: XYG
REML criterion at convergence: -3197.028
Random effects:
 Groups    Name         Std.Dev.
 G         (Intercept)  1.02950
 Residual               0.03066
Number of obs: 1000, groups:  G, 100
Fixed Effects:
(Intercept)
       9.988
> rlmer(data=XYG, Y ~ 1 + (1|G))
Robust linear mixed model fit by DAStau
Formula: Y ~ 1 + (1 | G)
   Data: XYG
Random effects:
 Groups    Name         Std.Dev.
 G         (Intercept)  1.14192
 Residual               0.03073
Number of obs: 1000, groups: G, 100
Fixed Effects:
(Intercept)
       9.984
```

The interesting question is, what will happen when we add contamination?

2. Then, we contaminate 5% of the data with random noise with a large variance. This will change our data (and our `lmer` coefficients) greatly:

```
positions = sample(1:1000, 50, replace=T)
XYG[positions,"Y"] = rnorm(1,50,10)
```

3. `lmer` suffers greatly, and the estimates are very distant from their true values. Nevertheless, the `rlmer` function does a great job and the coefficients look good.

The `lmer` function suffers especially for the variance components, as they are rather more than 10 times off their true values. This greatly changes our conclusions: actually the group effect explains $1/(1+0.3) = 76\%$ of the variability of the model, which is a very different thing from what we would get if we did $11.95/(11.95+39.9)=23\%$.:

```
lmer(data=XYG, Y ~ 1 + (1|G))
rlmer(data=XYG, Y ~ 1 + (1|G))
```

The following is the resultant output:

```
> lmer(data=XYG, Y ~ 1 + (1|G))
Linear mixed model fit by REML ['lmerMod']
Formula: Y ~ 1 + (1 | G)
   Data: XYG
REML criterion at convergence: 7468.825
Random effects:
 Groups   Name        Std.Dev.
 G        (Intercept) 1.929
 Residual             9.974
Number of obs: 1000, groups:  G, 100
Fixed Effects:
(Intercept)
       12.3
> rlmer(data=XYG, Y ~ 1 + (1|G))
Robust linear mixed model fit by DAStau
Formula: Y ~ 1 + (1 | G)
   Data: XYG
Random effects:
 Groups   Name        Std.Dev.
 G        (Intercept) 1.14287
 Residual             0.03437
Number of obs: 1000, groups:  G, 100
Fixed Effects:
(Intercept)
      9.987
```

Of course, the conclusions for the fixed effects would change (there is a 50% difference from what `lmer` gets versus what we should get)

4. We can plot the results and look at the resulting weights. As we know, the large residuals here all come from contaminated observations. The model does a great job at down-weighing them:

```
model = rlmer(data=XYG, Y ~ 1 + (1|G))
plot(model)
```

For fitted values versus residuals, black dots have a high weight, meaning that they are flagged as outliers:

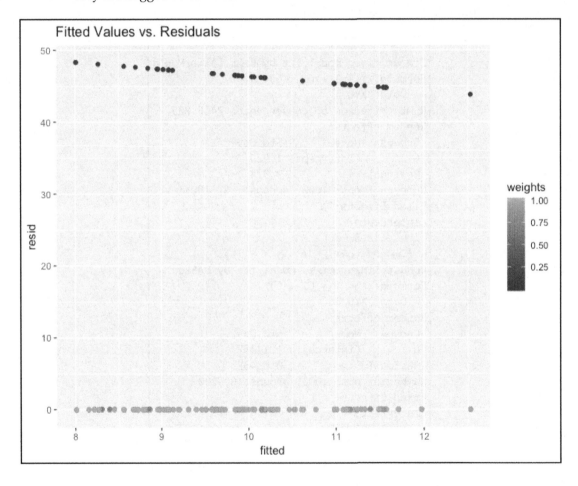

How it works...

When working with maximum likelihood, we derive the estimated coefficients by taking the partial derivatives of it and equating them to zero. We then find the expression for each coefficient in terms of the data. These derivatives are called scoring equations, and `robustlmm` works by making these equations more robust. This package uses several tricks to ensure that the impact of abnormal observations on these equations is small.

A detailed explanation of the algorithm can be found at `https://cran.r-project.org/web/packages/robustlmm/vignettes/rlmer.pdf`.

Choosing the best linear mixed model

When using OLS models, choosing the best one is not a complex task: we have a set of variables that we use, and we just pick whichever model has the lowest Akaike information criterion (AIC) (or any other appropriate metric that we choose).

Mixed models entail an extra level of complexity, as we can define the random effects in many ways. Resuming our previous example of `deal_size` versus `time_spent` and `salespeople`, we could choose a model with random effects only for the `deal_size` or both the `deal_size` and `salespeople`. We can also decide to add a random intercept or not, and we can force the model to assume that the shocks impacting each one of these are either, uncorrelated or correlated.

Choosing models by comparing the AIC is quite hard for mixed models, since we have a random and a fixed part. There are two types of analysis that we might be interested in: population parameters (fixed effects) and subject analysis (random effects predictions for the groups). This leads to two possible formulations of AIC, the **marginal AIC (mAIC)** and the **conditional AIC (cAIC)**. The former is used when we are interested in the fixed effects, whereas the latter is useful when we are interested in subject analysis. Another way of posing this, is that when we are interested in the predictive quality of a model, we should use the conditional AIC. On the other hand, if we are interested in the inference over the fixed effects, we should use the marginal AIC (the standard one that we get from lmer).

Getting ready

The cAIC4 package needs to be installed using `install.packages("cAIC4")`.

How to do it...

Computing the cAIC for mixed models is a nontrivial issue, but fortunately it can be done with the cAIC4 package. In this recipe we will formulate seven versions of our model for deal sizes; we will also add some noise variables into some of the models. If cAIC4 works as expected, it should penalize those models more than the rest:

1. First, we load the necessary libraries and dataset and then we generate four new variables that will have just noise. Ideally models having them, should receive a greater penalization:

```
library("lme4")
library("glmmLasso")
library(cAIC4)
set.seed(25)
data = read.csv("C:\\R_book\\sample_random_regression.csv")
data$clientid = as.factor(data$clientid)
data$ERR_1 = rnorm(100,0,10)
data$ERR_2 = rnorm(100,0,10)
data$ERR_3 = rnorm(100,0,10)
data$ERR_4 = rnorm(100,0,10)
```

2. We fit seven models and, as we will see, the third model will be the one being penalized the most. As can be seen here, m3 is the best model and for m6, m7, and m8, the more `irrelevant` the variables that we add, the worse the model performs:

```
m1 = lmer(data=data,deal_size ~ salespeople_involved +
time_spent_deal + (-1 +
salespeople_involved|clientid) + (-1 + time_spent_deal|clientid) )
m2 = lmer(data=data,deal_size ~ salespeople_involved +
time_spent_deal + (1  + salespeople_involved|clientid)  )
m3 = lmer(data=data,deal_size ~ salespeople_involved +
time_spent_deal + (1  + time_spent_deal +
salespeople_involved|clientid) )
m4 = lmer(data=data,deal_size ~ salespeople_involved +
time_spent_deal + ERR_1 + ERR_2 + ERR_3 + ERR_4  +  (1  +
time_spent_deal + salespeople_involved|clientid) )
m5 = lmer(data=data,deal_size ~ salespeople_involved +
time_spent_deal + ERR_1 + ERR_2 + ERR_3  + (1  + time_spent_deal +
```

```
salespeople_involved|clientid) )
m6 = lmer(data=data,deal_size ~ salespeople_involved +
time_spent_deal + ERR_1 + ERR_2  + (1  +   time_spent_deal +
salespeople_involved|clientid) )
m7 = lmer(data=data,deal_size ~ salespeople_involved +
time_spent_deal + ERR_1  + (1  + time_spent_deal +
salespeople_involved|clientid) )
```

3. Finally, we print the results and, obviously, m3 is the best model. A singular fit happens when the model is either too complex or has irrelevant variables. This happens because the ERR variables are just noise, so it can be that we get numerical errors just because of that:

```
cAIC(m1)$caic
cAIC(m2)$caic
cAIC(m3)$caic
cAIC(m4)$caic
cAIC(m5)$caic
cAIC(m6)$caic
cAIC(m7)$caic
```

The results are the following (note that the smallest AIC is, the better):

```
> cAIC(m1)$caic
[1] 769.6015
>
>
> cAIC(m2)$caic
[1] 771.1832
>
>
> cAIC(m3)$caic
[1] 765.4679
>
>
> cAIC(m4)$caic
[1] 775.5881
>
>
> cAIC(m5)$caic
[1] 773.8559
>
>
> cAIC(m6)$caic
singular fit
[1] 780.0531
>
>
> cAIC(m7)$caic
[1] 769.7357
```

How it works...

There are essentially two AICs that can be used in the context of mixed models. The first one is the **marginal AIC (mAIC)** and the second one is the **conditional AIC (cAIC)**. The former is useful when we are interested in the fixed effects part, whereas the latter is useful when our interest lies in the conditional predictions for each group.

A detailed discussion on the specifics of cAIC can be found at `https://arxiv.org/pdf/1803.05664.pdf`.

Mixed generalized linear models

Generalized linear models are a set of techniques that generalizes the linear regression model (which assumes that the dependent variable is Gaussian) into a wide variety of distributions for the response variable. This response can no longer be Gaussian, but can belong to any distribution that is part of the so-called exponential family. In fact, there are many distributions that fall into this category, such as the binomial, gamma, Poisson, or negative binomial distributions. This fact allows us to work with a wide array of situations, such as with count data, or binary responses, and so on.

Generalized linear models (referred to as GLMs in the literature) are defined by three things: first, a linear predictor that relates the covariates with the response variable; second, a probability distribution for the dependent variable from the exponential distribution; and finally, a link function that connects the linear predictor defined previously to the expected value of the response. Usually, these models are estimated using maximum likelihood.

GLMs formulated in the classical way are defined just over fixed effects. A coefficient is estimated for each variable, which relates each one of them to the expected values of the response. We can then get confidence intervals for each coefficient, but the underlying assumption behind OLS stills holds here: we assume that each observation is independent from the rest, and the effects that we estimate are *population* effects (conceptually, averages for all the population).

These models can be extended to accommodate for correlated observations belonging to the same subjects. The concept is the same one that we used for linear mixed effect models: for each variable (and intercept) we can define a random effect that varies per subject. As a consequence, the total effect for a variable can be decomposed as a fixed part and a random part. There is still an important consideration here: because the `link` function connecting the linear predictor to the target variable is generally nonlinear (except for the obvious exception of Gaussian models, which are just normal OLS models), the interpretation of each effect (whether fixed or fixed and random) is much harder.

GLMs that incorporate random effects are referred to **generalized linear mixed models (GLMMs)** and can be fitted using the `lme4` packages. In this recipe, we will show how to work with a Poisson distribution, although there are several other ones supported by this package.

Getting ready

The `glmm` package needs to be installed using `install.packages("glmm")`.

How to do it...

Use the following steps to analyze a GLMM:

1. We will use the `OrchardSprays` dataset, which is included in R. It contains data for an experiment *to assess the potency of various constituents of orchard sprays in repelling honeybees,* using a Latin square design. The `target` variable will be a `count` variable, and the treatment effect will be `treatment.rowpos` and `colpos` should ideally be assumed to be random effects. First, we load the libraries:

```
library(lme4)
library(emmeans)
library(MASS)
set.seed(10)
```

2. Let's ignore the random effects and fit this model using the regular GLM framework. Note that we specify `family=poisson()`:

```
fixed_std_model = glm(decrease ~
treatment,family=poisson(),data=OrchardSprays)
summary(fixed_std_model )
```

The following screenshot shows the GLM model—all of the effects are fixed:

```
Call:
glm(formula = decrease ~ treatment, family = poisson(), data = OrchardSprays)

Deviance Residuals:
    Min       1Q    Median       3Q      Max
-6.9617  -1.5516   -0.3743   0.7517   9.1888

Coefficients:
            Estimate Std. Error z value Pr(>|z|)
(Intercept)   1.5315     0.1644   9.316   <2e-16 ***
treatmentB    0.5000     0.2084   2.399   0.0164 *
treatmentC    1.6973     0.1788   9.492   <2e-16 ***
treatmentD    2.0239     0.1749  11.570   <2e-16 ***
treatmentE    2.6136     0.1703  15.346   <2e-16 ***
treatmentF    2.7026     0.1698  15.915   <2e-16 ***
treatmentG    2.6954     0.1699  15.868   <2e-16 ***
treatmentH    2.9711     0.1686  17.627   <2e-16 ***
---
Signif. codes:  0 '***' 0.001 '**' 0.01 '*' 0.05 '.' 0.1 ' ' 1

(Dispersion parameter for poisson family taken to be 1)

    Null deviance: 1904.73  on 63  degrees of freedom
Residual deviance:  438.95  on 56  degrees of freedom
AIC: 786.47

Number of Fisher Scoring iterations: 5
```

3. We can get the differences between the effects using the `emmeans` function:

```
emmeans(fixed_std_model, list(pairwise ~ treatment), adjust =
"tukey",type="response"
```

The differences between the effects can be obtained using emeans. The Tukey correction is used because we are doing multiple tests. If we do multiple tests using a fixed alpha value of i.e 0.05, the joint alpha will no longer be 0.05 (this is known as the multiple comparison problem):

```
$`emmeans of treatment`
treatment  rate     SE  df asymp.LCL asymp.UCL
A          4.62  0.760 Inf      3.35      6.38
B          7.62  0.976 Inf      5.93      9.80
C         25.25  1.777 Inf     22.00     28.98
D         35.00  2.092 Inf     31.13     39.35
E         63.12  2.809 Inf     57.85     68.88
F         69.00  2.937 Inf     63.48     75.00
G         68.50  2.926 Inf     63.00     74.48
H         90.25  3.359 Inf     83.90     97.08
```

Take a look at the following screenshot:

```
Confidence level used: 0.95
Intervals are back-transformed from the log scale

$`pairwise differences of treatment`
 contrast  ratio      SE  df z.ratio p.value
  A / B   0.6066 0.12639 Inf  -2.399 0.2415
  A / C   0.1832 0.03275 Inf  -9.492 <.0001
  A / D   0.1321 0.02311 Inf -11.570 <.0001
  A / E   0.0733 0.01248 Inf -15.346 <.0001
  A / F   0.0670 0.01138 Inf -15.915 <.0001
  A / G   0.0675 0.01147 Inf -15.868 <.0001
  A / H   0.0512 0.00864 Inf -17.627 <.0001
  B / C   0.3020 0.04412 Inf  -8.196 <.0001
  B / D   0.2179 0.03078 Inf -10.785 <.0001
  B / E   0.1208 0.01637 Inf -15.593 <.0001
  B / F   0.1105 0.01491 Inf -16.325 <.0001
  B / G   0.1113 0.01502 Inf -16.265 <.0001
  B / H   0.0845 0.01127 Inf -18.533 <.0001
  C / D   0.7214 0.06660 Inf  -3.537 0.0096
  C / E   0.4000 0.03330 Inf -11.006 <.0001
  C / F   0.3659 0.03009 Inf -12.225 <.0001
  C / G   0.3686 0.03034 Inf -12.125 <.0001
  C / H   0.2798 0.02227 Inf -16.003 <.0001
  D / E   0.5545 0.04131 Inf  -7.915 <.0001
  D / F   0.5072 0.03722 Inf  -9.251 <.0001
  D / G   0.5109 0.03753 Inf  -9.141 <.0001
  D / H   0.3878 0.02730 Inf -13.455 <.0001
  E / F   0.9149 0.05633 Inf  -1.445 0.8361
  E / G   0.9215 0.05684 Inf  -1.325 0.8897
  E / H   0.6994 0.04058 Inf  -6.162 <.0001
  F / G   1.0073 0.06074 Inf   0.121 1.0000
  F / H   0.7645 0.04323 Inf  -4.749 0.0001
  G / H   0.7590 0.04300 Inf  -4.867 <.0001

P value adjustment: tukey method for comparing a family of 8 estimates
Tests are performed on the log scale
```

4. Predicting is quite easy using the `predict` function. By default, these predictions will be on the log scale, so in order to force them onto the real scale, we specify `type="response"`:

```
predict(fixed_std_model,data.frame(treatment="D"),type="response")
```

Take a look at the following screenshot:

```
> predict(fixed_std_model,data.frame(treatment="D"),type="response")
 1
35
```

5. As usual, we can plot the results and check that there is no remaining structure in the residuals. We also need to check that the variance is stable (homoscedasticity). If the residuals are not, then the p-values and confidence intervals will be wrong:

```
plot(fixed_std_model)
```

For the residuals versus fitted values, the variability seems to increase with respect to the predicted values, but we will ignore this issue for the time being:

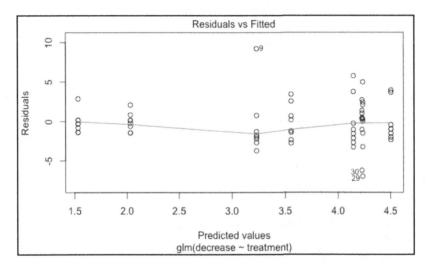

6. We now incorporate the random effects, and we fit our model using the `glmm` package. Note that we get a numerical error, meaning that no convergence has been achieved. One possible solution is to rerun the model, but using the previously estimated fixed effects as starting values for the numerical algorithm. Sometimes this fixes these issues, but not always:

```
model_1 = lme4::glmer(decrease ~ treatment + (1|colpos) +
(1|rowpos), family = poisson(), data = OrchardSprays)
ss <- getME(model_1,c("theta","fixef"))
model_2 <- update(model_1,start=ss)
summary(model_2)
```

GLMM model—fixed and random effects on a GLM model:

```
Generalized linear mixed model fit by maximum likelihood (Laplace Approximation) ['glmerMod']
 Family: poisson ( log )
Formula: decrease ~ treatment + (1 | colpos) + (1 | rowpos)
   Data: OrchardSprays

    AIC     BIC   logLik deviance df.resid
  667.6   689.2   -323.8   647.6       54

Scaled residuals:
    Min      1Q  Median      3Q     Max
-4.4858 -1.2184 -0.2889  0.8911  6.5399

Random effects:
 Groups Name        Variance Std.Dev.
 colpos (Intercept) 0.02496  0.1580
 rowpos (Intercept) 0.03792  0.1947
Number of obs: 64, groups:  colpos, 8; rowpos, 8

Fixed effects:
            Estimate Std. Error z value Pr(>|z|)
(Intercept)   1.5079     0.1867   8.076 6.68e-16 ***
treatmentB    0.4850     0.2083   2.329   0.0199 *
treatmentC    1.6776     0.1788   9.385  < 2e-16 ***
treatmentD    2.0067     0.1749  11.475  < 2e-16 ***
treatmentE    2.6155     0.1702  15.364  < 2e-16 ***
treatmentF    2.7070     0.1697  15.952  < 2e-16 ***
treatmentG    2.6908     0.1698  15.846  < 2e-16 ***
treatmentH    2.9691     0.1685  17.623  < 2e-16 ***
---
Signif. codes:  0 '***' 0.001 '**' 0.01 '*' 0.05 '.' 0.1 ' ' 1

Correlation of Fixed Effects:
           (Intr) trtmnB trtmnC trtmnD trtmnE trtmnF trtmnG
treatmentB -0.694
treatmentC -0.808  0.725
treatmentD -0.826  0.741  0.863
treatmentE -0.849  0.761  0.886  0.907
treatmentF -0.852  0.763  0.889  0.909  0.934
treatmentG -0.851  0.763  0.889  0.909  0.934  0.936
treatmentH -0.858  0.769  0.896  0.916  0.941  0.944  0.943
```

8. As in standard linear mixed effects models fitted by `lmer()`, we can get the random effects, the fixed effects, and the variance components:

```
ranef(model_2)
fixef(model_2)
VarCorr(model_2)
```

The following screenshot shows the random effects and fixed effects:

```
> ranef(model_2)
$colpos
  (Intercept)
1  0.20893166
2  0.21171940
3 -0.14365310
4 -0.01940481
5 -0.17732000
6 -0.08980566
7 -0.08152766
8  0.09836171

$rowpos
  (Intercept)
1  0.33434211
2  0.16578727
3  0.12408467
4 -0.15557697
5 -0.23460180
6 -0.16512827
7 -0.07662162
8  0.01880953

with conditional variances for "colpos" "rowpos"
> fixef(model_2)
(Intercept)  treatmentB  treatmentC  treatmentD  treatmentE  treatmentF  treatmentG  treatmentH
  1.5078872   0.4850256   1.6776380   2.0066968   2.6154742   2.7070001   2.6908219   2.9691472
> VarCorr(model_2)
 Groups Name          Std.Dev.
 colpos (Intercept) 0.15798
 rowpos (Intercept) 0.19474
```

9. The residuals should be checked as usual: essentially, we are looking for no remaining structure and constant variance (homoscedasticity):

```
plot(model_2, resid(., scaled=TRUE) ~ fitted(.) | colpos, abline = 0)
plot(model_2, resid(., scaled=TRUE) ~ fitted(.) | rowpos, abline = 0)
```

The following screenshot shows no evident structure is found on the residuals:

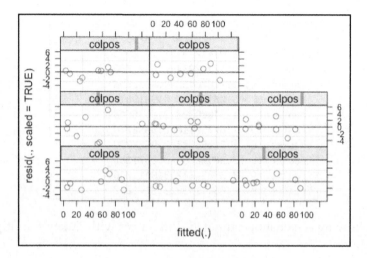

The following screenshot shows no evident structure is found on the residuals:

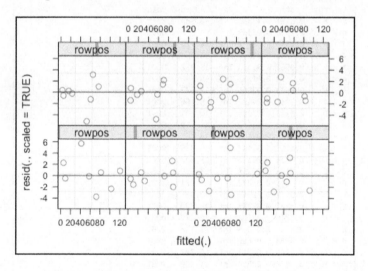

10. We can print, for example, confidence intervals for each effect using the `confint.merMod`, and we can also get the estimates contrasts using `emmeans` again:

```
confint.merMod(model_2)
emmeans(model_2, list(pairwise ~ treatment), adjust =
"tukey",type="response")]
```

The following screenshot the 95% confidence intervals:

```
Computing profile confidence intervals ...
                   2.5 %      97.5 %
.sig01        0.09442293 0.2976190
.sig02        0.12077033 0.3597700
(Intercept)   1.12576452 1.8632398
treatmentB    0.08171115 0.9019814
treatmentC    1.34000298 2.0435608
treatmentD    1.67758110 2.3658719
treatmentE    2.29653348 2.9665200
treatmentF    2.38922095 3.0571158
treatmentG    2.37281217 3.0411236
treatmentH    2.65411339 3.3171222
```

The following screenshot estimated differences with Tukey's multiple comparison correction:

```
$`pairwise differences of treatment`
 contrast ratio      SE df z.ratio p.value
 A / B    0.6157 0.12824 Inf  -2.329 0.2778
 A / C    0.1868 0.03339 Inf  -9.385 <.0001
 A / D    0.1344 0.02351 Inf -11.475 <.0001
 A / E    0.0731 0.01245 Inf -15.364 <.0001
 A / F    0.0667 0.01133 Inf -15.952 <.0001
 A / G    0.0678 0.01152 Inf -15.846 <.0001
 A / H    0.0513 0.00865 Inf -17.623 <.0001
 B / C    0.3034 0.04432 Inf  -8.166 <.0001
 B / D    0.2183 0.03085 Inf -10.771 <.0001
 B / E    0.1188 0.01610 Inf -15.718 <.0001
 B / F    0.1084 0.01463 Inf -16.463 <.0001
 B / G    0.1102 0.01487 Inf -16.339 <.0001
 B / H    0.0834 0.01112 Inf -18.632 <.0001
 C / D    0.7196 0.06654 Inf  -3.559 0.0089
 C / E    0.3915 0.03272 Inf -11.221 <.0001
 C / F    0.3572 0.02945 Inf -12.485 <.0001
 C / G    0.3631 0.02993 Inf -12.290 <.0001
 C / H    0.2749 0.02194 Inf -16.179 <.0001
 D / E    0.5440 0.04065 Inf  -8.148 <.0001
 D / F    0.4964 0.03659 Inf  -9.501 <.0001
 D / G    0.5045 0.03717 Inf  -9.287 <.0001
 D / H    0.3820 0.02699 Inf -13.620 <.0001
 E / F    0.9125 0.05644 Inf  -1.480 0.8184
 E / G    0.9274 0.05749 Inf  -1.215 0.9277
 E / H    0.7021 0.04093 Inf  -6.067 <.0001
 F / G    1.0163 0.06153 Inf   0.267 1.0000
 F / H    0.7694 0.04374 Inf  -4.611 0.0001
 G / H    0.7571 0.04318 Inf  -4.880 <.0001

P value adjustment: tukey method for comparing a family of 8 estimates
Tests are performed on the log scale
```

How it works...

Poisson models are appropriate when dealing with count data (non-negative integer data), which is usually severely skewed. A consequence of using Poisson distributions (and potentially, a problem) is that the mean and variance of the distribution are governed by the same parameter (`lambda`). Therefore, in a Poisson model, the residuals should always be checked, and special care needs to be taken with the variance/mean of them. If the variance is increasing as the mean increases, we should adjust our model and use the negative binomial distribution, which is a generalization of the Poisson distribution with an extra parameter to control the variance.

On a conceptual level, all the regular `lmer`/`lme4` functions that can be used for linear models can also be applied here for GLMs.

There's more...

Negative binomial models can be adjusted using the very same functions that we have used so far; but the problem is that we need to specify the `overdispersion` parameter manually (and we usually don't know it). The `glm.nb()` and the `glmer.nb()` are designed to account for this, and they take care of fitting the extra parameter.

Although some practitioners prefer to use negative binomial models over Poisson ones because it avoids the overdispersion problem entirely, the truth is that they are slightly more complex. Usually, complexity in statistics is paid for by having less precise estimates (and greater variability in the predictions).

Interestingly, the results do not change by much when compared with their Poisson counterparts. The `theta` parameter, which controls the extra variance, can be seen to be `6.7` with a standard deviation of just `1.46`, suggesting that using a negative binomial model might be a good idea:

```
fixed_std_model = glm.nb(decrease ~ treatment,data=OrchardSprays)
summary(fixed_std_model)
model_2 = lme4::glmer.nb(decrease ~ treatment + (1|colpos) + (1|rowpos),
data = OrchardSprays)
ss2 <- getME(model_2,c("theta","fixef"))
model_3 <- update(model_1,start=ss2)
summary(model_3)
```

The following screenshot shows the GLM model—all effects are fixed:

```
Call:
glm.nb(formula = decrease ~ treatment, data = OrchardSprays,
    init.theta = 6.700856316, link = log)

Deviance Residuals:
    Min       1Q    Median      3Q       Max
-2.4728  -0.7266  -0.2311   0.3033    3.5589

Coefficients:
            Estimate Std. Error z value Pr(>|z|)
(Intercept)   1.5315     0.2137   7.165 7.76e-13 ***
treatmentB    0.5000     0.2841   1.760   0.0785 .
treatmentC    1.6973     0.2632   6.448 1.13e-10 ***
treatmentD    2.0239     0.2606   7.766 8.07e-15 ***
treatmentE    2.6136     0.2575  10.149  < 2e-16 ***
treatmentF    2.7026     0.2572  10.508  < 2e-16 ***
treatmentG    2.6954     0.2572  10.479  < 2e-16 ***
treatmentH    2.9711     0.2564  11.590  < 2e-16 ***
---
Signif. codes:  0 '***' 0.001 '**' 0.01 '*' 0.05 '.' 0.1 ' ' 1

(Dispersion parameter for Negative Binomial(6.7009) family taken to be 1)

    Null deviance: 318.938  on 63  degrees of freedom
Residual deviance:  63.893  on 56  degrees of freedom
AIC: 527.16

Number of Fisher Scoring iterations: 1


          Theta:  6.70
      Std. Err.:  1.46

2 x log-likelihood:  -509.16
```

The following screenshot GLM model with mixed effects:

```
Generalized linear mixed model fit by maximum likelihood (Laplace Approximation) ['glmerMod']
 Family: Negative Binomial(8.6028)  ( log )
Formula: decrease ~ treatment + (1 | colpos) + (1 | rowpos)
   Data: OrchardSprays

    AIC      BIC   logLik deviance df.resid
  526.5    550.2   -252.2    504.5       53

Scaled residuals:
    Min      1Q  Median      3Q     Max
-1.7969 -0.5954 -0.0862  0.2879  4.0502

Random effects:
 Groups Name           Variance Std.Dev.
 colpos (Intercept) 0.003765 0.06136
 rowpos (Intercept) 0.031372 0.17712
Number of obs: 64, groups:  colpos, 8; rowpos, 8

Fixed effects:
            Estimate Std. Error z value Pr(>|z|)
(Intercept)   1.4986     0.2155   6.954 3.55e-12 ***
treatmentB    0.5262     0.2706   1.944   0.0519 .
treatmentC    1.6457     0.2498   6.587 4.47e-11 ***
treatmentD    2.0298     0.2456   8.263  < 2e-16 ***
treatmentE    2.6410     0.2429  10.874  < 2e-16 ***
treatmentF    2.7176     0.2426  11.202  < 2e-16 ***
treatmentG    2.7262     0.2422  11.254  < 2e-16 ***
treatmentH    2.9892     0.2410  12.405  < 2e-16 ***
---
Signif. codes:  0 '***' 0.001 '**' 0.01 '*' 0.05 '.' 0.1 ' ' 1

Correlation of Fixed Effects:
           (Intr) trtmnB trtmnC trtmnD trtmnE trtmnF trtmnG
treatmentB -0.721
treatmentC -0.775  0.619
treatmentD -0.794  0.633  0.685
treatmentE -0.805  0.641  0.689  0.707
treatmentF -0.805  0.643  0.695  0.707  0.717
treatmentG -0.806  0.642  0.691  0.707  0.717  0.716
treatmentH -0.810  0.645  0.696  0.710  0.721  0.720  0.721
```

Predictive Models Using the Caret Package

9

We will cover the following recipes in this chapter:

- Data splitting and general model fitting
- Preprocessing
- Variable importance and feature selection
- Model tuning
- Classification in caret and ROC curves
- Gradient boosting and class imbalance
- Lasso, Ridge, and Elasticnet in caret
- Logic regression

Introduction

The `caret` package has become the de facto package for dealing with regression and classification models in R, especially between machine learning practitioners. It is essentially a wrapper for many predictive modeling packages, providing a unified approach to deploying models, preprocessing data, tuning hyperparameters, and making feature selection. From a practical perspective, it really easy to switch between models while using the same functions.

It is very important to stress that some statistical and machine learning models have parameters and hyperparameters. The parameters are trained by whichever algorithm we use, and the hyperparameters need to be defined by the user. Hyperparameters essentially control how much overfitting or underfitting we have and they need to be tuned appropriately. There are essentially two ways of determining them:

- **Splitting the data between testing and training**: Fit the data in the `train` dataset and choose the best parameters that optimize a given metric over the testing dataset.
- **Working with the same dataset and doing cross-validation**: The idea is to split the data into multiple parts, train the model over *k-1* parts, and test it on the unused part. This is repeated at least *k* times.

The second method is much better than the first one for small datasets (because we are not really discarding data). The disadvantage is that we have multiple folds/parts, so the metrics need to be aggregated. The first one is easier to interpret and implement but is certainly a bad option for small datasets (usually a 75%-25% split is done – which means that 25% of the data is not used to train).

Data splitting and general model fitting

The `caret` package includes a set of very useful functions for splitting the data prior to modeling. This is often necessary, as we typically need to work with both `train` and `test` datasets.

In this exercise, we will work with the famous mushroom dataset, which can be obtained from the UCI Machine Learning Repository.

Getting ready

In order to run this recipe, the `caret` package needs to be installed using `install.packages("caret")`.

How to do it...

This dataset has 8,124 samples of mushrooms that can be either poisonous or edible; the objective is to predict which ones are edible or poisonous based on 22 categorical features that relate to the physical characteristics of each mushroom.

We will show different ways of partitioning this dataset using several `caret` tools:

1. First, we load the `caret` library and the `mushroom` dataset. This dataset does not contain the column names, so we need to add them after loading the data:

   ```
   library(caret)
   mushroom_data =
   read.csv("https://archive.ics.uci.edu/ml/machine-learning-databases
   /mushroom/agaricus-lepiota.data",head=FALSE)
   colnames(mushroom_data) = c("edible","cap-shape", "cap-surface",
   "cap-color","bruises","odor", "gill-attachment","gill-
   spacing","gill-size","gill-color","stalk-shape", "stalk-
   root","stalk-surface-above-ring","stalk-surface-below-ring","stalk-
   color-above-ring", "stalk-color-below-ring","veil-type","veil-
   color","ring-number","ring-type", "spore-print-
   color","population","habitat")
   ```

2. The first function that we will present here is the `createDataPartition()`. The first argument specifies what the `target` variable is (for classification problems, the partition will be generated according to this label—this means that the proportion of labels will be the same in the train and test splits). The `p =` parameter is used to specify the training size (obviously *1-p* will be the proportion of the data assigned to the `testing` dataset). The `list=FALSE` parameter is used to instruct R that we don't want to return a list, and `times=1` specifies that we want just one replication in the output. After we get the indices, we can build the test and test should be in the same font as `train` datasets.

   ```
   trainIndex <- createDataPartition(mushroom_data$edible, p = .75,
   list = FALSE,   times = 1)
   traindata <- mushroom_data[trainIndex,]
   testdata <- mushroom_data[-trainIndex,]
   ```

3. Let's compare the proportions of edible total for the main dataset, the `train` dataset, and the testing dataset. The proportions are the same:

```
total_proportion <-
nrow(mushroom_data[mushroom_data$edible=="e",])/nrow(mushroom_data)
train_proportion <-
nrow(traindata[traindata$edible=="e",])/nrow(traindata)
test_proportion   <-
nrow(testdata[testdata$edible=="e",])/nrow(testdata)
print(paste("p of edible in data=",round(total_proportion,3),
            "/p of edible in train=",round(train_proportion,3),
            "/p of edible in test=",round(test_proportion,3)))
```

The resulting proportions for the total dataset, the training one and the testing one:

```
> print(paste("p of edible in data=",round(total_proportion,3),
+             "/p of edible in train=",round(train_proportion,3),
+             "/p of edible in test=",round(test_proportion,3)))
[1] "p of edible in data= 0.518 /p of edible in train= 0.518 /p of edible in test= 0.518"
```

4. Another function in the `caret` package is the `createResample()` function. This generates several new samples of the same size as the data, using `bootstrap` (sampling observations with replacement - some of them will be repeated, and some of them won't even appear in the resulting sample):

```
bootstrap_sample <-
createResample(mushroom_data$edible,times=10,list=FALSE)
```

5. The final function that can be used to create partitions is the `createFolds()` function. We pass a vector of labels again, and we specify how many subsets of data we want, and whether we want to return a list or not. This function is similar to `createDataPartition()`, with the obvious difference that it can be used to generate more than two sets:

```
kfolds_results = createFolds(mushroom_data$edible, k=4,list=FALSE)
r1 = nrow(mushroom_data[kfolds_results==1 &
mushroom_data$edible=="e",])/nrow(mushroom_data[kfolds_results==1,]
)
r2 = nrow(mushroom_data[kfolds_results==2 &
mushroom_data$edible=="e",])/nrow(mushroom_data[kfolds_results==2,]
)
r3 = nrow(mushroom_data[kfolds_results==3 &
mushroom_data$edible=="e",])/nrow(mushroom_data[kfolds_results==3,]
)
```

```
r4 = nrow(mushroom_data[kfolds_results==4 &
mushroom_data$edible=="e",])/nrow(mushroom_data[kfolds_results==4,]
)
print(paste("proportion of edible in fold1=",r1,
            "/proportion of edible in fold2=",r2,
            "/proportion of edible in fold3=",r3,
            "/proportion of edible in fold4=",r4))
```

Take a look at the following screenshot:

```
> print(paste("proportion of edible in fold1=",r1,
+             "/proportion of edible in fold2=",r2,
+             "/proportion of edible in fold3=",r3,
+             "/proportion of edible in fold4=",r4))
[1] "proportion of edible in fold1= 0.517971442639094 /proportion of edible in fold2= 0.517971442639094 /proportion of edible in fold3
= 0.517971442639094 /proportion of edible in fold4= 0.517971442639094"
```

How it works...

The `caret` package uses random numbers to build the samples that we need. In the case of `createFolds` and `createDataPartition`, the concept is the same, with the obvious difference that the former generates two datasets, and the latter generates *k* of them.

There's more...

The `caret` package has also a function to select subsets of data from a time series. This is the `createTimeSlices()` function. It needs three parameters: the first one is the vector of data; the second one is the number of elements to keep in train; and the third one is the horizon (periods that are kept for the testing data). In this example, we will generate 10 random numbers that simulate a time series, and we will split it into training sets of 4 elements, and testing sets of 2.

```
r = rnorm(10,0,1)
createTimeSlices(r,4, horizon=2)
```

Take a look at the following screenshot:

```
> createTimeSlices(r,4,horizon=2)
$train
$train$Training4
[1] 1 2 3 4

$train$Training5
[1] 2 3 4 5

$train$Training6
[1] 3 4 5 6

$train$Training7
[1] 4 5 6 7

$train$Training8
[1] 5 6 7 8


$test
$test$Testing4
[1] 5 6

$test$Testing5
[1] 6 7

$test$Testing6
[1] 7 8

$test$Testing7
[1] 8 9

$test$Testing8
[1]  9 10
```

See also

The dataset can be found on UCI's official repository.

Dua, D. and Graff, C. (2019). UCI Machine Learning Repository [http://archive.ics.uci.edu/ml]. Irvine, CA: University of California, School of Information and Computer Science.

Preprocessing

The `caret` package allows us to do a variety of things for preprocessing our data, such as scaling, centering, removing variables with very low variability, and projecting it via principal components. The main workhorse for this is the `preProcess()` function.

In this recipe, we will explore how to undertake several data transformation steps, before modeling using the `Boston` dataset (included in the `MASS` package). This is a famous dataset containing house price indexes for several areas in Boston. The objective is to use several metrics for each area and predict the price index there. We will explain how to do it using random forests.

There are essentially two ways of doing this in `caret`:

- By calling the `preProcess=` `argument` in the `train` function (this is less flexible, but can be used with cross-validation)
- By calling the `preProcess()` function before calling `train` (this is more flexible, but requires testing and training datasets)

The first approach is usually done when we want to find the best hyperparameters in conjunction with a TuneGrid. On the other hand, the second approach gives us more control but can't be used with cross-validation: assume that we have our full dataset, and we make a certain transformation (such as imputing missing values) that will alter both the training and testing data in each fold. The problem will be that the testing data will be contaminated by data that we have learned from the training dataset. The idea behind k-fold cross validation is to split the data into several parts and use *k-1* of them for training and *1* for evaluation (ensuring that no part is ever used for both things). This is a usual approach for finding the best hyperparameters for any model.

Getting ready

The `caret` package needs to be installed using `install.packages("caret")`.

How to do it...

In this recipe, we will show how to do basic preprocessing with `caret`. We will use simulated data as if it had originated from a chemical test. The target will be each metal-sample strength, and the features will be the amount of each chemical/metal that is contained. Some of the features will have missing values, and the intention will be to impute them. We will use median imputation to fix them (the median for each feature will be used to fix each missing value). We have eight numeric features with missing values. The intention will be to create **support vector machines (SVMs)** for regression. SVMs are models that can be used for either regression or classification (we will explain how they work later in this recipe). For the time being, let's just remember that they have a C hyperparameter that (as usual) controls the overfitting.

The train function is the most important one in caret. It will fit the model that we specified, using a grid of hyper-parameters. It will find the best hyper-parameter out of that grid.

The first way of preprocessing in `caret` is by using the `preProcess=` argument in the `train` function. We can then perform cross-validation as usual and get the best hyperparameters. The preprocessing steps are calculated using the training data and then applied to the testing data; this is done for each fold. The other approach is to split the data into training and testing and apply preprocessing to both, making sure there is no information transfer there. The following are the detailed steps to be followed:

1. Load the data:

```
library(MASS)
library(caret)
library(RANN)
set.seed(100)
data <- read.csv("./metals.csv")
data = data[-1]
trainIndex <- createDataPartition(data$metal_strength, p = .75,
list = FALSE, times = 1)
traindata <- data[trainIndex,]
testdata <- data[-trainIndex,]
```

2. Get the train-test splits. We define one hyperparameter and we can train our model. We want to evaluate our model's performance on the testing data:

```
preprocess_object <-
preProcess(traindata[-1],method=c("medianImpute","scale","center"))
x_transformed <- predict(preprocess_object,traindata[-1])
combined_train_data <- cbind(x_transformed,traindata[1])
```

3. Train our model:

```
control <- trainControl(method="none")
tunegrid <- expand.grid(C=c(0.01))
m3 <- train(metal_strength~., data=combined_train_data,
method="svmLinear",
metric="RMSE", tuneGrid=tunegrid, trControl=control)
```

4. Once the predictions are computed, we get the **root mean square error (RMSE)**:

```
test_xdata   <- predict(preprocess_object,testdata[-1])
y_test_pred <- predict(m3,test_xdata)
postResample(pred = y_test_pred, obs = testdata$m)
```

Take a look at the following screenshot:

```
> postResample(pred = y_test_pred, obs = testdata$m)
    RMSE Rsquared       MAE
3.019687 0.444644 2.419719
```

5. If we wanted to recompute this with a different hyperparameter, we would retrain the model like this:

```
control <- trainControl(method="none")
tunegrid <- expand.grid(C=c(0.9))
m3 <- train(metal_strength~., data=combined_train_data,
method="svmLinear", metric="RMSE", tuneGrid=tunegrid,
trControl=control)
test_xdata   <- predict(preprocess_object,testdata[-1])
y_test_pred <- predict(m3,test_xdata)
postResample(pred = y_test_pred, obs = testdata$m)
```

The results look very similar to the previous one:

```
> postResample(pred = y_test_pred, obs = testdata$m)
    RMSE Rsquared       MAE
3.010622 0.450088 2.393453
```

6. Instead of calling the `preprocess` function, we can pass the preprocessing steps to the `train` function. This is usually the preferred approach when we want to perform cross-validation and transformations. Remember that `caret` correctly applies the transformations in the cross-validation, ensuring that no contamination occurs between the folds (training and testing):

```
control <-  trainControl(method="repeatedcv", number=4, repeats=1)
tunegrid <- expand.grid(C=c(0.01,0.1,0.2,0.3,0.4,0.5))
m3 <- train(metal_strength~., data=combined_train_data,
method="svmLinear",preProcess=c("medianImpute","scale","center")
,metric="RMSE", tuneGrid=tunegrid, trControl=control)
```

Using the train function with different hyper-parameters. Caret automatically chooses the best model for us:

```
> m3
Support Vector Machines with Linear Kernel

752 samples
  8 predictor

Pre-processing: median imputation (8), scaled (8), centered (8)
Resampling: Cross-Validated (4 fold, repeated 1 times)
Summary of sample sizes: 564, 564, 564, 564
Resampling results across tuning parameters:

  C     RMSE      Rsquared   MAE
  0.01  3.167553  0.4535466  2.501964
  0.10  3.151757  0.4619144  2.492518
  0.20  3.152360  0.4617206  2.491767
  0.30  3.149831  0.4622470  2.489312
  0.40  3.150668  0.4617750  2.490378
  0.50  3.151037  0.4617684  2.491050

RMSE was used to select the optimal model using the smallest value.
The final value used for the model was C = 0.3.
```

As can be seen here, we find that the optimal C is **0.3**.

How it works...

SVMs can be used for both regression and classification. The underlying idea is to generate a sequence of separating hyperplanes that separate the data as efficiently as possible. Conceptually, a separating hyperplane can be thought of as drawing a line on the floor that separates what is covered by a carpet, and where the furniture is. Of course, there will be overlaps (furniture sitting on top of the carpet), and the furniture might also be very close to the carpet. This defines a triple problem:

- The margin separating furniture from the carpet can be thin.
- We will usually have an overlap.
- The hyperplane separating the furniture and the carpet might not necessarily be linear; for example, a curve might separate them optimally.

SVMs solve the three problems by using a series of tricks, such as having a regularization parameter that controls how thin the margin should be (a thin margin will work well on the training data, but won't work on the testing data overfitting), or by using a kernel trick to allow us to find a hyperplane that separates the data well in a transformed (nonlinear) space.

The C hyper-parameter controls the model's regularization. Particularly, it controls the size of the separating hyperplane. A very good explanation can be found here: `https://stats.stackexchange.com/questions/31066/what-is-the-influence-of-c-in-svms-with-linear-kernel`.

The `caret` package applies whatever transformation we want to the training/testing data by using the list of preprocessing steps that we defined. You can check the `caret` package documentation for further information, as there are several other ones.

Variable importance and feature selection

When building a model, we want to keep only the relevant features and discard the nonrelevant ones. A model that uses redundant features will have a higher variance (that it, it will be less precise) and the predictions will not look that great. When building models, keeping redundant features is comparable to omitting the relevant ones.

Getting ready

The `caret` package needs to be installed using `install.packages("caret")`.

How to do it...

In this recipe, we will focus on removing irrelevant features from our models, extracting the importance for each feature, and how to use recursive elimination to select features from a preliminary model (this can be used later in a secondary model containing the right features).

We will work with the `Boston` dataset. The idea of this dataset is to predict the median property price, based on environmental variables, crime indexes, and so on. We will use a random forest model. Here, we will follow a manual approach for feature selection, where we will train a model, get each feature importance, and build a final model:

1. First, we load the `Boston` dataset, we define the control and the grid for the model, and then we train the model using the usual cross-validation:

```
library(MASS)
library(caret)
control <- trainControl(method="repeatedcv", number=4, repeats=1)
tunegrid  <- expand.grid(.mtry=c(2,3,4,5,6,7,8))
data <- Boston
result <- train(medv~., data=data, method="rf", metric="RMSE",
tuneGrid=tunegrid,
trControl=control,importance=TRUE)$finalModel
result
```

The following screenshot shows model results:

```
Call:
 randomForest(x = x, y = y, mtry = param$mtry, importance = TRUE)
               Type of random forest: regression
                     Number of trees: 500
No. of variables tried at each split: 7

        Mean of squared residuals: 9.941527
                  % Var explained: 88.22
```

2. After the model has been trained, we will get the predictions via the `varImp` function. This can also be obtained using the `importance()` function:

```
gbmImp <- varImp(result)
importance(result)
```

The following screenshot shows variable importance table:

```
> importance(result)
           %IncMSE IncNodePurity
crim      16.861785    1986.58738
zn         1.558330      74.09081
indus      9.546889    1568.62781
chas       2.505455      87.21040
nox       17.955073    2124.22826
rm        47.477796   15049.08565
age       13.089950     810.19076
dis       21.635264    2425.25057
rad        6.008844     207.38032
tax       11.713522     785.05155
ptratio   15.244567    1654.38507
black      9.659428     512.22050
lstat     36.523813   14796.48140
```

3. These can also be printed using the varImpPlot() function:

```
varImpPlot(result)
Variable importance plot
```

Take a look at the following screenshot:

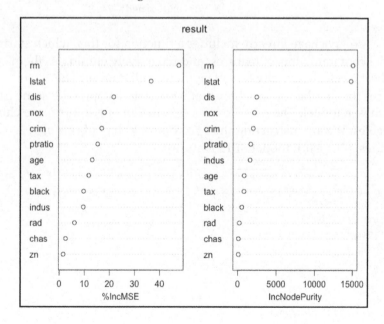

4. The model can be rebuilt using just two features (the ones that rank higher in both plots). It's not that surprising that a model with just two features performs reasonably closely to our full model with many extra variables. Nevertheless, what we really care about is which model gives the lowest RMSE, and obviously it would be rare for a model with two features to perform better than one with 13 of them. What could be a promising approach is to start with these two and keep adding more variables:

```
tunegrid <- expand.grid(.mtry=c(1))
result = train(medv~., data=data[,c("medv","rm","lstat")],
method="rf", metric="RMSE",
tuneGrid=tunegrid, trControl=control)$finalModel
result
```

The following screenshot shows model results for the two best variables:

```
Call:
 randomForest(x = x, y = y, mtry = param$mtry)
                Type of random forest: regression
                      Number of trees: 500
No. of variables tried at each split: 1

          Mean of squared residuals: 21.18228
                    % Var explained: 74.91
```

5. The `caret` package already includes a function for this, which starts with a large model containing lots of features, and recursively eliminates them. As we can see the best model is actually the one with the full dataset! The `print()` statement returns the number of variables that were tested along with some metrics, and the chosen model. The `predictors()` function only returns the chosen variables. We are instructing the `rfe` control to try subsets of 1, 2, 3, 4, and 5 features, plus a full model of 13 features:

```
control <- rfeControl(functions=rfFuncs, method="cv", number=10)
results <- rfe(as.matrix(data[-14]),as.matrix(data[14]),
sizes=c(1:5), rfeControl=control)
print(results)
predictors(results)
```

The following screenshot shows the result:

```
Recursive feature selection

Outer resampling method: Cross-Validated (10 fold)

Resampling performance over subset size:

 Variables  RMSE Rsquared   MAE RMSESD RsquaredSD  MAESD Selected
         1 6.574   0.5145 4.706 0.9108    0.11433 0.5566
         2 4.553   0.7570 3.122 0.5942    0.05851 0.3117
         3 3.844   0.8261 2.577 0.7870    0.07370 0.3623
         4 3.540   0.8584 2.394 0.5727    0.04900 0.2479
         5 3.511   0.8656 2.387 0.6134    0.05770 0.3051
        13 3.146   0.8916 2.141 0.4805    0.04053 0.2546        *

The top 5 variables (out of 13):
   rm, lstat, nox, dis, crim
```

```
plot(results, type=c("g", "o"))
RMSE (y-axis) and number of variables (x-axis)
```

The following screenshot shows the plotting results:

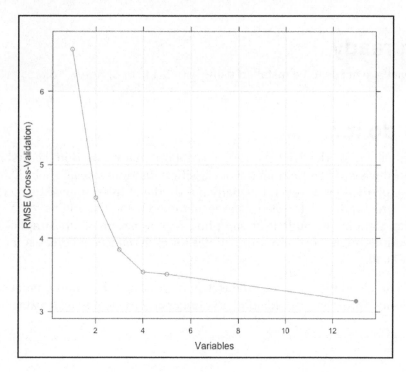

How it works...

The `varImpplot` function is described in caret's documentation. The variable importance plot that we used in this recipe, shows on the left the contribution to the reduction of the MSE (mean squared error) attributable to each feature; and on the right, the average purity increase (a pure node is a node that contains homogenous combinations of features). Pure nodes indicate that the tree (random forests are constructed using lots of trees) is correctly assigning similar sets of features to a similar target outcome. Good variables will obviously rank high on both scales. The `rfe` function (that we used in *Step 5*) works by building a large model (using random forests) containing all the features and eliminating them by their variable importance.

Model tuning

Most of the models that can be used with `caret` have certain hyperparameters. These are not estimated by each algorithm, but rather, need to be adjusted by the user. The strategy is to tune them in order to minimize some cross-validation error. `caret` has a variety of tools for tuning these hyperparameters that we will explore in this recipe.

Getting ready

The `caret` package needs to be installed using `install.packages("caret")`.

How to do it...

In this recipe, we will work with the `mushroom` dataset that we used in the first recipe of this chapter and we will fit a random forest classifier. Random forests are built by combining the predictions of several (usually hundreds) of trees, trained using different subsets of features, and bootstrapped datasets obtained using the original data. The way these bootstrap samples are built, is by sampling with replacement; this implies that some of the observations might appear multiple times for each dataset, whereas some of them won't appear at all:

1. We first load the `mushroom` dataset, and we assign the column names, as they are missing from the `.csv` file.Both the target and the features are categorical:

```
library(caret)
set.seed(11)
mushroom_data =
```

```
read.csv("https://archive.ics.uci.edu/ml/machine-learning-
databases/mushroom/agaricus-lepiota.data",head=FALSE)
colnames(mushroom_data) = c("edible","cap_shape", "cap_surface",
"cap_color","bruises","odor",
"gill_attachment","gill_spacing","gill_size","gill_color","stalk_sh
ape",
"stalk_root","stalk_surface_above_ring","stalk_surface_below_ring",
"stalk_color_above_ring",
"stalk_color_below_ring","veil_type","veil_color","ring_number","ri
ng_type",
"spore_print_color","population","habitat")
```

2. The objective of the data-processing part here will be to separate the target from the features, build the appropiate dummy variables for these features, and then join the features and target back. As a consequence, we save the target variables containing data on edible/nonedible mushrooms (the first column of our dataset). We also remove it from the dataset:

```
edible = mushroom_data[,1]
mushroom_data = mushroom_data[,-1]
```

3. We then remove the `veil_type` variable, which has only one level (it's constant and doesn't add anything to the model). After this is done, we generate the dummy model/expression containing the dataset and the expression. The `~ .` means that we want every variable to be transformed, and the `sep="__"` means that we want to create the column names in the format of `<factorname>__<level>`:

```
mushroom_data = mushroom_data[,-
which(colnames(mushroom_data)=="veil_type")]
mushroom_dummy_model = dummyVars(data=mushroom_data,~.,sep="__")
```

4. We then transform the dataset using the previous formula and we join both the dummies and the target variable laterally:

```
mushroom_data_model =
cbind(data.frame(predict(mushroom_dummy_model, mushroom_data)),
edible)
```

5. We then print the time, since this code takes some time to run. We define a control object that will manage how the grid search works. We will use repeated cross-validation (repeatedcv) with 4 folds and 1 repeat. This means that the data will be split into four parts, and four models will be estimated, one at a time. Each one of them will be trained in three folds, and evaluated in one. Because of repeated=1, this happens only once. There are several possible metrics we might be interested in, but since we are dealing with a balanced dataset, we can use the accuracy. The tunegrid variable holds a grid of values that will be tested: caret only allows us to tune the number of features that will be used (chosen at random) to train each tree (the objective of random forests is to train models that are as decorrelated as possible):

```
control = trainControl(method="repeatedcv", number=4, repeats=1)
metric = "Accuracy"
tunegrid = expand.grid(.mtry=c(2,5,7,10))
```

6. We then train the model by specifying that we want to model the edible target in terms of all the other variables in the dataset. The method that will be used here will be **random forests (RF)** and the other parameters correspond to the tunegrid and control objects that we defined previously:

```
rf_default = train(edible~., data=mushroom_data_model, method="rf",
metric=metric,
tuneGrid=tunegrid,  trControl=control)
```

7. We finally print the results of the model. Essentially, with either 5 or more for mtry, we get a 100% accuracy rate for the cross-validation samples. The kappa coefficient is similar to the accuracy, but it makes a correction by chance. For example, let's assume we have A and B labels, and we have a classifier that classifies 90% of the labels correctly. Depending on the proportion of A/B, this might be a spectacular classifier or a mediocre one.

For example, if the proportion was 50/50, classifying 90% of them correctly would be quite good. If, on the contrary, we had a 90/10 (or a 10/90), our 90% classifier would be mediocre. Why? Because in the latter case, if we assigned each label at random to A, we would still be on an approximate 90% accuracy rate; note that in the former case (50/50), we would be on a 50% accuracy rate. Cohen's kappa applies a correction to the ratio to account for this random chance agreement/accuracy. It will always be smaller than the regular accuracy. For balanced datasets, like the one we have here, Cohen's kappa will be roughly like the accuracy:

```
print(rf_default)
```

Take a look at the following screenshot:

```
Random Forest

8124 samples
 116 predictor
   2 classes: 'e', 'p'

No pre-processing
Resampling: Cross-Validated (4 fold, repeated 1 times)
Summary of sample sizes: 6093, 6093, 6093, 6093
Resampling results across tuning parameters:

  mtry  Accuracy   Kappa
   2    0.9767356  0.9533301
   5    1.0000000  1.0000000
   7    1.0000000  1.0000000
  10    1.0000000  1.0000000

Accuracy was used to select the optimal model using  the largest value.
The final value used for the model was mtry = 5.
```

8. There are several elements inside the tuned estimator, but in general we just want to get the best estimator using the full dataset. In order to achieve this, we can do the following:

```
rf_default$finalModel
```

How it works...

The dataset is split into *k* parts, and *k-1* parts are used for training and *1* for testing. In the testing part, the relevant metric is calculated (in this case, it's accuracy). This is done for each combination of hyperparameters that we have (in this case, we only have one of them). Finally, the model is retrained using the full dataset and those very same hyperparameters.

Even though this example works with a classification model, the same can be done for regression models as well (in this case, we need to adjust the metric accordingly).

The accuracy is usually a bad metric when the data is imbalanced, since models that work well for the most frequent class will be assumed to be better. In those cases, metrics such as the f1-score or the area under the **receiver operating characteristic (ROC)** curve are recommended.

Classification in caret and ROC curves

Classification models are harder to evaluate than regression models, because when we are classifying labels, we might have a severe imbalance. If, for example, we were predicting whether people are going to finish their university degrees or not, and 50% of people finish their degrees, the accuracy would be an ideal metric. But what happens when we have 95% of people finishing their degrees? In that case, the accuracy will be a very bad metric (maybe the model explains most of that 95% well, but doesn't work for the other 5% of the data).

There are several ways of assessing how well a classification model works that consider class imbalance. Apart from all these metrics, we can work with either ROC and precision-recall curves that allow us to choose a model that has the right performance for each label.

Remember that most classification models really output a probability that a sample belongs to class A or B. This probability is later transformed into a proper label (usually a 1/0 label) depending on whether this probability is greater or lower than a threshold. This threshold is usually assumed to be 0.5, but that doesn't need to be the case. By changing this threshold, we will alter the number of labels predicted to be 0 or 1.

More formally, we can define two metrics: the true positive rate, and the false positive rate. The former is the proportion of 1s correctly predicted as 1s, whereas the latter is the proportion of 0s incorrectly predicted as 0s. These metrics can be reversed, and we could replace the 1 by 0 in the previous statements. Let's suppose that we have the following predictions and true results:

Predictions	Real values
0.8	1
0.3	0

If we set up the threshold to be 0.1, both would be classified as 1s. The true positive rate is 100% but the false positive rate is 50%. If we change the threshold to 0.5, we get a true positive rate of 100% and a false positive rate of 0%. If we finally use a threshold of 0.9, we get a 0% true positive rate and a 0% false positive rate. We can obviously tune the threshold in order to achieve the right balance that we want for our model. This relationship can be plotted, yielding the ROC curve. Models can be compared by comparing the total area under the ROC curve (a good model will have a larger area, meaning that across all possible thresholds, it performs well). A nice thing about the ROC curve, is that the curve for a random model (one that randomly predicts 0s and 1s can be plotted and will actually be a 45-degree line).

Another way of posing this, is to define the so-called recall as the true positive rate, and the precision as the number of incorrectly predicted 1s (when they should be 0s) out of the total number of predicted 1s. By changing the threshold, the precision-recall values will change in the same way, yielding the precision-recall curve.

Many data scientists prefer the precision-recall curve over the ROC curve for highly imbalanced datasets. The reason is because precision-recall uses precision (it has the number of predicted 1s in the denominator – presumably low), whereas ROC uses a false positive rate (it has the number of 0s in the denominator – presumably high). This causes the precision-recall curve to change more drastically between models (a good model will have a substantial extra portion the reason why the area under the curve is used).

Getting ready

The MASS, PRROC, and precrec packages need to be installed using install.packages().

How to do it...

In this recipe, we will work with an imbalanced dataset and we will plot the ROC and precision-recall curves. The data contains:

1. We first load the dataset, and split it into training and testing data:

```
library(MASS)
library(caret)
library(PRROC)
library(precrec)
set.seed(10)
data = read.csv("./approved.csv")
data = data[,-c(1,7)]
data$Approved_ = "not_approved"
data$Approved_[data$Approved == 1] <- "approved"
data$Approved_ = as.factor(data$Approved_)
data = data[,-1]
trainIndex      <- createDataPartition(data$Approved_, p = .75,
list = FALSE,   times = 1)
traindata       <- data[trainIndex,]
testdata        <- data[-trainIndex,]
```

2. We fit a model using the training data, with a `tuneLength=10`. This means that caret will construct a grid for us containing 10 elements (using this, we don't even need to check what are the hyper-parameter names).

```
rctrl1 <- trainControl(method = "cv",number=5,classProbs =
TRUE,summaryFunction = twoClassSummary)
model1 <- train(Approved_~.,traindata,
method = "gbm", verbose=FALSE, trControl = rctrl1,metric="ROC",
tuneLength = 10)
```

3. We now predict the labels for the training data, and we print the confusion matrix. The model works really well for the not-approved, but it is not impressive for the approved class. It is important to realize that the accuracy is not a useful metric for these cases, as it is 94%, but that ignores the fact that the model underperforms for the approved ones. Kappa is obviously a much better metric:

```
predictions_train = predict(model1,traindata)
confusionMatrix(traindata$Approved_,predictions_train)
```

The following screenshot shows the model results:

```
Confusion Matrix and Statistics

                  Reference
Prediction      approved not_approved
  approved            13            5
  not_approved         0           67

               Accuracy : 0.9412
                 95% CI : (0.868, 0.9806)
    No Information Rate : 0.8471
    P-Value [Acc > NIR] : 0.006832

                  Kappa : 0.8039
 Mcnemar's Test P-Value : 0.073638

            Sensitivity : 1.0000
            Specificity : 0.9306
         Pos Pred Value : 0.7222
         Neg Pred Value : 1.0000
             Prevalence : 0.1529
         Detection Rate : 0.1529
   Detection Prevalence : 0.2118
      Balanced Accuracy : 0.9653

       'Positive' Class : approved
```

4. Now, we predict the same labels for the testing data. Obviously, our model doesn't work really well for the approved class. Kappa here is 51%, which makes sense given how badly our model works for the approved cases:

```
predictions_test = predict(model1,testdata)
confusionMatrix(testdata$Approved_,predictions_test)
```

The following screenshot shows confusion matrix for the test data:

```
Confusion Matrix and Statistics

                  Reference
Prediction      approved not_approved
  approved          3               3
  not_approved      1              21

               Accuracy : 0.8571
                 95% CI : (0.6733, 0.9597)
    No Information Rate : 0.8571
    P-Value [Acc > NIR] : 0.6292

                  Kappa : 0.5172
 Mcnemar's Test P-Value : 0.6171

            Sensitivity : 0.7500
            Specificity : 0.8750
         Pos Pred Value : 0.5000
         Neg Pred Value : 0.9545
             Prevalence : 0.1429
         Detection Rate : 0.1071
   Detection Prevalence : 0.2143
      Balanced Accuracy : 0.8125

       'Positive' Class : approved
```

5. Using the PRROC package, we plot the ROC curves for both the training and testing data. In practice, we almost never look at the ROC curve for the training data; we just display it here to gauge how much area we lose between the training and testing datasets:

```
plot.roc(traindata$Approved_,predict(model1, traindata,
type="prob")[,1],main="ROC curves,
black=train,red=test")
plot.roc(testdata$Approved_,predict(model1, testdata,
type="prob")[,1],col="red",add=TRUE)
```

The following screenshot ROC curves:

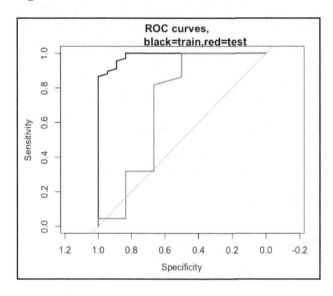

6. The precision-recall curve can be printed using the `precrec` package. We print it for the testing dataset:

```
par(mfrow=c(2,1))
sscurves <- evalmod(scores = predict(model1, traindata,
type="prob")[,2], labels = traindata$Approved_)
plot(sscurves)
sscurves <- evalmod(scores = predict(model1, testdata,
type="prob")[,2], labels = testdata$Approved_)
plot(sscurves)
```

The following screenshot ROC and precision-recall for the training data:

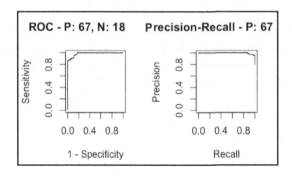

The following screenshot shows the ROC and precision-recall curve for the testing data:

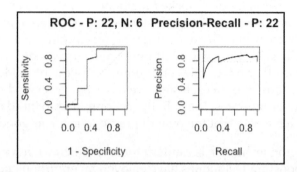

7. The most important part: we can get how well the model works across all possible thresholds using the following syntax. The AUC is 0.98 for the train data, and 0.70 for the test data. This big drop in the AUC could be seen in the ROC curves before.

```
auc(traindata$Approved_, predict(model1,traindata,type="prob")[,1])
auc(testdata$Approved_, predict(model1,testdata,type="prob")[,1])
```

How it works...

After we compute the predictions for our model, we can pass them, along with the real labels, to any proper function that computes the ROC and PR curves. These are obtained by changing the threshold and recomputing the TPR, FPR, recall, and precision.

ROC curves have two main advantages: they are robust to class imbalance (accuracy is not robust in any way), and they allow us to compare models irrepective of the threshold. They allow us to compare models along all possible thresholds. This is much better than for example the F1 score, or Cohen's Kappa because they need us to fix a threshold (they are usually calculated assuming a threshold of 0.5). It is worth noting that classification models can work well for certain thresholds and wrongly for other thresholds. So having a way of comparing among different ones is of prime importance. This is why the AUC (and also the area under the precision-recall curve) are the main tool that data-scientists use for choosing among different models.

Gradient boosting and class imbalance

Ensembles of models (several models stacked together) can be conceptualized into two main groups: bagging and boosting. Bagging stands for bootstrap aggregation, meaning that several submodels are trained by bootstrapping (resampling with replacement) over the dataset. Each dataset will obviously be different and each model will yield different results. Boosting, on the other hand relies on training subsequent models using the residuals from the previous step. In each step, we have an aggregated model and a new model that is trained over those residuals. Both are combined to build a new combined model optimally (in such a way that the overall predictions are as good as possible).

The most famous bagging technique is random forests, which we have used previously in this chapter. Several boosting techniques have enjoyed an enormous popularity over recent years, gradient boosting being the most.

A separate topic is class imbalance, which causes major changes regarding how we should assess our models' performance. The main problem is that when the data is imbalanced, the model will adjust to predict the dominating class to the detriment of the other ones. It is not strange to see cases when a model predicts all the labels to belong to the most common class. There are essentially three ways of fixing this problem:

- **Upsampling**, meaning that we resample with replacement from the least frequent classes
- **Downsampling**, which is the same as the previous method, but samples less from the most common classes
- **Synthetic minority oversampling technique** (**SMOTE**): this one generates new observations
- **Weighting the classes** (usually an inversely proportional weight to each weight according to the class frequency)

The first three can be applied with any classification technique in `caret`, whereas the last can be applied only if the underlying method accepts it.

Getting ready

The `caret` package needs to be installed using `install.packages("caret")`.

How to do it...

In this exercise, we will use gradient boosting with a real dataset containing wine types. Here we will have three classes, and they are slightly imbalanced:

1. We first load the modeling dataset and prepare the modeling data:

```
library(MASS)
library(PRROC)
library(precrec)
set.seed(10)
data = read.csv("./approved.csv")
data = data[,-c(1,7)]
data$Approved_ = "not_approved"
data$Approved_[data$Approved == 1] <- "approved"
data$Approved_ = as.factor(data$Approved_)
data = data[,-1]
```

2. We split the data into training and testing groups:

```
trainIndex          <- createDataPartition(data$Approved_, p = .75,
list = FALSE,   times = 1)
traindata           <- data[trainIndex,]
testdata            <- data[-trainIndex,]
```

3. We then fit our first model; let's call it `baseline`:

```
rctrl1              <- trainControl(method      =
"cv",number=5,classProbs = TRUE,summaryFunction =
twoClassSummary)
baseline            <- train(Approved_~.,traindata,   method      =
"gbm",   verbose=FALSE, trControl   = rctrl1,
 metric="ROC", tuneLength = 10)
```

4. We then apply upsampling:

```
rctrl1 <- trainControl(method       =
"cv",number=5,sampling="up",classProbs =   TRUE,summaryFunction =
twoClassSummary)
up <- train(Approved_~.,traindata,   method       = "gbm",
verbose=FALSE, trControl   = rctrl1, metric="ROC", tuneLength = 10)
```

5. We then apply SMOTE:

```
rctrl1   <- trainControl(method =
"cv",number=5,sampling="smote",classProbs = TRUE,summaryFunction =
twoClassSummary)
smote   <- train(Approved_~.,traindata, method = "gbm",
verbose=FALSE, trControl  = rctrl1, metric="ROC", tuneLength = 10)
```

6. Let's predict the labels for the testing data:

```
predictions_baseline = predict(baseline,testdata,type="prob")
predictions_up       = predict(up,testdata,type="prob")
predictions_smote     = predict(up,testdata,type="prob")
```

7. Finally, let's build the confusion matrices for each case. Let's start with the `baseline` model:

```
confusionMatrix(testdata$Approved_,predict(baseline,testdata))
```

The following screenshot shows the baseline model:

```
Confusion Matrix and Statistics

                  Reference
Prediction      approved not_approved
   approved          3             3
   not_approved      1            21

                 Accuracy : 0.8571
                   95% CI : (0.6733, 0.9597)
      No Information Rate : 0.8571
      P-Value [Acc > NIR] : 0.6292

                    Kappa : 0.5172
 Mcnemar's Test P-Value : 0.6171

              Sensitivity : 0.7500
              Specificity : 0.8750
           Pos Pred Value : 0.5000
           Neg Pred Value : 0.9545
               Prevalence : 0.1429
           Detection Rate : 0.1071
     Detection Prevalence : 0.2143
        Balanced Accuracy : 0.8125

         'Positive' Class : approved
```

8. Now, there is the model based on the data with upsampling:

```
confusionMatrix(testdata$Approved_,predict(up,testdata))
```

Take a look at the following screenshot:

```
Confusion Matrix and Statistics

                  Reference
Prediction      approved not_approved
  approved             4            2
  not_approved         4           18

                Accuracy : 0.7857
                  95% CI : (0.5905, 0.917)
     No Information Rate : 0.7143
     P-Value [Acc > NIR] : 0.2718

                   Kappa : 0.4324
 Mcnemar's Test P-Value : 0.6831

             Sensitivity : 0.5000
             Specificity : 0.9000
          Pos Pred Value : 0.6667
          Neg Pred Value : 0.8182
              Prevalence : 0.2857
          Detection Rate : 0.1429
    Detection Prevalence : 0.2143
       Balanced Accuracy : 0.7000

        'Positive' Class : approved
```

9. We now evaluate the confusion matrix for the SMOTE processed data:

```
confusionMatrix(testdata$Approved_,predict(smote,testdata))
```

The following screenshot shows SMOTE results:

```
Confusion Matrix and Statistics

                  Reference
Prediction      approved not_approved
   approved           3            3
   not_approved       1           21

               Accuracy : 0.8571
                 95% CI : (0.6733, 0.9597)
    No Information Rate : 0.8571
    P-Value [Acc > NIR] : 0.6292

                  Kappa : 0.5172
 Mcnemar's Test P-Value : 0.6171

            Sensitivity : 0.7500
            Specificity : 0.8750
         Pos Pred Value : 0.5000
         Neg Pred Value : 0.9545
             Prevalence : 0.1429
         Detection Rate : 0.1071
   Detection Prevalence : 0.2143
      Balanced Accuracy : 0.8125

       'Positive' Class : approved
```

10. Let's print the **area under the curve (AUC)** for the three models:

```
> roc(testdata$Approved_,predict(baseline,testdata,type="prob")$approved)

Call:
roc.default(response = testdata$Approved_, predictor = predict(baseline,     testdata, type = "prob")$approved)

Data: predict(baseline, testdata, type = "prob")$approved in 6 controls (testdata$Approved_ approved) > 22 cases (testdata$Approved_ not_approved).
Area under the curve: 0.7008
> roc(testdata$Approved_,predict(up,testdata,type="prob")$approved)

Call:
roc.default(response = testdata$Approved_, predictor = predict(up,     testdata, type = "prob")$approved)

Data: predict(up, testdata, type = "prob")$approved in 6 controls (testdata$Approved_ approved) > 22 cases (testdata$Approved_ not_approved).
Area under the curve: 0.7083
> roc(testdata$Approved_,predict(smote,testdata,type="prob")$approved)

Call:
roc.default(response = testdata$Approved_, predictor = predict(smote,     testdata, type = "prob")$approved)

Data: predict(smote, testdata, type = "prob")$approved in 6 controls (testdata$Approved_ approved) > 22 cases (testdata$Approved_ not_approved).
Area under the curve: 0.7197
```

11. Evidently, SMOTE and upsampling achieve a better performance for the approved class, but which model is working best? Here, we will just print the output for the SMOTE case. The metrics here are modified and are expressed in terms of precision-recall instead of FPR/TPR. The metric used usually is the F1 score, which is the harmonic mean of precision and recall:

```
confusionMatrix(testdata$Approved_,predict(baseline,testdata),mode="prec_re
call")
```

The following screenshot shows baseline outputs - precision/recall:

```
Confusion Matrix and Statistics

                    Reference
Prediction      approved not_approved
  approved             3            3
  not_approved         1           21

               Accuracy : 0.8571
                 95% CI : (0.6733, 0.9597)
    No Information Rate : 0.8571
    P-Value [Acc > NIR] : 0.6292

                  Kappa : 0.5172
 Mcnemar's Test P-Value : 0.6171

              Precision : 0.5000
                 Recall : 0.7500
                     F1 : 0.6000
             Prevalence : 0.1429
         Detection Rate : 0.1071
   Detection Prevalence : 0.2143
      Balanced Accuracy : 0.8125

       'Positive' Class : approved
```

Take a look at the following screenshot:

```
confusionMatrix(testdata$Approved_,predict(up,testdata),mode="prec_recall")
```

The following screenshot shows Upsampling outputs - precision/recall:

```
Confusion Matrix and Statistics

                   Reference
Prediction     approved not_approved
   approved          4            2
   not_approved      4           18

                       Accuracy : 0.7857
                         95% CI : (0.5905, 0.917)
            No Information Rate : 0.7143
            P-Value [Acc > NIR] : 0.2718

                          Kappa : 0.4324
       Mcnemar's Test P-Value : 0.6831

                      Precision : 0.6667
                         Recall : 0.5000
                             F1 : 0.5714
                     Prevalence : 0.2857
                 Detection Rate : 0.1429
           Detection Prevalence : 0.2143
              Balanced Accuracy : 0.7000

               'Positive' Class : approved
```

Take a look at the following screenshot:

```
confusionMatrix(testdata$Approved_,predict(smote,testdata),mode="prec_recal
l")
```

The following screenshot shows SMOTE results:

```
Confusion Matrix and Statistics

                     Reference
Prediction        approved not_approved
   approved              4             2
   not_approved          3            19


               Accuracy : 0.8214
                 95% CI : (0.6311, 0.9394)
    No Information Rate : 0.75
    P-Value [Acc > NIR] : 0.2638

                  Kappa : 0.5
 Mcnemar's Test P-Value : 1.0000

              Precision : 0.6667
                 Recall : 0.5714
                     F1 : 0.6154
             Prevalence : 0.2500
         Detection Rate : 0.1429
   Detection Prevalence : 0.2143
      Balanced Accuracy : 0.7381

       'Positive' Class : approved
```

How it works...

Gradient boosting works by building a sequence of models that are fitted iteratively to the data. For any step, a model is fitted to the data and residuals are obtained. A new model is fitted to those residuals, and the new model is joined to the previous one by summing them using an appropriate weight.

The SMOTE algorithm, presented here, works differently by finding the K-nearest neighbors for each sample in the small group. Then one of those is picked up as a reference point, and random numbers between 0 and 1 are drawn and multiplied by that vector of features that was picked.

Lasso, ridge, and elasticnet in caret

We have already discussed **ordinary least squares (OLS)** and its related techniques, lasso and ridge, in the context of linear regression. In this recipe, we will see how easily these techniques can be implemented in `caret` and how to tune the corresponding hyperparameters.

OLS is designed to find the estimates that minimize the square distances between the observations and the predicted values of a linear model. There are three reasons why this approach might not be ideal:

- If the number of predictors is greater than the number of samples, OLS cannot be used. This is not usually a problem, since in most of the practical cases we have, n>p.
- If we have lots of variables of dubious importance, OLS will still estimate a coefficient for each one of them. After the model is estimated, we will need to do some variable selection and discard the irrelevant ones (usually using t- or p-values). When we have lots of variables, this is very tedious to do manually, so we need to rely on an automatic approach.
- Even if everything works as expected in OLS and we manage to remove the irrelevant features, the resulting OLS model might not be very good. Maybe it could be improved by sacrificing some bias (forcing some coefficients to be smaller than they should be in order to gain via a reduction in variance). This is the best and most frequent reason why lasso, ridge, and elasticnet are used.

Getting ready

The `caret` package needs to be installed using `install.packages("caret")`.

How to do it...

The handy `train()` function in `caret` will allow us to find the best hyperparameters for these models. In this recipe, we will use the `longley` dataset, which is included in R's standard datasets library. This dataset contains the number of people employed (which is our target variable), and several features (such as the number of unemployed, the year, the GNP, the GNP deflator, and the population). There are two challenges here; it only contains annual data from 1947 to 1962, and some of the variables are highly colinear:

1. Let's first load the dataset, and build a simple `lm()` model that will serve as a reference. As can be seen below, we have three variables with a low significance. This model is obviously not very promising as it is, because it contains nonsignificant variables inside it (that is, the predictions will have a huge variance). We set the seed to `100` for reproducibility purposes:

    ```
    set.seed(100)
    library(caret)
    summary(lm(data=longley,Employed~.))
    ```

2. We now set up a train control that will be used among the different models:

    ```
    rctrl1 <- trainControl(method    = "cv",number=5)
    ```

3. We retrain the `lm()` model and we focus our attention on the RMSE. Here we get an RMSE of 0.39, which will be our baseline:

    ```
    ols_       <- train(Employed~.,longley, method     = "lm",
    trControl  = rctrl1,   tuneLength = 4,metric="RMSE",
    preProc    = c("center", "scale"))
    ```

The following screenshot shows model results:

```
Linear Regression

16 samples
 6 predictor

Pre-processing: centered (6), scaled (6)
Resampling: Cross-Validated (7 fold)
Summary of sample sizes: 14, 13, 13, 14, 14, 14, ...
Resampling results:

  RMSE       Rsquared
  0.3958705  0.999043

Tuning parameter 'intercept' was held constant at a value of TRUE
```

4. We do the same exercise for the lasso model, and we get a RMSE of 0.369 for a fraction parameter that equals 0.54:

```
lasso_ <- train(Employed~.,longley, method = "lasso", trControl =
rctrl1, tuneLength = 10,metric="RMSE",  preProc = c("center",
"scale"))
```

The following screenshot shows Lasso results:

```
The lasso

16 samples
 6 predictor

Pre-processing: centered (6), scaled (6)
Resampling: Cross-validated (7 fold)
Summary of sample sizes: 14, 14, 13, 14, 13, 14, ...
Resampling results across tuning parameters:

   fraction    RMSE        Rsquared
   0.1000000   2.0163297   0.9983535
   0.1888889   0.8871784   0.9983535
   0.2777778   0.5064000   0.9996527
   0.3666667   0.4786030   0.9997923
   0.4555556   0.3950334   0.9993535
   0.5444444   0.3691649   0.9992959
   0.6333333   0.3942011   0.9991461
   0.7222222   0.3963325   0.9990120
   0.8111111   0.4022890   0.9987205
   0.9000000   0.4044215   0.9985525

RMSE was used to select the optimal model using  the smallest value.
The final value used for the model was fraction = 0.5444444.
```

5. Doing the same for ridge, we get an RMSE of 0.362. So far, this is the best model:

```
ridge_ <- train(Employed~.,longley, method = "ridge",  trControl =
rctrl1, tuneLength = 10,metric="RMSE", preProc = c("center",
"scale"))
```

The following screenshot shows Ridge results:

```
Ridge Regression

16 samples
 6 predictor

Pre-processing: centered (6), scaled (6)
Resampling: Cross-validated (7 fold)
Summary of sample sizes: 14, 14, 14, 13, 14, 14, ...
Resampling results across tuning parameters:

  lambda         RMSE        Rsquared
  0.0000000000   0.4161288   0.9974995
  0.0001000000   0.3888210   0.9974647
  0.0002371374   0.3725052   0.9973616
  0.0005623413   0.3625536   0.9970605
  0.0013335214   0.3722161   0.9964052
  0.0031622777   0.4134904   0.9953960
  0.0074989421   0.4447313   0.9943925
  0.0177827941   0.4578839   0.9937277
  0.0421696503   0.4658095   0.9930094
  0.1000000000   0.5286827   0.9906528

RMSE was used to select the optimal model using  the smallest value.
The final value used for the model was lambda = 0.0005623413.
```

6. Finally, for `elasticnet`, the RMSE is 0.34. We conclude that this is the best model based on the ones we have tested:

```
elasticnet_ <- train(Employed~.,longley, method     = "glmnet",
trControl  = rctrl1, tuneLength = 10,metric="RMSE", preProc    =
c("center", "scale"))
```

Take a look at the following screenshot:

```
0.8    0.542568144   0.8250467   0.9975710
0.8    1.253402784   1.3779181   0.9974856
0.8    2.895522997   2.7206532   0.9974589
0.9    0.001545254   0.3502197   0.9972639
0.9    0.003569736   0.3408876   0.9971775
0.9    0.008246553   0.3346229   0.9967991
0.9    0.019050608   0.3713379   0.9963457
0.9    0.044009375   0.4677234   0.9956117
0.9    0.101667364   0.5640010   0.9964296
0.9    0.234864797   0.6740046   0.9978305
0.9    0.542568144   0.8336168   0.9976902
0.9    1.253402784   1.4628706   0.9975585
0.9    2.895522997   2.9890655   0.9975556
1.0    0.001545254   0.3398837   0.9973507
1.0    0.003569736   0.3289765   0.9972444
1.0    0.008246553   0.3289986   0.9967737
1.0    0.019050608   0.3640645   0.9963612
1.0    0.044009375   0.4913479   0.9957447
1.0    0.101667364   0.5567210   0.9969338
1.0    0.234864797   0.6563954   0.9978855
1.0    0.542568144   0.8211473   0.9978855
1.0    1.253402784   1.5201484   0.9978855
1.0    2.895522997   3.2526324   0.9978855

RMSE was used to select the optimal model using  the smallest value.
The final values used for the model were alpha = 1 and lambda = 0.003569736.
```

7. We can still use the `varImp` function to get the relative importance of each variable. For example, let's see what the importance is for the `elasticnet` model (which is our best model here):

```
varImp((elasticnet_))
```

The following screenshot shows the variable importance vector:

```
> varImp((elasticnet_))
glmnet variable importance

                  Overall
Year              100.00
Unemployed         26.34
Population         11.51
Armed.Forces       10.80
GNP                 0.00
GNP.deflator        0.00
```

How it works...

OLS works by minimizing the residual sum of squares, assuming a linear model. Both lasso and ridge assume the same idea, but with the difference of adding a penalization. Lasso adds an L1 one, whereas ridge adds an L2 one. This means that lasso results will be pushed towards zero (maybe exactly zero), and ridge will be pushed towards zero (but not exactly zero). Therefore, Lasso works almost as a variable selection tool: the irrelevant coefficients will receive a zero coefficient, thus being effectively dropped from the model. GLMNET is a mixture of both ridge and lasso, that is usually preferred by data scientists. The reason is that not only the amount of regularization, but also the mix of L2/L1 regularization can be tuned.

Logic regression

In some scenarios, all the features in our datasets will be 1/0 dummies (1 flagging the presence of an attribute, and 0 otherwise). These can obviously be accommodated using any usual regression or classification technique. But the problem is that we wouldn't be truly analyzing the interactions between them, unless we add all possible interaction terms (this is usually a tedious task—and we would potentially need to add an enormour amount of combinations).

The relevant question in these cases, is whether the presence of an attribute in conjunction with the presence or absence of other attributes causes an effect. Logic regression can be used in both regression and classification models, and the objective is to find the best possible sets of interactions that cause the highest accuracy (for classification models) or the lowest RMSE (for regression models). Logic regression is usually used in experiments where we can control the presence of an attribute, although sometimes it appears in other nonexperimental cases.

Getting ready

The `caret` package needs to installed in order to run this recipe using
`install.packages("caret")`.

How to do it...

In the following example, we will load data for the 2019 season for the Los Angeles Lakers. We will have one dummy for each player, flagging if that player was part of the starting team that night, plus an extra dummy that flags if the team is playing at home or away. The objective is to predict if the team won that night using just those dummies as explanatory variables. Ideally, we would like our model to capture those complicated interactions that might occur (that is, Player *X* might perform much better if Player *Y* was present):

1. We first load the dataset and we propose our first logic model:

    ```
    library(caret)
    set.seed(10)
    baseketball_data_2019 = read.csv("./lakers_.csv")
    baseketball_data_2019 = baseketball_data_2019[,-c(1,2)]
    ```

2. It will have two hyperparameters that will be tuned by `caret` (`treesize` and `ntrees`). Not surprisingly, the results are not good, and the kappa is even negative—meaning that the model is worse than one model that classifies the data randomly:

    ```
    rctrl1 <- trainControl(method = "cv",number=5)
    baseketball_data_2019$win = as.factor(baseketball_data_2019$win)
    model1 <- train(win~.,baseketball_data_2019, method = "logreg",
    metric = "Accuracy", trControl  = rctrl1, tuneLength = 4)
    ```

    The following screenshot shows logic model results:

```
Logic Regression

24 samples
13 predictors
 2 classes: '0', '1'

No pre-processing
Resampling: Cross-Validated (5 fold)
Summary of sample sizes: 20, 19, 19, 19, 19
Resampling results across tuning parameters:

  ntrees  treesize  Accuracy  Kappa
  2       4         0.40      -0.26545455
  2       8         0.36      -0.33818182
  2       16        0.40      -0.26545455
  2       32        0.32      -0.39878788
  3       4         0.48      -0.05030303
  3       8         0.40      -0.23212121
  3       16        0.40      -0.26545455
  3       32        0.32      -0.39878788
  4       4         0.28      -0.47151515
  4       8         0.32      -0.39878788
  4       16        0.32      -0.36545455
  4       32        0.32      -0.36895105

Accuracy was used to select the optimal model using the largest value.
The final values used for the model were treesize = 4 and ntrees = 3.
```

How it works...

When using standard techniques, we usually need to rely on very simple interactions (usually two-way interactions) that are built by adding term to the model, such as: *var1 x var2*. This is not very practical in many cases, when we have lots of features. The underlying algorithm for logic regression explores (as much as possible) the combination space by intelligently evaluating some of these combinations.

Unfortunately, this model reflects (again) how difficult it is to predict sports results. At the end, each game is not only determined by variables that we can measure, but also on specific game situations that are difficult to predict.

In essence, the logic regression model works by finding a set of **logic expressions** (*Lj*) and a **set of weights** (*β*) that can explain the expected value of a variable:

$$g(E[Y]) = \beta_0 + \sum_{j=1}^{t} \beta_j L_j$$

The logic expressions could be similar to this one (or more complex):

$$L_j = (X_1 \vee X_2)$$

There are several ways of solving this problem: the usual one is to formulate a starting model and use a stochastic search algorithm that proposes different moves (changes or additions to the logic expressions).

10
Bayesian Networks and Hidden Markov Models

We will cover the following recipes in this chapter:

- A discrete Bayesian Network using `bnlearn`
- Conditional independence tests
- Continuous and hybrid Bayesian Networks via `bnlearn`
- Interactive visualization of BNs with the `bnviewer` package
- An introductory hidden Markov model
- Regime switching in financial data using HMMs

Introduction

This chapter discusses two powerful techniques used in advanced statistics. The first one, **Bayesian networks** (usually referred to as **BNs**), is a graphical model based on Bayesian theory, which is used to represent probabilistic relationships between several variables. The second one, the **hidden Markov model** (**HMM**), is a model that can handle both observable and non-observable variables that affect a dependent variable. In the simplest scenario, we might observe whether people arrive at an office with an umbrella or not, with the intention of deducing whether it was raining or not.

This chapter is divided into two parts: there are four recipes dedicated to BNs and three recipes dedicated to HMMs.

A discrete Bayesian network via bnlearn

Bayesian networks are probabilistic graphical models used for understanding how different variables interact with each other. They are built by exploiting the conditional dependencies of each variable using Bayesian theory. For example, let's assume that we have three variables: **sleep quality**, **diet quality**, and **work performance**. For the sake of simplicity, let's also assume that each variable can only take two values: high and low. In our usual regression or classification framework, we would model one of these variables in terms of all the rest. Of course, we would need to take care to choose a dependent variable that is caused by the covariates in some way (in order to make an inference in a regression context, causality needs to flow from the covariates to the dependent variable). BNs operate differently, and in this case, we could define several networks (for example, these two):

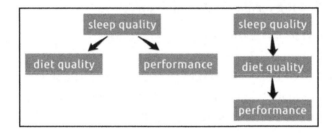

Note that we are, in principle, establishing a causal ordering between the variables, but causality in BNs (as in any other model actually) needs to be treated with a lot of care. The main problem is that we are imposing it, but not formally deriving it mathematically. The mechanics of BNs can work regardless of whether **sleep quality** causes **diet quality** and whether this last one causes **performance**, or vice versa. This is why deducing causality from a BN is usually wrong.

A nice aspect of BNs is that we can easily map how conditional probabilities change when modeled as an interconnected system. This can be done in two ways: as a bottom-up strategy, given a high or low performance, we can find out what's the most likely sleep-diet status to have caused it; or, as a top-down (predictive) approach: given a sleep-diet combination, find out what the most likely performance? There are essentially two ways of defining BNs, and there is a third one that is a combination of these two:

- **Expert-defined**: External knowledge is used to build the structure of the network. This is what we did in the previous example.
- **Data-driven**: The data is used to dictate what an appropriate configuration of the network would be by using an appropriate algorithm.

Getting ready

The bnlearn package needs to be installed using install.packages("bnlearn").

How to do it...

In this recipe, we will work with a dataset containing several features for the employees of a certain company: the area, the sleep quality, whether they recently had a child, diet quality, travel time and performance. In this example, all these features have two levels, but that is obviously not a requirement:

1. First, we load the dataset, we define the network, and we plot it. We could use several networks, but this one is a reasonable one to begin with. Note that the performance (maybe the most relevant variable for us here) is impacted by two variables: diet_quality and travel_time. Presumably, people that must travel more are more tired and perform worse at work; also, people who are not eating well, may feel too tired to work well. Both variables depend on other variables:

```
library(bnlearn)
data = read.csv("./employee_data.csv")[-1]
dag =
model2network("[Area][travel_time|Area][performance|travel_time:die
t_quality]
[Recently_had_child][Sleep_quality|Recently_had_child:Area][diet_qu
ality|Sleep_quality]")
plot(dag)
```

This plot shows how the different variables are connected:

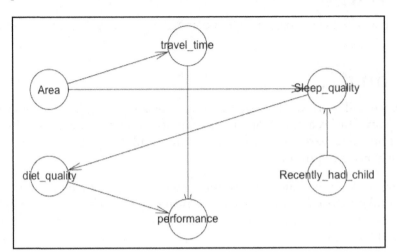

2. We now fit the model using two arguments: the structure that we specified and the data. The data frame containing the data needs to have the exact same column names as the model that we defined, and there cannot be any extra variables:

```
fitted = bn.fit(dag, data)
```

3. Once the model has been fitted, we can execute queries, which are essentially predictions for conditional probabilities. For example, let's see what the predicted probabilities are that the employee has a high performance level given that they live in a SUBURBAN or URBAN area:

```
cpquery(fitted, (performance=="HIGH"), (Area=="URBAN"))
cpquery(fitted, (performance=="HIGH"), (Area=="SUBURBAN"))
```

The following screenshot shows result:

```
> cpquery(fitted, (performance=="HIGH"), (Area=="URBAN"))
[1] 0.7796
> cpquery(fitted, (performance=="HIGH"), (Area=="SUBURBAN"))
[1] 0.6857835
```

4. We do a similar exercise, now querying the probability that the performance is HIGH given that `travel_time` is HIGH and `sleep_quality` is HIGH, and given that `sleep_quality` is LOW. These are predictive queries:

```
cpquery(fitted, (performance=="HIGH"), (travel_time=="HIGH" &
Sleep_quality=="HIGH"))
cpquery(fitted, (performance=="HIGH"), (travel_time=="HIGH" &
Sleep_quality=="LOW"))
```

The following screenshot shows the results of the query:

```
> cpquery(fitted, (performance=="HIGH"), (travel_time=="HIGH" & Sleep_quality=="HIGH"))
[1] 0.6323752
> cpquery(fitted, (performance=="HIGH"), (travel_time=="HIGH" & Sleep_quality=="LOW"))
[1] 0.5307557
```

5. A different query could be, given that the someone's performance is HIGH/LOW, what is the probability that the person in question is sleeping well or not?:

```
cpquery(fitted, (Sleep_quality=="HIGH"), (performance=="HIGH"))
cpquery(fitted, (Sleep_quality=="LOW") , (performance=="HIGH"))
```

Take a look at the following screenshot:

```
> cpquery(fitted, (Sleep_quality=="HIGH"), (performance=="HIGH"))
[1] 0.5980094
> cpquery(fitted, (Sleep_quality=="LOW") , (performance=="HIGH"))
[1] 0.3983425
```

6. We can plot the results for each node. For example, let's see how the conditional probabilities for `diet_quality` change according to the node that is connected to it (`sleep_quality`). The orange columns refer to each `sleep_quality` level, and the rows refer to each `diet_quality` level:

```
bn.fit.dotplot(fitted$diet_quality)
Conditional probabilities for diet_quality
```

Take a look at the following screenshot:

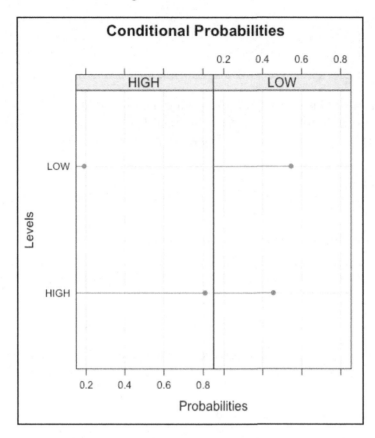

7. We have already stated that there are essentially two ways of building Bayesian networks: the expert approach (which is what we have used so far—specifying how the nodes are connected), and the automatic way. The latter relies on several sophisticated algorithms estimate the best structure. We can do this using the `hc()` function. Unfortunately, when we have lots of variables, it is very difficult not to rely on this fully automatic approach (the `maxp=` parameter specifies the maximum number of ascendants that a node can have):

```
dag2 = hc(data, maxp=2)
plot(dag2)
```

This plot shows how the different variables are connected:

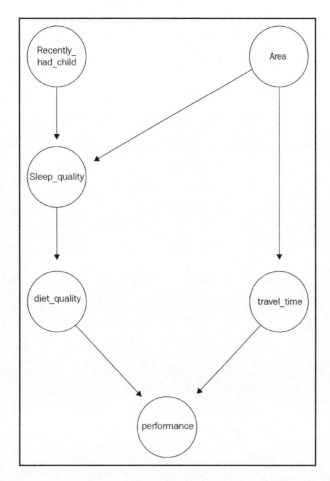

8. The automatic model that we get doesn't make any sense at all. The beautiful thing about BNs is that we can build hybrid structures, which use some expert knowledge in conjunction with an automatic approach. We have two interesting parameters: the `blacklist=` parameter specifies which connections we don't want to have, and the `whitelist=` specifies which connections we want to have. The automatic algorithm will complement these connections that we specify in `whitelist`.

Once we have the structure, we can fit it as usual:

```
whitelist =
data.frame(from=c("travel_time","diet_quality"),to=c("performance",
"performance"))
dag2 = hc(data,maxp=2,whitelist=whitelist)
plot(dag2)
fitted2 <- bn.fit(dag2,data)
```

This plot shows how the different variables are connected:

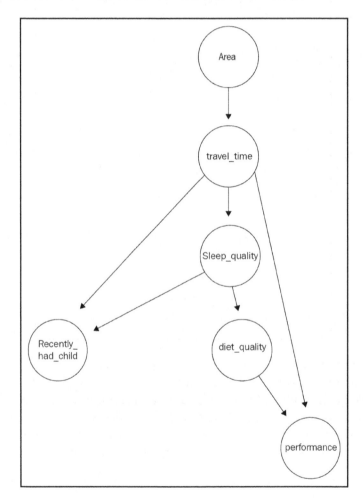

How it works...

The `bnlearn` package is the `de facto` package for BNs in R. It includes several powerful algorithms for automatic detection of the best structure, designed for very large problems. As we saw in this recipe, these can be used for both fully automatic learning and hybrid learning (expert + automatic learning). The `hc()` function that we used here, uses either the hill-climbing or the tabu search greedy algorithm (check the *See also* section of this recipe).

There's more...

A relevant question is: given a series of competing models, `bn1` and `bn2`, how can we choose the best model? There are several approaches for choosing the best one, and most of them rely on information metrics such as the **Akaike information criterion (AIC).** These can be computed using the `score()` function and an appropriate `type=` parameter. The first model (the expert-based one) has a lower AIC than the hybrid one; in consequence, we should keep that model:

```
score(dag, data, type = "aic")
score(dag2, data, type = "aic")
```

The following screenshot shows AIC values for both models:

```
> score(dag, data, type = "aic")
[1] -115.7599
> score(dag2, data, type = "aic")
[1] -110.9179
```

See also

The creators of the `bnlearn` package have written an excellent book, which discusses every algorithm used in this package in a lot of detail.

Scutari, M. and Denis, J.B (2015). *Bayesian Networks with Examples in R*. Florida, United States.

Conditional independence tests

In the previous recipe, we first started with an expert-defined model, and we then showed how to do it using an automatic approach. But this last one didn't work too well for our case, as the resulting model didn't make much sense. We finally decided to include some arcs, which were then complemented by the automatic algorithm using the `whitelist=` parameter.

Independence tests are used by the automatic algorithms to find out reasonable structures, but they can also be employed by the user in the expert decision process. More concretely, we might want to add a new node, and using these independence tests, we can decide whether adding it makes sense or not.

Getting ready

In order to run this recipe, the `bnlearn` package needs to be installed using `install.packages("bnlearn")`.

How to do it...

In this recipe, we will use independence tests to complement our expert model defined in the previous recipe:

1. We load the necessary libraries and the dataset. Then, we create our model, which is based on the same one we used in the previous recipe. Ultimately, we are interested in improving our starting model:

```
library(bnlearn)
library(ggplot2)
data = read.csv("./employee_data.csv")[-1]
dag =
model2network("[Area][travel_time|Area][performance|travel_time:die
t_quality]
[Recently_had_child][Sleep_quality|Recently_had_child:Area][diet_qu
ality|Sleep_quality]")
```

2. Let's run a first test to check whether the performance is independent of the `sleep_quality`, once we control for the performance ascendants. In other words, we are testing whether `sleep_quality` is associated with `sleep_quality`, controlling (conditional on) for the arcs that we have already used. In this case, independence is not rejected as the p-value is high. In consequence, we shouldn't add that arc:

```
ci.test("performance", "Sleep_quality", c("diet_quality",
"travel_time"), test = "mi", data = data)
```

The following screenshot shows conditional test—is the performance independent of the `sleep_quality`, once we already know the `diet_quality` and `travel_time`?:

```
            Mutual Information (disc.)

data:  performance ~ Sleep_quality | diet_quality + travel_time
mi = 1.7261, df = 4, p-value = 0.786
alternative hypothesis: true value is greater than 0
```

3. We then replicate the same exercise, but now testing if the `diet_quality` is independent of the area, once we control for the `sleep_quality`. We don't reject the independence hypothesis:

```
ci.test("diet_quality", "Area", c("Sleep_quality"), test = "mi",
data = data)
```

The following screenshot shows conditional test—is the `diet_quality` independent of the area once we control for the the `sleep_quality`?:

```
            Mutual Information (disc.)

data:  diet_quality ~ Area | Sleep_quality
mi = 0.53934, df = 2, p-value = 0.7636
alternative hypothesis: true value is greater than 0
```

4. We can also test whether an existing arc is statistically relevant (to decide whether we should keep it or remove it). Evidently, this arc is relevant and shouldn't be removed, as the p-value is small:

```
ci.test("travel_time", "Area", test = "mi", data = data)
```

The following screenshot shows the travel time independent of the area:

```
            Mutual Information (disc.)

data:  travel_time ~ Area
mi = 13.809, df = 1, p-value = 0.0002024
alternative hypothesis: true value is greater than 0
```

5. Actually, the `bnlearn` package has a very useful function for this, called `arc.strength()`. It will report the conditional tests for each arc. This can be used with large networks to trim arcs that are not relevant. This can be plotted quite easily by using the `ggplot()` function:

```
arc_strengths = arc.strength(dag, data = data, criterion = "mi")
ggplot(data=arc_strengths,
aes(x=paste0(arc_strengths$from,"->",arc_strengths$to),
y=strength)) + geom_bar(stat="identity") + theme(axis.text.x =
element_text(angle = 90, hjust = 1),axis.title.x=element_blank())
```

The following screenshot is the strength for each variable:

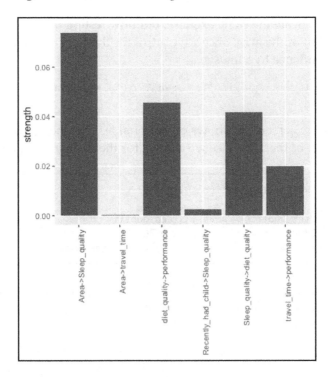

How it works...

The conditional independence tests depend on the nature of the variables involved. For categorical variables, the mutual information test is used, and for continuous ones the correlation coefficient is used. Conceptually, the mutual information measures how much information is shared between two random variables. On the other hand the correlation test evaluates if the correlation coefficient is statistically different from 0.

There's more...

There's a useful concept for analyzing BNs, which is directed separation (d-separation). We say that sets (or variables) *X*, *Y* are d-separated if all the paths between them are blocked. For example, if we have a graph containing *Z*->*X* and *Z*->*Y*, *X* and *Y* are not d-separated because there's an unblocked path between *X* and *Y*. But, if we condition on *Z*, then *X* and *Y* are d-separated. Another way of putting this is that once we know *Z*'s value, *X* and *Y* are independent. Note that we are associating dependence with connectedness.

In other words, d-separation is especially useful for understanding which sets of variables are independent/dependent of other ones. This is particularly useful when we have large networks with hundreds of arcs (in these cases, visual inspection cannot be done):

```
dsep(dag,"travel_time","Recently_had_child")
dsep(dag,"travel_time","Sleep_quality")
dsep(dag,"travel_time","Sleep_quality","Area")
```

After running the preceding, we'll get the following output:

```
> dsep(dag,"travel_time","Recently_had_child")
[1] TRUE
> dsep(dag,"travel_time","Sleep_quality")
[1] FALSE
> dsep(dag,"travel_time","Sleep_quality","Area")
[1] TRUE
```

Continuous and hybrid Bayesian networks via bnlearn

The previous framework can be extended to deal with continuous data, and a mixture of continuous and discrete data. From an operational perspective, nothing changes much with respect to the methods that we have discussed in the previous recipe. It is worth noting that `bnlearn` requires that continuous data be `gaussian`, which might not work in some cases.

Getting ready

The `bnlearn` package needs to be installed using `install.packages("bnlearn")`.

How to do it...

In the following example, we will work with the `abalone` dataset (hosted by the UCI Machine Learning Repository), which contains 4,176 measurements taken for shellfish (sex, length, diameter, height, the number of rings, and several weight metrics). The number of rings is the most important variable, as it determines the age of each specimen. But counting the number of rings is a tedious and costly process, since it needs to be done by cutting each specimen and using a microscope. In general, predictive models are built to predict the number of rings in terms of all the other variables.

In our case, we will formulate a BN model where all the variables are interconnected. We will assume that the sex determines the diameter, height, and length. And, on a secondary level, these three variables will determine several weight attributes. Finally, the weight features will determine the number of rings.

It's worth noting that we have one categorical feature (sex) and eight numeric ones. Of those numeric ones, the number of rings is an integer variable). Among those numeric ones, the number of rings is the only integer based variable. But this is problematic, since Gaussian variables can't be integer based.

1. First, we load the data and apply the column names and logarithms to the `rings` column:

   ```
   data =
   read.csv("https://archive.ics.uci.edu/ml/machine-learning-databases
   /abalone/abalone.data")
   colnames(data) =
   c("sex","length","diameter","height","whole_weight","shucked_weight
   ```

```
",   "viscera_weight","shell_weight","rings") data$rings     =
log(data$rings)
```

2. We define our model using the `model2network()` function, and we plot the graph using `graphviz.plot()`:

```
dag = model2network("[sex][length|sex][diameter|sex][height|sex]
[whole_weight|length:diameter:height][shucked_weight|length:diamete
r:height]
[viscera_weight|length:diameter:height][shell_weight|length:diamete
r:height]
[rings|whole_weight:shucked_weight:viscera_weight:shell_weight]")
parm = list(nodes = nodes(dag), arcs = arcs(dag),col = "black",
textCol = "black")
graphviz.plot(dag, highlight = parm)
```

This plot shows how the different variables are connected:

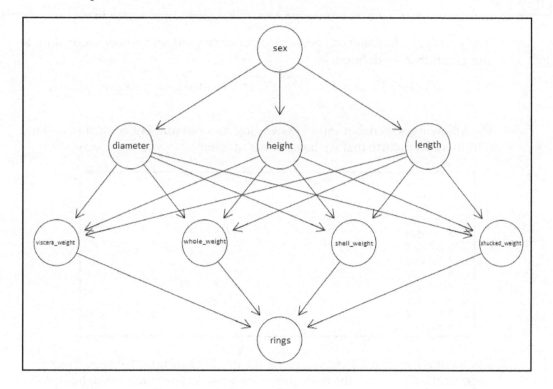

3. We fit our model as usual:

```
fitted = bn.fit(dag, data)
```

4. We can run queries as we did for categorical models. Here, we want to know if probability of it being a male, given that we have a high weight and large diameter, is larger than when the weight is low and the diameter is small. As expected, for the first case, it is more likely to be an adult, whereas in the second case, it is more likely to be either a female or an infant:

```
cpquery(fitted, event = (sex == "M"),evidence =
list(diameter=0.65,whole_weight=.8), method = "lw")
cpquery(fitted, event = (sex == "M"),evidence =
list(diameter=0.15,whole_weight=.8), method = "lw")
```

The following screenshot shows resulting query probabilities:

```
> cpquery(fitted, event = (sex == "M"),evidence = list(diameter=0.65,whole_weight=.8), method = "lw")
[1] 0.7029717
> cpquery(fitted, event = (sex == "M"),evidence = list(diameter=0.15,whole_weight=.8), method = "lw")
[1] 0.1890514
```

5. The `cpdist()` function can be used to generate random numbers according to the graph that we defined:

```
cpdist(fitted, nodes = c("height"),evidence = (viscera_weight >
0.4))
```

The following screenshot shows generating random number according to the conditional structure that we have in our model:

```
> cpdist(fitted, nodes = c("height"),evidence = (viscera_weight > 0.4))
      height
1   0.1422997
2   0.2006702
3   0.1655565
4   0.2107666
5   0.1884822
6   0.1556774
7   0.1931824
8   0.1035670
9   0.1453130
10  0.1531892
```

6. BN models can be predicted by using the predict function. We need three arguments: the model, the node that we want to predict, and the dataset:

```
head(predict(fitted,"rings",data))
head(predict(fitted,"whole_weight",data))
```

Take a look at the following screenshot:

```
> head(predict(fitted,"rings",data))
[1] 1.997482 2.257931 2.134850 1.979325 2.087611 2.521133
> head(predict(fitted,"whole_weight",data))
[1] 0.1706331 0.8539106 0.5759641 0.0993662 0.3762936 0.8709074
```

How it works...

Hybrid (Gaussian and categorical) models and Gaussian models work in a similar fashion to the categorical ones we used in the previous recipes. There is a minor point worth discussing, namely that categorical nodes cannot depend on continuous nodes.

See also

The `abalone` dataset can be found on UCI's official repository. It is an excellent source for machine learning datasets for both classification and regression.

Dua, D. and Graff, C. (2019). UCI Machine Learning Repository (`http://archive.ics.uci.edu/ml`). Irvine, CA: University of California, School of Information and Computer Science.

Interactive visualization of BNs with the bnviewer package

Visualizing our Bayesian networks is very important, especially when dealing with large networks that we have found algorithmically using one of the `bnlearn` included algorithms. Plotting them is easy, but ideally, we need an interactive tool for visualizing properly how the different nodes are connected.

Getting ready

The `bnlearn` and the `bnviewer` packages need to be installed using `install.packages()`.

How to do it...

We will work with the same network used for the previous exercise, and we will plot the network using the `bnviewer` package:

1. We formulate the same model as before, with the same code:

```
library("bnviewer")
library("bnlearn")
data =
read.csv("https://archive.ics.uci.edu/ml/machine-learning-databases
/abalone/abalone.data")
colnames(data) =
c("sex","length","diameter","height","whole_weight",
"shucked_weight",
"viscera_weight", "shell_weight","rings")
data$rings = log(data$rings)
dag = model2network("[sex][length|sex][diameter|sex][height|sex]
[whole_weight|length:diameter:height][shucked_weight|length:diamete
r:height]
[viscera_weight|length:diameter:height][shell_weight|length:diamete
r:height]
[rings|whole_weight:shucked_weight:viscera_weight:shell_weight]")
parm = list(nodes = nodes(dag), arcs = arcs(dag),col = "black",
textCol = "black")
```

2. Let's view the network. The layout parameter controls how the plot is rendered (essentially controlling the shape of the diagram. The diagram looks beautiful, but the nicest thing is that we can click on any node:

```
viewer(dag, bayesianNetwork.width = "100%", bayesianNetwork.height
= "80vh",
bayesianNetwork.layout = "layout_with_sugiyama",
bayesianNetwork.title = "Abalone network",
bayesianNetwork.subtitle = "User defined
network",bayesianNetwork.footer = "Fig. 1 - live diagram")
```

The following screenshot is the network that we defined for the `abalone` dataset:

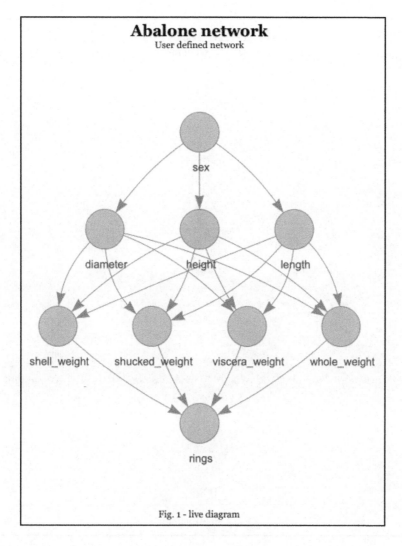

3. Let's, for example, click on a random node:

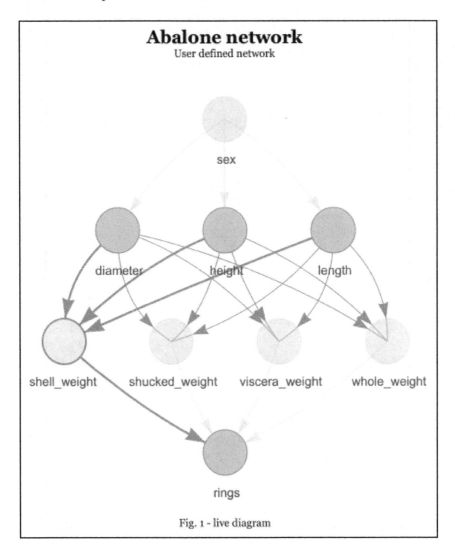

4. We can now change the layout using the `layout` parameter:

```
viewer(dag, bayesianNetwork.width    = "100%",
bayesianNetwork.height = "80vh",
bayesianNetwork.layout = "layout_as_tree", bayesianNetwork.title
= "Abalone network",
bayesianNetwork.subtitle = "User defined network",
bayesianNetwork.footer   = "Fig. 1 – live diagram")
```

The following screenshot is our network for the `abalone` dataset using a different theme:

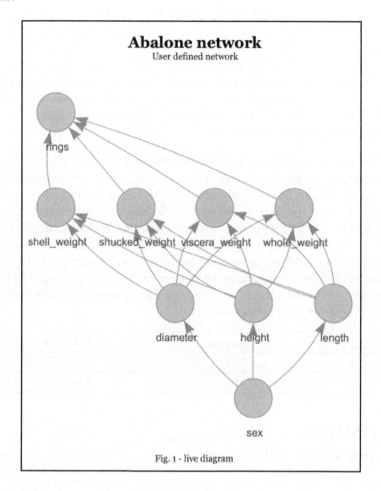

Abalone network
User defined network

Fig. 1 - live diagram

How it works...

The `bnviewer` package parses the model structure from `bnlearn`, and builds the corresponding diagram. When we click on a node, the arcs that are connected to it are highlighted so we can identify the node ascendants and descendants easily.

An introductory hidden Markov model

So far in this book, we have worked with observable variables, such as prices or quantities. But what happens when we have an unobserved variable? Let's suppose that we observe the number of people that walk over a street that has an underground station. This variable can, in principle, be modeled as a Poisson random variable (since it is count data). The number of people walking over this street depends on many variables, among them whether the station is open or closed. Let's further assume that we don't observe whether the station is open or not. We want to estimate whether the station is open or not based on the number of people that we observe.

It's tempting to model the station status based on the amount of people walking, possibly using logistic regression or any other tool. The problem is that our dependent variable cannot be observed! **Hidden Markov models (HMMs)** assume that there is an unobserved variable that governs how the dependent variable behaves; in particular, it assumes that the unobserved state behaves according to a Markov chain (each state probability depends only on the previous state). For example, in our subway example, we assume that there exists a matrix that governs the transition from open to closed. Let's suppose that the rows reflect the current state and the columns reflect the next state: for example, cell (1,1) reflects the probability that an open station today remains open tomorrow, and cell (1,2) reflects the probability that an open station gets closed:

State	Open	Closed
Open	0.9	0.1
Closed	0.1	0.9

Getting ready

The `depmixS4` package needs to be installed using `install.packages("depmixS4")`.

How to do it...

In this recipe, we will load a dataset containing how many people walk on a street, the weather (rainy or sunny), and a hidden variable state (whether the station is closed or open). The objective will be to determine what's the most likely status for the station, given that we can't observe it:

1. We first load the dataset. It contains the following columns: ID, people, state, and weather. The state variable (flagging whether the station is open or closed) would typically be hidden/unavailable, but we have it here so we can compare our model versus the true values:

```
data = read.csv("./subway_data.csv")
```

2. We create an extra column called weather_sunny, which will flag whether the weather was sunny or not (this is a standard dummy variables creation approach), as depmixS4 can't work with factor columns:

```
data$weather_sunny = 0
data$weather_sunny[data$weather=="sunny"] = 1
```

3. We formulate our model. We will have two variables: an intercept and the weather_sunny variable. After that, we fit our model; bear in mind that we are not using the state variable because, in theory, it should be hidden (unavailable). The family= parameter specifies the distribution for the dependent variable:

```
hmm <- depmix(data$people ~ 1  + data$weather_sunny, family =
poisson(), nstates = 2, data=data, respstart=c(10,10,10,10))
hmmfit <- fit(hmm, verbose = TRUE)
```

4. We get the posterior probabilities for the hidden state, and we print the predicted state probabilities along with the observed number of people. The two states can be estimated well, and we can see that whenever the probability of the station being open is low, the number of people is low as well. In order to do a proper analysis, let's check our data:

```
post_probs <- posterior(hmmfit)
layout(1:2)
plot(data$people,type="l")
data$state_pred = post_probs$state
matplot(post_probs[,-1], type='l', main='Regime Posterior
Probabilities', ylab='Probability')
legend(x='topright', c('Flat-Bear','Bull'), fill=1:3, bty='n')
```

The following screenshot shows the number of people and the **Posterior Probabilities** for each state:

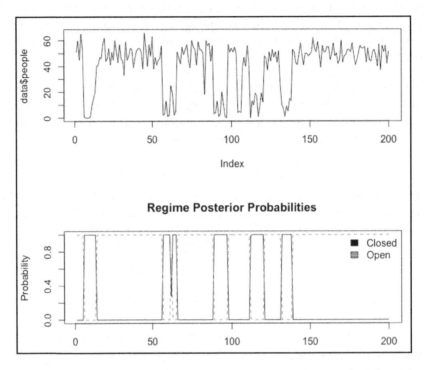

5. Let's print the results using the `tables` command. Column 1 would be our predicted **closed** state, and column 2 would be our predicted **open** state. Obviously, our model works quite well, and we predict almost all the observations correctly (the diagonal elements are the correctly predicted ones):

```
> table(data$state,data$state_pred)

          1   2
closed   41   1
open      1 157
```

How it works...

The mathematics of HMMs are rather complex, but on a conceptual level, we could factorize the likelihood between terms, involving the observed variables and the unobserved ones. The usual way of estimating these models is by using the Expectation-Maximization algorithm. It works by iteratively taking expectations for the unobserved effects, and maximizing the log-likelihood.

There's more...

The `depmixS4` package assumes by default that the unobserved states are governed by a multinomial model. This means that, in principle, the transition probability between two states, s1 and s2, depends on the current state s1. This can be extended using the `transition=` option and specifying covariates for those transitions.

Let's suppose that we now observe another variable called `machinery_road` that flags whether machinery/equipment was seen on the same day around the area. It's likely that whenever the station is closed, maintenance is going to be done on it. In consequence, whether we see machinery around the station should help explain the transition between open and closed and vice versa:

```
data = read.csv("./subway_data_extended.csv")
data$weather_sunny = 0
data$weather_sunny[data$weather=="sunny"] = 1
hmm      <- depmix(data = data, people ~ 1 + weather_sunny, transition=~1 +
machinery_road,  family = poisson(), nstates = 2, respstart=c(10,10,10,10)
)
hmmfit <- fit(hmm, verbose = TRUE)
post_probs <- posterior(hmmfit)
data$state_pred = post_probs$state
```

And after doing this, we get the same regime posterior probabilities.

Regime switching in financial data via HMM

Regime switching models are usually used in finance, as it is assumed that there is an unobserved market state (let's call it market sentiment) that governs stock prices. This market sentiment can be loosely associated to a bull or a bear market.

Getting ready

The `depmixS4` package needs to be installed using `install.packages("depmixS4")`.

How to do it...

In the following recipe, we will work with the returns for the Pampa Energia S.A. ADR stock prices:

1. First, we load the data and the necessary packages, and we calculate the returns. As can be seen here, they seem reasonably Gaussian (further testing could be performed here):

```
library('depmixS4')
datas = read.csv("./hist_PAM20190304.csv")[5]
returns = diff(datas$cierre)/datas$cierre[-length(datas$cierre)]
plot(returns,type="l")
returns = data.frame(returns =returns)
hist(returns$returns,main="Histogram of returns")
```

The following screenshot is the **Histogram of returns**: the data seems reasonably Gaussian:

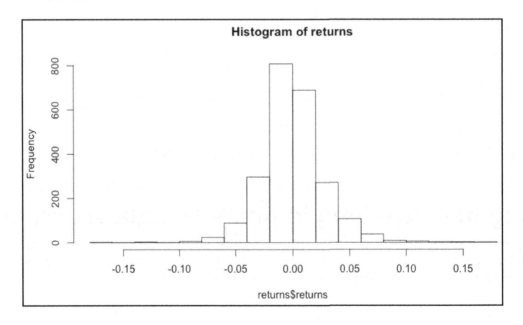

2. We fit our model, where we will have just an intercept, a Gaussian distribution for the returns and two unobserved states (these would be a bear or a bull market):

```
hmm <- depmix(returns ~ 1, family = gaussian(), nstates = 2,
data=data.frame(returns=returns))
```

3. Once we define the model, we can fit it:

```
hmmfit <- fit(hmm, verbose = FALSE)
```

The following screenshot shows HMM model output:

```
> hmmfit <- fit(hmm, verbose = FALSE)
converged at iteration 65 with logLik: 5336.259
```

4. Let's plot the predicted states, the probabilities for each state, and the series' values. The third plot is very important, as it shows the 0/1 states. As we can see, the bear market seems to dominate up to observation 1,000, and then the market is really bullish up to observation 1,800. We finally have another bear market again:

```
post_probs <- posterior(hmmfit)
layout(1:4)
plot(datas$cierre,type="l")
plot(returns$returns,type="l")
plot(post_probs$state, type='s', main='True Regimes', xlab='',
ylab='Regime')
matplot(post_probs[,-1], type='l', main='Regime Posterior
Probabilities', ylab='Probability')
legend(x='topright', c('Flat-Bear','Bull'), fill=1:3, bty='n')
```

The following screenshot shows the stock prices, returns, **True Regimes**, and **Posterior Probabilities**:

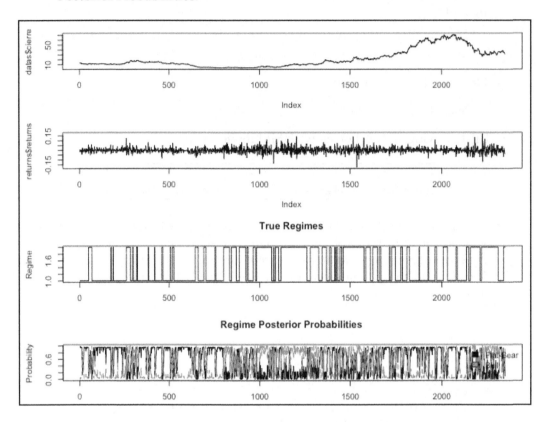

5. We can do the same exercise but with three states. The problem is not computational, but conceptual: interpreting more than two states is not easy, even though the resulting model might be better than one with just two states.

How it works...

This package uses the **expectation-maximization** (**EM**) algorithm, which is covered in a lot of detail in the package documentation. As explained in the previous recipe, the EM algorithm works by alternating between taking expectation and maximization operators. A good technical explanation of the EM algorithm, and HMM can be found on `https://cs.nyu.edu/~mohri/asr12/lecture_8.pdf`.

There's more...

We could try modeling the same data but using three states, and we can use the resulting AIC to choose which model to use. But the more states we have, the harder they are to interpret:

```
hmm <- depmix(returns ~ 1, family = gaussian(), nstates = 3,
data=data.frame(returns=returns))
```

Other Books You May Enjoy

If you enjoyed this book, you may be interested in these other books by Packt:

Generative Adversarial Networks Projects
Kailash Ahirwar

ISBN: 9781789136678

- Train a network on the 3D ShapeNet dataset to generate realistic shapes
- Generate anime characters using the Keras implementation of DCGAN
- Implement an SRGAN network to generate high-resolution images
- Train Age-cGAN on Wiki-Cropped images to improve face verification
- Use Conditional GANs for image-to-image translation
- Understand the generator and discriminator implementations of StackGAN in Keras

Generative Adversarial Networks Cookbook
Josh Kalin

ISBN: 9781789139907

- Structure a GAN architecture in pseudocode
- Understand the common architecture for each of the GAN models you will build
- Implement different GAN architectures in TensorFlow and Keras
- Use different datasets to enable neural network functionality in GAN models
- Combine different GAN models and learn how to fine-tune them
- Produce a model that can take 2D images and produce 3D models
- Develop a GAN to do style transfer with Pix2Pix

Leave a review - let other readers know what you think

Please share your thoughts on this book with others by leaving a review on the site that you bought it from. If you purchased the book from Amazon, please leave us an honest review on this book's Amazon page. This is vital so that other potential readers can see and use your unbiased opinion to make purchasing decisions, we can understand what our customers think about our products, and our authors can see your feedback on the title that they have worked with Packt to create. It will only take a few minutes of your time, but is valuable to other potential customers, our authors, and Packt. Thank you!

Index

J

JAGS
  GLM model, using 201, 204

K

Kruskal-Wallis 207

L

Lasso
  in caret 384, 385, 388, 389
leaflet package
  used, for displaying geographical data 58, 59, 60
leverage metric 151, 152, 153, 156, 157
linear mixed model
  selecting 335, 336, 338
linear regression model
  formulating 165, 167, 169
  working 169
linear regression
  variable selection 132, 133, 135, 138
LOESS regression
  about 214, 215, 218
  working 149, 217
  working with 145, 146, 148, 149, 150
logic regression
  about 389, 390
  working 391

M

Mann-Whitney-Wilcoxon test 206
marginal AIC (mAIC) 335, 338
Markov Chain Monte Carlo (MCMC) 160
maximum likelihood estimation
  about 10, 11, 12, 13, 14, 91
  working 12
MCMC algorithm
  coding 176, 178, 180, 182
  working 183
mean squared error (MSE) 149
Metropolis Hastings (MH) 177
mixed effects models
  about 88
  plots 312, 315, 316, 318, 320, 321

mixed generalized linear models
  about 338, 339, 341, 342, 344, 345, 347, 349
  working 347
model
  tuning 366, 367, 368, 369
  using, for prediction 198, 200
moving-average (MA) 264
multiple distributions
  random numbers, generating from 21, 22, 23
multivariate analysis of variance (MANOVA)
  about 103, 104, 107, 222
  working 106
multivariate t-test
  about 100, 101, 102
  working 102

N

nested designs 326, 327, 328, 329, 330
nonlinear mixed effects models
  about 322, 323, 326
  working 325
nonparametric ANOVA
  estimating 208
  working 209
nonparametric multivariate tests
  with npmv package 222, 223, 225
nonparametric tests
  used, for equality of medians 206, 207
npmv package
  used, for nonparametric multivariate tests 222, 223, 225

O

ordinary least squares (OLS) 384
ordinary least squares estimates
  about 110, 205, 308
  computing 110, 111, 113
  working 113

P

p-values
  used, for variable selection 132
paired t-test
  about 71, 72, 73, 74
  working 73

partial autocorrelation function (PACF) 275
plot3d package
  used, for 3-D visualization 26, 27, 28
plots
  for mixed effects models 312, 315, 316, 318, 320, 321
posterior density
  obtaining, in STAN 159, 161, 162, 164
preprocessing
  data 357, 358, 361
priors
  assigning 171, 173, 175, 176
  impact 173
  parameters, deciding for 171, 172
  support, defining 171

Q

qclust package
  robust Gaussian mixture models, using 253, 255, 258
quantiles
  calculating 14, 15, 17

R

R6 classes
  using 46, 47, 48, 49
random effects
  about 88, 89, 92
  working 91
random number generators (RNGs) 14
random numbers
  generating, from multiple distributions 21, 22, 23
random sampling 31, 32, 33, 35
Rcpp package
  C++, using in R 38, 40, 41
receiver operating characteristic (ROC) 369
Regime
  switching, in financial data via HMM 417, 419, 421
repeated measures
  about 93, 94, 96, 98, 99
  working 98
residuals metric 151, 152, 153, 156, 157
restricted maximum likelihood (REML) 91
ridge regression

about 141, 142
  in caret 384, 385, 388, 389
robust ANOVA
  with robust package 245, 246, 247, 248
robust clustering 258, 259, 261
robust covariance matrices
  estimating 237, 238, 240, 241
robust Gaussian mixture models
  with qclust package 253, 255, 258
robust linear regression
  about 232, 234, 236
  working 236
robust logistic regression 241, 242
robust mixed effects models
  with robustlmm 331, 332, 334, 335
robust principal components
  about 249, 250
  working 252
robustlmm
  robust mixed effects models, using 331, 332, 334, 335
root mean square error (RMSE) 359

S

sandwich estimators
  implementing 129, 130
  working 132
SARIMAX model 270, 271, 273, 274
Scheirer-Ray-Hare test 207
seasonality model 270, 271, 273, 274
SemiPar package
  used, for semiparametric regression 226, 228, 229
semiparametric regression
  with SemiPar package 225, 226, 228, 229
sequences
  clustering, with TraMineR package 55, 56, 57
  modeling, with TraMineR package 50, 52, 53, 54
sequential sum of squares 84
Shapiro-Wilk statistic 81
sjPlot package
  used, for reporting linear regression results 113, 115, 116
Spearman rank correlation test